The Life of
John Middleton Murry

Die geistigsten Menschen, vorausgesetzt, dass sie die
mutigsten sind, erleben auch bei Weitem die schmerz-
haftesten Tragödien: aber eben deshalb ehren sie
das Leben, weil es ihnen seine grösste Gegnerschaft
entgegenstellt.

— NIETZSCHE

by the same author

*

THE TRAGIC PHILOSOPHER
A Study of Friedrich Nietzsche

THE LIFE OF
John Middleton Murry

————◦◦◦◦◦◦————

F. A. LEA

1960
OXFORD UNIVERSITY PRESS
NEW YORK

FOR M.K.

EM^cC

CONTENTS

————◦◦◦◦◦————

[v]

CONTENTS

Part III: 1931–1939

Part IV: 1939–1957

ILLUSTRATIONS

facing page

Permission to reproduce plates 1, 2, 5, 17, 18 has been kindly given by Mr Richard Murry, plates 4, 6–12, 16, 25, 26 by Mrs Michael Church and plates 19, 24, 29, 33, 34, 35 by Mrs Middleton Murry.

PREFACE

❧❧❦❧❧

THE 'OFFICIAL BIOGRAPHY' IS suspect – rightly. Appointed
by the literary executors of the deceased, inhibited by the
scruples of his relatives, friends and 'others still living', the
author is not expected to produce more than a faint outline – a bas-
relief at best, and that so draped in fig-leaves as rather to pique the
reader's curiosity than appease it. This being the official biography of
John Middleton Murry, inasmuch as it was commissioned by his widow
and elder son, it may be as well to set my cards on the table at the
outset.

When, in April 1957, Mrs Middleton Murry first suggested to me
that, as a friend of some twenty years' standing, I should write her
husband's life, I felt it to be an honour and privilege. I still do. Because
I did, I was daunted, both by the responsibility itself and by fears lest
I should be prevented from discharging it loyally by deference to others'
wishes. My fears proved groundless. Few biographers, official or otherwise, can ever have been treated to such generous consideration and
co-operation on the part of family and friends alike. From the day I
agreed to the suggestion, Mrs Murry herself placed unreservedly at my
disposal all the relevant documents in her possession – books, manuscripts, letters, diaries; while Miss Ruth Baker, Mr Murry's former
secretary, was tireless in seeking out papers that would otherwise have
been overlooked. Whatever merit this book may have – and its chief
merit must lie in the material drawn from these sources – is due to them
above all.

Out of respect for what appears to have been one of Murry's own
last expressed wishes, I have refrained from citing the material in his
journals relating to his tragic third marriage. I have also withheld the
names of some half-dozen persons referred to in the narrative. I do not
think that these reservations affect its veracity: and they are the only ones.

[ix]

To have gone beyond this, to have presented Murry either exclusively as a public man or as a pattern of all the conventional virtues, would have been an unpardonable solecism. His virtues were of a different order; and of these the greatest, and the least conventional, was his honesty. Falsification, especially idealization, in biography shocked him as deeply as the framing of an experiment would a conscientious biologist. Nobody, he said, could understand even his public life who did not understand his private; and if ever a man strove, not only to understand, but to record, the truth about both, it was he. In his uncompleted autobiography, *Between Two Worlds*, he discarded the fig-leaf and set a precedent in self-revelation which incurred charges of 'exhibitionism' as strident as those of 'humbug' would have been if he had done otherwise. His journals reflect a submission to the injunction, 'know thyself', the cumulative effect of which is almost overpowering in its objectivity. If a man's life was worth recording at all, he maintained, it was worth recording truthfully; and he would have agreed with Carlyle that any man's life truthfully recorded was worth recording.

Largely because of this, his own life must be one of the most fully documented in the annals of literature. His forty-odd books – as personal in their way as his conversations – constitute only a tithe of his total output, as journalist, lecturer, diarist and correspondent. For months at a stretch, it would be possible to follow his movements, including the movements of his mind, from day to day, almost from hour to hour. *Hinc meae lacrymae.* More than once, in the course of this study, I was tempted to envy a fellow-biographer, of whose subject, a fourth-century saint, all that seemed to be known was the date of his death and a handful of dubious miracles. Ideally, the official biography should be a straightforward recital of events, leaving interpretation and evaluation to others. In this case, the necessity for stringent selection has ruled out any such possibility. So once more I had better state at the outset what consideration has governed my approach.

The Middleton Murry I have tried to present is first and foremost the moralist: that is to say, the man whose criticism, politics, theology, farming, were one and all expressions of an overriding need to determine (as he put it) 'what is good for man, $T\grave{o}$ $\varepsilon \tilde{v}$ $Z\widehat{\eta}\nu$'. No one can be more conscious than I of the limitations imposed by this perspective. It has meant bolting the door on a number of side-alleys promising unique views or glimpses of the Georgian and post-Georgian literary scene. Readers more interested in Murry's associates than in himself are bound to be disappointed. It has meant, again, passing hurriedly over books like *The Problem of Style* to dwell on others like *The Necessity of Communism*, which, though intrinsically much less valuable, are of greater biographical consequence. On the other hand, it must be allowed that, until Murry has been studied as a figure in his own right, no complete understanding will be possible even of Katherine Mansfield or D. H. Lawrence; and it may be hoped that one effect of this study will be to stimulate other writers – or better, other thinkers – to examine his particular contributions to various branches of knowledge more attentively than they have done in the past.

To name all those who have given me help is impossible. I trust that the references at the back will be read as acknowledgements by those whose material I have availed myself of directly; and that the many others whose letters and reminiscences have contributed indirectly will not think me any the less grateful because I have omitted to thank them individually. I must, however, express my particular indebtedness to Mr E. G. Collieu, of Brasenose College, Oxford, for information concerning Murry's student years, and to the following for sequences of letters extending over considerable periods: Mr H. P. Collins, Mme Katherine de Coninck, Mr L. G. Duke, C.B.E., Mr T. S. Eliot, O.M., Miss N. Gill, Mr J. P. Hogan, Prof. G. Wilson Knight, Mr Philip Landon (Emeritus Fellow of Trinity College, Oxford), Miss Mary Murry, Mr Richard Murry, Mrs Max Plowman, Sir Richard Rees, Mr Navin Sullivan, Mr A. W. Votier, Mrs Clare Walter, Mr J. H. Watson, Mr Henry Williamson, Mr W. B. Wordsworth and Mrs Marcelle Young. I am also very greatly indebted to Sir Richard Rees, Mr Richard Murry, Mr Colin Murry and Mr and Mrs J. P. Hogan for reading the manuscript and giving me the benefit of their criticism.

For permission to quote from the letters of D. H. Lawrence, published and unpublished, I am obliged to Messrs Laurence Pollinger, Ltd and Wm. Heinemann, Ltd; to quote from Katherine Mansfield's *Letters* and *Journal*, to Messrs Constable, Ltd and the Society of Authors; and to quote substantial passages from Murry's published work, to Messrs Jonathan Cape, Ltd.

In conclusion, I wish to tender my sincere apologies to anyone to whom I may inadvertently have given pain, either by the facts I have publicized or by the opinions I have expressed.

F. A. LEA

1 December 1958

PART I

1889–1923

I

FIRST YEARS

❦❦❦❦❦❦

THE MURRYS FIRST LOOM out of the Celtic Twilight early in the nineteenth century, with 'Thomas Murry Senior of the Parish of Hubberstone County of Pembroke Shipwright'. Thomas's mother was a Welsh-speaking, steeple-hatted native of Anglesey; his father may have hailed from Ireland, where the name is not uncommon in seventeenth- and eighteenth-century records: but his further ancestry is uncertain, and immaterial. All that concerns us is that he had two sons, Thomas Junior, born 1831, and John, born 1835, who, he did solemnly and sincerely declare, were likewise apprenticed to the shipwright's trade.

These two began life by plying the ferry between Milford Haven and Haverfordwest. Later, the Hungry Forties bearing hard on the family, this proved an inadequate livelihood. As long as a crust of bread remained in the house, their father used to aver, his old mother (of the steeple hat) should not be sent to the Union: but often a crust of bread was literally all that did remain; and by their early twenties both boys were forced to migrate to Sheerness Dockyards, where he himself eventually joined them. The memory of those early privations seems to have exerted a decisive influence on their lives – and not only on theirs.

Thomas Junior, whose mortal fear of the Union survived into his ninety-second year, would take his son out into the streets and point to the crossing-sweeper at work, reminding him that such would be his own lot unless he worked hard at the Docks. The lesson went home. The boy (another Thomas) worked so hard that he hoisted himself clean out of the proletariat, ending his days as inspector of the Government Ordnance Factory at Dum-Dum – and father of Mary Murry, the novelist.

John was a rougher diamond. He would supplement his meagre earnings by pocketing copper bolts from the Docks and disposing of them outside, until, getting wind of the transaction, his employers confronted him with a constable at the gates. Arrested, searched, and severely admonished, he thereupon vowed revenge on that constable, and seized the first occasion to wreak it. Unfortunately, it was the occasion of his father's funeral. It was just as the long procession was winding round Sheerness Green that he happened to catch sight of his enemy, and, throwing discretion with frock-coat to the winds, proceeded to settle the account. But this lesson too went home. His son (another John), who had been sitting beside him in the carriage, was so appalled by the squalor of the scene – the constable being borne off to hospital, his father to gaol, while the cortège paused open-mouthed – that he, like his cousin, turned his back on the proletariat for ever, ending his days as a Civil Service pensioner – and father of John Middleton Murry.

This second John was evidently endowed with a formidable energy and determination. At the time of the funeral, 1871, he cannot have been more than eleven, and, as the only responsible member of a large and feckless family, he had his sisters' welfare as well as his own to consider. Yet by dint of sheer hard work, without a word of encouragement from anybody, he succeeded in teaching himself to write, in securing a post at Somerset House – first as boy-messenger, then as a temporary clerk at £1 a week – and, by his twenty-eighth year, in laying aside enough to marry and set up house on his own, in Ethnard Road, Peckham.

His wife, Emily – née Wheeler – loyally reinforced his efforts. While he, to earn a further sixpence an hour, trudged from Somerset House to a Penny Bank in the Brompton Road, toiling as a cashier till midnight, she took in lodgers at home. Their life together, for the first few years, was confined to the small hours and Sundays. That was the price to be paid, in the 1880s, for rising above your station. She knew it and did not complain. If she submitted as a wife, however, she must have grieved as a girl: for she was only eighteen when they married, and, though no better off than he – she brought a dowry of £30 – less obsessed by the spectre of poverty. By nature gay where he was dour, tender where he was hard, reckless where he was circumspect, she never completely resigned herself to the meagreness of their existence. She would day-dream of gipsies and caravans. The couple, indeed, were of singularly opposite temperaments – and the opposites emerged in their son.

Born on August 6, 1889, John Middleton Murry was pronounced a beautiful baby, and good-looking he was always to be. Yet his very face was a *coincidentia oppositorum*. Look at any portrait, or pen-portrait, of him in middle life. What have those large, luminous, contemplative eyes, so easily flooded with tears, to do with that combative chin; those finely chiselled, fastidious lips with that coarse, thrice-broken nose? Nowadays heredity is discounted, circumstance deemed all-important: but if that chin was his father's so was the forcefulness it betokened, and if those eyes were his mother's so was the sensibility. What nature had proposed, no doubt, nurture disposed: but the traits coexisted from the start – and not always peacefully.

As the first son of an only son, he was naturally the apple of his grandfather's eye. By this time, the shipwright had retired to a pub in Bow Road, The Ordell Arms, and there the baby was taken to see him. Once, when his aunt had gone off, first to fight somebody, then to play tip-cat, leaving him squatting outside in the street, the old man, outraged by such negligence, descended from on high like Jehovah and felled her to the ground. His outbursts, both of fury and of affection, however, were already nearing their end. It must have been soon after this that the family were summoned to his deathbed:

> I sat there, on a chest at the end of his bed, in a reefer coat with gold anchor-buttons, staring at him, half-frightened . . . Everybody was sent out of the room by a motion of his head, and I sat there alone, staring at him with big eyes. Every now and then he would say something to me, which I could not catch; it seemed to get lost in his bushy black beard, as he struggled to lift himself to get a full sight of me. At last I understood what he wanted and pulled a chair close to his bedside and perched myself upon it. And we looked at one another. How long I sat there, looking at him, he looking at me, I cannot say. I know it was a long time, and that I was not tired. I know it was a long time, because I was dimly conscious that the misgivings of my parents at leaving me alone with him, were being increased into restiveness and anxiety by the length of my stay. But they dared not interfere . . . They were afraid of the dying lion. I was afraid, and not afraid. I knew him as a lion; but I knew also that he would never dart his paw on me. And as I looked at him, and felt something of the speech that was in his eyes when he looked at me, my little heart was *weh* with a grief unspeakable.[1]

This was when Murry was three. Thenceforward, his glimpses of his grandfather's world were few and fleeting. His gaze was turned, willy-nilly, in quite another direction.

[5]

To him, it was a picturesque world, at least in retrospect. He liked to recall the odd, Dickensian characters who frequented it – the old gentleman, for instance, who had lately retired from the profession of catching black beetles in Buckingham Palace. But his romantic leanings were not shared. To his father, it was a world of perdition, such characters a *memento mori*. John Murry felt always as though he were skirting an abyss, where one false step would be fatal. And the feeling was not unwarranted. Of all classes of late Victorian society, the lower middle class had most to fear. The proletariat itself was secure by comparison, if only because it could sink no lower. This haunting sense of insecurity determined his every move, exacerbated his feverish efforts to better himself, and infected all who came within his reach. Nothing was more dreaded in that household than his work-frayed temper, and nothing so sure to provoke it as the least suggestion of back-sliding.

Furthermore, he was an idealist. Not for himself alone had he pinched and scraped and denied himself and his wife. Just as far as he, by his own unaided exertions, had risen above the rank of his parents, so far, he was resolved, should his son rise above his own; and nothing was to distract or divert him. Nor was the ideal itself indeterminate: it was incarnate before his eyes. Day by day from the high places of the War Office there descended those tangled screeds which it was his duty and privilege to transcribe; day by day he beheld the exalted beings from whom they emanated. 'They arrived at ten o'clock, in hansom cabs when it was wet; they went to lunch at their clubs at one, and returned at three. They drafted more letters till half-past four, and then they departed. One or two of them stayed during lunch-time, in case war broke out in the interval; and they had elegant meals brought to them in their rooms.' [2] It was to this empyrean that his son was destined.

The end was laid down before the child was out of his cradle. The sole doubt related to means. Clearly, the key was education: but what was that? John Murry could not be sure, but he knew at least that it meant the three R's, and History, and Latin. The three R's, therefore, it was, from the moment the boy could speak. By the age of two he was reading the newspapers aloud to the clients of The Ordell Arms; at two-and-a-half he was sent to school – the Rolles Road Board School. Then came sums, and dates, and tags from *The Victoria Spelling Book* – *multum in parvo*, *noli me tangere* – to be conned by rote and repeated Sunday mornings. At seven he was doing quadratics, author – already – of a treatise on Gothic Architecture, and top of the Bellendon Road

Higher Grade Board School. It was merely a question of time before he should stand for a scholarship.

'The only moral imperative I knew in my youth was: "Thou shalt work".' [3] It is rather horrible to contemplate, this forcible feeding, and he himself looked back on it with horror. 'It involved the complete obliteration of a child's childhood.' [4] It involved, in other words, an atrophy of the sensuous, a hypertrophy of the intellectual, from which he never recovered. Probably it was accountable for his short-sightedness too, and for a susceptibility to minor ailments that robbed his manhood of at least as many working-hours as he had had to put in as a boy. At the age of eleven, his aunt said, he was just 'a little old man'.[5]

Mention of this aunt, however, recalls the other side of his nurture – the maternal side. For John Murry did not have things all his own way. By 1893 he had saved up enough to move from Peckham to East Dulwich, and there, instead of lodgers, his wife's mother and sister shared the house. Much of the boy's spare time, therefore, was passed in the company of three women, all of whom he adored. His grandmother, he writes, 'had an instinct for life':

> She had known what hard times were; she had been through a kind of poverty which even my father's family had never known: yet she was completely unsoured. She had brought up her two daughters – my mother and my aunt – to be gentle and generous. They had learned from her to be tender. Experience has taught me that this quality of tenderness in woman, which my grandmother possessed so abundantly and which flowed on through her two daughters, is rarer than I imagined. After all, these were the only women I knew: and this quality was the same in them all. They were all gentle and generous.[6]

This grandmother used to take him for carefree holidays in Hastings, where he was allowed to play with the dustman's children and get as grubby as he pleased – indulgences that would have shocked his father. As for Aunt Doll, then a girl in her teens, she was less an aunt than a playmate herself – and something more. 'I used always to see in you my ideal of beauty',[7] he told her years afterwards; at the same time confessing how 'terribly hurt' he had been when she took it into her head to marry. Even then he was 'a woman's man'.

In a chilly and intimidating world, these three stood for warmth and security. They ensured that whatever else he was starved for, he was not starved for affection: and that was something he never forgot. The same letter to his aunt, of condolence on the death of her son, concludes:

[7]

'Days come when I would give up everything to be a child again and sit in the kitchen while you and Mum laughed and laughed and laughed – you remember how? – at something I could never quite make out. This letter is only to let you know that in my heart I return all that love you gave me. I love you still and always will.' [7] Since these words were written from Bandol, during one of the happiest spells of Murry's life, his childhood, though drab, could not have been altogether joyless.

Indeed, it was not altogether drab. If Sunday mornings were darkened by homework, the afternoons were redeemed by Sunday School – an hour of purely secular enjoyment, consecrated to readings from Kingston and Ballantyne. Romance entered Coplestone Road in the small person of Edith Pinnington next door, to whom he paid tongue-tied courtship, and in whose eyes he distinguished himself by beating her father at ping-pong. At ping-pong itself – a novelty in the 'nineties, and the first of the long succession of ball-games to enlist his enthusiasm – he was something of an infant prodigy. Then, there were the annual excursions to Margate, Brighton or Yarmouth, on which even John Murry could relax: and once, 'seized by an unaccustomed spirit of adventure',[8] he took the whole family to Jersey. That was in 1896. To the same year belonged 'the most glowing memory' [9] of all, and perhaps the most lastingly effective – Beerbohm Tree's production of *Julius Caesar* at His Majesty's, which they watched from high up in the ninepennies:

> From the beginning I was spell-bound. I had not read *Julius Caesar* – nor indeed any Shakespeare at all. But the whole thing was marvellous to me. Rome – the crowds – Caesar – the togas – the swords – the eagles – the storm – the lightning – the growls at Anthony – and then the cheers. I was in ecstasy. And then – wonder of wonders – the scene between Brutus and Cassius in the tent. The tears streamed down my face. Whether, in any sense, I understood the play, I have no idea. But it was all unbearably splendid and beautiful to me.[10]

Half a century later, reading in her autobiography that it was this same production which had opened 'the world of theatrical enchantment' to Lady Cynthia Asquith, Murry felt as if they 'shared a secret'.[9]

And yet, 'the terrors of childhood are much more real to me than the joys'.[11] Perhaps he exaggerated his nervousness. It took some pluck to steal a lift on the back of a dray, at the risk of the driver's whip; and one of his school-fellows at Bellenden Road remembers him as a ringleader of mischief. But nervous he was, harrowed by night-horrors, unable to go to bed without a knotted towel for company. Fear was in the air he breathed. Every bit as much as his father, he felt that at any moment the ground might cave in under his feet. The very mythology which, like most children, he evolved and half-believed, reflected this abiding *Angst*. It centred, he recalled, on two deities: God, whose 'business was to punish you for wickedness', and the Power, who had 'one sole activity – to "git you, ef you don't watch out" '.[12] Before both he walked in fear and trembling. Nowhere, except with his grandmother, mother and aunt, could he ever feel really secure. And when, at the age of eleven, he did succeed in winning a scholarship, the last familiar landmark fell away. The sentence of exile became irrevocable.

'The sense of being a stranger in a strange land', he was to write in 1931, 'dates back further than I can remember.' [13] That was his father's legacy. The measures taken by John Murry to ensure his son's security defeated their end. The higher he rose in the social scale, the better he adapted himself outwardly to one milieu after another, the more of an impostor he would feel, the more rootless, the more homeless, the more complete an outsider. Perdurably established by his strange education were, on the one hand, a craving for some setting to which he could *belong* without pretence, on the other a critical intelligence that would make it all the harder to satisfy. At the same time – and this was his mother's legacy – his very touchstone of *belonging* would remain the kitchen at Coplestone Road. Only where his affections as well as his intelligence were engaged would he ever be completely at one, with his setting or himself. The interplay, the conflict, the conciliation, of these two factors make up the history of his life – a life 'like the Scriptures, figurative', inasmuch as it epitomizes the quest of the common man in a century of breakneck social transition.

His entry into Christ's Hospital, in the first month of the first year of the century, January 1901, was itself symbolic. It was in response to the mounting pressure of a million John Murrys that the great Tudor foundation had thrown six scholarships open to Board School boys. Murry's was one of the first six. The night his success was announced, his aunt remembered, he behaved 'like a little maniac, dancing round the room and crying "I've passed! I've passed!" ' [5] till she and his mother were positively alarmed. No doubt his father's jubilation was scarcely inferior to his own. Christ's Hospital had been recommended by no less a person than his former chief at the War Office, himself an Old Blue. The first milestone, at least, had been passed on the high road to Somerset House.

The school was still situated in Newgate Street. The Grecians' Cloister, in the centre of the buildings, was the same that Coleridge had adorned. The oak-panelled wards, with their great open hearths, were as steeped in tradition as a church. Everything was venerable, impressive – to a small boy accustomed to the narrow thoroughfares and narrower minds of East Dulwich, more than a little overpowering. Christ's Hospital, at first, was 'a kind of bewildering dream, with brief intervals of lucid wakefulness'.[14] But not, it would seem, a bad dream. Murry's first extant letter, dated January 25, 1901, deserves to be quoted, if only for the sake of the opening, with its characteristically scrupulous, even pedantic, reservation:

Dear Mother,

'What is your name and where do you live?' Everyone asks me that question until I would like to punch the head of every impertinent questioner that speaks to me. Wait till I've been here a little longer and I'll teach a lesson to some of the smaller ones.

We went up for a little exam. this morning in Arithmetic and I got on allright. In the afternoon we had one in Algebra. These are to ascertain which form we are to be placed in.

Make beds. wash. BREAKFAST. Brush boots. SCHOOL (2 hrs.). Play. Dinner. Play. SCHOOL (2 hrs.) play. tea. School. to Bed. Such is the daily routine of Christ's Hospital. I'm not quite mummy sick yet though I'm always thinking of you and Dad and all my Royal Family. Send to the Warden the Saturday after next for me to go out. I ought to have brought some goodies in with me like the other fellows did, for the tuck shop is always packed, not in the ordinary sense of the word, but just like sardines in a tin. By the bye you might get me a couple of tins of decent bloater paste.

We saw the headmaster this morning and a very nice ~~fellow~~ gentleman he is.

Send some stamps use my sixpence to help pay for this.

I s'pose I shall have to have a 'lastly' to my little sermon so I'll have it now.   Jack.

No doubt the Royal Family was much in the news at that moment. 'Mafeking' and 'Ladysmith' were scrawled over the staircase walls; 'and I remember', Murry wrote fifty years later, 'that though I was only 9 or 10 a wave of nausea and foreboding (mentally quite incomprehensible) swept over me on Mafeking night'.[15] His mother's 'goodies' were a more present affliction, consisting, alas, of seedcakes so repulsive that he could neither eat them himself nor offer them to his friends – with the result that his furtive sorties to the dustbin gained him a quite undeserved reputation for consuming his parcels in secret.

Boys whose homes were in London were allowed out on Saturday afternoons. This had its advantages. To the children of Bellendon Road, his silver buttons, leather girdle and yellow stockings were objects of envy and admiration – an admiration he lost no time in exploiting. One of them, Victor Cooley, remembers being severely reprimanded for his addiction to Omar Khayyam – a corrupting influence. Murry himself carried a copy of 'Elia.' On the other hand, there were drawbacks. For one thing, he was acutely embarrassed by his aunt's deference to the school beadle, whenever she came to collect him; for another, his father, having never got over his being placed second instead of first on the scholarship list, would subject him week by week to a searching inquisition on his place in class *vis-à-vis* his rival, Allen – and Allen, though eight months his junior, was far ahead. When, after several terms' evasion, this awful truth came to light, there was an explosion that shattered the household: which, perhaps, was why Murry remembered Allen's birthday to the end of his life.

If he had become 'lethargic' in class, however (and that is not surprising – nature was bound to get its own back sooner or later), he was neither idle nor unambitious. The same letter which describes (indiscreetly) life at school as 'one long holiday',[16] speaks of his spending every playtime in the library; and he was already resolved on becoming, like Coleridge, a Grecian – one of the select band of sixth-formers destined for university scholarships: 'Won't I think myself someone when I'm one which I count as being a dead certainty if I like to try. When I shall have 15 big buttons instead of 7 small ones.'[16]

Moreover, traits were emerging, not indeed of the future Civil Servant, but of the real Middleton Murry. Together with two other scholars, Allen and Downie, he had soon formed a little circle of initiates, among whom he was the acknowledged leader. It was on his initiative that they decided to set up a 'Republic'. Allen, as mathematician of the group, was appointed Chancellor of the Exchequer; an artist, co-opted to design the postage stamps, became Postmaster General; and Murry himself, of course, as President, drafted the Constitution. The Republic was followed by a newspaper. All had to pool their resources to purchase a jellygraph, while he, Editor-in-Chief this time, contributed the leading articles. And no doubt there were further projects, since (Sir Harold Downie recalls) it was noticeable that each new enthusiasm enlisted a new band of collaborators.

This was while the school was in London. With the removal of Christ's Hospital to Horsham, in the summer of 1902, more orthodox pastimes engrossed him. His old 'blind hunger for the country' [17] met at last, he became, in spite of his short-sightedness, a good enough cricketer to end up as House Captain of Maine A, and a really able swimmer. Cricket, indeed, never lost its fascination for him. In his sixties he still could, and frequently did, recall every detail of a match at the Oval, which his father had taken him to that summer; he even acquired the objectionable practice of taking a portable radio on to the beach in order to listen in to Tests.

At the same time, life at Horsham was so rich and strange that nothing could well have prevented him from feeling, ever more acutely, the contrast presented by his home. The Murrys had moved, via Ewell and Kingston, to Hampton Wick; and he had been blessed with a small brother, Arthur (hereinafter called Richard, the name by which he was to be known) – and 'blessed' is the word, for he was never happier, then or afterwards, than in the company of very small children. But it was the holidays now that were become a bewildering dream. 'My parents and I lived in complete aloofness.' [18] They had neither interests nor tastes in common; and 'one holiday it struck me suddenly, with an awful despair and a guilty consciousness of treachery, that there was not a single object in the whole house which I should have been glad to have for its own sake. This was, in its own small way, a tragic realization.' [19] It was, since it meant a deepening shame, both of his class and of his parents themselves.

In his autobiography, *Between Two Worlds*, he has told of the days of suspense he endured when his father was due to visit the school; of his panic fear lest John Murry should disgrace him in the eyes of his housemaster (a groundless fear, Sainte-Croix being well aware of his origins, and many blue-coat boys no better off); and of the odd compensatory fantasy he evolved afterwards. According to Downie, he would have had his schoolfellows believe that his father belonged to the Indian Civil Service and had just come to bid good-bye at the end of another furlough. Such tales never quite imposed on them, and made him more mysterious than popular.

Perhaps it was to escape the ordeal of Hampton Wick that, in the summer of 1907, he and another seventeen-year-old stumped up all they possessed – £9 between them – to go on a walking-tour of Brittany. In the days before youth hostels, this was something of an adventure, and he was understandably proud of it. His account of the trip, *A Fortnight in Brittany for £4.10.0.*, still survives, though his numerous attempts to get it published came to nothing. Written in a competent, undistinguished prose, with occasional lapses into Lamb, and neatly rounded off with a list of 'Expenses (in detail)', it proves that he had already acquired a working knowledge of French, and that he was deeply impressed with the hospitality of the countryside. It does not add that the hospitality of Morlaix extended to making both of them tipsy, nor that they were so exhausted by the end that he, at least, had to be carried ashore.

Meanwhile, whatever his shame of his family, he was justifying their expectations academically. His 'lethargy' did not outlast the move to Horsham. Although he himself gives us to understand that among his contemporaries he was 'definitely one of the least literary',[20] that was not their impression. On the contrary, to them he appeared very much of a bibliophile, with his choice selection of Restoration dramatists and eighteenth-century essayists, his beautiful Temple Shakespeares, which he saved up to buy as they came out, and the little volume of Ford which he took to chapel because it looked like a Bible. His taste for poetry had been aroused by Lucretius, and for literary criticism by Quiller-Couch – whose *Adventures in Criticism* had led him on to Coleridge and Arnold, the first of his heroes. To his utter astonishment, moreover – for he could never rid himself of the idea that he was comparatively backward – he was awarded, at sixteen, the Charles Lamb Medal for an essay on 'Literature and Journalism' and at eighteen, the Gold Medal for Classics, a year before his time. He was the obvious choice for editor of the school magazine – and he had encompassed his fifteen big buttons.

That meant that once again he would have to stand for a scholarship. Christ's Hospital had given him all it had to give. It had shaped him, 'the spiritual waif of modern industrial society',[21] into the semblance of a gentleman, with a gentleman's accent, a gentleman's manners and a gentleman's accomplishments. Now it was Oxford's turn. He sat for the examination in the summer of 1908, and once again with success. At any time prior to the twentieth century, his obvious destination would have been the Church.

II

ASCENDING CURVE

❧————◆◦◇◦◆————❧

IN 1908 BOARD SCHOOL boys can scarcely have numbered more
than a dozen at Oxford and Cambridge together. Murry himself
knew of only two, and both had come by way of Christ's Hospital.
Few schools were well enough endowed to provide exhibitions; and
without exhibitions worth £70 in addition to a scholarship worth
£100, he could not have afforded to go up. As it was, he was by no
means badly off. Many a student today, recalling what the pound
could buy then, would consider him fortunate.

His own feelings, as the autumn approached, were fearfully mixed.
Oxford meant another plunge into the unknown; and what made it all
the more daunting was the reputation of the college he had been
assigned to, Brasenose. It was rumoured to be a 'tough' college. His
trepidation was such that not only did he 'sidle into Oxford and out
of it by a devious route through Guildford and Reading, rather than
face two London termini, and the piracy of a connecting cab', but he
would, he says, have 'run to the ends of the earth' [1] rather than betray
the yet more devious route by which he had reached a university at all.

However, as so often happens, rumour had outlasted reality. The
Vice Principal of Brasenose at that time was a disciple of Pater,
F. W. Bussell, and under the influence of this remarkable man (while
posing as a Tory squire, a pluralist with ten livings in Norfolk, he was
reputed to have read – and remembered – the whole *Encyclopaedia
Britannica*), the character of the college had already undergone a
change. From being exclusively athletic and social, it was inclining
towards the academic. Straws in the wind had been the foundation of
a literary Pater Society by two undergraduates, Frederick Goodyear
and Charles Mellows, and of a college magazine, *The Brazen Nose*. It
was Goodyear who greeted Murry on the night of his arrival with an
invitation to join the Society.

[14]

He was swept from the start into a social and intellectual whirl which left no time for misgivings. 'I am enjoying myself up here immensely', he wrote to his aunt (whose photograph hung in his study as it had at Christ's Hospital): 'Of course it's all so strange at first, but one falls into it immediately without that irksome fledgling stage which you have when at school. A couple of decent rooms all to one's self, good food, – and you don't know how much we appreciate that after what we got at school – comfortable rooms, some pocket-money, everything that goes to make life pleasant to people of my age.' [2] The food never ceased to impress him. He could not understand how anyone could complain, as some young aristocrats did, preferring to cook a simple meal for themselves in their rooms. But if their assumptions abashed him, he concealed it effectively. Only one of his contemporaries recalls that he was 'noticeably reticent' about his origins. Others deny that he betrayed any class-consciousness whatever.

He was, of course, taking Classics. Courses in English were happily unknown. Outside the broad demesne of Latin and Greek, supplying a permanent standard of excellence, the student of those days could read what authors he chose, and read them as sources of pleasure, not as samples of schools. He could even lose himself in a book and discover a taste of his own: whilst for those who wished to discuss, there were societies innumerable. Through these Murry quickly made friends. The Pater Society introduced him to Michael Sadleir and two younger men, Philip Landon and Leonard Duke; the intercollegiate Milton Society (which Goodyear also prevailed on him to join) to a group of exceptionally able undergraduates, mostly from Trinity, including Joyce Cary and E. H. W. Meyerstein, Arnold Toynbee, Thomas Higham, Duncan Macgregor, F. R. Barry and Philip Mitchell. It was of this group that he wrote:

> They were a little older than the average undergraduate. Some of them had come on from Scottish universities, while Joyce had put in a year at an art school. Something had intervened for them between the public school and the university, which made the difference. They were neither overgrown sixth-form boys, like me, nor pass-men up for a good time. There was nothing precious about them, yet their intellectual interests were various and widespread; and they judged for themselves. To me they were vastly stimulating: I can hardly have been that to them. [1]

The last sentence is unwarranted. 'Murry certainly contributed more than his fair share to the informal education of his contemporaries', writes Higham (now Dean of Trinity), and his statement is supported by Meyerstein and others. Although no orator, in congenial company such as this he could always be a good talker; Cary described him as 'brilliant in dialectics'; and his personality was already impressive. 'With his white face, black hair and aquiline features', says Duke, 'he always reminded me of the portraits of Dante: there was a look almost of spirituality, humanized by his quaint way of holding his head on one side, and his smile – rather shy than sly.' Donald Gladding also 'got the impression of a future poet or saint'. Some found him verging on the sentimental or precious, but all emphasize his good looks – only spoilt, according to Sadleir, by 'his ungainly, lunging walk'.*

Since several of these friends were fine athletes as well as intellectuals, Murry was able, he tells us, 'to make my athletic contribution to the college, so to speak, vicariously'.³ But this was not the whole truth. Although his attempts at rowing ended, on one occasion at least, in his being thrown into the river, he rose to be captain of the Hornets, the Brasenose Cricket XI. Altogether, his first two years at Oxford were so fully occupied that it is less surprising to learn that he was usually up till one or two in the morning than that he continued to make progress in the Classics. Fortunately, his tutor, H. F. Fox, was a man he could love and admire – Fox lives again in *Between Two Worlds* – and in those days admiration and love invariably called forth his best.

His first vacations were spent at home. His parents had prepared him a snuggery – very small, but with its jars of tobacco and lines of books very impressive to his small brother. A carpenter living next door, who worked at Hampton Court, gave him his first lessons in woodwork, helping him to fashion a cigarette-box and cribbage-marker out of Palace timber; and he adorned the walls with copies of pictures, good enough, in Richard's opinion, to belie his own belief that he had no talent whatever for draughtsmanship. It was a cosy retreat, and, like most undergraduates, he worked harder at home than at college.

During the Long Vacation of 1909, however, Fox invited him and three others for a month at Snape, in Suffolk, studying and sailing on the Alde. As a schoolboy, he had passed evening after evening

---

* Murry himself attributed this to the necessity of keeping pace with the bigger boys at Christ's Hospital, when they marched to a band.

dreaming of cruising with his friends; now the reality proved as good as the dream. 'What was probably at best good fun to my companions was a wild delight to me. When they went off to play golf, I would take out the boat alone, and generally succeed in running myself aground. Then I waited, blissfully, for them to return and extricate me. The estuary of the Alde was then a marvellous piece of country – soaked in sunshine – and for the first time in my life I entered into a care-free, country existence which I felt to be my rightful heritage.' That reading-party was decisive. He could no longer endure the idea of spending his vacations alone in a suburb; and 'as soon as my month was over . . . my mind was filled with a single purpose – to find some place in the country where I could live'.[4] The upshot was that he took a room in a farmhouse, a few miles from Stow-on-the-Wold, and spent the next two vacations there.

These too were bliss. After a hard struggle to overcome his shyness, the farmer and his wife took Murry to their hearts. Trafalgar Farm became his home in a way that Lutterworth, Cedars Road, had never been. For a spell, he was simply one of the Peachey family. They were the originals of the Williamsons in *The Things We Are*, and he let them believe that he, like the hero of his novel, had only a mother, who lived abroad on a pension. But 'I suppose that I was as near as I ever could be to my real self in the kitchen at Waterloo. There I had no need, and therefore no desire, to defend a precarious position.'[5] This brief interlude of 'reality' and unalloyed happiness stamped itself so indelibly on his memory that the chapters devoted to it in his autobiography are among the most vivid he ever wrote. J. D. Beresford once cited them as evidence that he might (despite *The Things We Are*) have become a novelist of distinction.

Probably it was Peachey who implanted in Murry that hankering after a farm of his own which found such belated fruition. It was certainly he who infected him with his own passion for hunting (which another reviewer, Winifred Holtby, cited as proof of his egocentricity). For a time he could contemplate no career that did not entail riding. That Christmas, accordingly, he broke the grim news to his father that, instead of trying for Somerset House, he would enter the Indian Civil Service – at the same time extracting £30 for the purchase of a horse. Then, as an eligible suitor, he proceeded to fall in love. His courtship (conducted on horseback) was auspicious. Fate and the vicar's niece smiled; and when, towards the end of the Easter Vacation of 1910, news reached Trafalgar Farm that he had not only been awarded the Bridgeman Prize for an essay, but was one of four Brasenose men (a record since 1898) to win a first in Honour Moderations, his prospects seemed to be assured.

Unluckily – or luckily – just at this moment the Peacheys had another visitor, a young French officer of the submarine service, Maurice Larrouy, who had stopped with them before to learn English. In his spare time Larrouy wrote novels, under the name of René Milan, and naturally he was interested to meet an Englishman of literary leanings: more especially as Murry, having lately supported with 'mournful optimism' (*The Brazen Nose*) Sadleir's attempts to win Oxford for the Symbolists, was now endeavouring to read them. Larrouy pointed out the absurdity of studying Rimbaud or Mallarmé before one could converse intelligibly with a French porter. If he, Larrouy, could find time to visit England, Murry could afford a vacation in Paris. In fact, it was imperative that he should, if he dreamed of becoming a critic – was Paris not the capital of culture? He would make the arrangements himself.

If Murry was really dreaming of becoming a critic, his decision to enter the Indian Civil Service must have died almost as soon as it was born. But that is what we should expect. His life at this time was entirely fluid, ready for any mould it was poured into. He had no convictions of his own. What passed for his personal convictions were, like most people's, those of the circles he moved in: only he, moving in so many, never had time to consolidate them. He just conformed to the expectations of his associates, adopting *persona* after *persona*. The Cotswold *persona* had been one – the best-fitting so far, but no more secure for that. Now he would have to try on another. For Larrouy, after he had left, pressed home the attack by post, and was reinforced by Cary and Sadleir. Reluctantly, Murry acquiesced.

Consequently, instead of returning to Trafalgar Farm for the summer, he took a tutorship at Hopetown, Northumberland, coaching and golfing with Lord Charles Hope, in order to pay for the excursion. And in fact he never returned. His sweetheart he saw once more, as she happened to be passing through Oxford; the Peacheys, without a line of explanation or affection, gratitude or regret, he let drop out of his life for ever. The Christmas Vacation of 1910–11 found him alone in Paris.

At first, he was very much alone. Larrouy had booked him a room

at the Hôtel de l'Univers, Rue Gay Lussac, but given him no introductions. Cary, who knew the Latin Quarter well, was not due to join
him until the New Year. Left to his own devices, he quietly adopted a
routine. It was dictated partly by his poverty (though why he should
have been so poor is obscure), and partly by his shrinking from every
fresh human contact. The mornings were spent at the picture galleries,
the afternoons in reading or writing, the evenings at one or other of
the cafés frequented by students, where he took his first and only meal
of the day and sat on till after midnight.

Left Bank cafés, however, are no place for solitude. Within a week
of his arrival at most, the art-students had found him out. If he was
not an artist himself, he was something still better – a votary of the
arts. His impressionability, his receptivity to their ideas, his naïve and
unconcealed admiration for their devotion to the *métier*, won him
their hearts. They invited him to their tables, they showed off before
him – and he loved it. He was even delighted when they asked him
to lend them money, since that proved that they thought him one of
themselves, and would have been ashamed to hold back, though it
meant wiring to Cary for more. 'I have made two score of acquaintances and three *friends*',[6] he was exclaiming in a letter to Landon soon
after Christmas; one of these friends, a Pole named Ouritz, was
'nothing less than a genius':[7]

> I met him and three others in a cheap café; on a night when one of them
> had made 40 francs out of a dealer for some hackwork. They invited me
> to share their wine and I became one of the party: we talked in a weird
> mélange of French (they can hardly speak French) – German and Italian.
> How we talked! From ten o'clock to three in the morning in praise of
> Nietzsche and Schopenhauer – and Art. It will be many years before Art
> becomes so real a thing in speech to me again. For to Ouritz it was a thing
> to die for and live for – to sink one's whole being in. And so we talked –
> and I became a hero among a company of heroes. Ouritz is indeed $\acute{\varrho}\mu\acute{\iota}$
> $\theta\varepsilon o\varsigma$ – light eyes and flaxen hair – flushed with good wine towards the
> end he climbed upon the table and chanted a part of the kalevala: – a
> wonderful thing that every true Lothringian knows from his cradle. And
> we parted after I had bound myself with many oaths to visit them.[6]

The genius of Ouritz seems to have manifested itself chiefly in the
kalevala and the confusion of his studio, where Murry posed for his
portrait next day. But what mattered to him more by far than the quality
of their achievement (which he had no means of judging anyway) was

the enthusiasm of all these young men. That was intoxicating. He was caught up in a world quite different from any he had hitherto known – a world of which Art was the pivot and pole. He goes on:

> I have come to see and see clearly how living and quivering a thing is Art; here in Paris it is a Life-force you can feel – and perhaps you will find when I come back that a heresy or two has taken root in my brain on the question. At all events L'Art pour L'Art has a different but a much more real meaning now to my soul: because I have seen it lived and heard it worshipped and watched the sacrifices made for it. And so you can read between the lines that my life here has been fuller than it ever had been before. I have got clear on things that shifted vaguely before me and the whole vividness and directness has reacted back upon me and given me myself an end to live for – which will be a life of Art as far as I can make it so.[6]

What that meant in practical terms was that he would apply for a Senior Hulme Scholarship, spend a year and a half at the Sorbonne under Bergson, a further year and a half in Germany, and then either 'be a don or starve in Paris as a journalist'.[6]

Ostensibly it was to attend Bergson's lectures that he had come to Paris on this occasion. 'I never went', he states in Coming to London – giving the lie to some of his letters. But he was studying L'Evolution Créatrice. Bergson was the chosen philosopher of many of the young Post-Impressionists, and already he seems to have seen himself as a theoretical exponent of the movement. What else could 'a life of Art' denote, so far as he was concerned?

The years 1910–11 were the heyday of Fauvism in France. Thanks to Cary he had come all prepared to be impressed by it – his first letter extolling a poster whose 'yellow-greens screamed in a discord which was the consummation of a perfect harmony';[8] and soon he was meeting some of its representatives. One in particular commanded his admiration – John Duncan Fergusson, the Scottish artist. Again, it was more by his personality than his paintings: only whereas the bohemianism of Ouritz quickly palled, the rhythm of Fergusson did not. A man some years older than Murry, he had the engaging habit of referring to anyone he respected – anyone, that is, 'who put up, consciously or unconsciously, some resistance to the disease of mechanical uniformity' – as an 'artist':

> The effect of this was (though he never formulated it) that he, in his capacity of a painter of pictures, was a representative and peculiar cham-

pion of this tribe of men. If he stuck to his guns, and faced without flinch-
ing the unpopularity he knew was coming to him through abandoning his
earlier and very saleable manner, he was, in his function of advance-guard,
somehow clearing the way for future freedom for the tribe. Again, it
followed that it was unseemly for an artist to live uncleanly or in disorder:
he must embody a natural discipline of his own. His rhythm must be his
own rhythm: but rhythm he must have. In other words, art was not a
profession. No man could be a professional artist. By profession he might
be a painter, a writer, or equally well a boxer or a boot-black; whether he
was an artist or not depended on what he was in himself. Art was a quality
of being – an achievement of, or an effort towards integrity.[9]

Fergusson's influence on Murry, like his friendship, was lasting. The
first-fruits of their desultory discussions was the idea of a new magazine, to be entitled *Rhythm*.

Bliss was it in that dawn to be alive! To Murry, the Post-Impressionist resurgence veritably was a dawn – 'There are great artists
working here to-day'[8] – and, like Wordsworth at a similar climacteric,
he had fallen in love. How much of his enthusiasm, of his sense of
identification with the French school, sprang from his passion for
Marguéritte, how far his decision to attend the Sorbonne was really
motivated by that, he himself might have found it hard to say. Rive
Gauche, Fauvism, Marguéritte – to him they were all one 'sensation'.
That it played some part, however, and probably the largest part, he
would have been the last to deny, and his whole future life would
confirm. Its motto might have been: *Cherchez la femme*.

Not that he was exceptionally passionate – quite the contrary.
Francis Carco's description of him at this time, spending night after
night with the *petites femmes* and sending them flowers on the morrow
(a practice which he, Carco, shamed him out of) is on a par with his
statement that Murry was already *Times* correspondent. He may well
have given Carco to understand such things – for he could not shake
off the 'tyrannous pretence of manifold experience in another's presence'[10] – but in truth his intellectual precocity was matched by an
emotional immaturity peculiar even in an Englishman. '*C'était un
adolescent au teint clair, aux yeux pétillants d'intélligence et d'ironie, qui
cachait mal, sous ses allures décidées, une grande pudeur.*'[11] His very
attractiveness to women was bound up with that *grande pudeur*. They
sensed his craving for affection, and it brought out the mother as well
as the mistress.

It was not only the art-students of the Café d'Harcourt who had sought him out. From the first he had been an object of interest to the *petites femmes*. 'It is a job to write a reasoned critical letter', he had confessed to Landon soon after his arrival, 'with Yvonne and the rest of them clasping your neck and reading every word, that they can't understand.'[7] Yvonne, demonstrative, vulgar, vain, was of one breed; Marguéritte of quite another. An unsophisticated country girl from the Corrèze, not long resident in Paris, not yet subdued to the life, '*J'ai fait mes bêtises*', she acknowledged, but she was only too ready to renounce them – as she did, the moment she had enticed him to bed. She took a job as a sempstress – while he, completely oblivious to all but this new enchantment, promised her an allowance of 10s. a week. By the time Cary arrived in Paris, 'worldly-wise, *and* sweet',[12] it was already too late for his warnings. In Marguéritte, Murry had found the warmth and security he craved; in him she had found – or thought she had found – a husband.

Thus, for the first time, both the demands of his nature were fulfilled: intelligence and affection were at one. For the first time, in the Paris of Fauvism and Marguéritte, he could feel that he *belonged*. And, within a matter of weeks, the conciliation was finding expression in the first of his writings to bear the unmistakable Murry impress: an essay on 'Art and Philosophy', produced in one of those moments of 'inspiration' which (he told Landon) visited him in Paris alone, during which 'I really see visions for some hours on end; and I understand things that I never understood before'.[13]

The essay shows him at the top of his enthusiasm for Bergson. At the same time it shows just what Bergson had come to mean to him. Life, it tells us, proceeds by 'unending creations', of which the artist's are the type and continuation. Since no analysis of the old will suffice to predict the new, reason, in order to apprehend life, must be transformed into intuition, 'that point, as it were, at which the reason becomes most wholly itself, and by its own heightened working conquers the crude opposition of subject and object, from which at a lower level it cannot become free'. By the same token – this being the artist's prerogative – philosophy must be transformed into a 'recognition of the rational supremacy of art'.

Art, in other words, expresses a new wholeness of the personality, a unity to which the intellect is merely instrumental. Here the implicit has become explicit. This essay, immature as it is, diffuse, hortatory, seeking to make up by emphasis for all that it lacks in definition, is none the less the authentic forerunner of *Things to Come*, just as *Rhythm*, in whose first number it appeared, was to be the forerunner of *The Adelphi*.

Truly that vacation in Paris marked a climacteric in Murry's development; and it is no surprise to learn that it was followed by a 'fearful revulsion' [13] from Oxford. To return from the delicacy of those evenings with Marguéritte to the pruriences of the man with whom, to his outspoken regret, he had elected to share rooms in Ship Street, from the fervid debates of the Quarter to 'the pointlessly subtle and insincerely clever' [14] discussions of the Pater Society, was almost more than he could bear. For a week or two he was actually ill. 'Another year and a half', he mourned to his aunt, 'is a terribly long time before one can be up and doing – although I'm afraid it will be very quaint things that I shall do in life.' [15]

He put a brave face upon it; he took part in college activities as usual, composing the Brasenose Ale Verses for the annual Shrove Tuesday celebrations, opening discussions on 'Mysticism and Literature' and 'Criticism and Art'; to none of his friends, except Cary, did he breathe a word of his love. But his heart was no longer in the business. He had left it behind in Paris – and where his heart was, there went much of his treasure also. By Easter his resources were so exiguous that it was only by raising £10 from family and long-suffering friends that he was able to go back at all.

Go back he nevertheless did – and immediately the spell reasserted itself. Not that he saw much of Marguéritte now. While he occupied her rooms at No. 36 Rue des Ecoles, she had gone to live with a relative, who insisted upon her returning at nights. But his time was blissfully occupied, roaming the streets, reading the Symbolists, chatting with painters and poets into the small hours of the morning. He was, he told Landon, sunk in 'a coma of happiness' [16] – a coma so deep, in fact, that before he awoke to what was happening, he had left his pocket-book in one of the cafés and lost every sou he possessed. Still, in response to his frantic cards, Landon, Duke and Cary stumped up; and still he stayed, living on doughnuts, chestnuts and (if one of his letters is to be trusted) hashish, or scrounging meals from his friends.

The idea of *Rhythm* had by this time taken definite shape. He had interested Goodyear and Sadleir. Sadleir's father, a connoisseur and collector of paintings, had subscribed £50 to the venture, and Michael himself was to join him in Paris. Fergusson remembers their calling at his studio one morning for permission to use a picture of his, then on exhibition, for the cover of the opening number. He promised to design a new one, and also to act as art editor – on condition that the price of the magazine did not exceed a shilling. Only at that, he pointed out, could it hope to circulate in Aberdeen and Perthshire.

Actually, Fergusson never supposed that it would last beyond one or two numbers. But these young men were enthusiastic, and their enthusiasm was contagious. Very soon Murry was able to announce an imposing list of contributors, including, on the artistic side, Othon Friesz and Anne Estelle Rice, Derain, Van Dongen, Peploe and Picasso; on the literary, Francis Carco, Edouard Gazanin and Tristan Dérème, 'the three leaders of the young fantaisiste movement'. *Rhythm*, he informed Landon, was to be the organ of Modernism:

> Modernism means, when I use it, Bergsonism in Philosophy – that is a really *Creative* Evolution with only in the end an Intuition to put the individual at its heart roots; an intuition which is the raising of Personality to the nth degree, a conscious concentration of vision. This I cannot pause to enlarge on now. I hope next term every week to have a gathering of those people who are really heart and soul with us, who stand for Progress in a real sense in Art matters, whereat we can discuss matters. Incidentally it does touch politics very very intimately and I am a yellow Syndicalist; that too I can't explain.
>
> Now Bergsonism stands for Post Impressionism in its essential meaning – and not in the sense of the Grafton Exhibition: it stands for a certain symbolism in poetry on the one hand; and a certain definite rejection of suggestion on the other. It stands equally for Debussy and Maehler in music; for Fantaisisme in Modern French literature, and generally if you like for 'guts' and bloodiness.
>
> Now, there is a lot to explain there, and doubtless you will demand it next term till then it must wait; but without seeing the connexions between the elements, you may see the general drift of the idea, on which the venture is to be run. It is to be kept absolutely cosmopolitan – no suggestion of connexion with Oxford; so that I want you to leave my name or anything local out of the question – Oxford is almost the negation of our idea. We will have no Shavianism or False Aestheticism . . . But still we want more younger men from England – young men in London: who have not gone thro' the unenthusiastic aesthetic atmosphere of Oxford: How to get them is the problem?
>
> We are arranging to have the paper distributed in Edinburgh, Glasgow, Manchester, London, Oxford, Cambridge, Paris, New York, and Munich

and all over the world by subscription. My heart is absolutely in it, and now that I know that there are so many other men over the world with the same enthusiasms and the same disgusts I have a new interest in Life. I am playing with every penny I have in the cause.

Schools have gone to glory as far as I'm concerned. I sink or rise to my proper place in Paris and Oxford fades away.[17]

In *Between Two Worlds* all this side of Murry's life in Paris is totally eclipsed by his love-affair and its painful dénouement. Of the circumstances attending the birth of the magazine he retained 'no memory at all'.[18] His own narrative, accordingly, gives a quite false impression, both of its importance to him at the time and of the extent to which he was the moving spirit. For all their vagueness and youthful didacticism, his letters leave no doubt that he was, as he appeared to Fergusson and others, a much more positive and enterprising person than he himself would have us believe. And perhaps if the course of true love had run smooth, his contributions to the earlier numbers would not have been so feeble as they were.

The trouble was, that though Oxford might fade away from his mind, there could be no question of his fading away from Oxford. Apart from his scholarship and exhibitions, he had not a penny of his own to play with. To have gone down now would have meant throwing away all his advantages and declining into some office that would leave neither leisure nor energy for editing. Upon his enduring another four terms depended whatever future he aspired to. *Rhythm* itself depended upon it.

Yet here was Marguéritte, trustfully waiting for the word that would make her his wife – and he dearly longing to speak it. Cary was right: he had landed himself in an impossible position. Paris had kindled all his latent idealism, only, it seemed, to dash water on it. She, who had meant security to him, now meant the very reverse. 'If I had had any money, even the chance of the tiniest job in Paris – or indeed in England – if, like Joyce Cary, I had had £300 a year of my own – or even a *quarter* of that – I should have married Marguéritte. There is no earthly doubt about it. And what, I wonder, would my life have been then? Something unimaginably different?'[19]

As it was, his second vacation in Paris drew to a close, like the first, without the word being spoken. He went back to Oxford promising to return in the summer – but this time resenting the love (or was it now only pity?) which had compelled the promise. 'Every time that he wrote a letter he watched himself with disgusted curiosity construct phrases of deep affection; every time he received a letter from her, a wave of sentiment, which he knew for false at the very moment that it made him cry, broke over him and urged him on to yet another hypocrisy. Thus the affair dragged on monotonously.'[20] He continued to send Marguéritte money, though it meant begging the College for an advance on his October allowance; continued to hold out the prospect of rejoining her at the end of the term. But there is a point at which indecision itself amounts to decision.

When at last the summer term did end, instead of returning directly he took, first a tutorship in Devon, stag-hunting and tickling for trout with the young Lord Fortescue, then a month in Heidelberg, 'working ten hours a day in the hottest weather that ever was'[21] to master the rudiments of German. Only late in September did he finally wend his way, via Cologne, towards Paris – and then beset with such violent alternations of longing and resentment as he has depicted in the opening pages of *Still Life*. 'All that remained of that chaotic interplay of argument and objection was the deep knowledge that to part finally was right, that all else was wrong, and that he was too weak to do what was right.'[22]

He was too weak to tell Marguéritte to her face that they had come to the parting of the ways, too weak to inflict her pain on himself. Had he plucked up the courage, would everything have turned out happily after all? He came to believe that it would have done. But at the time, after twenty-four hours spent in Paris miserably trying to make up his mind, he turned tail and fled – for Hampton Wick. The pang of that betrayal was to haunt him for twenty-eight years, the shame of it to the end of his life.

III

TAKING OFF

—————◆◆◆◆◆—————

THE QUARTERLY *Rhythm*, which made its appearance in June 1911, was a remarkable achievement for a couple of undergraduates. It is not surprising that it should have won a *succès d'estime* in Oxford, where Vice Principal Bussell himself was to be heard reciting over and over, with a delighted chuckle, the conclusion of a prose-poem by Carco: '*Absolumment nu! Absolumment nu!*' But Murry's intention was realized: there was nothing in the magazine itself to betray its undergraduate origins, nor was the small band of readers located mainly within the University. It was emphatically, aggressively cosmopolitan, aiming directly at those who had been excited, the winter before, by the first Post-Impressionist exhibition at the Grafton Gallery.

Of that exhibition Arnold Bennett had written in *The New Age*: 'I have permitted myself to suspect that supposing some young writer were to come along and do in words what these men have done in paint, I might conceivably be disgusted with nearly the whole of modern fiction, and I might have to begin again. This awkward experience will in all probability not happen to me, but it might happen to a younger writer than me.' Whether or not Murry read this comment – and Bennett was one of the few English authors of the older generation whom he did read – it chimed exactly with his purpose. He wanted *Rhythm* to do in words what the Post-Impressionists had done in paint; and though he was disappointed – for the literary side was never up to the artistic – the handsome typography of the St Catherine Press offset the weakness of the articles, while the numerous black-and-white illustrations, selected by Fergusson, went far towards justifying their claims. The first two numbers alone included work by S. J. Peploe, Anne Estelle Rice, Othon Friesz and Picasso.

His own contribution to the opening number was the essay, 'Art and Philosophy'. By the time this appeared, however, the precarious unity it commemorated was already a thing of the past. Meyerstein, who must have observed Murry shrewdly, had the impression that 'his mind was divided; he seemed to look at existence now with the reason, now with the passions . . . he did not apparently admit that the claims of emotion and intellect must be worked into some kind of unity'.[1] Even if he had still admitted that, it would have been beyond his power to achieve, now and for a long while to come.

In the throes of what he soon afterwards called 'the most terrible mental struggle a man can undergo, when his love for a woman turns to pity'[2] (whatever struggle Murry underwent would always be 'the most terrible'), he was in no condition to philosophize that summer. As his letters show, he was trying desperately to salve his self-esteem with the unguent of self-pity and self-dramatization. The examples of Dowson and Wilde, Flaubert and Baudelaire, are appealed to in turn: 'There's no road to the poem that burns and the words that bite. Only the old Vivez and that means Souffrez . . . Live, suffer, and you may win out – and you may leave just enough ashes to cover the bottom of an urn neglected nameless in a cobwebbed niche.'[3] The sententiousness, the affectation of superiority in experience, are painful.

It was not that he felt himself a 'cad'. That would have implied that he genuinely subscribed to the code of his milieu. It was precisely because he did not, that he was divided against himself. He had betrayed the one value that was truly his own, although it was only by betraying it that he had discovered it – what Keats would have called 'the holiness of the heart's affections'. He would never do so again. He had, in fact, sacrificed the claims of emotion to those of intellect, only to learn that the sacrifice gained him nothing. The material security it brought turned to dust and ashes in his mouth. If he was in no condition to philosophize, much less was he in a condition to work – unless a preoccupation with Plato's aesthetics may be termed work in the academic sense. His career at Oxford was effectively over. Though he lingered on another two terms, sharing new rooms with Cary in Holywell, he no longer made even a pretence of attending lectures. His real life, such as it was, was lived elsewhere.

Rhythm, originating in revulsion from Oxford, served to intensify it. Seeking in London 'some counterpart to that wonderful republic of art in Paris',[4] he was led by Fergusson to Dan Rider's bookshop, in St Martin's Lane. It was a poor counterpart, but the best. There, in his café behind the shop, Rider would treat struggling authors to cake, cups of tea and, on special occasions, the company of Frank Harris. Murry, as an editor, was received with respect by the coterie, which included such up-and-coming talents as Lovat Fraser, Holbrook Jackson and Hugh Kingsmill. As a shame-faced seducer, he could draw comfort from their man-of-the-world cynicism: for ' "Life" was the *specialité de la maison*; and "Life" consisted, essentially, in love-affairs with women'.[5] Once again, he soon absorbed, or appeared to absorb, the tone of the house, even transposing it into a Dowsonesque poem, with the title 'Life':

> *No, let her go her way,*
> *Laugh with her lovers of a single day*
> *For the joy of bought embraces. She is fair,*
> *Her breasts like towers, and her chestnut hair*
> *Flowing and fragrant, and her dancing eyes*
> *Will burst with passion. Have not these their price?*
> *But we were more than lovers of a night.*
> *And we were fools. Like fools we turned our light*
> *Into the darkness of a vain regret . . .*[6]

All this, however, was mere bravado. Not merely was he inwardly shocked by Kingsmill's language, but his first attempt to live up to the code was his last. One miserable assignation outside Oxford, ending in an attack of gonorrhoea, was enough to show up these pretensions, at least to himself. The poem had hardly appeared, in fact, before he was involved again, and this time finally – with Mrs George Bowden, *alias* Katherine Mansfield.

Katherine was twenty-four when Murry met her – ten months older than himself. Like him, she had rebelled against a bourgeois home and upbringing – though her father, the prosperous, complacent Chairman of the Bank of New Zealand, was more indulgent than his, taking a genuine, if bewildered, pride in her first attempts at fiction, and giving way to her importunate demand to be allowed to leave Wellington for London in her twentieth year. Like him, she had spent some months on the Continent, in Paris, Belgium, Germany and Geneva – and incidentally been so struck by the Post-Impressionists that she could refer to Van Gogh as one of her writing masters. Under the influence of Wilde, moreover, she, like him, had set out in search of 'life' – and 'life' for her meant much the same as it did at Dan Rider's. One 'adventure' had ended in a miscarriage, another in an abortion, a third in an operation for peritonitis which had permanently injured her health, making it unlikely, if not impossible, that she would ever bear a child. In 1909 she had married, for the sake of security, only to desert her husband the following day. Now, though without abating her desire to *épater le bourgeois*, she was inwardly longing to start afresh.

To Murry, the bitter short stories she had just published, *In a German Pension*, equally with the one she had sent in to *Rhythm*, 'The Woman at the Store', seemed to express, with a power he envied, his own 'revulsion from life'.[7] He was eager to meet the authoress; and W. L. George obligingly arranged an introduction – anticipating, it appears, a lively clash of temperaments, since both had acquired reputations which neither could properly sustain, he as a sardonic young Bergsonian, she as a cynical wit. They took to each other at sight.

This was in December 1911, when Murry was spending a dismal vacation with his parents at Wandsworth, quarrelling with his father about late nights and borrowing from Aunt Doll to pay his keep. Soon afterwards Katherine went back to Geneva, he to Oxford. But a correspondence had sprung up *à propos* of *Rhythm*, and before the end of the term they were meeting again, at her flat in Clovelly Mansions, Gray's Inn Road. There he caught his first glimpse of her young brother, Leslie, who had just been buying a car to take back to New Zealand, 'very impressive to me – a denizen of the strange and inaccessible world of wealth';[8] and there they tea-ed *tête-à-tête*. It was not many minutes before he found himself confiding his aversion to university life, his incapacity for work, his mostly ineffectual attempts to escape from dons and duns by way of free-lance journalism. She promptly decided that he must come down, without troubling about the remaining three months that would secure him a first in Greats.

It was a characteristic beginning. The initiative was always to be hers: and he, whose 'whole life seemed to be histrionic, broken by one only impulse to throw himself into another's keeping, and thus be rid of the unending necessity of choosing and acting the part he chose',[9] acquiesced in it thankfully. Had it been otherwise, she would not have been drawn to him as she was. Little though he suspected it at the time, his very diffidence and dependence were his asset. She had had enough – much more than enough – of the conquering male. Only a few months before, she had been on the point of adopting a child.

It was on Katherine's initiative that he came down from Oxford that spring; on hers that he cut adrift from his parents, taking a room in her flat; on hers that – at the third time of asking – he became her lover. The story has been told so often and so well that there is no need to go over it again. But the fact of Murry's backwardness, or bashfulness – which, even then, it took a kind of apocalyptic vision of the indifference of the universe to overcome – cannot be stressed too hard. Embarrassing though these details may be to some, and piquant to others, they are the key to much of his career. What can be read between the lines of his novel, *Still Life*, with its curiously infantile ardours, is confirmed by his intimate journals. It was a bashfulness, not only of heart, but of body.

At the time they met, there were good reasons for this. 'It's hard to explain: but two things worked together in me: a very deep sense of guilt for my treachery to Marguéritte, which made me feel unworthy of a woman's tenderness, combined with the sense of defilement produced by the gonorrhoea.' [10] These, however, will hardly account for the strength and duration of his recoil – for, he goes on: 'I was a terribly "innocent" lover. It was only when we were settling in at Runcton, and I happened to read one or two passionate love-letters from S. V., an Austrian journalist . . . in which he spoke of kissing her breasts, that I plucked up courage and dared to kiss them . . . Beyond that I never made love to her – right to the end.' [10] There were no caresses, no preliminaries; their love-making (such as it was) was a climax without crescendo. Some deep repression must have been at work, which it is tempting to associate with his confession elsewhere that he had been the victim, at the age of fourteen, of an 'indecent assault'. The bare fact that he, so candid in print, could never bring himself to mention this incident, tells a tale: it left 'a scar inside me somewhere'.[11] It had set him off on the schoolboy habit of masturbation – a habit he 'had no doubt at all . . . was a deadly sin';[12] and it was responsible, he knew, for his violent repugnance to homosexuality. One cannot escape the suspicion that it was responsible for more than he knew.

However that may be, Katherine made no attempt to initiate him. On the contrary:

Looking back, it seems to me now that at first she was enchanted by my innocence, and wanted to preserve it, and (to be in harmony) to put away her own 'experience', which was considerable and much of it an unhappy memory. She wanted to annihilate her past. Of that I am *sure*. She never mentioned it to me – her past (I mean) so far as it consisted of relations with men – and I was made to feel that any reference to, or curiosity about, it would be unwelcome, and hurting. Not that I was curious about it. My attitude was that if she wanted to tell me about it, she would: if not, she knew best. But I was deeply conscious that she wanted to start afresh, and that she was in some way afraid of my making any contact with her past.[10]

Not merely did she never confide in him, as he did in her, but even when they finally realized that their hopes of a child were to be disappointed, she never divulged the cause: she gave him to understand that it lay with him. In Murry she found a child as much as a husband, a 'symbol and incarnation of her lost innocence';[13] in Katherine he found a mother as much as a wife, a symbol and incarnation of security. It was not until forty years later that he learned the facts of her earlier life – from Anthony Alpers's *Katherine Mansfield: A Biography*.

From the outset he idealized her. 'She was a woman simple and lovely in all her ways,' he writes in *Between Two Worlds*: 'I do not think it ever entered my head, at any time, to criticise her in any way.'[14] Not all his friends were equally uncritical – much less his family. Believing, in the simplicity of his heart, that 'when they met Katherine, they could not fail to see that there had been method in the madness of their son',[15] he soon took her to visit his parents. The result was as might have been expected. Their horror, on learning that he was cohabiting with a married woman, was such as to embolden his mother and aunt to pay a return visit to Clovelly Mansions, for the purpose of taking him away. It was years before he met them again. Of his Oxford friends, Goodyear, Meyerstein and Elliot Crooke survived. Duke, who saw only 'a dumpy young woman with bobbed hair', features no more in the correspondence; the last letter Landon received from Murry, dated May 17, 1912, announced his imminent departure, via Poland and Russia, for China; and it was not very long before Sadleir, finding his editorial judgements brushed aside as the velleities of an incorrigible bourgeois, withdrew, or was ousted, from *Rhythm*.

Still, the first two years of their life together were happy ones, what hardships did come their way serving mainly to unite them more closely. New friends took the places of the old – Gordon Campbell, the Irish barrister, whose generosity was so often their mainstay; and Gilbert Cannan, the novelist, who christened them 'the Tigers', after a woodcut in *Rhythm*. (Softened, via 'Tig', to 'Wig', this became Murry's permanent nickname for Katherine.) They were still young enough to enjoy shocking the respectable. At The Duke of York, in Theobald's Road, where they supped, he in his old fisherman's jersey, she in her exotic coiffures, were taken for a music-hall turn – and the music-halls did, in fact, see much of them, though as patrons, not performers: as, of course, did the *Ballet Russe*. Back in their flat, guests would be enchanted or embarrassed, as the case might be, to find themselves the focus of much secret conspiracy and laughter; while Katherine's wit at their expense, like her many accomplished poses, never ceased to command Murry's admiration.

His former tutor, Fox, moreover, having failed to persuade him to stay at Oxford, but secured his promise to return for his Finals (which he did, winning a tolerable second), presented him that April to J. A. Spender, editor of *The Westminster Gazette*: with the result that he was taken on as a reviewer, and, quickly acquiring the professional journalist's knack of reading a book at a glance, was soon making up to £5 a week. With this as well as Katherine's allowance of £100 a year, they ought to have been very well off.

Unfortunately *Rhythm*, now changed to a monthly, absorbed much of their time and income. Partly because it had brought them together, and partly because of the ferocious attacks launched on it month by month in *The New Age* (to which both had contributed formerly), they made it a point of honour to keep the magazine in being, even when it was obvious that it could never pay its way. In the summer of 1912 Katherine's publisher, 'Stephen Swift', agreed to take over the publication, paying them £10 a month as editors. They forthwith rented and furnished a house of their own – Runcton Cottage, near Chichester – only to learn, within three months, not merely that Swift was bankrupt, but that he had bequeathed them a debt of £400. From that time forward, the whole of Katherine's allowance went in monthly instalments to the printers.

Reading the old files today, it is possible to trace other vicissitudes, as the Post-Impressionist fireworks of the earlier numbers give way, first to the rising star of Frank Harris, then to the Georgian constellation. The Frank Harris cult was short-lived, reaching its apogee in July 1912, with Murry's dithyrambic likening of Harris to

Shakespeare, 'Who is the Man?' – the genesis and bathetic sequel of which he has recounted in *Between Two Worlds*. This is, of course, a preposterous effusion, as he was the first to realize, when 'the greatest short-story writer England has ever possessed' turned out to be the most unscrupulous plagiarist. But it has a redeeming side. Not only is genuine admiration, however naïve, preferable to affectation or indifference, but the ideal of which Harris was the unworthy embodiment was not itself unworthy:

> Fifty years ago the man Shakespeare was unknown . . . Here was an artist whom all the world confesses supreme, who must by the same confession have been the supreme man of the last one thousand years, utterly unknown. To recreate this soul was one of the highest tasks that a great artist could undertake. To achieve where Coleridge and Goethe failed needed a man on a spiritual equality with William Shakespeare, perhaps without the supreme poetic gift, yet for intellect and power of divination his spiritual equal.

That Murry should already have divined that prerequisite of the ideal Shakespeare-critic is perhaps as deserving of notice as the fact, recorded by Kingsmill, that he burst into tears and fled at the voice of the great man's displeasure.*

The Georgians flooded in in the wake of Edward Marsh, who helped to salvage *Rhythm* at the time of the bankruptcy, and installed W. W. Gibson on the staff. According to Murry, he also gave them £100. According to Marsh, he merely guaranteed their overdraft with his balance, while Murry guaranteed repayment with his life – and then defaulted on the lot. Be that as it may, it was owing to him that *Rhythm* became, for a time, the centre of 'the Georgian literary scene'. In his memoirs, Marsh recalls 'the *Rhythm* luncheons at Treviglio's in Soho, where the brilliant contributors met and resourcefully plotted to keep the brave little paper going for another month.'[16] The Cheshire Cheese and the Café Royal were other favourite rendezvous; whilst the office in Chancery Lane, which was also the Murrys' home, became a resort for many of the most promising writers and artists of the younger generation. It was there that they won the friendship of D. H. Lawrence, and lost that of Henri Gaudier-Brzeska.

Of Lawrence and Gaudier, Murry used always to say that they were

---

* Harris himself atoned for his unkindness by contributing two paragraphs to the following number – on the inevitable martyrdom of 'men of large and original minds'.

'the only two indisputable men of genius' [17] he had ever met. What he meant by that is explained in *Between Two Worlds*: they were distinguished by 'a kind of profound animal spontaneity, but not on the animal level. They were complete human beings, but with the grace and poise and quickness of an animal in *all* their human doings.' [18] Unhappily, his relations with both were catastrophic, the one a brief epitome of the other.

Gaudier fell in love with the Murrys – the expression is hardly too strong – when they were on the point of moving to Runcton. In a burst of confidence, he insisted on their taking Sophie, his mistress, to live with them – which they weakly consented to do. Shortly afterwards, on a surprise visit to the cottage, he overheard them lamenting their concession – Murry pleading with Katherine not to be intolerant of Sophie, if only for the sake of the paper, Katherine retorting that *she* was responsible . . . And that was the end. His passionate affection turned overnight to passionate hatred, egged on by Sophie and reinforced by 'George Banks', the cartoonist – who had known Murry in Paris, and believed herself slighted by him – Gaudier became their implacable enemy, repeatedly raiding the office and continually threatening fresh violence. It was not until *Rhythm* closed down that Murry was able to breathe freely again.

It closed down finally in July 1913 – and none too soon. Changing the name to *The Blue Review* had not sufficed to popularize it in England, while the French had lost interest with Albert Rothenstein's appointment as art editor. It had become a burden even to the editors, since, though Katherine had taken to living at Cholesbury, in Buckinghamshire, Murry himself was tied to Chancery Lane, seeing her only at week-ends. Now, having first exchanged the dingy office for a flat in Chaucer Mansions, Baron's Court, they could begin to look further afield.

The Lawrences were beckoning from Lerici. That was out of the question. But Paris, which they had not revisited since their 'honeymoon' excursion the summer before, was a possibility. That December, accordingly, Murry exchanged his secure appointment with the *Westminster* for the chance of reviewing French books in *The Times Literary Supplement*; and on the strength, or weakness, of this he and Katherine transported their worldly possessions to No. 31 Rue de Tournon, hard by the Jardins de Luxembourg.

He had always liked that quarter. The Punch-and-Judy shows

fascinated him nearly as much as the harlequinades of the *Commedia dell' arte* – where he was moved to tears by the love-lorn Pierrot, thrumming a lute while the wicked Harlequin made off with Columbine. He was looking forward eagerly to showing Katherine around. Carco, who met them at the Gare St Lazare, describes him as '*ivre de bonheur*' – though highly conscious of his new responsibilities: '*Il avait une façon de nous guider, de nous protéger que je ne lui connaissais pas. Ce n'était plus le même homme. Sa distraction avait fait place à une éspèce de déférence, de prévenance, de gratitude envers Katherine qui m'attendrissait presque.*' [19] It was arranged that Carco should give Katherine French lessons, while Murry attended to his connexions.

Alas, his '*air digne, important*' was scarcely warranted by the situation. It might impose on Carco, who was so far *attendrissé* as to borrow 100 francs, but not on the estate agents, who demanded a reference before handing over the keys, nor on *The Times* Correspondent who, while supplying it, wondered aloud what Murry would find to do there. It was not long before he was wondering himself. His contributions, not merely to the *Literary Supplement*, but even to the hospitable *Westminster*, were returned with disheartening frequency. His earnings fell from £12 a week to 30s. To make ends meet at all, they had to resort to Katherine's allowance, and that meant the end of monthly instalments to the printers.

Within two months of their brave departure, Murry was back in London, filing a petition of bankruptcy (as he ought to have done eighteen months sooner); within another fortnight, Katherine had rejoined him. The resourceful Carco disposed of their possessions around the Paris *bordels*; the generous Campbell presented them with nineteen sovereigns; the magnanimous Spender, less surprised by the prodigal's return, took Murry back on to the *Westminster* as a full-time reviewer and art-critic – and art-critic he had to remain, until the outbreak of the War.

Of this, their first break for freedom, two memories alone survived the ignominious débâcle:

A glimpse, late at night, in the Café Weber of a tall slim man in black with a sickly yellow face: that was Marcel Proust. A glimpse, in full daylight, through the windows of his little shop in the rue de la Sorbonne, where the *Cahiers de la Quinzaine* were sold, of a man with pince-nez set awry on his nose, tying up a parcel: that was Charles Péguy. I admired him, and admire him still. If I could have had my way (I dreamed) that is how I would live: publishing my friends' works and mine in a little shop with my own hands – keeping the books, taking the cash, tying the parcels.[20]

This was to be a recurrent dream, which Murry would make more than one attempt to realize. But what works of his own would he have found to publish in the winter of 1913? One poem, *The Critic in Judgement*, and one book, *The Art of the Novel, and Other Essays*, which was probably (for the manuscript has vanished) little more than a collection of reviews. He had only just started *Still Life*.

His unproductiveness during these years was not due mainly, as he liked to think at the time, to the routine pressure of reviewing. He really had nothing to say. He still had no convictions of his own, not even critical convictions: at most a stubborn recalcitrance to the prevailing cult of 'form', which, even he could see, threw no light on the felt significance of a Dostoevsky as compared with a James. His taste in poetry was improving – James Stephens had given place to Baudelaire, Dowson to Milton; he would read the *Areopagitica* to Katherine till his eyes were blurred with emotion. But the only effect of the emotion was to set him philosophizing, and the philosophy was of no effect at all.

'Even at this time, I was a person who could not rest until he had rendered to himself some account of his deepest experiences.'[21] To that extent, his philosophizing was real – a foretaste, at least, of that 'true intellectual life' which, in a review of Benda's *La Chute*, he contrasted with *'le caressement des idées qu'il avait connu comme tous ceux de sa classe au sortir du collège'*.[2] If he turned to Plato, it was for the answer to a question set by an experience, not an examiner; and there were moments when the answers he found evoked an emotion as overpowering as the poetry itself. *The Critic in Judgement* commemorates one such moment. The Critic is rapt into ecstasy by the idea of an ultimate harmony in the soul of man: 'somehow within that are all philosophies comprehended, all beauties, all desires'.[22]

Significantly, however, in the poem as originally conceived (for it was only indirectly 'inspired'), the Critic was to awaken from his trance 'half crying with shame and vexation' to find 'some ghastly book'[22] in front of him, waiting to be reviewed. These intellectual ecstasies, even when Murry shared them, as he sometimes did, with Campbell, bore no relation to his day-to-day existence. Involving but a part of himself, they dissolved into an all-pervading scepticism.

No wonder Katherine was impatient of them. 'Mysticism', she declared tartly in *Rhythm*, 'is a "passionate" admiration for that which has no reality at all'; and again, while he was at work on the poem, 'Jack can't fry a sausage without thinking about God!'

'The moral values of the intellectual and the family life', Jack retorts, in the review of *La Chute*, 'are at least equal. There is no fundamental rightness in the victory of instinct over the intellect; and the tragedy is that they cannot be reconciled' – even by a Bergsonian 'Intuition'.[2] This repudiation of Bergson – the first of Murry's *volte faces* – is eloquent of his inward division.

Just as long as he felt secure of Katherine's affection, he could indulge the intellectual side of his nature, confident that he was choosing 'the better part'.[2] But only let Katherine turn away, or appeal to his pity, and all his cloud-capp'd towers collapsed on the moment: the other side took control. 'I was loosely compacted of a consciousness and an unknown; and there was no vital relation between them.' [23] His efforts to find something he could truthfully call 'himself' would issue in endless introspection: and then this very self-analysis seemed to provide the one thread of continuity.

His last article in *The Blue Review* – an article on 'Mr Bennett, Stendhal and the Modern Novel', which was probably the germ of his book of essays – shows him in the act of making a virtue out of this necessity. 'For a revelation of the human soul in a character of fiction', he concludes here, 'demands what philosophers call the continuity of the self, and demands that this continuity should be made explicit. Throughout its development the soul must be self-conscious, analysing its motives and feelings, making the psychological evolution plain to us . . .' [24] This being the recipe he actually adopted for his novel (the earlier part of which is modelled on *La Chute*, even to the heroine's name), it is not surprising that it was dead.

Still Life was, in fact, still-born. It was the kind of novel which, had it been written thirty years later, and in French, might have won wide acclaim. As it was, the only readers who had a good word for it were Leo Myers and Edward Garnett. It brought Murry £8 10s. in royalties, against £9 spent on typing, and deserved no better.

IV

CLIMAX

————⟡⟡⟡————

ON JULY 13, 1914, Murry and Katherine were witnesses at the Lawrences' wedding in London. This was the culmination of a month's steadily growing intimacy between the two couples, whilst the Lawrences were staying with the Campbells in Selwood Terrace, the Murrys moving uncomfortably from one Chelsea lodging to another. Now they all had holidays in view. Within three weeks, the outbreak of the War – for which they were as unprepared as the least prophetic of their countrymen – had thrown their plans to the winds, and them into one another's arms. Murry's life, for the next eighteen months, seems to vibrate in a magnetic field, with Katherine for one pole and Lawrence for the other.

The mutual attraction is easy to understand. Few people met Lawrence at that time without being jerked out of their orbits. Newly enfranchised by his early triumphs, still unembittered by reverses, gay, confident, sensitive, alert and alive in a way that made even the average sensual man feel moribund, he must have burst on Murry's vision as a star that 'stuck fiery off indeed'; and to him, Murry's very impressionability, his readiness to credit him with a wisdom far exceeding his own, would be powerful recommendations. To a great extent, it was an attraction of opposites.

But the similarities were still more striking. With the Lawrences, as with the Gaudier-Brzeskas, it counted for something that the Murrys, like themselves, were living together unmarried. In those days that still implied a certain measure of ostracism, and therefore of independence – especially as Katherine, like Frieda and Sophie, was an alien. It counted for most of all that the two men themselves were, if not aliens, *déracinés*. Not only was Lawrence, like Murry, in quest of a setting to belong to, but even his touchstone was the same – namely his relationship with his wife. Of no other of his friends was that so true; of none, certainly, was it so true that all his thinking as well as his doing was related to this one over-riding concern. The identical quest that was to carry Lawrence around the globe was to be the driving-force of Murry's career. Hence, among other things, their recurrent, calamitous attempts, in face of the War, to constitute a community of friends.

Neither of them, luckily, was fit for military service. Murry, to be sure, caught up in the first wave of mob-enthusiasm, spent all night outside the French Embassy, chanting '*A bas les Allemands!*' and next day went with Kingsmill to Putney to enlist in a cyclists' battalion. But, having come to his senses, he had no difficulty in getting a medical certificate that would ensure his discharge. Only six weeks before, he had been laid up with pleurisy: the doctor suspected tuberculosis.

He and Katherine, accordingly, after house-hunting vainly in the neighbourhoods of St Merryn and Rye, took a cottage at The Lee, in Buckinghamshire, two miles distant from the Lawrences' Chesham. Rose Tree Cottage, damp, ugly and remote from every convenience as it was, was better than nothing, Murry being an enthusiastic cyclist and Lawrence a capable decorator. There they established themselves on October 26, and there all four could arrange to meet almost daily.

It was not a happy arrangement. For one thing, the women were far from participating in their menfolk's taste for neighbourly living: long afterwards Frieda confessed that she had resented Lawrence's interest in Murry, and it is more than probable that Katherine resented Murry's in Lawrence. For another, the men themselves disapproved of each other's marriages. If Murry, sharing Katherine's dislike of Frieda, was repelled by Lawrence's dependence upon her, Lawrence was no less distressed by Murry's 'child-love', and by his want of any conviction or purpose beyond it. Already the summer before, he had told Murry bluntly that Katherine was 'unfulfilled', and that he, least of anyone, had cause to poke fun at psycho-analysis. Earlier still, in a long, wise, affectionate letter, he had exhorted him to pull himself together, 'be more natural and positive' and 'give her a man to be satisfied with':

> If you are disintegrated, then get integrated again. Don't be a coward. If you are disintegrated your first duty is to yourself, and you may use Katherine – her money and everything – to get right again. You're not well, man. Then have the courage to get well. If you are strong again, and a bit complete, *she'll* be satisfied with you. She'll love you hard enough.

But don't you see, at this rate, you distrain on her day by day and month by month. I've done it myself.[1]

But integration was never achieved by exhortation, nor were Lawrence's own raucous and ineffectual attempts to assert his independence reassuring. The only result of this would be to set Murry delving more feverishly into himself, projecting himself more vertiginously into the empyrean of intellectual ecstasy. When not immersed in his novel, 'analysing my own inward life to immobility' [2] (was that why he called it *Still Life?*), he was engaging with Campbell again in week-end-long discussions on Dostoevsky. These indulgences of the 'masculine', intellectual side of his nature were partly a pitiful effort to assert his own independence; partly, as he recognized later, a compensation for his inferiority to both Lawrence and Katherine on the 'feminine', intuitive side.

Poor Murry! One cannot but feel sorry for him, toiling away at that dreary novel between two writers of genius, both of them pre-eminently endowed with the very quality he most conspicuously lacked. Of Katherine he wrote: 'I knew I was her inferior in many ways, but I could have accepted them all save one. She had an immediate contact with life which was completely denied to me.' [3] It was even truer of Lawrence, a man of 'more than usual organic sensibility' if there ever was one; a man, moreover, to whom the written word, be it a novel, a poem or a letter, came naturally as its swoop to the hawk. Twenty years afterwards, Murry was to draw on this very experience for a characterization of Wordsworth and Coleridge, which ranks among the best of his studies.[4] He, like Coleridge, 'rear'd in the great city, pent mid cloisters dim', could only admire such spontaneity; and although Lawrence won his heart by denouncing the education that had denied it him, it would have taken a man of more heroic proportions than either himself or Coleridge to feel admiration untinged with envy.

Of course, there were cheerful interludes. There were the days when he would join Lawrence in some straightforward practical job, decorating, painting boxes or cooking – days when he learned, for the first time in his life, what it meant to be at one with a fellow-being on a level deeper than the intellectual. 'Then "the flow", as Lawrence called it, was really between himself and another. We did not have to, we did not want to, talk; and it was good between us, better than I have ever known with a living man.' [5] The memory of those days was to exert a lasting influence on his life. There were the evenings, too, when Samuel Koteliansky would join them, and the five would sing Hebrew or Creole songs together, and day-dream of the island Rananim, where they were all to escape from the War and live happily ever after. But it was not Rananim that Katherine wanted.

The 'true intellectual life' was in full swing at Rose Tree Cottage, and she detested it. 'Finished *Crime and Punishment*. Very bad I thought it too,' was her *Journal* entry for February 4, 1915. Lying there on her bed (for the roof leaked, and she suffered from fibrositis), she would conjure up before her mind's eye everything most unlike The Lee, everyone most unlike Murry: Paris in spring, the Jardins de Luxembourg, Carco 'with his confidence, and his warm sensational life . . .' [6]

If only she had the money to go there! 'J. doesn't want money, and won't earn money',[7] she wailed – forgetful that only six weeks before, when he had wanted to get on with a review (and reviews were seldom commissioned nowadays) she had accused him of being 'just like a little dog whining outside a door'.[8] Nothing he could do was right. 'Don't believe the conjugal "we"', she told Koteliansky: 'It's not worth protesting but it's not really true of me – never.' [9] A Christmas party at the Cannans' ended in her making love to Mark Gertler in the music-room, to the horror and indignation of the Lawrences.

They could not understand Murry's complaisance. Neither, perhaps, could Katherine. By February she was exchanging a passionate correspondence with Carco, which she made no attempt to conceal; yet when she spoke to him about it, 'he refused to take it at all seriously'.[10] It must have been exasperating. In truth, he did not believe in it. He did not believe in it even when, having secured some money from her brother, she resolved to put an end to their 'three years idyll' [7] and actually went to France.

That, however, was the end of the Buckinghamshire idyll: for by then the Lawrences had already moved to Greatham, in Sussex, and Campbell, no doubt sensing her disapproval, had, to Murry's intense distress, abruptly discontinued his visits. At one stroke almost, both his sanctuaries, of the heart and the mind, had collapsed. And he could not subsist on his own. Left high and dry at The Lee (or rather, low and wet, with a feverish cold), he tried to resume work on *Still Life*, only to find the loneliness insupportable – and make for Greatham himself.

Lawrence, of course, was triumphant. Not only was his diagnosis confirmed, but all Murry's craving for affection was now concentrated upon him – and he made the most of it. After all, he too was feeling his isolation. The moment Murry arrived, his cold turned to influenza by the long wet tramp from the station, Lawrence set to nursing him body and soul. Now, he felt, they could really get down to the business of creating a setting for themselves. It was at this juncture, as his letters show, that his affection and esteem touched high-water mark. To Lady Ottoline Morrell, he was writing on February 22:

> Murry is here because Katherine has gone to Paris. He is one of the men of the future – you will see. He is with me for the Revolution. He is just finishing his novel – his first – *very* good.* At present he is my partner – the only man who quite simply is with me. One day he'll be ahead of me. Because he'll build up the temple if I carve out the way – the place.[11]

He spoke in the same strain to Murry himself – and Murry, not unnaturally, was bewildered. For, though his anxiety to please would lead him on to verbal agreement, the 'Revolution' meant nothing whatever to him. His one real desire was 'to live in a warm atmosphere of love'.[12] And though his own affection for Lawrence was sealed in those few days at Greatham, for better or for worse, he had by no means given up Katherine. On the contrary, he continued to write to her day by day, in spite of getting no replies, exactly as if nothing had happened. He could not believe that she would really forsake him for Carco. And he was right. Before the end of the month she was back again, disillusioned as he had expected.

'The excitement of the adventure which had sustained her was short-lived, and there was a severe reaction,' [13] he writes in his edition of her *Letters*. His journal is more explicit: 'She wanted me to remain an innocent lover: and then she got bored with me for being an unexciting one. Hence her stupid and deeply disappointing affair with Carco . . . From the Carco folly she reacted violently; and I was made the paradigm of innocence and fidelity' [14] – which in fact he was. But the adventure had served a purpose. Though Katherine paid two more visits to Paris that spring – and the Lawrences, putting them down to the same motive as the first, shook their heads over Murry's obtuseness – his letters no longer went unanswered. While she, at the Quai aux Fleurs, was engaged on the first draft of *Prelude*, he, at Notting Hill

---

* cf. 'It is the kind of wriggling self-abuse I can't make head or tail of': Lawrence on *Still Life*, in a letter to Koteliansky, Dec. 15, 1916.

Gate, was translating Tchehov with Koteliansky. *Still Life* was done with for good, and so was Rose Tree Cottage, with all that it stood for. That summer, they transferred their possessions from The Lee to No. 5 Acacia Road, St John's Wood, and settled down to work in harmony.

Once again, it was the Lawrences who had determined the locality, they themselves having taken a house in the near-by Vale of Health. But this time the 'aspegs', as Katherine called them, were altogether better, outwardly as well as inwardly. Not only was their new villa really pleasant, with a garden behind (where Murry added badminton to his repertory of ball-games), but the company was no longer so restricted, other friends, new and old, coming to enrich their lives.

There was Koteliansky, for one, now a near neighbour and constant visitor. Murry depicts him in a note written many years later:

> In the old days he was very nice. He had a remarkable face: he looked like some Assyrian king – a Sargon or Sennacherib – with an impressive hooked Semitic nose, a fine head of coarse black curly hair, and massive features: very dark eyes with pince-nez (I see the gesture of adjusting them), and he closed his full mouth with a snap when he passed sentence . . .
> He had pathetically extravagant notions of the power and prestige of literature: which I think were derived from his worship of the great Russian figures when he was a Jewish boy, emancipating himself from the narrow circle of ideas of the Ghetto . . . He was naive and intolerant; but he had a curious kind of moral authority, particularly amongst fellow-Jews. Gertler and Sydney Schiff, for example, were really awed by him. In his limited way his integrity was remarkable; and so was his prejudice and his obstinacy. 'You call Kot a great rock', said B. D. once to me, '*I* call him a bloody mule.' [15]

It was Koteliansky who said of Katherine that 'she had the greatest talent for being a human being he had ever known';[15] and who, when the Murrys left Acacia Road, took over her little attic room (from which they had all watched the first Zeppelin raid on London), making it his home till he died, in January 1955.

Then there was Dorothy Brett, who was to prove a faithful friend to them both – and who, in her *Lawrence and Brett*, portrays Murry and Katherine in their turn, with an artist's eye:

> Katherine Mansfield and Murry appear. Katherine small, her sleek dark hair brushed close to her head, her fringe sleeked down over her white forehead: she dresses nearly always in black with a touch of white or

scarlet or a rich, deep purple. This evening she is dressed in black. Her movements are quaintly restricted; controlled, small, reserved gestures. The dark eyes glance about much like a bird's, the pale face is a quiet mask, full of hidden laughter, wit, and gaiety. But she is cautious, a bit suspicious and on her guard. Middleton Murry rolls in with the gait of a sailor, his curly dark hair is getting a bit thin on top. He is nervous, shy, a small man. The eyes are large and hazel, with a strange unseeing look; the nose is curved one side and perfectly straight the other, due to its having been broken. His lips are finely cut, the mouth sensitive, the chin determined. A fine and beautiful head, more masculine than Gertler; the head of a poet, of a recluse, of a dreamer. When the shyness wears off him, he also is full of fun.[16]

The scene of this sketch is Brett's studio in Earl's Court Road, where they sometimes went to parties that summer, and where she painted the first of her several portraits of Murry.

Best of all, for Katherine especially, was the company of her brother Leslie, whom the War had brought back to England as a soldier. He spent his first leave at Acacia Road; and it was his conversation, no doubt, that focused her imagination once more on their childhood days in New Zealand – the stuff of her finest stories. Altogether, life in London was nearly as sociable as it had been secluded in Buckinghamshire.

Meanwhile, Lawrence was promoting the Revolution by means of lectures and a fortnightly periodical, for which Koteliansky supplied the business management and Murry the title, *The Signature*. This, it hardly needs saying, was a harebrained venture in the second year of the War – as Lawrence himself saw in retrospect, fathering it on to Murry. The subscribers, though they included Bernard Shaw, Albert Rothenstein, Frank Swinnerton, Clifford Bax and Lytton Strachey, never numbered more than a hundred or two; and of the 'six papers on social and personal freedom by D. H. Lawrence and J. M. Murry' announced in the prospectus, only three ever appeared. It closed down early in November. Still, it gave both of them a chance to express their feelings and, to some extent, clarify their thoughts.

For Lawrence, the War had meant the collapse of all his hopes and ideals; for Murry, an intense aggravation of his habitual *Angst*. As Katherine reminded him later, 'it was a supreme justification of all you had trembled towards (like a compass) all your life'.[17] Feeling no solidarity with any class of society, he could share none of the patriotic emotions, base or noble; sharing none of these, he was feeling more uprooted than ever. Indeed, his fear and hatred of the mob bordered on counter-hysteria: and unlike Lawrence, he had nothing to pit against it. Though he was shedding his second-hand values, he had still not grown any new ones. He could neither bear the thought of dying before his purpose was accomplished, nor define that purpose itself, except in such vague terms as 'to achieve art'. It was to assign some content to this phrase that he undertook his own long, rambling, stilted contribution to *The Signature*, 'There was a Little Man'.

He was not entirely unsuccessful. He discovered, at least, that the only art that concerned him was that which he could understand as 'the expression of a striving soul', in which he could recognize 'an intimate personal possibility'. To achieve art was to realize that possibility. The essay is shot through with foregleams of a later knowledge. As a whole, however, it bears pathetic witness to the futility of his attempts to unearth an 'identical self' by means of introspection; and even before it was finished, the helpless division it reflects was manifest again in his life.

The St John's Wood idyll was cut short as abruptly as the Buckinghamshire, and more tragically. Leslie's leave had ended in September. On October 7 he was killed, accidentally while giving a demonstration of grenade-throwing. From that moment forward, Katherine could abide the house no longer – the associations were too recent and heartrending. Once again she insisted upon going to France, and this time Murry had to escort her.

It proved a miserable expedition. Nursing her grief, she locked herself away in a private world which she shared with no one but Leslie. 'You know I can never be Jack's lover again,' she apostrophized him in her *Journal*: 'You have me. You're in my flesh as well as my soul. I give Jack my "surplus" love, but to you I hold and to you I give my deepest love. Jack is no more than . . . anybody might be.' [18] This was too much even for Murry. He who, believing that 'love was, by its essence, free',[19] had made no attempt to withhold her from Carco, was now tormented by jealousy – all the more despicable, he felt, for being jealousy of a dead man. On the beach at Cassis, when she broke into a passion of weeping, he burst into a towering rage; and then, unable to endure the sense of exclusion, fled for England – ostensibly to attend to *The Signature*, actually, as before, to seek consolation with Lawrence.

Though Katherine had assured him that there was nothing he could do to help, this was rather pusillanimous of him. In after years he reproached himself bitterly for it, likening it to Coleridge's abandonment of Sara to accompany the Wordsworths to Germany. And this time February's *rapport* was not forthcoming. Lawrence received him as he deserved. 'Murry turned up on Friday, to my moderate surprise,' he wrote to Katherine on December 12: 'He doesn't look very well, tells us of his dreadful experience in France, and is *very* chirpy. At the present I am not very much in sympathy with him.' Yet the episode had a good outcome: it brought the equivocal relationship between Murry and Katherine to a climax.

Left to herself at Bandol, she quickly awoke to realities. Waiting impatiently for the posts, she began to realize how much, after all, he still meant to her, how dependent she was on his love. Never dreaming (although it was war-time) that posts might be delayed,* she worked herself up into an orgy of self-pity and reproach: 'Oh Jack, I appeal even to your imagination as a novelist – do not leave me like this without news. It is so cruel – cruel. I weep bitterly as I write.' [20] And he, of course, as ever by an appeal to his pity, was stung awake too: saw himself losing her for ever, saw all his cloud-capp'd ivory towers come toppling down once more, as the other side of his nature took control:

> Why did I leave you? I keep on asking myself the question, and I find no answer. I can remember nothing of what urged me back. It must have been strong and overwhelming – but it is all gone. There is no printing-press – that vanished like smoke. There is no England. There is only you, whom I left. Why, how, did it all seem so simple and natural then, and now it is like a nightmare that never ends? [21]

Even then, when he was on the point of departure for Bandol, a belated assurance of Katherine's relief at receiving his letters was enough to stay Murry's hand. 'If all that mattered was the reality of the love that was between us, and one was sure of that once more, why should we not stay as we were?' [22] But only for a moment. The bitterness of her disappointment on this occasion, when she had already found a villa for the two of them, overbore all hesitation. He, in his

---

* As late as July 1916, she was reproaching Murry in her best Little Governess manner, because one of his letters had miscarried: 'You are a funny boy, and you *do* rather offend me.'

turn, realized how dependent he was upon her – and New Year's Day 1916 found them united at Bandol.

'The Villa Pauline – it was to be a memory of beatitude between us for ever.' [23] The ensuing two and a half months were the happiest of their life together. Always until then, Murry says, they had held something back; now they surrendered to each other unreservedly: and 'the victory over ourselves that had been won passed naturally into all our doings. I who was wont to explore myself with such sick and sensitive fingers, forgot myself entirely. There was Katherine, there was the book I was writing: both engrossed me.' [23] The book was *Fyodor Dostoevsky, a Critical Study*, and it was his first original achievement.

It had been commissioned by Secker over two years before, to pay off a £30 debt on *Rhythm*; but as often as he had tried to begin it, he had found that he really had nothing to say. Now, reading the four major novels through once again from beginning to end, with the new self-abeyance conferred by his love, he became, all at once, completely receptive to the personality and purpose informing them. 'Suddenly the whole thing had fallen into pattern; and I was, for the first time, the victim of the strange sensation of being hardly more than the amanuensis of a book that wrote itself':

> For the first time in my life, I had the experience of certitude. It was no question of my opinion of Dostoevsky; I had no opinion of Dostoevsky: and if I expressed any personal opinions about him in the book, they were certainly exaggerated and probably wrong. All that happened – I speak, of course, of my sensation only – was that the objective 'pattern' of Dostoevsky had declared itself, through me as instrument. [24]

The Dostoevsky who 'fascinated and perplexed and stimulated' [24] Murry, was the Dostoevsky who pushed scepticism to its furthest limit, only to find it paralysing and deathly; who could neither renounce the intellect, in the name of a Bergsonian Intuition (since 'the man who is most truly man can acquiesce in no limitations to his knowledge' [25]) nor live in the meaningless universe it exposed (that 'metaphysical terror and obscenity which is the appointed end of the striving of the human consciousness' [26]): who, therefore, could only dream at the last of a change in the nature of consciousness – 'the sudden revelation of a new consciousness, when all eternity shall be gathered into a moment, when there shall be no more division between the body and the soul and no more barriers between the knower and that which is known, when there shall be no more time'.[27]

This Dostoevsky was *anima naturaliter christiana*, inasmuch as the sole reality to which he might have been reconciled was one that validated love, the love he saw embodied in Jesus; yet all the less able to believe in Jesus's God because 'that being whom he recognized for perfect . . . had been made to suffer the last extremity of bodily agony upon the Cross'.[28] For him, 'God' could only be the synonym for such a reality, 'faith' for the consciousness of it; and it was this consciousness, which he imputed to Alyosha Karamazov, that he spent his own life in search of:

> He knew that belief in God as a person, the faith of religion as we understand religion, was denied him for ever. He asked for no more than a way of life. What must he *do* to be saved? The posing of that terrible problem and the attempt to answer it with something more than barren silence, forms the deep argument of his greatest books.[25]

It was this argument that Murry tried to elucidate. He was not concerned with Dostoevsky as an artist – his book was not literary criticism. He was concerned with Dostoevsky as a seeker, who simply made use of the novel as a vehicle for his explorations; a philosopher, indeed, though not in the academic sense:

> Abstract thought was for him not merely a fascinating occupation, as it is with many philosophers so called, not a habit of mind learned in a school, but an awful necessity upon which his life depended. It was born anew in him from the shock of his contact with life itself. All his life long the eye of his soul was turned to the contemplation of Pain.[29]

The Dostoevsky who concerned Murry, in short, was the 'striving soul', and it was this that declared itself through him.

Since, however, he himself was drawn to the novels by a precisely similar necessity – since, in wrestling with them, he was wrestling with a problem of his own – the elucidation was mutual. The same existential approach that enabled him to bring to Dostoevsky an understanding that was new in England, enabled him likewise to take from Dostoevsky an aspiration that became integral to his life. Comprehending his own division, he transcended it; and by virtue of that transcendence, recognized, in the creation of Alyosha above all, an 'intimate personal possibility':

> He has the waking consciousness of the harmony of all things . . . His

mind tyrannizes not over his body, nor his body oppresses his mind. He is a being beautiful, conscious only of his unity, and feeling within himself that which binds him to all humanity, the knowledge that he is the appointed end of all their striving.[30]

That now became Murry's dream also. Whether it was more than a dream, he did not profess to know.

1. J. M. M., c. 1891   2. J. M. M., c. 1903

3. Christ's Hospital, Newgate Street: The Grecians' Cloister

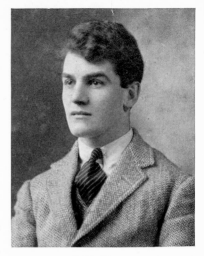

4

5. J. M. M., c. 1909

4, 6. J. M. M. with Katherine Mansfield, Clovelly Mansions, 1912

V

STRANGE SEAS OF THOUGHT

❧───⟪❀⟫───❧

HIS THREE MONTHS' FRUITFUL seclusion at Bandol changed Murry decisively. He remarked the change himself when he came to write his autobiography: 'It's quite noticeable that a new solidity came into my writing and my thinking in 1916 – in particular, there is an amazing contrast between the letters I wrote to Katherine in Dec. 1915 and those of Jan. 1917. I have no doubt that the crucial moment of change was at the Villa Pauline: when for the first time, both in love and work, I lost self-consciousness ... Anyway, I do feel that in 1916 I became, for good or ill, a definite "somebody", a real person.' ¹ That was true. Both in love and work he had acquired standards of his own; and the consequences were quickly apparent – not least in his relations with Lawrence.

Frieda once told William Gerhardi that she and her husband used to look on Murry and Katherine as 'children to be helped out of their troubles'. Hitherto that may have been true. Now the roles were reversed. At all events, it was in response to Lawrence's almost desperate appeals that the Murrys reluctantly gave up the Villa Pauline and made their way back to England. Though they were perfectly happy where they were, their books were finished, and his need for companionship sounded greater than theirs for solitude. 'Out of the disciples, there was one Judas,' he was crying: 'In modern life, there are twelve Judases in the twelve disciples.' ² He had found them a cottage next to his own in Cornwall, and his excitement on hearing that they would take it was schoolboyish: 'We are so delighted. What a joyful day, when you arrive, and we meet you in St Ives station, which is on the edge of the sea!' ³

'It was a cold, slatey-grey day in early April when we arrived at

St Ives,' Murry recalls: 'The white gulls wheeled about, crying desolately: and our hearts sank. We tried to be gay, not to disappoint Lawrence, as we drove out to the Tinner's Arms at Zennor; but we felt like weeping. Our fairy-tale was over.' [4] A day or two later, he was giving vent to his feelings by painting their chairs a funereal black; whilst Lawrence himself, telling Koteliansky of the proceedings, was constrained to add: 'But we are as yet rather strange and un-accustomed to each other. It is so difficult to re-establish an old footing, after a lapse during which we have all endured a good deal of misery.' [5] The old footing was never to be re-established.

It was not only Murry who had changed. Lawrence had too. Read-ing his books and correspondence today, one remarks it instantly. It is as though one of the wings which had borne him so superbly up to the middle of *The Rainbow*, were riddled with shot. He falters in mid-flight – sinks – rises – sinks again, the old confidence and direc-tion lost for ever. Down there in Cornwall, he was sheltering as far as possible out of earshot of the guns and beaters. If he could, he would have lapsed from consciousness altogether, at least until his wounds were healed. He was, in fact, in the throes of his first attempt to find community on the pre-conscious level: with his wife, of course, and with real or imaginary primitives – the most evident symptom being more violent dissensions than ever. 'I don't know which disgusts me worse,' Katherine wrote that May, after a spirited account of one of his brawls with Frieda, which had ended in Murry's acting the peace-maker, 'When they are loving and playing with each other or when they are roaring at each other.' [6]

Katherine was repelled by Lawrence's now ineradicable obsession with sex. His house, she said, ought to be called 'The Phallus', and Frieda cordially agreed. It was about the only thing they did agree upon. But Murry was not much more sympathetic. If he and Katherine were not children to be helped, neither were they children to be moulded. Sure of himself as he was, he no longer wanted Lawrence's help with his *Dostoevsky*, much less to be weaned from his 'spiritual' love. That that was morbid, Lawrence was more than ever convinced – he was demonstrating his conviction in *Women in Love* – but if the alternative to 'spiritual' love was a frenzy of hatred, to marriage as the be-all and end-all, 'blood-brotherhood' between men, what could Murry do but recoil? He felt no need now to assent even verbally to Lawrence's propositions: and nothing is so exasperating to a prophet as to be revered as a man and yet ignored as a teacher. 'If I love you and you know I love you, isn't that enough?' he inquired naïvely. 'I hate your love, I *hate it*,' Lawrence burst out: 'You're an obscene bug, sucking my life away!' [7] Clearly, it was time for them to part.

An American scholar, E. C. Gilbert, thinks that Lawrence's disappointment with Murry was critical in his life, that it was this that precipitated him finally into the cult of 'mindlessness'. It may be so. Murry's disappointment with Lawrence was certainly critical in his own. Henceforward both men would expect less of their friends, and consequently more of their women – seeking in the one intimate relation, whether spiritual or sensual, a refuge from the impersonal horror of the War. They would go on growing, but in opposite directions; and though their opposition would be part of their fascination for each other, it would only be by 'pretending a bit' [8] that they could coexist at close quarters. The Higher Tregerthen reunion served mainly to bring that home to them. It lasted a bare two months. In June, the Murrys moved over to Mylor, on the less forbidding south coast of the peninsula. 'They should have a soft valley, with leaves and the ring-dove cooing,' [9] was Lawrence's comment.

Unfortunately, it was too late by that time to resume the fairy-tale of Bandol either. Katherine had resisted the reunion from the start. Sitting apart in her room, smoking and projecting cynical stories, she had been as miserable at Higher Tregerthen as at The Lee, and it seems to have had the same effect on her. According to Lawrence, she was once again in reaction against Murry, and thinking of leaving him – for Denmark this time. Be that as it may, she divided most of the summer between visits to London and Garsington, leaving Murry to fend for himself. His memories of Mylor were mainly of being on his own.

A year or even six months before, he would not have been able to endure that. He would have rejoined the Lawrences. As it was, he turned his solitude to good account, reading intensively in Rousseau (who reminded him of Lawrence), Nietzsche, Sainte-Beuve, De Quincey. *Dostoevsky*, he tells us, had loosened his critical muscles, and 'there were few periods in my life when I devoured books more eagerly than I did now. I was conscious of the stirrings of a new power to connect what I read; at any rate it all began to fall into some kind of pattern, and I was coming to believe that my once doubtful hope of having an independent mind might prove to be not wholly unfounded.' [10] It was from these months of tolerable loneliness that he dated the beginnings of his 'philosophy of acceptance'.[11]

But they were only a few, for the War was closing in. He had kept out of it as long as he could; soon no escape would be possible. Already the beaters were up in Cornwall. He and Lawrence had hardly parted before both were summoned to report at Bodmin for medical examinations; and this time Murry was warned that unless he bestirred himself, he was liable to be conscripted for navvying. By the early autumn, therefore, he was following in Katherine's footsteps – and none too soon. In London, his attempts to secure an interpretership failed ignominiously – all the posts had been filled long ago. It was fortunate that he was well known and respected at Garsington.

Lady Ottoline Morrell, having rebelled against a conventional aristocratic upbringing, and constituted herself the generous (if not always tactful) patroness of half the young intelligentsia of Britain, had little sympathy for the military. She had induced her husband to wreck his parliamentary career by employing conscientious objectors, like Clive Bell and Edward Garnett, on his estate, and their home, the seventeenth-century Manor House, was now the resort of a multitude of writers and artists, having little in common but a certain aversion to the War and a boundless ingratitude to herself. Murry and Katherine were no exceptions. He had spent the Christmas of 1915 there, and she had been often since; as the moving spirits of plays and *tableaux vivants* – a regular feature of the entertainment – they were always made welcome. In return, both gained a reputation as mischief-makers. But that was later. In the meantime, with the help of J. T. Sheppard, he got taken on as a translator at the War Office.

Thus, by a roundabout route, he had reached the destination prescribed by his father – and it was good-bye to small magazines, country cottages, flittings; good-bye to Bohemia and poverty. For the next two and a half years, he was to be attached to M.I.7, for the next four and a half to London. The *Wanderjahre* were over.

As it happened, neither the work nor the workers at Watergate House proved as uncongenial as he had feared. On the contrary, his colleagues, who included, besides Sheppard himself, Mgr Ronald Knox, Adrian Boult, D. L. Murray and, later on, J. W. N. Sullivan, 'formed a rare combination of ability and humanity'.[12] He liked them all, with Murray and Sullivan in particular striking up fairly close friendships. And the common task of extracting from the newspapers of the Central

Powers a picture of their economic, political and moral conditions, roused all his zeal. Within six months he was appointed editor of *The Daily Review of the Foreign Press*, a confidential sheet circulated among heads of Government departments; within twelve, he had doubled his salary of £5 a week. 1918 was to find him Chief Censor, 1920 O.B.E. This is not surprising. Murry was no writer of genius, but a man of uncommon ability who happened to have taken up writing. He would have excelled at anything that engrossed his whole attention, and his whole attention was now focused on the War.

'I had a prodigious faculty for work in those days,' [13] he writes. He had indeed. In addition to this, and to his regular reviews of French books for the *Literary Supplement*, he now began contributing articles to Massingham's *Nation*, on the European situation. His speciality being Austrian affairs, he was aware, as the general public was not permitted to be, that Austria at least was prepared to contract out of the War, and was hoping against hope that the British Government would be induced to negotiate:

> 'Europe' had suddenly become real and precious to me. It would be hard to explain what I meant by it – it was almost identical with Humanity. And now that I could not turn away from Europe, and my eyes were riveted on its agonies every day, I saw how precious and precarious it was. Now, *all* my friends who had entered the War were dead. Goodyear had gone the way of all the rest. It was all one happening. In them, and those like them, Europe was murdering its own soul. If Europe could awake to what was happening, then the life, the soul, the consciousness would be saved, and those men would not have died in vain. But if Europe did not awake, and the thing went on to the bitter end – then, there was no hope, no hope any more. Victory or defeat, it was all one. Europe would be dead.[13]

This was the tenor of his articles, as it was of the conversations he sought with 'politicians who were "interested" in peace' [13] – Lady Ottoline's relative, Lord Henry Bentinck, for example, whom he admired, and Ramsay MacDonald, whom he did not. It was also the bond between himself and H. M. Tomlinson, whom he met for the first time on *The Nation*. Needless to say, their pleas went unheeded. Though he remained persuaded to the end of his days that a timely initiative on the part of the British in 1917 might have spared Europe much of the agony of the next thirty years, the only result of his own was that he was reported to the Supreme Head of the War Office as a 'security risk'; it was lucky for him that the self-appointed *agent provocateur* (subsequently ennobled by the Chamberlain Government) was despatched about his business.

With all these commitments, however, he was straining his powers to the limit: and he had no home-life to relax into. For, far from sharing his new preoccupation with 'Europe', Katherine reacted to it as he had done, two years before, to her absorption in her own bereavement. It must have been with a wry understanding that he received her letter of January 17, 1917: 'My one overwhelming feeling is that we both must be free to write this year, and that even our full life together must mark time for that.' They were then boarding with Dorothy Brett at No. 3 Gower Street. Whereas he would have liked a flat of their own, she required a studio in addition – and even flats were hard for an unmarried couple to come by. With the spring, they moved to separate apartments, she at No. 114a Church Street, Chelsea, he at No. 47 Redcliffe Road.

It was a poor arrangement for them both. Had he been the man that one of her biographers thinks he ought to have been – 'another man than he, a man . . . all action and resolution' [14] – he might have insisted upon her forgoing her studio for the time being and providing him with a breakfast. As it was, though they met every evening for supper, neither was properly fed, and each felt bereft. Katherine, according to an intimate friend, would roam the streets after dark, rather than stay in the house alone; and he, before the end of the summer, was on the brink of a nervous breakdown. The War preyed on him; he was visited by morbid fantasies. 'Once I was obsessed for days with the notion of climbing on to the plinth of one of the lions in Trafalgar Square and shooting myself as a protest against the horror'; [15] at other times, 'I walked about the streets during the air-raids in the hope of kindly death'. [16] It is odd that they never ran into each other.

As the year wore on, this nihilism gave way to something more significant – something he was wont to call an 'intellectual ecstasy', though it had little in common with the experience he had shared with Campbell. That had been an intoxication with the abstract idea of an ultimate harmony, of the One; this was the apprehension of a harmony in experience itself, of the One in the Many – 'a lucid ecstasy of self-immolation before the blind and beautiful power of Necessity, an almost exultant acceptance of the wreck of hope'. [17] Sometimes this would take him unawares, as an immediate conviction of the 'meaningfulness' of existence; sometimes it was the consummation of a sustained effort to discover a 'pattern' in his experience, analogous to the 'pattern' revealed in Dostoevsky: that is to say, to envisage it in such a way that intellect and emotion were at one. In either case, since such an integration could be purchased only by the renunciation of all the hopes and desires that make up what is ordinarily known as the 'self' – by a self-annihilation, in fact – he neither could nor did regard it as his *own* at all, but rather as a divine visitation.

This it was that he would communicate to Sullivan in those 'wonderful conversations' they held after office hours, 'on Dostoevsky and the "higher" consciousness'. Sullivan recalled them fifteen years later in his autobiographical novel, *But for the Grace of God*:

> They would last for hours, and during them he would mount, as it were, from one transcendental height to another, the ascent culminating with some such remark as 'the inhuman is the highest form of the human', and in the ensuing silence he would gaze vaguely at a corner of the ceiling with a faint, wondering smile . . . The impression made by these conversations, which often affected me as revelations, was permanent. I have always found, since then, that the literature or music that most matters to me is that which reveals this superior consciousness.[18]

Sullivan, who shared the same revulsion against the mass-hysteria of the time, the same sense of isolation, and, as this record goes to show, the same intimations of a change of consciousness, became Murry's chief confidant.

Nevertheless, it is by no arbitrary decree of the ascetics that mysticism is associated with malnutrition. Abruptly, one morning, after days of solving the problem of food by ignoring it, and nights of such 'beatific wakefulness',[19] Murry found himself unable to get up. The doctor was called in; he was pronounced, once again, in imminent danger of tuberculosis, and ordered two months' sick-leave. This was in November 1917. He spent the two months at Garsington: and it was there that he was launched decisively on those strange seas of thought which were to be his for the next thirty years.

It was there, to begin with, that he discovered Keats:

> That autumn Sir Sydney Colvin's *Life of Keats* was published. It lay in my way at Garsington, and I read it. I had never read any life of Keats before; nor even a word of his letters. His poetry I admired, as one admires a lovely thing, which has never entered into one's soul. But the fragments from the letters in Colvin's *Life* stirred me deeply. I began to

read the poetry with a new understanding – a very partial understanding, for there is no end to the process of understanding Keats, but a real one. The barriers were down. Though it might take me a lifetime to explore the world of human feeling and thought before me, the gate at least was open, and I had entered in. One evening, sitting in an armchair in the drawing-room, I re-read *The Fall of Hyperion*.[20]

How deeply those fragments from Keats's letters must have stirred him one can guess, remembering that they included most of the passages concerning 'the poetic character' which he was to make so intimately his own. But it was *The Fall of Hyperion* that really gripped him:

> *Every sole man hath days of joy and pain,*
> *Whether his labours be sublime or low –*
> *The pain alone, the joy alone, distinct:*
> *Only the dreamer venoms all his days,*
> *Bearing more woes than all his sins deserve.*

Here Murry recognized his own condition. Even Katherine had 'the pain alone, the joy alone, distinct': this was what estranged them now. ('Jack, *must* you look so ill?' she burst out irritably one evening at table, to the amused surprise of the other guests.) Here what he knew for an idiosyncrasy, and perhaps a weakness, was revealed beyond doubt as a privilege. And that was not all. In the poet's vision of Moneta, he recognized the blind and beautiful power of Necessity itself – only seen, not as he had seen it, through a glass darkly, but face to face:

> What I had groped for and glimpsed, there was seen; that of which I was afraid, there was realised. A kind of chill crept over me, a foreboding sense that I had not paid the price of the knowledge that was there, and that it would have to be paid. The vanward cloud of evil days had spent their malice; that was true. Was I not at peace and resting now? But,
>
> > The sullen rear
> > Was with its stored thunder labouring up.
>
> Yet, at the very instant that I was chilled with the premonition of disaster, I was thrilled with the ecstasy of discovery. This was for me; this was mine: to this voice my ears were sensitive.[21]

The 'invisible writing' had become a legible writing on the wall.

This was a critical discovery in more senses than one. It was not only that Murry had found, in his own experience, a clue to Keats; he had found in Keats a clue to his experience. For it should not be forgotten that he himself, at this time, was in his own eyes primarily a poet. He was, indeed, engaged on *Cinnamon and Angelica* – a verse play that fully deserved Katherine's praise, and which stands in much the same relation to his final achievement as *Thyrsis* does to Arnold's. Now everything fell into place: the pattern was unmistakable. On the one hand, poetry was revealed as the very voice of the Unknown God – hence its compulsive power, which had so long bewitched and bewildered him; on the other, he himself was revealed as being tempered to make a poet without illusions – a great poet.

> '*None can usurp this height*', return'd that shade,
> '*But those to whom the miseries of the world
> Are misery, and will not let them rest*'.

Murry copied those lines on the flyleaf of his *Dostoevsky*, adding that he would have them printed there in any future edition. It must have seemed as though nothing was wanting to his realization of the new consciousness but some further, more intimate experience of 'the miseries of the world'. And that was not long delayed.

It was while he was still under the impact of this discovery that Katherine came down again – chilled through by the icy ride from the station. Next day she took to her bed with a temperature. Neither of them treated it seriously. It was he who was suspected of consumption, and, though they agreed that they had been neglecting themselves and decided to live together again, she would hear nothing of a comfortable flat. She liked the 'impermanency' of Redcliffe Road, she said, and talked gaily of going off to France. She had barely had time to notify her landlord, however, before the truth was out. It was by no whim of her own, but by doctor's orders, that she would have to leave England for the winter.

So this was how the Beauty of Necessity was to be revealed! Murry foresaw it all. 'The grim sense of foreboding that had been gathering in me fairly took possession of me. I was engulfed in a black wave of unfaith.' [22] All his fears for himself were transferred overnight to Katherine. Never does it seem to have occurred to him that her illness need be no more disastrous than his own. No, though he tried to suppress his misgivings, to give rein to the inextinguishable hope that all might be well, the precedent of Keats, combining with his inveterate

Angst, overbore all consideration: 'Behind my confidence was a despair; and likewise, behind my despair, a confidence. But the confidence behind my despair was not a confidence in any future happiness: on the contrary, it was a confidence in a power that wrought beauty out of human disaster. My veiled goddess dwelt with beauty, indeed; but with "Beauty that must die".' [23] No wonder Katherine took leave of him with relief! At the end of December, he returned to London; on January 7, 1918, she set off for Bandol.

On the nightmare of the next three months it is needless to enlarge. The story of Katherine's journey, in unheated trains besieged by riotous soldiers; of her arrival in a town turned totally strange by the War; of her loneliness and homesickness, illness and terror; of her vain efforts to get back through Paris, when the city was under bombardment and all communication with England cut off – that story is told in the agonizing letters she posted Murry day by day. Enough that when she did reach London again, on April 11, 'she was barely recognizable. She looked as though she had been for months in some fearful prison.' [24] And he? According to one of his colleagues, he too looked as though he were being 'led to execution'. Those three months were more crucial in both their lives even than the corresponding three of 1916. On May 3 – at the South Kensington registry office, in the presence of Fergusson and Dorothy Brett – they were married at last: but the ceremony, which was to have meant so much, was a travesty of itself. They were scarcely the same couple as had parted at the beginning of the year.

There was really no possibility now of Katherine's recovering. 'The hardships she had suffered had given pthisis a secure hold upon her.' [25] Six months later, two eminent specialists were to tell Murry plainly that her only hope lay in entering a sanatorium – and that she refused to face. Ironically, she who had been so unwilling to live with him and keep house when she was well, now that she was incapable of it, desired nothing else as much. It was all he could do to prevail on her, six weeks after her return, to go down to Looe, in Cornwall, where Anne Estelle Rice had found a suitable hotel, while he prepared a house for them to live in – the first they had owned, and the last they were to occupy in England – No. 2 Portland Villas, Hampstead.

As for him, the cast of his mind was determined for years to come. It was during those months that he wrote the 'Induction to an Unwritten Poem' and 'The Daughter of Necessity' – memorials, both,

to that almost exultant acceptance of the wreck of hope which was
to remain his religion till Katherine's death:

> *Love not the scapegoat of humanity.*
> *Love me no longer: yea, love thou not aught;*
> *And love not love, for this shall surely be*
> *A sudden spear thrust through thy living thought,*
> *A poison that will chill thy warmest blood,*
> *To strange adventure in the desert brought*
> *Or in the frozen wastes of the great flood,*
> *Within the toils of lonely knowledge caught*
> *Of that which lies beyond the evil and the good.*[26]

In the 'Induction' – the most powerful, though not the best, of his
poems – Murry seeks to convey the actual sensation of that self-
immolation before the blind and beautiful power which he was wont
to call (after Spinoza, whom he read for the first time that spring)
amor intellectualis dei – and might better have called *amor fati*. In
'The Daughter of Necessity', it is the accompanying sense of being a
vehicle or instrument of this power that finds its first characteristic
expression:

> He went out blind, he returns with sight; so that he comprehends the
> necessity which drove him forth and compels him to return. While he was
> in the wilderness he believed that his purpose was that he should express
> himself. At the moment when his steps turn homewards he has realised
> that his purpose is that life should be expressed through him. He is
> become the finger of the hand of Necessity.[27]

Sullivan was right to discern in this essay the key to *The Evolution of
an Intellectual*. It is the key to nearly all Murry's work.

For him, Katherine's illness and the War now constituted a single
event (was her fate not 'as much a circumstance of the war as any
death at the front'?[28]): for, just as he had no hope of her recovering,
so he had none of England's. On the contrary, 'God has spewed
England out of his mouth,' he wrote that February, in a moment of
bitter disgust with Government demagogy: 'And I am very sad,
because I love England.' [29] The nearer the Armistice drew, the more
evident it became that the fine flower of a generation had been sacrificed for nothing: 'They, and the ideals for which they gave up their
lives, ideals which were incarnate in them, were forgotten. And what
was remembered? Not they, but profits and possessions and revenge –

everything which they despised, that was remembered.' [30] Of this
event, Katherine's suffering was the symbol.

It is noticeable how, under the strain of separation – when their
correspondence seemed to be, and probably was, affected by telepathy
– both he and she turned by a common instinct towards the great
Romantics. 'We belong to these people,' he exclaims in another of his
letters: 'And just as Keats, Lamb, Coleridge, Shelley, Wordsworth
fed themselves on the Elizabethans, we must feed on them both.' [31]
In 'these people' they heard the voice of the authentic England; and
there were times when they heard it nowhere else, when to him, at
least, it seemed as if they themselves were its sole surviving
representatives:

> No, my darling, you and I are English, and because we are truly English
> we are set apart from our generation. That has gone a whoring after
> strange gods, and only you and I and Wordsworth and Coleridge, Lamb
> Keats and Shelley abide. I am in that state of mind, not seldom with me
> now, when I can see symbols in everything. Your having gone to Paris
> on the day when the great German attack began now seems to me as
> inevitable as all our correspondences. You are the perfect flower of
> England – the thing that Shakespeare dreamed, and almost embodied in
> Cleopatra (in the moment you and I know by heart) – therefore they
> drive at you. I know I become fantastic; but these fantastic ideas of mine
> are true somehow, ils n'agissent qu'au niveau de leur source, as Rousseau
> said of his own ideas, – and that means that everyone else in the world
> will think them mad save only you.[32]

Fantastic they were: but in the War, Murry felt, the nature of reality
itself had been laid bare – a reality utterly indifferent, if not positively
inimical, to beauty and love. If he was to reconcile himself to this,
therefore – and reconciliation was the sole alternative to futile revolt
or evasion – it could only be by discovering a 'meaning' here too, a
beauty not his own to which he could respond with a love not his own.
And that was what he was doing.

Was there not, after all, a certain inhuman justice in the very fact
that, as others had lost their physical lives, he was condemned to lose
his spiritual? If the destruction of all his second-hand values had been
a retribution, since 'there are moments when each man is secretly
convinced that in himself he bore the seeds of this great disruption,
by reason of his own disharmony',[33] so likewise was that of his one
genuine value, his naïve faith in love. This was his penalty for avoiding

the War and turning to love as a refuge. Now that even this was being taken from him, he could persuade himself that he had been spared for a purpose, 'to experience, in full consciousness, the *meaning* of their disaster':[34] to expiate his guilt and his generation's by becoming their spokesman, and arraigning the actual England in the name of the ideal.

It was this persuasion that drew him to Rousseau, who, a century and a half before, had exposed the fallacy of their common faith in Progress. The essay on Rousseau in *Aspects of Literature* was written in March 1918, with the same sense of complete understanding, he told Katherine, as he had experienced with Dostoevsky. It was this also that drew him to Wordsworth, who, in his 'patriotic' sonnets, had discharged such a mission at the time of the Napoleonic Wars: 'Wordsworth alone could speak for me. And I feel that if I am spared I shall do again what Wordsworth did.' [32]

Murry, alas, was not to be a second Wordsworth. The 'Unwritten Poem' was to be in prose. It was in the articles succeeding 'The Daughter of Necessity' that he assumed the prophetic mantle. Yet how well, on the whole, it became him! He might be a second Rousseau. There were not many writers in those days with the integrity, the courage and the foresight to indict, as he did, the iniquity of Versailles; still fewer to lay bare the root of the War, when the simple concept of 'German guilt' was held to justify every measure of self-interest:

What had really happened was that modern civilisation had incredibly increased the physical power of man. It had first made him a unit in a herd; and, secondly, armed the herd with such appliances for destroying its similars as made one single man more dangerous than ten thousand of his great-grandfathers. But instead of the attempt being made to magnify his moral consciousness in proportion, the physical intensification had so occupied the energies of the world that it was tacitly agreed to assume that the moral development proceeded *pari passu* with the material. Somehow, exactly how no-one knew, they were the same thing. They were, in fact, totally different. The result was that war broke upon a race of men only half conscious of their strength, and vaguely believing that the strength itself was a guarantee against the misuse of it. Once the issue was engaged between the new giant organisms there was no stopping the slaughter. Imagination, so far from being commensurably developed and organised, had remained, roughly speaking, at the pre-civilisation level. There were no adequate spiritual controls. The problem is how to create them. The first step towards its solution will be the creation of the general sense that they are lacking and necessary; and the first step towards this is to demonstrate the equivocal nature of civilisation.[35]

Nowadays this may be a commonplace among political thinkers (if not their opposites, political actors), but it was not a commonplace in January 1919. There is much that is truly prophetic in *The Evolution of an Intellectual*, and still more that is self-prophetic. In a fluid, faltering fashion, practically every theme of Murry's later work is anticipated in these essays. It is strange to think that the last of them was his first in *The Athenaeum* – that he should have been set up at precisely this moment to be 'a light to lighten the intelligentsia'.[36]

7. D. H. Lawrence, Katherine, Frieda Lawrence, J. M. M., Selwood Terrace, 1914

8. S. Koteliansky with Katherine, Portland Villas, 1920

9. Katherine

10. J. M. M. with Katherine, Menton, 1920

11. J. M. M. (centre) with Katherine and Richard Murry, Portland Villas, 1920

VI

'THE ATHENAEUM'

'IT WAS ABOUT THE end of 1828', writes Carlyle in *The Life of John Sterling*, 'that readers of periodical literature, and quidnuncs in those departments, began to report the appearance, in a Paper called the *Athenaeum*, of writings showing a superior brilliancy and height of aim.' By 1919, when Arthur Rowntree purchased the Paper, both brilliancy and height of aim had long departed. It had only just survived the War, as a monthly 'Journal of Reconstruction' scrappily edited by Arthur Greenwood; and history would scarcely have repeated itself had he not reconstituted it entirely as a weekly 'Journal of English and Foreign Literature, Science, the Fine Arts, Music and the Drama', and, by a stroke of inspiration, offered Murry the editorship.

'The new opening seemed to come as a godsend,' Murry writes, 'for our financial difficulties were considerable.' [1] 'The Elephant' (as they called No. 2 Portland Villas, on account of its towering greyness) was carrying at that time, besides himself and Katherine, her friend Ida Baker and two domestic servants – to say nothing of the cats – whilst doctors' fees were mounting. Moreover, whether Rowntree knew it or not, Murry was still an undischarged bankrupt, not legally entitled to borrow. It was as much for economy's sake as Katherine's that they had been thinking of leaving England that spring. As it was, he closed with the offer of £800 p.a. enthusiastically: and was given six hectic weeks to prepare the April number.

If brilliancy and height of aim ensured prosperity, the Paper should have seen another century. One of his first initiatives was to secure from Santayana the *Soliloquies in England* and from Valéry *La Crise de l'Esprit* – both of which have become classics. The majority of his regular contributors were younger, many of them personal acquaintances, but nearly all outstanding. Under his editorship, *The Athenaeum* was to publish, as Frank Swinnerton recalls, 'a truly astonishing number of articles and reviews and letters written by men and women who have since taken leading places in the literary world' [2] – and, he might have added, taken leading places largely through its agency.

Lawrence was enlisted of course. Despite his emphatic 'I have done with the Murries (*sic*), both, for ever' [3] of three years before, he had been visiting Katherine in Hampstead, and responded promptly to the call. 'The Whistling of the Birds' featured in the opening number, over the pseudonym 'Grantorto'. If his next contribution was unacceptable, and he relapsed into sullen hostility, that was not for want of efforts on Murry's part to 'give him a leg-up',[4] by praising *Sons and Lovers* and upholding a reprint of *The Rainbow*. Perhaps 'the outlaw of modern English literature' [5] was envious in his turn.

Koteliansky, on the other hand, embarrassed the editor by the quantity of his translations from the Russian; Katherine came into her own as a reviewer of fiction; and Watergate House was well represented. Those of Murry's colleagues who had hoped that M.I.7 would survive into peace-time, and admired what they took for his astuteness, had no cause to regret it. Sullivan was appointed assistant editor; Sheppard and Murray were regular reviewers. (He also secured Murray a post on the *Literary Supplement*.) As for Garsington, it supplied an entire contingent, including, besides the Bloomsbury phalanx – 'the Woolves', as the Murrys called them, the Stracheys, Clive Bell, Roger Fry and E. M. Forster – Aldous Huxley and T. S. Eliot, both of whom won their spurs in this field. Huxley was the second assistant editor; Eliot would have been, if Murry had had his way (he 'wrestled with Rowntree to get him £500 a year').[6] In the event, he was impressed for literary criticism, on the strength of *Prufrock* – which fact, according to Eliot, illustrates Murry's 'erratic and intuitive nature'.

How was it then that *The Athenaeum* lasted barely two more years? Perhaps Shaw had the answer. His finger on the public pulse, he may already have realized what nobody else did, that the literary reviews, numerous and influential as they still were compared to their present-day counterparts, had had their day. Not that the market for responsible criticism was any smaller than fifty or a hundred years before – it had never been large – but costs of production were geared to the mass-circulation newspapers. Only an editor prepared to compromise with Fleet Street methods could hope to compete, and Murry was the last man for that.

The editorial office was at No. 10 Adelphi Terrace, on the floor below Shaw's flat. Murry had not been installed many weeks before he was greeted with a postcard from Ireland: 'They tell me that the Athenaeum is now *the* paper. I thought the poor old thing was dead. How did you get into my house? When I come home somewhere towards the end of September I shall look in on you on my way upstairs.' [7] Shaw did look in – or rather, he burst in, delivering himself of this oracular pronouncement: '*You* won't make a good editor: you write too well yourself.' It was, as Murry said, 'a two-edged compliment',[8] since he badly needed to make a good editor – but both edges cut.

Though the paper's forbidding format was not his responsibility – he repeatedly urged something more attractive – its unrelieved earnestness was. He had no flair for the lighter side of literature. It was a year before it occurred to him that it was 'perhaps a little too frigid and impersonal for the ordinary man' and might be improved by 'a page of literary *causerie*', costing 'no effort';[9] a year before he even thought of including a short story – and then, one suspects, mainly for Katherine's benefit. The only competition he launched, for an essay on 'English Literature since 1914', seems to have discouraged any further attempt in that direction – perhaps because, whereas he had favoured an unknown, Herbert Read, the other two judges, George Saintsbury and Robert Bridges, insisted on awarding the prize to Katherine's former friend William Orton, for a piece sprinkled with praise of the editor. Consisting almost exclusively of reviews, *The Athenaeum* was aimed at an *élite* and foredoomed to failure.

If Murry had accepted the editorship primarily for financial reasons, however, he saw in it also a grand opportunity to uphold the 'true' values of England and Europe: and here he was more successful. It was at this period that he wrote of Edith Cavell, 'She was that most exquisite product of a true civilisation, the patriot who has passed beyond patriotism, whose instinctive love of her own country has been refined in the furnace of a higher and more devouring loyalty into a passionate devotion to all that her country is not and may be.' [10] It was in this spirit that he set out to combat, as far as he dared, the jingoism of the Northcliffe years – those years when an editor could be dubbed (as he was) 'Bolshevist and pro-German' for proposing that Einstein be offered a professorship in Britain.

The Athenaeum was not a political journal: his sector was clearly defined. But what disgusted him even more than the vengefulness and vulgarity of Versailles was the fact that so few shared his disgust – that so many men of letters, in particular, had emerged from the War not merely unchanged but confirmed in their breezy optimism. This seemed to him, as it did to Katherine, a veritable *trahison des clercs*, and it was on this that they concentrated their fire.

There was to be no log-rolling in *The Athenaeum* camp. It was a novel by Virginia Woolf that called forth Katherine's protest, in her letter of November 10, 1919, 'The novel can't just leave the war out', and his own reply four days later:

> I agree with every word you say about Virginia and the war . . . So few people have felt the war; and for us who have, the work of those who have not – if it pretends to be true at all – must sound a lie. And we're not arbitrary in requiring the truth from them. The War *is* Life; not a strange aberration of Life, but a revelation of it. It is a test we must apply; it must be allowed for in any truth that is to touch us.[11]

If that applied to the Bloomsburys, how much more to the Georgians? To Murry and Katherine, the 'sickening falsity' [12] of contemporary life seemed to reach a head in their erstwhile allies. Hence the historic feud between *The Athenaeum* and *The London Mercury*, the new Georgian organ edited by J. C. Squire.

In the long run, this feud probably did more harm than good. Whatever their failings, these poets were popular – the last who were; and the only result of their discrediting was that poetry ceased to be read. As on many other occasions, Murry would have done better to have remembered his motto from Tchehov, 'plus values only'. Yet, since it was mainly responsible for his reputation at that time – a reputation that was a mystery to himself – his attack on their anthology *Georgian Poetry* is still worth recalling:

> There is nothing disturbing about them; *ils peuvent être mis dans toutes les mains*; they are kind, generous, even noble. They sympathise with animate and inanimate nature. They have shining foreheads with big bumps of benevolence, like Flora Casby's father, and one inclines to believe that their eyes must be frequently filmed with an honest tear, if only because their vision is blurred. They are fond of lists of names which never suggest things; they are sparing of similes. If they use them they are careful to see that they are not too definite, for a definite simile makes havoc of their constructions, by applying to them a certain test of reality.
> But it is impossible to be serious about them. The more stupid of them

supply the matter for a good laugh; the more clever the stuff of a more
recondite amazement. What *is* one to do when Mr. Monro apostrophises
the force of Gravity in such words as these? –

> By leave of you man places stone on stone;
> He scatters seed: you are at once the prop
> Among the long roots of his fragile crop
> You manufacture for him, and insure
> House, harvest, implement, and furniture,
> And hold them all secure.

We are not surprised to learn further that

> I rest my body on your grass,
> And let my brain repose in you.

All that remains to be said is that Mr. Monro is fond of dogs ('Can you
smell the rose?' he says to Dog: 'ah, no!') and inclined to fish – both of
which are Georgian inclinations.[13]

An incidental and unexpected result of this review was that Murry
was invited to the *Mercury* office, to be taken aside by Edward Shanks
and told that he had hurt the editor in a very delicate spot – his own
dog, to which he was devoted, having passed away a day or two before.
It is doubtful whether Murry was repentant: like many childless
couples, he and Katherine were cat-lovers.

Like many men nervous in society, moreover, he was far more
combative than he ever admitted. He had thoroughly enjoyed being
threatened with an action by the President of the Royal Institute for
a criticism ending, 'the only thing to be said about the R.I. is R.I.P.' [14]
He was certainly enjoying this cat-and-dog fight, his gusto being all
the greater for the relative opulence of the *Mercury* (he could never
forget a barrel of beer glimpsed in that office). 'There's no doubt it's
a fight to finish between us and them,' he exclaims in another letter to
Katherine, 'them is the "Georgians" *en masse*. It's a queer feeling I
begin to have now: that we're making literary history.' [15]

It would be a grave mistake, none the less, to imagine him still
animated by the undergraduate iconoclasm of *Rhythm*. Though his
polemics may have made his reputation, they do not make him important. They were only the obverse of a serious, indeed tense, endeavour to define his own artistic and literary values. It is this that
raises his articles, in both *The Athenaeum* and *The Nation*, above the

ruck of reviews. Already he was as much a traditionalist as a revolutionary. 'The superiority that prevails to-day', he was writing in an obituary on Renoir, 'takes the form of always trying either to lead or react against the fashion. A real superiority ignores the fashion; it rejects the humility which is *bête* and the beauty which is null. It throws down the false gods only in order that it may revere the true gods with a more self-forgetful devotion.' [16] He had no use now for Modernism for its own sake, whether it took the form of pseudo-negro sculpture or the poems of E. E. Cummings. His exaltation of Epstein implied no belittling of Sickert (both of whom thought him one of the best art-critics of the day); his overrating of Eliot no underrating of De la Mare. What he was pitting against the spurious traditionalism of the Georgians was the genuine tradition of the Romantics. This was what he wished to see prolonged in forms appropriate to the age – and did see prolonged, for example, by Hopkins, Edward Thomas and Owen, whom he was the first English critic to salute.

His two essays on Keats, in *The Athenaeum* and *The Nation*, are typical, and vital. In the first of these, he joins hands with Eliot (whom at this date he lost no occasion to publicize) in deploring 'the undiscriminating submission of a century' [17] to the *Poems* of 1820. But, unlike Eliot, he deplores it in the name of Keats. It is the spirit of the Romantics themselves that he pits against the letter. And this is how, in the second essay, he tries to define that spirit:

> When all the turmoil of aesthetic debate is over, the simple fact remains that the highest triumphs of art are possible only to those who have achieved in themselves a purity of soul ... The purity of the great artist is based upon a profound acceptance of experience, and the endeavour always to find some point of hidden strength within himself from which he can at once submit himself to life and comprehend it ... We may say that Keats, during his last year of poetic activity, came to believe that the poet was in some sort the scapegoat of humanity, one who fronted experience on behalf of mankind.[18]

To front experience on behalf of mankind: that was Murry's ideal; and it was as much an ethical ideal as an aesthetic: 'The vital centre of our ethics is also the vital centre of our art.' [19] It was, indeed, about this time that Eliot first shocked and then illuminated him by calling him primarily a 'moralist'. His criticism, from the outset, was a quest for values, 'a determination of what is good for man'. Hence his objection to *l'art pour l'art*, and his insistence on the necessity of establishing a hierarchy. That art was best in kind which expressed and communicated a comprehension of life; that greatest which comprehended life most completely. This was the standard by which he set head and top of twentieth-century writers Tchehov and Thomas Hardy.

The Athenaeum sailed under the banner of Hardy. 'Mr Hardy can speak for all that is noble in England as no poet since Wordsworth has been able,' [20] he declaimed in one editorial; and scarcely a month went by without some similar salvo. His admiration became almost a 'monomania'.[21] Not content with dedicating his *Poems, 1916–20* 'To Thomas Hardy . . . in Devotion and Gratitude', he out-Hardyed Hardy himself by despatching personally a poem on the old man's death. (The reply was perfect: 'The verses are very striking I think, and they will keep. It will be for others to judge of their contents. I must limit myself to admiring their form.')[22] Of all his critical essays, 'The Poetry of Thomas Hardy' cost him the greatest pains, yet he felt himself richly rewarded by a further reply, enjoining him, with the help of the principles laid down in it, to 'throw a flood of light on the history and art of poetry'.[23]

That 'profound acquiescence' [24] in all experience which he divined in Hardy's work, however, Murry himself was very far from attaining. His own nearest approach was still the *amor intellectualis* – and by that he could not live. His heart revolted against it. He was still 'lost in a sort of purgatory blind', and the despair breaks out again and again in his essays. Sometimes it is despair of ever passing from ecstatic to serene acceptance: 'The effort of contemplation so austere and self-regardless is too great to be maintained; we have not the strength to be Spinozas for more than a moment.' [25] Sometimes it is despair of the experience itself: 'It is a megalomania, a sublime self-deception.' [26] These intrusions lend an individual and unmistakable *timbre* to *Aspects of Literature*. What Carlyle wrote of Sterling's *Athenaeum* papers applies exactly to these: 'Good reading still, those Papers, for the less-furnished mind, – thrice excellent reading compared with what is usually going. For the rest, a grand melancholy is the prevailing impression they leave; – partly as if, while the surface was so blooming and opulent, the heart of them was still vacant, sad and cold.'

This period of his life, in fact, which some less-furnished minds still look on as Murry's best, appeared to himself, in retrospect, that of his 'supreme unreality'.[27] Isolated by his inward division, yet more by the personal anguish that exacerbated it, he felt as remote from his allies as his opponents. He had many acquaintances in the literary world – we hear of week-ends with H. G. Wells (whom, despite his admiration, he thought a snob) and Lytton Strachey (whom he liked as well as admired): but they had no common ground. He had a number of friends, Tomlinson and De la Mare in particular: but even to them he could not force himself to speak of what lay nearest his heart. Small wonder he appeared odd and abstracted – 'inhuman' to them, though 'human, all-too-human' to himself. One day he showed Tomlinson a poem he had written:

> scratch through the silver of illusion's glass
> Their name at least that a faint light be thrown
> Upon the further chamber's basalt floor . . .

'*Your* floor', Tomlinson chuckled, '*would* be bloody basalt.' [28]

The only literary man with whom he felt something in common was Eliot: and that, he surmised, mainly because Eliot 'lived in the same *kind* of isolation. Not that I could really enter his world, or he mine; but there was a strange feeling of kinship between us.' [29] It was Murry who reviewed *Ara Vos Prec* in *The Athenaeum*, Eliot who reviewed *Cinnamon and Angelica*. 'He's the only critic of literature that I think anything of,' [30] he told Katherine on this occasion.

With Katherine herself, of course, it was different. Not only did she make her name by her reviews, but 'she entered into the project enthusiastically',[1] as her letters prove. Alone of his contributors, she shared his ideals completely. But, throughout the winters of 1919 and 1920, Katherine was living abroad; and the very division which their suffering exacerbated, exacerbated their suffering in its turn. It was as though Murry's head were in London, his heart on the Riviera.

Their relation was a paradoxical one. Since 'the natural consequence of social insecurity is the search for the security of love',[31] its intensity and exclusiveness were proportionate to its precariousness. The sense of being strangers together in a strange land runs through all their correspondence. They habitually thought of themselves as babes in the wood. Theirs was, indeed, what Katherine called it, 'child-love' – 'the most marvellous, the most radiant love that this world knows',[32] perhaps: but child-love unnaturally prolonged by childlessness, and exalted into an ideal that no human being could live up to. Thus one might have expected their common suffering to have drawn them yet more closely together.

And so it did – up to a point. But, as Katherine also said, she had always 'been the man and he had been the woman and he had been called upon to make no real efforts'.[32] It was precisely his dependence, his timidity, his naïvety, that had attracted her: had he been 'a man . . . all action and resolution' she would never have married him. And her illness, at the same moment that it made them all-in-all to each other, brought that situation to an end: rendering her, materially and morally, dependent upon him, and him less capable than ever of shouldering the responsibility. For he had no 'point of hidden strength within himself' from which to do so. Poised helplessly between his craving for affection, and the exultant acceptance of a reality which denied it, he was devoid alike of a conviction that could command the whole of his being and of the courage of such a conviction.

Not that he failed entirely to rise to the occasion. Materially 'he stood it marvellously'.[32] It would be easy enough to prove that the accusations of Katherine's *Journal* and *Letters* – to say nothing of her conversations with Sydney Schiff – were for the most part as unjust to him as to Ida Baker, but for whose devotion she would not have lived as long as she did. In matters of finance, in particular, he was far the more realistic. It was certainly not he who 'refused to face what it meant – living alone together for two years on not much money';[32] it was he who tried to make her face it, and got smartly rebuffed for his pains. Morally, however, he was a broken reed.

If he had only been completely confident in 'a power that wrought beauty out of human disaster', he might have given her the faith she needed – a faith that would have enabled her to make the best of what years remained. As it was:

I was haunted by the fear of Katherine's death. Katherine dead: it was a condition which I could not conjecture or imagine. My life would be gone, yet I should be living. It would be, and it was unthinkable. Towards the end of her life Katherine quoted in her Journal as speaking to her heart the line:

Lo! I have made Love all my religion.

'Who wrote that?' she asked. The answer is that I wrote it, and at this time. I wrote it in a little book which she was not meant to see. She had forgotten that. She had forgotten it, I think, because she had blotted it out of her memory, for it was a line from a poem in which I had tried to ease my heart, and strengthen my courage, against the thought of her death. She had come upon it unawares, and it had pierced her heart, as well it might, that I should thus have meditated on the possibility of her death.[33]

Katherine, who also identified herself with Keats, no more relished the role of the dying Tom than Murry did that of Fanny Brawne. Far from accepting a faith so insecure, she bitterly resented (as who would not?) her death's being regarded, not merely as a foregone conclusion, but as part of a necessary educative experience.

Alternatively, if he had only been less dependent upon her love as his one security, his one assurance of his own 'validity', he might have insisted on her going to the sanatorium which was her sole chance of life. As it was:

I was haunted too by the feeling that I had failed: that it was somehow my duty to have warded off death from her even at the sacrifice of Love itself. I ought to have had the courage to hurt her – to wound her even to the heart – by sending her away to the sanatorium. Not all my gratitude to Dr Sorapure could put that doubt at rest.[33]

Katherine being haunted likewise, they took refuge together in a dream, which they knew to be a dream – the Heron Farm, where they and their children (and occasionally M. Georges Duhamel) would live happily ever after.

In these circumstances, their decision that Katherine should spend the winters on the Riviera was probably the best compromise attainable. After all, she could not recover in London nor he earn money abroad: and no doubt, if common sense had been the arbiter, they would have faced a six months' separation resignedly. He, at any rate, could have done, for it was not Katherine he needed, but only her love: assured of that, he could subsist on his own indefinitely, 'a monk without a monastery'.[34] Unfortunately, that was just the trouble. That was just what made it impossible for her to do so. That was what drove her, sick, lonely and terrified at Ospedaletti, to post him those cruel verses printed in the *Letters* and *Journal*.

That was in December 1919; and here was his first reaction (the italics are Katherine's):

My own darling,

This morning in bed I got your Thursday letter and the verses called 'The New Husband'! I've wired to you to-day to say I'm coming out for Christmas. I feel there's not much I can say.

I don't think that at any time *I've* had a bigger blow than that letter and these verses. Even now they hardly seem like a letter and verses – more like a *snake* with a terrible sting. But it's kind of you to tell me you have those feelings: far better, for me anyhow, than keeping them from me. You have too great a burden to bear; you can't carry it. Whether *I* can manage mine, I don't know. We'll see when I get out to you.

What is certain is that this can't go on – something must change. What can go on – I don't know yet. My faith at present is that my coming out for a little while will put you right. But I don't see why it should. *I feel that everything depends upon me; that I have to do something quite definite, very quickly.* But I don't know what it is, and *my* faculty for doing anything has been suddenly paralysed. At the moment when *I* have to balance in the middle of the tight-rope *I* have begun to hesitate.

My plan is to try to get the paper in *some sort* (*!*) of order for three weeks ahead during this week, and leave here at the end of the week. The return fare second class is just over £14, so I'm hoping to do it for £20. I mention money, because it's important. But I'll explain these things when I get there.

As you know already, I'm ready to chuck the paper any moment; but I must see my way to money. I've said this many times; but I say it again, because, though I feel you don't agree with me, it's fundamental to any decision I take. At present I'm trying to clear up the remains of last year's debts. Until they are cleared I shall stick to the A. That's callous, I suppose. But I can't help it. You know my position as a bankrupt. I dare not leave our debts unpaid – I'm not supposed to have any. Once we're straight – and if things were to go moderately well I shall be straight by April (as I hoped to be by December) – I'll do anything. But *I know* that to cut off with little money coming in and heavy debts would mean inevitable disaster.

If I felt certain that my being there would really make things right until May, then nothing would matter. But now I can't pretend to a certainty I don't feel. We'll just have to leave it and see. Anyhow, I just couldn't go on with the A. if you were to go on feeling like this. I'm absolutely incapable of work, now. That sounds, and is, selfish. But you have told me the truth; and I must tell the truth. I'm not made of steel, myself. And it's becoming a great effort to do what I have to do sanely – do you think I can do anything with this ringing in my ears.

> Who's your man to leave you be
> Ill and cold in a far country?
> Who's the husband, who's the stone
> Could leave a child like you alone?

There's nothing to say to that. All that I implore you is to say what you want. That will help.

No, no, no – all this is too hard. I don't mean it – something different. But I must keep sane. I'm coming quickly, darling – then we'll see, we'll see.[35]

Across the envelope, Katherine has scribbled:

This letter killed the Mouse, made the Worm creep underground and banished the Dream Child for ever. Before I had received it I had learned to live *for* Love and *by* Love. I had given myself up – and a kind of third creature *US* was what I lived by. After I had read it, quite apart from me, my own self returned *and* all my horror of death vanished. From this date I simply *don't care* about death! No question of heroics or life not being worth living or anything like it. I simply feel alone again. Voilà.

Even though Murry repented instantly, writing next day, 'Forget all about that horrible letter', her reaction seems excessive. 'The New Husband', after all, was a curious memento of US; she can hardly have expected him to like it. Yet Katherine must have echoed his cry, 'But why in God's name, I ask myself now, did we not originally arrange to have Xmas together? I feel it would have spared you half the torment of your loneliness. What a blind fool I am!' The simple answer was that his fear of her death had completely overshadowed hers. Of Katherine as an independent being, with fears, hopes, needs of her own, he was scarcely aware: if he had been, he could not have idealized her as he did. It took 'The New Husband' to open his eyes – and, incidentally, induce him to ask Rowntree for a rise of £200.

Their fortnight at Ospedaletti was happier than might have been expected after this, despite his being laid up with neuralgia. It was arranged between them that he should look for a house in Sussex, where they could live together in future; he returned to England enthused by the example of an Englishman out there who was making £400 a year by the cultivation of roses: 'That's the way to live!' But whereas a decision, for Murry, meant action, and a thick line drawn under the past, for Katherine it was not so easy to start afresh.

He would say, and he meant it, that because her happy letters made him happy, he wrote her happy ones in return – expecting them to have the same effect. Here, for instance, was his reply to the news of her escape from Ospedaletti to the blessed hospitality of Menton:

[76]

My own darling,

Two gorgeous letters from you this morning telling me that you really are at Menton, that you're happy, that the doctor has given good reports – everything that I was longing and praying for – except one thing. What *is* your real address? I've only had it as it came on the telegram. I made it out to be L'Hermitage, rue P. Morillot, Menton. And some of my letters sent to that address seem to have reached you. But to-day I received from the P.O. an official notification that a telegram I sent to Murry, Hermitage, rue Morillot, Menton on January 19 was not delivered, because you were unknown. That's absolutely bewildering – unless perhaps you weren't actually in Menton on the 19th, and 20th. But then I should have thought that they knew you were coming. However, since you didn't actually get there until Jan. 21, I shall presume that the address is correct and that the telegram wasn't delivered because you weren't there. But, just to set my mind at rest, will you copy out your address and put it prominently at the top of your next letter.

You will, I hope, have got the notes which I sent you from Sussex. I came back without having found a house, but with the firm conviction that Sussex is a county of *incomparable* beauty, and that I must try might and main to find something there. I walked 30 miles on Saturday and Sunday. The walk on Sunday was divine. Darling, I'm sure you wouldn't believe what the South Downs can be on their day even in January. There was a bright, pale-blue sky, with tufts of cloud. We were walking on the lower slope of the Downs on the north side. Below us, gently sloping away to the right were miles on miles of the Sussex weald rolling away to the north. The strangest and most wonderful thing about it was the colour – it seemed to be all golden, with dark brown splashes where the woods were, and every now and then a glimmer of vivid green. I can't describe it; it needs patience and art. But it made a profound impression upon me – of wideness and peace, a queer sense that the country instead of being alien wanted to protect and shelter you, almost to lull you into her own richness. I felt that you and I could grow wise and unfretted there, that the note of hysteria would go out of all that I did.

Well, well, if I didn't find anything, I had a day's sheer happiness, and I came nearer to a knowledge of what I want than I was before. When I got back this morning I found the enclosed note waiting for me. I have made up my mind to go down and see it to-morrow, even though it's the day before press-day. One can't afford to take risks, the demand for houses in the country is so portentous. You see if its anything like, the rent is so small that we can take it on the spot, even if we change it for something else. Hold thumbs – what if it were the real thing – an old farmhouse!

Your reviews came to-day – Hurrah! The next number of the paper won't be flat anyhow.

I'm working like a horse. My goodness, but what a difference your letters have made.

How's money – let me know, please. Wig for ever![36]

This, strange to say, was the 'abnormally selfish letter from Jack' [37] which hurt Katherine so much, provoking her fresh outburst of January 31. Again, her reaction seems extravagant ('It doesn't seem very bad to me', Murry himself wrote at the top, thirty years afterwards). Yet again, it was not so much his seeming omission to send her £10, instead of asking 'How's money?' that cut her (in fact, he had already posted all he had, £13, to Ospedaletti) as his inability really to enter into her feelings of loneliness and relief. Even to put oneself in the other's shoes, after all, is only to judge the other by oneself – and that is what he did, habitually. His reply to this outburst was a meek confession of failure:

My own darling,

This seems to be the first evening since I came back from Italy when I have been able to sit down and write to you calmly – not dashing off a few lines in time to catch a train, or to write a review. I feel that I have allowed myself to become an appalling machine, and that you have felt it in my letters, as you could not fail to feel it; and so you have been left without the sympathy I should have given.

There is, Wig, a certain amount of real insensibility in me. I think that has been proved now. I must just accept it: I hate it, and try to kill it. But the fact remains that I never realised how much you were suffering in Ospedaletti, nor how great would be your anxiety about money in Menton. Both those things you had a right to expect of me as your lover – and, there's no doubt in my own mind that I failed in them both.

Certainly, to be quite fair to myself, I have found it hard to keep going. My power of concentration has weakened, and it now takes me a good deal more energy than it did two or three years ago to do the same amount of work. But I don't believe very much in the argument. I feel, on the contrary, that there have been times when I have, not consciously or deliberately, turned my sympathy away from you. Something of the kind you must have felt.

Perhaps it all comes back to the fact that I am able to do nothing without an effort, neither to work nor to love. It's what I mean when I say I'm no good as a lover – our old quarrel of years ago about the enamel spoon. I think that at bottom it's no worse, and no better than that. You managed to bear with it when you were well – that was your generosity – and now when you are ill it becomes intolerable.

Don't let it become intolerable, Wig. Believe at least that my thoughts are not as cold and brutal as my words sometimes seem to be. That in fact I do give you my all, and if it's a poor one, it's because I have no more to give. You have the whole of me, darling, and when it fails, as it has failed so often I know, just remember that I would have given more if I had had it. It's not much consolation – it's certainly not the rich comfort I should be giving you, but it may be some. I mean that though I am a jagged, flowerless, and inhospitable rock, I am a rock. If I'm not beautiful or life-giving, I'm also not treacherous.

I don't suppose I have explained what I mean. I do try to give, Wig darling, try desperately sometimes because I know how much you need it, and from me. But the spring whence richness comes seems to dry up. I become a barren and dry land where no water is. I feel like a tree must feel in the winter. It knows it is not dead, yet it cannot know that it is alive – it has neither voice nor leaves. The only thing to do would be to cut it open. But you can't cut me open. Things that you, being you, might read in a movement of my hand or a glance of my eyes when we are together are lost altogether in my bald letters. The more I try to make my letters live, the less I seem able to.

You see, my darling, it's wrong for us to be apart. That is what it comes to at the last. You can understand my harshness, blackness, my habit of silence when you are near me, and make allowances: but when we are so far away that is impossible, yet it is more necessary than ever.

The only thing is for you to get well – to make up your mind that I am the same Boge all the while – not the Boge I ought to be, but a better Boge than I look at the distance. Get well, my darling, and lets put an end to this time of torture. Your voice is sweet, but mine is harsh when we call from so far away.

Well, my darling Worm, I'll tell you what news there is in my next letter. This one is all explanation, of something perhaps which cannot be explained. But as your telegram to-day said, *of course I love you* and love you for all I am worth, with all that I have.[38]

Murry wanted them to live together, there is no doubt of that. He spent every week-end that month cycling or tramping the countryside, sometimes alone, sometimes with his brother or Sullivan, in search of a suitable home. He found a house where she could have lived even in winter (and long afterwards regretted that he had not insisted on their taking it); when she rejected that idea, he bought a charming cottage to which they could retire later on, Broomies, on Chailey

Common. But always Katherine suspected – and one cannot escape her suspicion – that he wanted it more for her sake than his own. '*Amabare amabam*': he said it himself in *Between Two Worlds*.

Let it be admitted, nevertheless, that few could have coped with Katherine more patiently. Nowhere in all his writings or reported conversations is there anything resembling the malicious gossip she so often indulged in about him – and he had much besides that to put up with. Irritable, suspicious, demanding, her normal oscillations of temperament magnified to earthquakes by disease, she would accuse him of not reading her letters, yet misquote his most innocent remarks, reading sinister meanings into them which never were, or could have been, intended. What a tirade followed his 'feeble joke',[39] for example, 'I've also insured my life for £1000 in case I break my neck house-hunting':[40] 'It is terrific torture – terrific. Don't you care about ME at all? If I must bear it, I *must*, but I'm nearly at the end of my tether when you say such things.' [41] Or his mild reproach to her for thinking that he would be anything but delighted by her reconciliation with Ida, 'I must say, I hated your picture of me being thin-lipped and angry over it: your idea of me seems to get a long way from the reality':[40] in her reply that becomes, 'Everything I thought at the Casetta got "a long way from reality",' [41] and further proof of his insensibility. 'Don't give me up entirely,' [42] he pleaded, i.e. 'Don't think me entirely insensitive': [43] 'Your coldness is killing me,' was the response – and it was neither the first nor the last wire of its kind.

He had but to inquire whether she still had a soft spot for Beatrice Hastings, who had written asking for work, to receive a 'deeply hurt': he ought to have known that she had had a tiff with Beatrice four years before. He had but to go to a party, reported by a common acquaintance, to receive a 'don't drink any more wine', and a succession of curtain-lectures. This particular wire, as it happened, was opened by the maid at Portland Villas, with what portentous reflections may be imagined. Then the furore over that photograph of her, which he gave to Constables! It was not until thirty years later that an explanation for this dawned upon him – that she might have had it taken for Carco. At the time, he was simply 'knocked sideways'.[44]

This was in November 1920; and it was under the impact of this, when Katherine actually broke off communications, that he committed his one more serious offence, of embarking on a mild flirtation. That he was 'starving for some feminine warmth and tenderness' is

[80]

understandable – '*how* one is starved for it when one has spent years tending, and anxious for, a sick wife!' [44] – and there were women in plenty willing to supply his need. The wonder is that as long as Katherine lived, he never gave way to his inclinations beyond an occasional kiss or caress. Yet even that Katherine 'took very hard, as her letters show. And I felt a horrible sort of double guilt – for hurting Katherine and for hurting Elizabeth, by writing her the cold and formal letters on which Katherine insisted . . . Katherine would not hear a word in defence of Elizabeth, and I resented being compelled to behave brutally towards her.' Finally, 'I explained to Elizabeth that I was completely in love with Katherine, that she was seriously ill, and that whatever she wanted me to do, I must do – however hard or unjust or against the grain it might be. And, as I remember, Elizabeth took it very well.' [44] All the same, it was 'a little hard. While she was well, I had to be the companion of her "innocent" self; and when she was ill, I had to be "the man without a temperament".' [45]

The Elizabeth in question was Princess Elizabeth Bibesco, whom Murry met from time to time at The Wharfe, the country seat of the Asquiths. Katherine might not have heard of their friendship, but for some letters which reached him at Menton over Christmas. As it was, she was deeply upset; and still more so when, shortly after his return to England, she learned that they had taken leave of each other in person. The appearance of a story by Princess Bibesco in *The Athenaeum* for January 14 was the occasion of a final wire, announcing the end of her own contributions. The episode, so innocent in itself, and yet, because he had kept it secret, so deleterious to their relationship, was the germ of his novel, *The Voyage*.

Introverts are seldom good letter-writers, and Murry was no exception. Set beside Katherine's, his side of their correspondence would be scarcely more than a foil – laboured, clumsy, often transparently tired. There must have been many weeks when his emotional reserves were exhausted, and he badly needed a 'blood-transfusion' – weeks when 'the feel of not to feel it' made him, as he said, like a tree in winter. 'We are both abnormal,' she wrote once: 'I have too much vitality – and you not enough.' [46] She might have added that she had little to do but write letters, whereas he had to squeeze his out between endless articles and reviews. All in all, it speaks much for his devotion that, throughout those long separations, he hardly ever let a day go by without sending one at least; and still more, that their cumulative effect is to inspire a singular affection for the writer. It is not merely that one sympathizes with his bewilderment, 'the awful feeling that all that I may write may have an effect utterly different from what I meant':[47] their very lameness and awkwardness are touching. One ceases to marvel (if one ever did) that she should have awaited them so eagerly, or cherished them – and him – to the last, 'in spite of all'.

Moreover, to what love he knew he was loyal. When the storm broke over that photograph and his consequent flirtation, he did not hesitate. The paper was losing heavily; he had already decided to relinquish it in April. She being seriously ill, he resigned on the spot. February 1921 saw *The Athenaeum* merged in *The Nation*, Murry and Katherine reunited at Menton.

VII

DEATH IN LIFE

———————◆◆◆◆◆◆◆———————

M URRY'S ANNOUNCEMENT OF THE ending of *The Athenaeum*
caused widespread regret. It was 'the one hope of literary
decency in England',[1] Wells mourned, adding that he would
gladly have stepped in to save it, had he known before. 'I am more
sorry than I can say that you should be going', wrote De la Mare,
'though at the same time I rejoice for K. M.'[2] Only Lawrence as usual
struck a discordant note. 'I hear the Athenaeum lost £5000 a year under
our friend the mud-worm,' he was jeering to Koteliansky: 'I hear he is
– or was – on the Riviera with K. – who is doing the last-gasp touch . . .
K. also announcing that the *Rowntrees* couldn't bear *her* writing. Ah
me, we have become important. Two mud-worms they are, playing
into each other's long mud-bellies.'[3] But then Lawrence had been
promised a blow on the face if the editor ever met him again, after his
vicious attack on Katherine the winter before ('You are a loathsome
reptile – I hope you will die . . .').[4]

Murry's own regrets were altogether outweighed by relief. Not that
he was glad to see the paper go down – he had been hoping to hand it
over to a successor. But as far as he was personally concerned, it had
served its turn. It had established his reputation as a critic, so that he
could now afford to live abroad on his earnings; and his labours were
appropriately rewarded by two invitations: one from Sir Walter
Raleigh, to deliver a course of six lectures at Oxford; and one, which,
he valued still more highly, from Hardy, to visit him in Dorset. His
reconciliation with Katherine this spring, moreover, bore more than a
casual resemblance to that of five years before – and as at Bandol, so
at Menton, issued in a new creative spell. His lectures, *The Problem of
Style*, were themselves its first-fruits.

To his disappointment, Katherine would hear nothing of living in
Sussex. She had conceived a positive aversion to England, and was

anxious to try the Spahlinger treatment for tuberculosis, now being practised in Switzerland. When he set off for Oxford in May, therefore, she went on to Montreux. But, compared with the partings of the past, this was 'a trivial affair'.[5] The letters they exchanged day by day were eloquent of what he called their 'new love', the 'state of grace'[6] they had reached:

> For some reason or other, I can't give you an account of my doings in Oxford. It's all so awfully unreal. Not that the people aren't very nice to me . . . but it's a world I left years and years ago. I love Oxford; but in the way I love my father. We're utterly strange to each other. Sometimes, when I'm dining at the high table the clock stops ticking and I hear everything from an incredible distance – and it's so strange.
>
> Yesterday afternoon I went to see the cricket in the Parks – it was lovely. Great tall trees, smooth grass, bright sunshine, a slow clapping when a man came out to bat, the muffled click as he hit the ball. A dream game – so remote it was from me. And how I enjoyed my own remoteness!
>
> How intimately I have *grown in* to you lately! With everyone else, everywhere else I am a kind of bemused spectator. Life seems like the slow dropping of water into a deep well. Fascinating and very far away. A curious deep happiness is hidden somewhere inside me.
>
> Well, darling -- we've had a strangely mixed time together – but if it had been a time of unmixed suffering it would still have been worth the price to get to the condition we're in now.[7]

So he wrote on May 19: and for once the deep happiness persisted.

Looking forward as he was to a long stay abroad, Murry had plenty to do that month. Broomies had to be sold (the 'Elephant' was already disposed of), Alpine equipment to be bought, his family to be said good-bye to – for, by pretending to be married sooner than they were, he and Katherine had long since conciliated his parents. Indeed, his mother had told him, 'You have taught me to believe in something I once dreamed of but never believed in again – perfect love and perfect happiness';[8] and it was while visiting them that he persuaded his father, who was on the point of retiring, to let Richard take up art as a career. He could sympathize with the boy's struggle – as could Katherine, whose own father chose this moment to stop her allowance.

Oxford also, in spite of its remoteness, responded well to his lectures ('especially the young ladies', Mark Gertler reported). Instead of dwindling after the first, as he had expected, his audience of 250 grew; instead of finding them obscure, as he had feared – for he was pursuing a typical voyage of discovery, rather than formulating pre-determined conclusions – the dons were so favourably impressed that *The Problem of Style* became a standard work, to be reprinted more often than anything else he ever wrote. Had he wished, he could easily have secured a permanent university appointment.

Even so, 'thank God I never became a Don!' [9] The high point of the excursion, for him, was that long-awaited meeting with Hardy on the 24th, an account of which (published thirteen years later) he wrote down the following day, thinking it unlikely that they would ever see each other again. 'The old man was everything I had dreamed – everything,' [10] he told Katherine. After that he was impatient to be gone. The last lecture was hardly finished before he was heading for Switzerland, and June 9 found them once more together, at the Chalet des Sapins, Montana.

'The peace of the Chalet des Sapins was the peace of the Villa Pauline in a new dimension,' he writes; the months July to December 1921, 'the most fruitful period of Katherine's writing life'.[11] He might have added that it was the most fruitful of his own to date. Although he wrote no more poetry – which, only twelve months before, he had still thought of as his 'chief concern' [12] – it was during these months that he produced, in addition to *The Things We Are* and the first half of *The Voyage*, most of the finest of the critical essays assembled in *Countries of the Mind (1st Series)*. Evidently *The Problem of Style*, like *Dostoevsky* five years before, had loosened his critical muscles, and helped to show him where his true strength lay.

Not that the novels are important in themselves. They were primarily Murry's method of discovering that he was no more a novelist than a poet. That he lacked the power of a Tchehov or a Katherine to communicate 'a sense of the quality of life as a whole' [13] by investing a particular scene with 'the weight and force of the universal',[14] he already knew. This presupposed, as he had said in his lectures, 'an unusually rich accumulation of sensuous perceptions' [15] – and his own was unusually poor. He had yet to learn that he likewise lacked the power of a Proust or a Joyce to communicate it by a 'presentation of his immediate consciousness'.[16] As always, he could convince himself only by experiment. Yet the time he spent on these works was not wasted. For one thing, however slight, they are by no means negligible: it was not merely personal friendship that led De la Mare to praise the atmospheric effects of *The Things We Are*, while *The Voyage* reveals a real power of creative extrapolation. For another, their composition was a valuable, if not indispensable, part of his education as a critic. It is noteworthy that much of what he wrote about *Ulysses* the following March applies *mutatis mutandis* to *The Things We Are* – and that Joyce was sufficiently impressed by the review to seek him out in Paris.

When it came to literary criticism, on the other hand, Murry's very weaknesses turned to strength, for not only was his susceptibility to the lightest nuance of feeling in poetry proportionate (like the blind man's touch) to his everyday impercipience, but both by propensity and practice he was superbly equipped to formulate an emotional response intellectually. Virginia Woolf once called him 'the most intellectual of all modern critics'. That as he told Katherine, was untrue, at least as she had meant it:

> Whatever I am I am not intellectual critic at all. It is true I try to give my views an intellectual statement, because that is the only method I have. If I were a born writer, I should express myself in your way. But my attitude is almost exactly like yours. I can't treat art as a clever game, and I am (to myself anyhow) always notoriously weakest in the examination of the technical side of a work. My test is extremely simple. If a work awakens a profound response in me, then I sit up and try to find out what it is that is working on me. In other words I am an absolutely emotional critic. What may seem intellectual is only my method of explaining the nature of the emotion.[17]

But it was Katherine herself who touched the heart of the matter, when she divined in him the poet *manqué*.

Aspects of Literature was the work of a minor poet *manqué*. In that, as she saw, lay the origin of its worst fault – Murry's deplorable tendency to 'show his wounds'. 'If you speak for your generation,' she admonished him, 'speak, but don't say "I speak for my generation", for the force is then gone from your cry. When you know you are a voice crying in the wilderness, *cry*, but don't say "I am a voice crying in the wilderness".' To turn away from the object of his emotion, and describe the emotion instead, is precisely the minor poet's temptation. *Aspects of Literature*, like *The Evolution of an Intellectual*, was largely vitiated by it. No more penetrating judgement on these books was passed than Katherine's letters of December 5 and 8, 1919.

By contrast, *Countries of the Mind* is the work of a major poet *manqué*, since here the bifocalism has given way to a single-minded absorption in the object. Here we see Murry's very lack of 'determined character' turn to advantage, as, obstructed by no hard crust of acquired convictions, he loses himself in the work or the man before him. If these essays are not literary criticism as that is now understood, they are something infinitely rarer and more precious.

He was lucky in his centenaries that year. Like Dostoevsky, Flaubert, Baudelaire and Amiel were all born in 1821; and, like Dostoevsky, all three were men with whom, by virtue of some kindred potentiality, he could identify himself up to a point. Moreover, Bruce Richmond, the editor of the *Literary Supplement*, commissioned articles well in advance, so that he had time to master his material. But this capacity for entering into and making his own a wide variety of viewpoints – related to his youthful adoption of one *persona* after another – was always to be Murry's *forte*. It was no accident that those months were the occasion also of his first deep draught of Shakespeare.

He had studied Shakespeare before, of course. On *The Athenaeum* he had made a point of reviewing Shakespeare criticism and personally reporting the Stratford Festival; while his letters to Katherine, abounding in tributes to the poet's conception of love – 'that perfect harmony between the physical and the imaginative' [18] – show that he had already discovered, in Portia, Perdita and Imogen, his lifelong ideal of womanhood. Now, however, conscious of the connexion between his own self-abeyance in love and work, he sensed a similar connexion in the dramatist. It was, he surmised, precisely that capacity for losing himself in the creatures of his imagination which had predisposed Shakespeare to create such embodiments of love – and, conversely, precisely that loyalty to love which had enabled him, ultimately, to comprehend all his experience in a 'vision of life as a whole'. [19]

That this conclusion was important to Murry hardly needs saying. It must powerfully have reinforced his instinctive faith in 'the holiness of the heart's affections'. The opening essay of *Countries of the Mind* is virtually a declaration of that faith; and so, in a different way, is the conclusion of the essay on Amiel – a minor Dostoevsky, a Dostoevsky without an Alyosha:

> 'It [love] can even become religion.' When we have sifted away all the contradictions in Amiel, this positive indication alone is left in our hands; when we have followed him along all the paths by which he sought peace in vain, this road alone remains open through 'the high uno'erleaped mountains of necessity'. It was Amiel's bitter fate that he could not enter upon it. [20]

In Amiel, as in Dostoevsky, Murry 'found himself' – or part of himself. But he could never have done so, had he not been wholly absorbed in finding Amiel.

Those early months at Montana were not only the most fruitful, but the most peaceful, that he and Katherine had passed together since Bandol. The chalet was well heated and comfortable, their daily routine unvarying. From breakfast till lunch, and from tea till supper, they worked. In the afternoons he went skiing or skating, or, if she was feeling strong enough to accompany him, collecting wild flowers and mushrooms. At night they read to each other – poems, novels, plays. Katherine 'came nearer to following a regime than ever before or after';[21] and, rightly or wrongly, Murry believed that if only they had stayed, her life might have been prolonged by years.

Why, then, did they not stay? According to him, 'the very quality of our happiness at the Chalet des Sapins set in motion in Katherine the overwhelming desire to be "well", in order that we should be completer friends, companions and lovers than we were'.[11] And that, no doubt, was a large part of the truth. Although too many specialists had driven the facts home for him to cherish any such illusion, she could not altogether banish the hope of a 'miracle'. Already by the end of the year, her inveterate restiveness was reviving; and then it needed only a letter from Koteliansky, with news of yet another novel treatment for tuberculosis, to bring it to a head. Nothing could restrain her from investigating this forthwith. On January 30, 1922, she and Ida Baker set out for Paris to consult Dr Manoukhin – and the spell was broken.

Her restiveness, however, was not due to this cause alone. The mere fact that neither spoke openly of what both knew only too well – that their peace was stolen from time – seems to have persuaded her that their relation was not yet 'pure', and that if a remedy could be found for this falsity, bound up as it was with her illness, her illness might be remedied too. The very quality of their unhappiness, in other words, set in motion an overwhelming desire to separate, in order that she should be 'well'. This was the persuasion that attracted her to *Cosmic Anatomy*, the book sent to Murry at the instance of A. R. Orage, editor of *The New English Weekly*.

Murry, who disliked the occult teachings of the book, was sceptical; but his scepticism only reinforced her conviction. And so, unhappily, did his reaction to the Manoukhin experiment. For, cursing Koteliansky in his heart, and clinging to the chalet as 'a symbol of salvation and sanity',[22] he delayed departure, even after Katherine had resolved to stay on in Paris and begin the new treatment at once – characteristically leaving it to her to decide whether he should join her or finish his novel. Naturally, she told him to finish it – but with such 'an obvious "oh!" ' [23] that he was filled with shame and set off for Paris there and then. Only that had been wanting to prove to her that their 'new love' was no different from the old after all, and that nothing short of some drastic step on her part would ever put it right. 'God! how terrible are one's failures in *love*,' he wrote long afterwards, recalling the episode: 'They haunt the secretest places of one's soul for years and years – for *ever*. Even though they are, in a sense, tiny and almost trivial, they are enormous and *absolute*. And what good would it do to "open them to God"? God himself cannot pardon them.' [24]

The effect was not immediately apparent. The four months from February 4 which they spent together at the Victoria Palace Hotel, Rue Blaise Desgoffe, were comparatively peaceful too. They mixed with the Russian colony, which included Dmitri Merezhkovsky and Ivan Bunin; and it was then that Murry made the acquaintance of most of the leading French men of letters, to whom he was already well known as the 'presenter' of Proust and Gide to the English public – Valéry and Charles Du Bos, for example, who became his friends and lifelong admirers. But if his and Katherine's veneration for the Russians was dashed by their patronizing attitude towards Tchehov ('*ah, oui, il était charmant*' [25] was Bunin's sole reminiscence of the hero), it was soon more materially shaken by the failure of the Manoukhin cure. The spring found her no better than she had been at Montana; the predicted miracle had come to nothing; and by June 4, when they retraced their steps forlornly to Switzerland, her thoughts were already turning elsewhere.

All the physical treatments had failed: there remained only the psychological – and that, for her, meant the occult. That July she took leave of Murry, descending to Sierre, while he remained at Randogne. In August she set out for England – ostensibly to consult Dr Sorapure, actually to contact Orage and the circle surrounding Ouspensky. As usual, he accompanied her: but they had reached the parting of the ways. 'It was at this moment that, unknown to me, she bade me farewell, and wrote me the letter to be given to me after her death.' [26]

'It was a sad business after so long a pilgrimage together.' [27] Nine years had gone by that summer since their 'honeymoon' trip to Paris.

Carco, who chanced on them now as they were passing through the city, was shocked by the change in both. Katherine could no longer walk – only drive in a car beside the river. '*Jack me parut vieilli: il n'avait plus cet air d'extrême jeunesse ni cette fraicheur qui séduisait si rapidement chez lui. Ses traits s'étaient creusés. Son menton, accentué. Ses yeux, jadis très clairs, semblaient avoir perdu leur transparence.*' [28] It is not surprising.

Katherine had resumed her old initiative, on the spiritual plane. Confident in her new-found faith, she discussed Murry's scepticism with Koteliansky more in sorrow than in anger. 'You know', she wrote that month, 'I am deeply sorry for Murry':

> He is like a man under a curse. That is not melodrama. That is why I am determined to remain his friend and to make him free of his own will. Special cases need special methods. There is no general treatment for all. But, dear precious friend, I must not speak against him to you. Yet we both know too much for that to be necessary ... Now that I am no longer in a false position with Murry. Now that I am, in the true sense of the word 'free' I look at him differently. His situation is very serious. But who am I to say anyone is beyond hope – to withdraw my heart if there is even the smallest chance of keeping them.[29]

It was true enough: Murry *was* like a man under a curse. Katherine was not more distressed by his 'unreality' than he was himself. He, no less than she, was travailed by the thought of 'rebirth' – 'haunted', like the hero of *The Things We Are*, 'by bits of the New Testament'.[30] Only, the teachings of Ouspensky and Gurdjieff, which had come to mean everything to her, not merely meant nothing to him, but were positively repugnant. Although, in Hampstead, they occupied adjoining houses – she Dorothy Brett's, he Boris Anrep's, in Pond Street – there was little or no communication between them:

> Had I been older and wiser, maybe I should have been more tolerant, understanding the import of Blake's profound saying: 'Everything possible to be believed is an image of truth.' But at that time I felt that the only thing that remained to me – my own integrity – was at stake. It was not that I felt superior to Orage, or J. D. Beresford, or James Young, or Maurice Nicoll, who were among Ouspensky's disciples: still less did I feel superior to Katherine. But I was very certain that it would be treachery to myself to follow them. I could scarcely bear to discuss the doctrines of Ouspensky with Katherine. The gulf between us was painful to us

both; and living under the same roof became a kind of torture. I could not bear it. In a few days I went into the country to live with Vivian Locke-Ellis at Selsfield.[26]

Locke-Ellis, the poet, had been, and was to remain, a generous friend. His ingeniously modernized seventeenth-century mansion near East Grinstead had served Murry as a model for the home he had been looking for in Sussex two years before. Now it became his own, so far as he had one. Katherine came down once or twice; he paid week-end visits to Hampstead. Otherwise they hardly saw each other again before her departure for Paris at the end of September.

This year, 1922, was as barren a period of his life as 1921 had been fruitful. Apart from his weekly reviews in *The Nation and Athenaeum* and the pot-boilers collected in *Pencillings* (oddly enough, one of the lightest as well as the slightest of his books), its only fruits were a lecture on 'The Nature of Poetry' and an essay on 'Russian Literature' – both distraught with those intimations of a harmony which seemed for ever beyond his reach. There were, he says, still 'moments when, in spite of all, it seemed clear to me that life, with all its shipwreck of human hopes – its "pain, misery, heartbreak and oppression", as Keats put it – was incomparably beautiful . . . But I felt it a kind of hypocrisy, a kind of desperate play-acting, to try to write out of that vision when I had sunk back to the condition of a wounded and suffering animal.' [31] Only in Shakespeare and Tchehov could he find any assurance that this was not a deception – that the nature of things was not, as reason declared that it must be, finally and implacably opposed to the nature of love.

The essay on 'Russian Literature' concludes with a passage on Tchehov:

'Good-bye, my treasure!' There is the magic that makes a paradise of a desert of human hopes. We look again, we listen: yes, the harmony is there. And if the harmony is where Tchehov found it, then it is everywhere. He is, in the great company of men of genius, the latest-born. He comes, the youngest son, and there is no inheritance for him. The great estate of human life has been divided: so he goes off alone into the waste and desolate places, the dreary commonplace wildernesses of the spirit, which are as like the wildernesses of the heroic writers, as the waste ground in a modern city is like the majestic jungles of the Amazon. Tchehov goes there, without hope, without belief; it is the last of all forlorn quests: and he brings back the Grail in his hands.[32]

It was after he had just written these words, Murry always remembered, that, glancing at the *Literary Supplement*, he caught sight of the announcement of a new poem by Eliot, entitled *The Waste Land*. The coincidence so struck him that he wrote to Eliot, who came down to Selsfield, and, to his further surprise, informed him that there was a traditional, even technical, connexion between the Waste Land and the Grail – on which, indeed, his poem was based. 'I came nearer to Tom Eliot in that day than I had ever been before, or ever was afterwards.' [26]

Murry always attached a peculiar, sometimes superstitious, importance to omens: and this was not the only one. In his utter despair and gnawing sense of failure, now that Katherine had left him, he was ready to explore almost any path, however uncongenial, that promised a way out of 'this extreme condition of non-being',[33] this 'death in life'. He even overcame his prejudice against the occult so far as to join hands with Locke-Ellis and Sullivan in their tumbler-turning experiments. In fact, he was 'amazed and disturbed by the relevance and apparent profundity of many of the answers'; and one night, in order to test the oracle, it was arranged that he should sit apart from the two with their fingers on the glass and frame his questions in thought alone:

> Then I put the only question which truly concerned me. 'What shall I do to be saved?' I don't think I put the question in that articulate form. As I remember it, I simply asked 'What shall I do?' Then, rather slowly, but completely without hesitation, a strange answer was spelt out before my eyes . . . The answer was 'Christ's Coat'. I was at the same moment overwhelmed and bewildered . . . The meaning of the answer, or part of its meaning, was quickly clear to me. Christ's 'coat without seam' – the vesture which was not parted among the soldiers, but for which they cast lots – has a hallowed place in Christian tradition. The interpretation seemed at the time obvious to me: I must become whole. It told me, indeed, nothing that I did not know, in some sense, already: but it unlockedt he knowledge from its dumb cradle – and set it before my imagination with a vividness that was almost terrifying.[34]

He was so impressed on this occasion that he kept the paper with the answer in his pocket-book for twenty years. At the same time, he became immediately convinced that the whole phenomenon was 'exceedingly unhealthy (to put it mildly)',[35] and from that day forward refused to have anything further to do with it.

Instead, mainly under the influence of a friend whom he had met at

Garsington, and now came to know more intimately, he turned towards Yoga. Miller (as we shall call him) was a practising Yogi, who
had long ago discerned 'some considerable spiritual significance' [36] in
Poems: 1916–20. He was also – and this counted for more – a family
man, with an attractive wife and four small sons, who welcomed 'Mr
Miltony Murry' into their household. When, in November, Katherine
entered the Gurdjieff Institute at Fontainebleau, and Murry felt it impossible for himself to go on living in the relative luxury of Selsfield,
Miller found him a villa next to his own at Ditchling, in Sussex, and
there proceeded to initiate him.

After all, he and Katherine were not so remote from each other.
'You see, my love', she wrote that December, 'the question is always:
"*Who am I?*" and until that is answered I don't see how one can really
direct anything in oneself.' [37] 'Who am I?' – It was the very question
Murry had been asking for months. 'You have rather a horror of anything at all . . . Eastern, haven't you?' [38] she inquired again. By return
of post he was able to tell her that he was at that moment immersed in
Raja Yoga: 'So you see, darling, if you have your Salzmanns, whom I
should dearly love to know, I have my Millers, whom I would dearly
love *you* to know. And every letter of yours that I get now makes me
feel more than ever that we are marching along parallel paths – parallel
paths which converge, and that the day is not so terribly far distant
when we shall be ready for one another.' [39]

But even *Raja Yoga*, 'absorbing and very exciting' [40] as he had found
it at first, palled; even Miller could supply no answer to the only
question that truly concerned him. 'I sat still, I breathed rhythmically,
I tried to make my mind a blank, and once I distinctly saw shining
bright in the dark behind my closed eyelids, the *crux ansata*. I duly reported it, and was told that it was the symbol of eternal life. If I had
been told it was the symbol of eternal death, I should have been moved
just as much, or as little.' [27] This might be some men's path to the Self,
he was willing to admit: it was not his own – and once again the old
revulsion overcame him.

With that, he threw in his hand. There seemed to be nothing further
he could do – except 'dash his head against the wall'. Katherine had forbidden him to visit her before Easter: 'I cannot see you until the old
Wig has disappeared.' [41] Sullivan, whose wife had also left him, came
to share Wayside Cottage; and together they whiled away the time
playing chess, learning to drive, listening to records of Beethoven –

whose late quartets became, and remained, Murry's 'only music'.[42] It was Katherine who arrived first at the destination.

Suddenly, on New Year's Eve, she wrote again, inviting him to come out to her the following week. There was to be a great feast, a formal inauguration of the Institute, and she wanted him to be present; Mme Tchehov herself might be there . . . He arrived at Fontainebleau on January 9, 1923, to find 'a being transfigured by love, absolutely secure in love':

> She told me she had felt that her love for me had had to die. 'It was killing us both', she said. And it had died. 'I felt that I could not bear it, – tearing my heart away from yours. But I managed to do it.' I gathered somehow that it was part of the spiritual discipline of the place, as she conceived it, thus to sacrifice one's earthly affections. But I made no comment. I was happy to see her happy. 'But now I have come through, at last', she said. 'My love for you has all come back to me, renewed and purified – and greater than ever. That was why I wanted you to come.' [26]

All that afternoon, as she showed him around the Institute, Katherine was radiant. She presented him to some of her friends – Orage, whom he had not seen for years, Salzmann, Dr James Young the psychiatrist, whom he met for the first time now, Adele Kafian. 'There was a blend of simplicity and seriousness in most of the people I met there, and in the company as a whole, which impressed me deeply.' [43] It was his first glimpse of a real community, such as he and Lawrence had so often dreamed of. But she would be leaving it soon, Katherine said – it had given her all that she needed. She would like him to take a cottage in England, where she could write and he cultivate the land. He desired nothing better – it was what he had been urging for years.

Then, at ten o'clock, after listening to some music on the gramophone, they started upstairs. 'She forgot every caution', Adele Kafian says, and – whether from 'excess of joy' [44] or in order to show how much better she was – 'ran up quickly, as any healthy person might do, without touching the banisters'.[45] Immediately, a spasm of coughing seized her, succeeded, as she reached her room, by a violent haemorrhage. She collapsed on her bed. ' "I believe. . . I am going. . . to die", she whispered.' [46] Murry ran for a doctor. Young and two others were at hand. 'Wisely, I suppose, they thrust me out of the room, though her eyes were imploring me.' [47] Within half an hour, she was dead.

She had left him the letter written at Sierre, dated August 7, 1922:

Dearest Bogey,

I have been on the point of writing this letter for days. My heart has been behaving in such a curious fashion that I can't imagine it means nothing. So, as I should hate to leave you unprepared, I'll just try and jot down what comes into my mind. All my manuscripts I leave entirely to you to do what you like with. Go through them one day, dear love, and destroy all you do not use. Please destroy all letters you do not wish to keep and all papers. You know my love of tidiness. Have a clean sweep, Bogey, and leave all fair – will you?

Books are yours, of course, and so are my personal possessions. L. M. had better distribute my clothes. Give your Mother my fur coat, will you? Chaddie and Jeanne must choose what they want, and I suppose Vera would like something. My small pearl ring – the 'daisy' one – I should like to wear. The other – give to Richard's love when you know her – if you approve of the idea.

I seem, after all, to have nothing to leave and nobody to leave things to. De la Mare I should like to remember, and Richard. But you will give a book or some small thing to whoever wishes . . . Monies, of course, are all yours. In fact, my dearest dear, I leave everything to you – to the secret you whose lips I kissed this morning. In spite of everything – how happy we have been! I feel no other lovers have walked the earth together more joyfully – in spite of all.

Farewell – my precious love,

I am for ever and ever

Your

WIG.

PART II

1923–1931

———◦—◦✦◦—◦———

VIII

REBIRTH

KATHERINE'S DEATH SPELT FOR Murry the end of an old life and the beginning of a new. The old life had lasted thirty-three years: to the onlooker, years of steady advance in the world, to the inlooker (and he was nothing if not that) of steady estrangement. He had won a small but recognized place for himself in English letters; he was the most influential literary critic of the day; and 'it would be the greatest mistake in the world', William Rothenstein was writing at this moment, in his *Contemporary Portraits*, 'to regard Mr Murry's spirit as wholly critical. One cannot tell what he will write next. The theatre is as yet unattempted.* Might he become an English Tchehov?' It was only in his own estimate that he figured first and foremost as the husband of Katherine Mansfield and the friend (or enemy) of D. H. Lawrence.

The new life would also last thirty-three years: to the onlooker, years of steady estrangement, to the inlooker of steady advance. Little by little he would lose all influence with his contemporaries, and be remembered by his juniors, if remembered at all, merely as a foil to his friends. That it was during these years that his most original work was accomplished, that he became, what he had not been before, a thinker and teacher in his own right, would be admitted only by the few.

This new life, however, did not follow directly upon the old. Katherine's death left him wandering 'between two worlds' indeed – 'one dead, the other powerless to be born'. In retrospect, the ensuing four or five weeks seemed to him always like a phantasma or a hideous dream:

> The thing had happened. I was alone. The shock was so great that I lived for some weeks in a kind of numbness. Unreal myself, I moved in

---

*Actually, *Cinnamon and Angelica* was intended for the theatre.

an unreal world, as it were a painted scenery. Katherine's funeral, the negociations with the Pompes Funèbres, supercilious at my blind insistence on a simple coffin, the fantastic *éloge* in the cold Protestant *temple*, for which the Pastor had asked me for notes, the cortège to the municipal cemetery – it was the beginning of a chilly phantasmagoria, which, as far as I knew, might go on and on for ever.[1]

Friends were kind; letters of condolence poured in from high and low: but his alienation was now complete. The inward division which had been debilitating him for years, between the craving of his heart for the security of love, and the knowledge of his mind that love was doomed, had reached an extremity. 'What I chiefly remember about this strange period of my life is that I had no coherent self at all. No action of mine was veritably my own. Everything I did, or might do, was equally sensible or equally absurd.'[1] It is not to be wondered at that most of his actions were absurd, and some grotesque.

From this *ne plus ultra* of isolation, he fled: first of all, to his friends at Ditchling. There, he says, Mrs Miller hugged him to her bosom 'in a simple womanly way', and for a moment he did taste relief:

> But she took it in a different sense. I will not say a wrong one, because she may have known what I needed better than I. But when, one day, her husband, with the simple seriousness that made him attractive to me, explained to me that she was a rare woman because she had had four little boys, and that he was willing for her to leave him and come to me, I felt that I was being carried out of my depth. When, shortly after, his wife completed my bewilderment by telling me, like a Sybil, that 'I must come to her as myself, not as the bereaved husband of Katherine Mansfield', I fled to London.[1]

Murry still had his room in Pond Street: and there, had he been in his right mind, he might have stayed quiet and alone. But loneliness was the last thing he wanted; loneliness was exactly what terrified him; and once again he reacted hysterically – first entreating 'a faithful woman friend' (with whom he had flirted mildly some four years before) to marry him, 'if he was really cornered';[1] then, when she had given proof of her willingness, flying to the arms of a prostitute, 'and that was misery'.[2] It was only after this, when the very ignominy of his position became unbearable, that he gave up trying to escape:

> Gradually, I became convinced that the only thing to do was to go away and be really alone: simply because it was unworthy and ignominious

to be with people to whom I must pretend a relation which I did not feel. I should at least regain some dignity in my own eyes. Once so much was decided, things happened quickly. I was offered an isolated furnished cottage in Ashdown Forest, which I gratefully accepted. I quickly made my preparations, and set off on a motor-bicycle I had lately learned to ride . . . As the dusk came on, I began to be troubled. I was going to be, I was determined to be, really alone.

I found myself vaguely terrified of what might happen to me; and the fear grew the nearer I approached my destination. I was required to do or to endure something now from which I could not escape. The plunge into the unknown which had haunted me for weeks, and from which in one form I had withdrawn, because the form was alien to me, now confronted me in a form which I knew to be my own, and I must take it. It was as though I were being compelled to explore a dark cave alone, and I was afraid. But there was no possibility of retreat. To run away from this would be a final ignominy, from which I should not recover.

That was my feeling, and it was compulsive. But I had not the faintest notion of what I should, or could do: and now the memory of what I actually did is faint to me. I am positive of two things: I had no plans, and I had no hesitations. Something that had to happen was going to happen.[1]

Of what did happen, either on the night of his arrival at The Old Farm, Twyford, or shortly afterwards – he himself could not remember which – Murry published an account some four months later, which can only be reproduced as it stands:

Then in the dark, in the dead, still house, I sat at the table facing the fire. I sat there motionless for hours, while I tried to face the truth that I was alone. As I had wanted to turn back, so now I longed to turn away. There was in me something that simply would not look, and, again and again, as it turned its eyes away, I took its head in my two hands and held its face towards what I had to see. Slowly and with an effort I made myself conscious that I was physically alone. Prompted by some instinct, I tried to force this consciousness into every part of my body. Slowly I succeeded. At last I had the sensation that I *was* in my hands and feet, that where they ended I also ended, as at a frontier of my being, and beyond that frontier stretched out the vast immensities, of space, of the universe, of the illimitable, something that was other than I. Where I ended, it began – other, strange, terrible, menacing. It did not know me, would never acknowledge me, denied me utterly. Yet out upon this, from the fragile rampart of my own body, I found the courage to peer, to glance, at last to gaze steadily. And I became aware of myself as a little island against whose slender shores a cold, dark, boundless ocean lapped devouring. Somehow, in that moment, I knew I had reached a pinnacle of personal being. I was I, as I had never been before – and never should be again . . .

What happened then? If I could tell you that I should tell you a secret indeed. But a moment came when the darkness of that ocean changed to light, the cold to warmth; when it swept in one great wave over the shores and frontiers of my self; when it bathed me and I was renewed; when the room was filled with a presence, and I knew I was not alone – that I never could be alone any more, that the universe beyond held no menace, for I was part of it, that in some way for which I had sought in vain so many years, I *belonged*, and because I belonged, I was no longer I, but something different, which could never be afraid in the old ways, or cowardly with the old cowardice. And the love I had lost was still mine, but now more durable, being knit into the very substance of the universe I had feared. And the friends whose words had been so meaningless were bound to me, and I to them, for ever. And if it should prove that I had work to do, or a part to play, I should no longer draw back at the last.[3]

This, Murry always insisted, was 'the one entirely revolutionary happening'[4] of his life. It was, in fact, the birth of that new life, of which the remainder of this book is an outline.

Essential to the mystical experience is the suspension, or obliteration, of the subject-object distinction: in other words, an immediate assurance of the consubstantiality of knower and known. Since normal cognition presupposes this distinction, and language reflects normal cognition, the experience is, as every mystic has testified, ineffable: 'what can be shown cannot be said'. And Murry, who had endorsed that sentence of Wittgenstein's some six months before, made no further attempts to express it. As often as he was called upon to do so he referred his readers to the passage above.

The implications of such an assurance, on the other hand, are innumerable: and these he did revert to, stressing now one and now another. Here we need indicate only two.

In the first place, it stands to reason that the *consciousness* of consubstantiality belongs (or is felt to belong) neither to knower nor to known. It veritably is a new kind of consciousness – 'timeless', because the perception of time is a function of normal cognition; 'detached', because events exist for it in their own right, not as means to an end. The activities of the subject (including normal cognition), the activities of the object (including the most inimical), are envisaged alike without moral or aesthetic bias. Murry himself adds, elsewhere:

> For a brief and timeless period of beatitude life seemed to pour into me from every created thing. Everything about me shone in the incredible radiance of its own simple reality. And love went out from me to all things: a love not my own, a love that it was impossible to imagine could ever be mine, a love which enveloped me and all creation, a love which was our common life, and upheld us all, like children, to the lips of God.[5]

When, probably the following year, he read in Meister Eckhart's *Sermons*, 'The re-born soul is as the eye, which having gazed into the sun, thenceforward sees the sun in everything,' he experienced 'a shock of delighted recognition'.[6] This was the Divine Vision itself.

In the second place, since this seemingly miraculous translation from an extremity of isolation to a corresponding extremity of communion cannot but seem, to the man in whom it takes place, itself the recompense and justification for all that he has hitherto endured – all the striving and despair that were its preconditions – it confers a new unity upon him. In the contemplation of a universe which, instead of being indifferent or hostile, seems mysteriously to have endorsed his aspirations, heart and mind are at one: 'All things work together for good.' It was this realization – that the universe was, after all, 'harmonious', a 'Vale of Soul-making' – that Murry summed up by his watchword, 'Faith in Life'.

Now at last he *'belonged'* – to the universe, if not to society: and, knowing that he belonged, could submit patiently to further experience, instead of running away from it. For the first time since childhood he was whole: and, knowing that he was whole, was wholly possessed by his conviction. In fact, in the relief of being rid once and for all of his morbid, debilitating introspection, the joy of being simply obedient to the promptings of his new-found unity, he felt, for a few months at least, as though not only past events but present were working together for good. Like Carlyle, at a similar climacteric, he could scarcely resist belief in a 'special Providence'. 'I veritably believed that some sort of endorsement by the Universe was guaranteed to all my doings, and that I could do no wrong.'[7]

Naturally, he did a good deal: mystics generally do in the first flush of their illumination. Yet the belief was intelligible enough: that it is we who are endowed with the capacity for turning whatever befalls to account is never an easy thought to entertain. And in his case, a succession of coincidences rendered it practically inescapable. It was at this juncture, most decisively, that he received Lawrence's *Fantasia of the Unconscious*.

He had not seen Lawrence since 1918; nor had they corresponded until the previous winter, when, mollified by a friendly postcard to Katherine and by the tone of *Aaron's Rod*, Murry had sent him a letter 'suggesting, I suppose, that our relation should be renewed'.[8] In the loneliness of Wayside Cottage he had been in a mood for renewing relations (Koteliansky, too, had been forgiven); and Lawrence, who had never really believed in Katherine's illness any more than he did in his own, was shocked by her death. 'I wish it needn't all have been as it has been: I do wish it,' [9] he wrote. The *Fantasia*, following hard on these words, arrived at the psychological moment. Murry read it on March 10. Next day, 'This book contains all my deep beliefs – all,' [10] he was exclaiming.

Here was the man who, of all his contemporaries, meant most to him, proclaiming, on the one hand that 'spiritual love', when it becomes the be-all and end-all of man's life, ends in the disaster of pthisis; on the other, that the rational consciousness must be subordinated to the whole being, and that 'we have to break away, back to the great unison of manhood in some passionate *purpose*'. '*De te fabula narratur.*' [11] What wonder if, in his 'new half-convalescent, half-confident condition', Murry found this 'completely convincing'?[12] If *this* was what Lawrence stood for, then he, Murry, was his man. Away with all reservations! In the next number of *The Nation and Athenaeum*, he wrote the book up in terms of ecstatic enthusiasm.

More vividly than anything else, this review reveals his state of mind. Its opening sentence strikes the keynote: 'Things in this life are not wholly fortuitous.' It cannot have been merely by chance, he affirms, that this book should have dropped into his hands just when he was emerging from Jung's *Psychological Types*: 'Into the dry and deadly, the positively tindery atmosphere left by Jung, came the bright spark of Lawrence. There was an exhilarating explosion.' The echoes of the explosion are audible. Not only does he present the *Fantasia* as the answer to the one real question, 'What must I do to be saved?' – pronouncing all writing unconcerned with this 'irrelevant'; but, suiting the action to the word, he heads his own article 'Relevancy', and, for the first time, discards all pretence of impersonality. It is written in a style as informal and discursive as Lawrence's own. On the other hand, perhaps 'we journalists have learned that we must be irrelevant to make our living', he concludes significantly: 'I dare say we must. We shall see.' [13]

'We shall see.' Very obviously, Murry himself would not be content with irrelevancy much longer. He, too, now had an answer to the one real question – thoughts 'different from Lawrence's thoughts, and yet related to them' [13] – clamouring for utterance. The prospect of endlessly turning out reviews of books that meant nothing whatever to him was not to be borne. In fact, the *Fantasia* had clinched his determination to have done with it for good and all. Within a week of writing this article, he had abruptly resigned all his regular literary work. He would launch an independent journal – a mouthpiece for Lawrence and himself.

It was a reckless step. Only a year before, warning a young correspondent, H. P. Collins, against the hazards of a journalistic career, 'I doubt whether there are half-a-dozen men who make a tolerable living out of reputable criticism,' he had written: 'Luckily, I happen to be one of them. But the more I reflect, the more it seems to me a matter of luck; and I have the suspicion that I exist only on sufferance.' [14] The fate of *The Athenaeum* was still fresh in his mind. He was under no illusion as to the risk. It meant reducing his income at a stroke from approximately £800 a year to £300.

Yet his enthusiasm carried all before it. It must have been at this moment that Tomlinson came to visit him in Sussex, and, on departing, confessed that he had been in two minds about coming, but was glad now, ' "For", said he, "I always wondered whether you had a soul at all: now I know you have." ' [15] Similarly, Koteliansky arrived in Pond Street one day 'in a sort of tender anguish' to tell Murry that he no longer doubted him: 'I see him now with a piece of string in his hands, knotting and unknotting it, as he told me of his new-born faith.' [16] They would start a magazine 'as big as a telephone-book',[17] he averred. Sullivan was equally keen; so was Locke-Ellis, who put up £400 for the venture. Lawrence himself, from New Mexico, gave it his blessing.

For a time there was talk of taking over *The New English Weekly*; and during the second week of April Murry went over to consult Orage, who was still at the Gurdjieff Institute. He seemed positively eager to part with it. In the end, however, a brand-new monthly was decided on, for which Sullivan proposed the title – *The Adelphi*. There was already a *Strand*, a *Pall-Mall*, a *Windsor*, he pointed out: and what could be more fitting, seeing that he and Murry had worked together so long at Watergate House and 10 Adelphi Terrace? It was only several years afterwards that Murry, recalling that 'Adelphi' meant 'brothers', applied the name retrospectively to the little group presiding over its birth – by which time they were brothers no longer.

So, *The Adelphi* it was: and for the next six weeks he was kept hectically busy again preparing an opening number. British Periodicals, founded to handle *The Athenaeum*, took over the publishing; an office was opened, appropriately, at No. 18 York Buildings, Adelphi; Koteliansky became business manager. Of Locke-Ellis's £400, £250 went into preliminary advertising.

In his own eyes, Murry was merely *locum tenens* till Lawrence should come back to England. Yet the convergence of their conclusions, and their apparent endorsement by his friends, had persuaded him, not merely that 'a single process manifests itself with such a difference in two human beings',[13] but that it might manifest itself in many. His contributors, at all events, however divergent their views, would be 'knit together by a common conviction'[18] – that the magazine should be 'a thoroughfare for all thoughts, not a select party'. In particular, he intended that it should present two sorts of 'truth': truth concerning the external world, as revealed to the scientific consciousness, and truth concerning the internal, as revealed to the artistic. If these came into collision, so much the better: then it would set working in its readers 'a process of inward struggle which would be, if they did not flinch from it, a beginning of new life'.[19] His own function, as editor, would be to point the way towards a reconciliation.

At the same time, the prospectus he drew up that spring shows that other, less mystical motives played a part – for it is at least as eloquent of Murry's revulsion from Bloomsbury as of any more positive belief. As a rarity now and a curiosity, it deserves quotation.

'The ADELPHI', it begins, 'aims at filling a place apart among contemporary magazines':

> Of magazines of fiction, of political and literary reviews, there are already enough and to spare. What is needed, and what THE ADELPHI is designed to supply, is a magazine in which subjects of vital interest to modern readers are treated with honesty and conviction. The standard by which the contents of THE ADELPHI will be decided is 'significance for life'.

Of LITERATURE, it goes on:

> We are bored to death by modern dilettantism. We are sick of 'Art'. Inspired by no living purpose, it has brought us nowhere. If modern literature is to be anything better than a pastime for railway journeys or a parlour game for effete intellectuals, it must be built upon some active conviction. Those who have something to say will know how to say it. Therefore, we hope that although the contents of THE ADELPHI may not be 'literary', they will be literature.

Of PHILOSOPHY:

> We believe that there is no such thing. There is science, and there is literature. What has lasted under the name of philosophy is either one or the other. But true literature and true science are always in a sense philosophical: they are occupied with reality. In this sense THE ADELPHI also will be philosophical.

Finally:

> THE ADELPHI will not be a high-brow magazine. It aims at being comprehensible and interesting to as many people as possible. But it will not be written down to suit the needs of an imaginary audience of the semi-educated and half-witted. We believe that a magazine to be really interesting to its readers must first be interesting to those who write it.

THE ADELPHI, in short, is to be everything that *The Athenaeum* was not – even to the total exclusion of reviews.

This is an oddly provocative document – 'brash' would not be too hard a word; and Shaw's retort, scrawled across the foot of his copy, was not altogether unmerited:

> Same old song! 'I have known four and twenty leaders of revolt.' You forgot to mention that it will be printed on paper in black ink, and will be dependent either on advertisements or charity. However, there is some novelty in the phrase 'filling a place apart'. It used to be 'supply a want'. But as it will do neither, it doesn't matter. Why not tell the truth? 'An energetic young journalist has deluded a capitalist into parting with sufficient cash to set him up as editor of a new mag. for a few months. So here goes!' [20]

Shaw's reaction, however, was exceptional. It 'sounds as if it were going to be the right sort of thing – the wanted thing',[21] Galsworthy pronounced; and that was the sentiment of most of the writers Murry approached. He had hit on the bright idea of a 'Contributors' Club', to consist of 'short paragraphs of 3–500 words, in which people can vent their anger and enthusiasm about any old thing';[22] and among the first to avail themselves of this were Galsworthy himself, Bennett, Wells and Swinnerton. He had secured Lawrence's permission to serialize the *Fantasia*, as yet unpublished in England; and in the opening number the 'Adelphi' themselves were well represented – Tomlinson, Sullivan, Koteliansky (translating Tchehov). All together, they made an imposing panel. There was good reason to anticipate a sale of up to 4,000.

It was only after the magazine had gone to press at the end of May, that Murry's confidence began to wane. The preparations had left no time for second thoughts. Now they came crowding in. He began to reflect on the financial sacrifice he had made – for he was to receive no salary as editor; to reflect, what was worse, on the awkwardness of a faith which, when it came to the point, was impossible to put into words. His introductory editorial had turned out vague in the extreme, and uncomfortably personal. Would he simply be dismissed as a crank?

His dilemma is plain to see. He was persuaded that the universe was 'harmonious', and that the knowledge of this conferred a new unity and spontaneity. He believed that the great Romantics, like Keats and Tchehov, Shakespeare and Beethoven, had arrived at a similar knowledge, revealing the harmony and communicating the unity through their works. Had he been a born artist, he would have done as they did. Being what he was, he could only affirm that these things were so – and even this he could only do by referring to personal experience.

He could not reveal the harmony. He could only say, Do as I did – neither deny in the name, nor affirm in the face, of reason the intuition that responds to those works – and sooner or later you will apprehend it for yourself:

Shall I say then, Read *Antony and Cleopatra* till the bugle-call of that unearthly challenge to human loyalty echoes in the remotest chamber of the soul? Or, Listen to the last piano sonatas of Beethoven, till you feel that in the high B of op. 109 all that human desire can imagine of the crystalline perfection of the ideal is cracked and shattered, *must* be cracked and shattered, with a faint, far-away sound of breaking that stabs the very quick of being; till you know that Beethoven faced this disaster, pressed its inevitability home against his heart, and saw what lay beyond and triumphed and was free? Or shall I say, Read Tchehov's *The Cherry Orchard*. Read and listen, till you know what secret harmony and high design lies within all human discomfiture, to be discovered only by those who feel, and feeling, do not turn their faces away?

These men, and other men like these, knew the secret of life. They fought for it and conquered. Listen to them. Learn to listen to them. Learn to wait for the silence which descends when the importunate mind grows weary of asking its unanswerable questions, and to discern what echoes are awakened in that stillness by the notes which these men plucked out of their souls. Learn to live by that music, earthly and divine, or even learn only to desire to live by it, and you also will triumph and be free.[23]

He could not communicate the unity. He could only say, This is what it feels like to live, neither from the head nor the heart, but from that which comprehends both:

> It is not easy to explain – this new security. 'If he could tell me in three words', writes someone, 'what he is confident *about*.' He is not confident about anything: simply he is confident. About himself? 'Well, well, this word myself has many meanings.' Confident about himself, if the self has all its old personal meaning burned away: if it is no longer something which he possesses, but which possesses him. Confident because he has found a master whom he must obey, who says unto him 'Do this and he doeth it'. Confident because he has acknowledged a destiny of which the end and process are unknown; confident because they are unknown: because everything matters and nothing matters, because he does not care and cares infinitely, because he loves men dearly and loves them not at all, because he is bound and free, waiting and not anxious, himself and not himself.[24]

This was the kind of writing to which Murry was compelled from the outset. He had tried, in his introductory editorial, to preserve a semblance of impersonality – tried again and again – only to find it impossible, and finally throw discretion to the winds. No wonder, by the beginning of June, he was feeling 'damnably naked'.[25]

Then came the shock. ' "It's gone with a *bang*." The voice of the business manager . . . seemed to explode over the telephone.' [26] Within a week *The Adelphi* had sold out; within a fortnight it had had to be reprinted, not once but three times over. More than 15,000 copies had been supplied – and still the demand went on. No such success had attended a new magazine within living memory. To Murry, in his exalted frame of mind, it could only seem like the ratification of his faith.

IX

JOURNALIST AT SEA

———◆◇◆◇◆———

Six months before his death, musing on the past, Murry wrote:

> I have the feeling that I have been completely outside the main stream
> of literature: that I don't 'belong' and indeed never have belonged.
> My concern has always been that of a moralist, and I have never been
> sufficient of the artist to be diverted from it. And yet the stubborn feeling
> persists that my 'concern' was shared in the old days by Lawrence and
> by Katherine: that I was, in some sense, their critical counterpart, and
> that the *kind* of seriousness we had has been lost. That distinguished us,
> absolutely, from the Bloomsburies. Eliot came nearer to it; but from him,
> too, there was an inevitable separation. None of us was, or ever could
> have become, capable of accepting dogmatic Christianity, as Eliot did.
> I am the sole remaining representative of our particular integrity, our
> particular concern. We were all socially outsiders, quite without the social
> and domestic tradition which the Bloomsburies, Aldous Huxley, and
> expatriate – *plus royaliste que le roi* – Eliot inherited. And, I think, experi-
> ence came more naked and direct to us than to the others. To us, there
> was a sense in which they were all 'phoneys' (in the nuance of *The Catcher
> in the Rye*). Love meant more to us: we needed it more.[1]

That is perfectly true: it 'places' Murry more exactly than any similar
attempt of his own or others. But it is the truth of a man no longer
engagé: able to scan the past with detachment. In the summer of 1923,
for all his revulsion against the Bloomsburies, he was still very far indeed from realizing how complete an outsider he was. If his friends'
enthusiasm had persuaded him that his 'concern' was held widely in
literary circles, the spectacular success of the first *Adelphi* went far towards convincing him that it was general. A great, a revolutionary
change of consciousness was imminent, inaugurating a society of
human brotherhood!

Such misjudgements are characteristic of the mystic. In the first flush

[110]

of his illumination he can scarcely bring himself to believe that what is so self-evident to himself can be less than evident to others. He has only to point it out, and they will exclaim in a chorus, '*But of course!*' Blake was not more misled by the coincidence of his vision with the French Revolution. 'Probably the greatest misfortune of my life', we find Murry writing to J. P. Hogan a few years afterwards, 'was that the Old Adelphi (quite unintentionally) made a popular appeal. It was a pure accident; and it misled me hopelessly into thinking that a great many people were interested in what I am interested in.' [2]

Of course it was not a *pure* accident. By 1923, the reality of the War and its aftermath had had time to seep in. It was a moment of disenchantment and hesitation, when the privileged few, the Bloomsburies and Huxleys, could take to the Ivory Tower or a studied cynicism, whereas the many, their belief in Progress undermined, were groping for something to take its place. The voice of one crying in the wilderness 'Faith in Life' could not fail to awake an answering chord, least of all when the faith in question was proclaimed as the answer to the War.

It is noticeable that many of the earliest and staunchest subscribers to *The Adelphi* hailed from the North, where the Nonconformist or Catholic Conscience was still strong, although the Churches were losing their hold. Hogan himself, then a Manchester clerk, was in this respect typical; so was J. H. Watson, a Durham blastfurnaceman, who has written of Murry:

> All kinds of people were attracted to his work. A railway signalman once stopped me in the street and said 'I believe you know Middleton Murry. He is my arch-priest.' On another occasion, I was with an ardent reader of the Adelphi magazine, and the new number had come out that day. He scanned Murry's article, and dragged me out along the street of a small industrial town. Each acquaintance he met, he stopped, said in a voice like Jove Himself, 'A new asceticism is upon us', and to support his words he hauled the magazine out of his pocket and added, 'It has it here.' Such powerful yeast as Murry leavened many lumps. He was perhaps never read by the mass of the people but those who did read were stirred and influenced to a great degree. Many shared my enthusiasm. [3]

Hogan and Watson were untypical in that they stuck to the magazine to the last. But the great majority of its readers were always men and women of their degree. To this extent, at least, Murry did realize his purpose of by-passing the literary intelligentsia and striking the man in the street.

Misled he was, nevertheless – and not only by the popular appeal. Perhaps his very modesty was to blame. It never occurred to him that it was he who had enthused his friends – that the appearance of a common conviction was largely of his own creating; much less that his own capacity for reconciling divergent viewpoints was anything out of the ordinary. 'If the fool would persist in his folly, he would become wise,' said Blake. Ultimately, Murry did. But in the summer of 1923, he was living in a fool's paradise – and the disillusionment came swift and sharp.

Had he witnessed Lawrence's reception of his letters (described by Wytter Bynner in his *Journey with Genius*), it might have come even sooner. For, whether or not Lawrence had ever believed in 'the necessity of that absolute spiritual regeneration, that passing beyond the intellectual consciousness',[4] which Murry divined in the *Fantasia*, he certainly did not believe in it now, two years after writing the book. On the contrary, there in New Mexico he was abandoning himself to the full tide of his recurrent revulsion against everything 'spiritual', 'western', 'civilized'. He had not even made up his mind to return to England when the June *Adelphi* reached him – and that was not calculated to encourage him. 'Oh dear', he wrote to Koteliansky, 'I was badly disappointed. It seemed to me so weak, apologetic, knock-kneed, with really nothing to justify its existence. A sort of beggar's whine through it all. Mr Wells' parsnips floating in warm butter. Mr Joiner screamingly ridiculous. No really! Is this the best possible in England? . . . One's got to *hit*, nowadays, not apologize.'[5]

Lawrence's opinion of his fellow-contributors was matched by theirs of him. The mildest judgement was Bennett's, 'very wild'.[6] Galsworthy and Tomlinson remonstrated, Wells expostulated: 'I have read as much as I can stand of the clotted nonsense of *Fantasia of the Unconscious.*'[7] And as usual, it was Wells who spoke for the multitude. When, in the July number, Lawrence categorically pronounced Jesus a 'failure', the fifteen thousand dropped abruptly to seven – and Murry faced the common conviction that he was ruining a promising review.

It was not only his loyalty to Lawrence that gave offence. So did his cult of Katherine. Encouraged by her cousin, Elizabeth Russell, urging him to 'publish all you *can*, as quickly as you can',[8] and, still more, by the precedent of Monkton Milnes, he had begun issuing her posthumous papers month by month in the magazine. 'I am old-fashioned enough', he had written two years before, in a review of Tchehov's *Notebooks*, 'to believe that it is almost a crime to make public fragments of an author's manuscripts which he obviously did not mean to show the world'; yet even then he had made an exception of Keats, since 'The letters to Fanny added something essential to our knowledge of Keats; and because that which they added was essential, though they may have diminished the esteem in which he was held in the '70s and '80s, they have increased it since. No-one regrets the publication of them now.' [9] In his own mind, there was always an affinity between Keats and Katherine – both were greater than their actual achievement – and Katherine, he thought, like Keats, now belonged to the world, not to John Middleton Murry.*

Unfortunately, on any showing, he carried his policy too far. There was much too much Katherine in *The Adelphi*. The photograph pre-fixed to the first number was appropriate – this was in some sense a memorial number; the commemorative verses of his own on the anni-versary of her death were not – especially as they were eight-year-old verses, re-conditioned for the occasion. For over two years, Katherine featured in every issue; she became the presiding genius of the paper – till even the friendly Bennett was forced to remonstrate, whilst with the unfriendly it became an article of faith that Murry was 'exploiting his wife's reputation'. The charge was ridiculous, of course. Had he wished to make money out of Katherine's remains, he would not have published them in *The Adelphi*, the only person to profit by that being Koteliansky, the business manager; had he wished to bask in her re-flected glory, he would not have included passages that could, and would, be used to blacken his name. But a charge does not have to be sensible in order to stick – and this one did. It is probably still current in the coteries.

To complete his discomfiture, it was not long before there was added the charge of 'profitably exploiting a new vein of self-disclosure' [10] by his own contributions: for, though his 'sudden and unprecedented out-burst into personal confession' [10] was inescapable, and anything but welcome to himself, there were few who could appreciate that, and

* In her will, dated August 14, 1922, Katherine had instructed Murry to 'publish as little as possible and to tear up and burn as much as possible. He will under-stand that I desire to leave as few traces of my camping ground as possible.' Her admirers, at least, should be grateful to him for attaching more weight to her letter of August 7.

fewer still who, sharing his experience, could read his words with 'a shock of delighted recognition'; whereas many could detect the arrogance that really disfigured them. The labels 'exhibitionist' and 'egotist' likewise stuck.

'Arrogance' is perhaps the wrong word: 'sectarianism' might be a better, since he was honestly convinced that it was every man's duty to face an isolation akin to his own, as the precondition of 'rebirth'. But seldom has even an editor been so prone to impute moral cowardice to whole classes of mankind – to all churchmen, for instance, or all light novelists. Reading the collection entitled *To the Unknown God*, one can only too easily understand Canon Orchard's reproach of pharisaism, and Leonard Woolf's damaging comparison of Murry's style to Mr Pecksniff's. As he confessed some years afterwards, 'I was completely upset, *bouleversé*, by my mystical experience. I was like a newly converted revivalist preacher, and in my order, committed the same offences against "good taste" as they in theirs.' [11]

Thus, it was not many months before the illusion of a common conviction was dispelled. Although he might still feel that he 'belonged', it was to no existing society, least of all to literary society. Already by the end of the year, *The Adelphi* had lost so much of its support that he was in two minds about continuing it at all. The article, 'Heads or Tails?' clearly reflects his bewilderment.

The vicissitudes of *The Adelphi*, however, were by no means alone in giving him to wonder whether a mystical experience was more of a blessing than a curse. The same factors that bedevilled his public life – his loyalty to Lawrence, in particular, and his fixation on Katherine – were meanwhile making havoc of his private life. In fact, in the case of Murry, the distinction between 'public' and 'private' is impossible to maintain – as he found himself. It belongs to that very world of convention from which the experience had delivered, or discharged, him. Whatever he was now, he was as a whole:

In a simple and subtle way, it changed the pattern of my life from within. While, on the one hand, it made me passive and receptive to experience, whatever it was, it gave me a criterion of the experience I would seek. I must move forward with my whole being, when I did move. I must wait, before any decisive movement, until my whole being 'could no other'. [12]

Well and good. But Murry's whole being could never be satisfied until both the great needs of his life were met: until his sense of 'belonging' was completed by the sense of belonging to a woman. From first to last, the very touchstone of any religion or society he adhered to was the quality of the marriage it sustained. Not that he any longer needed to be loved in order to be assured of his own 'validity': as his reckless launching of *The Adelphi* goes to show, the experience had rid him, momentarily at least, of his feverish insecurity. At the same time, it had released in him a new capacity to love. In a diffused, impersonal form, this was the motivation of his public activities, however fantastic; in a more concentrated, personal form, it motivated his private ones also, however absurd.

'In feeling my way to some sort of adjustment to this new dimension of experience', he writes, 'I did some very foolish things. In groping about for clues, I entangled myself with women, not in the ordinary sense of that phrase, but as it were touching them with my feelers, almost blindly, in order to discover whether they were the person to whom I was destined to respond with the whole of my being.' [12] Briefly, within two months at most of Katherine's death, and while he was still living at The Old Farm, Twyford, he had got himself practically betrothed.

Significantly, it was to a woman who had written to him about Katherine – a woman a couple of years older than she, who, for some reason, had both frightened and fascinated her in the old days at Chancery Lane. 'There was a peculiar recklessness in her manner and in her tones which made me feel that she would recognize no barriers at all,' [13] Katherine had written then. But now Murry heard in Vere's letter 'the voice of a captive princess, whom I longed to set free';[14] and, mounting his Rosinante – his Levis two-stroke – set forth without further ado for the enchanted castle of Chobham. His own letter of March 6, 1923, shows what happened:

> But it's the other side of all this, my dear. Will it really be any fun for you to hide in a hole with me? I keep on saying to myself: 'Perhaps she'll get sick of it' and asking 'What right have I to impose my conditions?' And yet, I'll own it was because I suddenly had the feeling that you might care to live with me the absurd kind of life which is the only one possible for me, that I asked.

They had arranged to meet again within a fortnight.

During that fortnight the *Fantasia* arrived. Murry promptly forwarded it to Vere, adjuring her to read it at once:

By reading this book – which is a joy to read – you'll never be able to feel that I appeared under false colours. I've got utterly sick of being told I'm charming. I hate my own charm. I don't believe in it. But if it is there, I detest it. You see, my dear, I don't want you to marry me because I may appear charming: nor because we're both a bit tired and weary. Neither of us *really* is. But because we're both out to make something positive out of it. We're not too old to be *profoundly* happy: we are too old to make a stupid mistake. And I don't want to appear, like a Homeric hero, in an iridiscent smoke-screen. I prefer to appear as Lawrence's book – that is as near to the naked J. M. M. as you can get without six months of me. Of course I am J. M. M. and not D. H. L. But we're blood-brothers and we've bought the same wisdom with different coin.[15]

What he wanted was not love, as he had known it in the past – 'I've had enough love, for I feel that the kind of unearthly love I'm inclined to ends inevitably in disaster' [16] – but something more down-to-earth, 'just a sort of fondness and loyalty'.[17] Above all, he wanted children.

What Vere thought of all this, we can only guess. What is certain is that their next meeting turned out a painful disappointment. 'You were quite right. There was a queer change in my mood between the Saturday and the Sunday. I didn't (as I once would have) make any attempt to conceal it. But what it was, or what its cause, I don't know . . .' [16] The cause was simple enough: Vere was not Katherine. When it came to the point, Murry found, not merely that pity was no substitute for love, but that without love his 'whole being' refused to move forward. He faced an invincible physical repugnance, intensified, as it happened, by the woman's confession that she might not be able to have children:

Then came the trouble. I, who definitely didn't want love, found that something in me wouldn't move without it. Instead of going out as it were to meet you, I discovered I was simply withdrawing myself again: just as though what there is of me wouldn't manifest except at the call of this thing I definitely didn't want. And that's where I am, my dear – inclined to wait till something happens inside me, – definitely afraid of acting until something does happen.[17]

And that was that. Although they continued to meet for a while, and Vere did secretarial work for *The Adelphi* (until Murry dismissed her), the engagement was at an end. It was this episode, no doubt, that prompted the story of Burlap in Huxley's *Point Counter Point*. Vere, far from setting Ethel Cobbett an example, a few years later became Mrs J. W. N. Sullivan – and thirty years later still (distance lending enchantment, perhaps) referred to it as one of 'the delightful things' [18] in her life. But Murry's reputation would have been better, had his intentions been less distressingly honourable.

While all this was going on, he had moved from Twyford: first back to Selsfield House, then, at the beginning of June, to a cottage of his own at Boxgrove, Chichester. At the same time, *The Adelphi* demanding regular visits to London, he retained his *pied-à-terre* in Pond Street, next door to Dorothy Brett's – where the 'Adelphi' met each Thursday evening to discuss the policy of the paper. Indeed, that summer and winter, for the first time for years, and the last, he was enjoying a comparatively sociable life, even attending dancing classes with his brother, now a professional artist, and renewing some of the literary contacts he had let slip. De la Mare (whose daughters conducted the classes) invited him to Manorbier for a week; Galsworthy prevailed on him to join the P.E.N. Club; and he was again in close touch with Eliot.

Not that he and Eliot had much in common intellectually now. *The Waste Land* had horrified Murry by its 'degradation of physical love' – 'a spiritual enormity' [19] he called this – and *The Criterion*, founded the previous year, stood for a Classicism in literature and religion which he found increasingly alien. But that did not prevent a measure of cooperation between the two editors; and of the warmth of feeling that survived through all their controversies, one note is sufficient witness:

My dear Tom,

    I have been looking for news from you these last few days most anxiously. No news worries me. Will you send me a wire? Is there *anything* I can do that will help?

    Dear old boy, I don't know what to say to you. I never do. But in my way believe me I love you – I think of you and feel for you continually. And there is this queer feeling that you and Vivien and I are bound together somehow.

John.[20]

It was that September that Murry made a special journey to Freiburg in Baden, to consult a doctor on Vivien Eliot's behalf – a partial record of which is contained in his article 'On Tolstoi and Other Things'.

However, he did not travel alone, nor was Tolstoi the main theme of his meditations, for it was also during that month that Frieda Lawrence arrived in London – to his surprise (though not to anyone's reading Bynner's reminiscences) completely out of love with her husband. 'She had had enough of Lawrence in his Mexican "moods", and in fact

she had left him. She felt – rightly enough – no more loyalty to him.' [21]
She had come to visit her children (her son remembers Murry taking
them to a performance of Fred. Carno's Mumming Birds); and, as she
too was going on to Germany, they travelled together as far as Freiburg.

Then took place another incident which, in view of his earlier dislike
of Frieda, shows how *bouleversé* he had been:

> On the journey we declared our love to each other. She was sweet and
> lovely, altogether adorable, and she wanted us to stay together in Freiburg
> for a few days anyhow, and I wanted it terribly. The idea of our sleeping
> together, waking in each other's arms, seemed like heaven on earth. I
> was worn out with the long strain of Katherine's illness, and Frieda's
> love was the promise of renewal. And Lawrence had been horrible to her
> in Mexico – something really had snapped between them. So I felt free
> to take Frieda, or thought I did; but when it came to the point, I didn't.
> I felt that, though he had treated me badly, still he had been my greatest
> friend (after Gordon let me down), and, at the very moment when the
> decision lay wholly with me, I said to F. 'No, my darling, I mustn't let
> Lorenzo down – I can't'. It was, I think, the one and only great renun-
> ciation I have made. And, I think, I'm glad I did. But it was a very *real*
> renunciation. [22]

These words were written in 1955, when Frieda had assured Murry
that by acting as he did, and persuading her to go back to Lawrence
(who, after all, was seriously ill), he averted 'an ugly tragedy'. [22] He
was not always so glad. There were moments when he blamed himself
heartily for what seemed, in retrospect, a merely conventional loyalty.
Whether he did right or wrong, however, there were liable to be com-
plications when, a couple of months later, Lawrence himself arrived
in London.

This reunion was a disappointment from the start. 'He looked
positively ill when I met him at the station: his face had a greenish
pallor. Almost the first words he spoke were: "I can't bear it." ' [23]
According to Murry, it was London Lawrence could not bear. According to Mrs Carswell, who was also present, it was the 'chumminess' he
had already discerned between Murry and Frieda. Be that as it may, he
was certainly in no mood to stay, let alone collaborate on *The Adelphi*.
On the contrary, England was played out, finished, doomed, he
asseverated; and the best thing the magazine could do was to 'attack
everything, everything; and explode in one blaze of denunciation'. [23]
Murry did not try to argue. By this time, he was so discouraged that

he was actually tempted to agree. And when Lawrence went on to propose that they return to New Mexico together, and start 'the nucleus of a new community' there, he was more than tempted – he fell. 'After all, since the main purpose of the *Adelphi* had been to make a place for Lawrence and Lawrence now refused it, why not give up? Lawrence said he needed me badly. Why not do what he wanted?' [24] Eight years previously, when a similar project had been broached, he had been shrewd enough to guess that Florida (it was Florida then, not New Mexico) was 'a state of mind, not a place'.[25] For the moment, he seems to have forgotten that.

Happily, it was only for the moment. He had but to look at what was really involved to have second, and wiser, thoughts. For one thing, the Lawrence for whom *The Adelphi* had been founded and the Lawrence of 1923 were two different beings (supposing the former ever to have existed, outside Murry's imagination). Whereas loyalty to the one was implicit in his own faith, loyalty to the other negated it: and, no matter how strong his personal affection, when it came to the point Murry could not bring himself to abandon his faith – his new-found faith in the spiritual, the western, the civilized, in all that the magazine stood for. Moreover, supposing he did go, what would, what must, ensue? He and Frieda knew only too well. 'There might have come out of it a strange *ménage à trois*. As woman, Frieda could have carried us both. But one thing is absolutely clear to me. If I had gone with Lawrence and Frieda, Frieda would have become my woman.' [26] That would hardly have been a service to Lawrence.

Once again, therefore, his 'whole being' refused to move forward; and, once again, in his frantic attempts to escape an impossible commitment, he began to do 'crazy things, for which Lawrence jeered at me, and which hurt Frieda – the supreme imbecility of *Jimmy and the Miner's Wife*'.[27] The miner's wife was a poetess of Mansfield (was the name a coincidence?), in whose verses he heard another captive princess, to whom he paid a flying visit, and who, like Vere, turned out no Dulcinea. This episode, needless to say, was a gift to Lawrence, whose satirical version, *Jimmy and the Desperate Woman*, featured in *The Criterion* next year. But did Lawrence himself ever realize why his victim was behaving so crazily?

Truly, the situation was ironical. Here was Murry, his 'blood-consciousness' aroused at last – for 'when I was drawn to Frieda, I wanted the riches of her body just as much as I wanted the generosity of her soul' [12] – being driven by his very efforts to escape it into such fantastic contortions; and there was the apostle of 'blood consciousness', deriding his idealism and exhorting him in God's name to 'untwist'! 'If only I had had the guts to say to him, "Yes, I *am* twisted, Lorenzo. And the reason is simple. I am trying to escape from the fact that Frieda and I are in love. And the way to untwist myself is equally simple. Not to try any more to escape from it. What have you to say to that?"' [12]

Lawrence must have realized, at bottom. What was apparent even to Koteliansky and Mrs Carswell cannot have been hidden from him. His story, *The Borderline*, proves it. So, in their different way, do *Jimmy* and *The Last Laugh* and *Smile*. It was not by chance that, from this time forward, Murry became, after Frieda herself, the object of his most vindictive attacks. He had exposed the pathetic pretensions with which Lawrence strove to conceal his dependence, from the world and himself; had proved that 'he was not, and never could be, Frieda's "lord and master". That was all a hollow sham.' [21] And if, for a man so resentful of the least obligation, to be dependent upon Frieda was bitter, to be dependent upon Murry for Frieda was unbearable. This it was that Lawrence could neither forget nor forgive.

And Murry, for his part, could never forget the glimpse he had caught of the real Lawrence – of the inward desolation and loneliness that prompted his frenetic outbursts. That was the meaning of their queer exchange at the Café Royal: when Lawrence, drunk and despairing, appealed to Murry not to 'betray' him: and he, drunk too but 'clairvoyant', [28] spoke the celebrated words, 'I love you, Lorenzo, but I won't promise not to betray you.' [29] They meant, as he explained later on, 'I am full of affection for you and pity for what you are suffering; but I won't promise to conceal my knowledge of why you are suffering.' [30] From this moment onwards, he said, Lawrence seemed to him 'a living dead man'. [31]

So – they too had reached the parting of the ways. For after this, the dénouement followed swiftly. He had given his reluctant consent to accompany Lawrence to Mexico as a friend; Lawrence went on to make him one of a retinue – and that was decisive. Personal friendship was one thing; 'impersonal' discipleship quite another. Even though, or because, the retinue consisted in the end only of Dorothy Brett, Murry's mind was made up to stay behind and stand by *The Adelphi*.

All the same, it was a much-sobered Murry who saw the three of them off at Waterloo on March 5, 1924. The magazine was on its last legs; his own had been knocked from underneath him. Of the exaltation of twelve months before, little indeed remained. How quickly and painfully he had been brought down to earth his next article, 'The Two Worlds', reveals:

A sense of proportion has descended upon him. He is not going to revolutionise the world. Is there then nothing he can do? What he can do is to try to create a nucleus, to gather together a sort of brotherhood, to build a milieu for himself, wherein his beliefs and aspirations shall find an echo and a response. And this time (such is his vow) the quality of the impulse must not be suffered to be degraded by the mechanism of its own expression. He dreams of a community whose force shall be measured not by the numbers of its professed adherents, but by the intensity and spontaneity of their devotion to the work before them: work on themselves, and work on the world without, shaping some small fragment of it into harmony with the world within.[32]

It is a far cry from this to 'The Cause of it All'.

X

ABBOTSBURY HARVEST

————◆◆❖◆◆————

IT WAS THROUGH *The Adelphi* that Murry met his second wife.
Violet le Maistre, descended on her father's side from Huguenot
refugees, and on her mother's from the poet Cowper, was a
versatile, vivacious, attractive girl of twenty-three, who had inherited,
along with the portraits and memorials of the poet adorning her
father's house at Oxshott, a lively ambition to paint and write herself.
Neither two select boarding-schools in Devon nor even a college of
dramatic art had sufficed to stifle her talent; she had read Katherine
Mansfield, of course; and one day, seeing a photograph of Murry in
the paper, had turned to a friend with the words, 'That's the man I'm
going to marry.'

During the autumn of 1923, she sent in some pieces to the magazine.
Murry returned them with a few encouraging words, suggesting that
she should work at something longer if she wanted a definite opinion;
and with that, forgot the matter. Not so Violet. Early next year she
wrote again. She had followed his advice, she said: would he please
keep his promise and read the longer stories enclosed? He read them,
accepting one.

She replied gratefully, and asked if she might bring some more in
person so that she could have some minutes talk with me. She came.
She was a slip of a girl, with wavy chestnut hair, an entire absence of
sophistication, and a simple determination to be a writer. 'Her voice was
soft and low – an excellent thing in woman', and there was, in the fragments of her writing, a lovely and incorrupt fidelity to the beauty seen
which, though hesitant, belonged to the same order as Katherine Mansfield's. I told her to read the stories of Tchehov, of whom she had never
heard; and I said I would do my best to criticise anything she sent to me.
At the end of about a month she came again to see me in the Adelphi,
and I took her out to tea in the Strand. We talked about Tchehov, whom

she had read assiduously in the meanwhile, and I expounded my view of his exquisite and heroic morality, without which so pure a perception of the beauty in all things was impossible.[1]

Tchehov was much in Murry's mind at this time. The essay on him published in *Discoveries* was his most articulate statement of faith to date.

But it was not only of Tchehov that he was thinking. 'While I was talking to her, the thought came to me that she was the very girl for my brother . . . She was too good not to be kept in the family, so to speak, though obviously she was not for me: 35 and old and battered.' [1] So he went on to talk about Richard, intimating that she would find him congenial, and that next time she came to tea, he would bring him along – as he did. Meanwhile, he added, he and Richard were arranging to go for a camping holiday.

Violet was disconcerted. Could they not meet once again before he left London, she asked. Of course. Murry readily agreed, and, being rather proud of his cooking, invited her to supper at his room in Pond Street. It was the first time he had ever done such a thing; and it was only then, while he was waiting for her to arrive, that he noticed his own impatience:

> She was late; and I was frightened lest the *filet* should spoil. I looked out of the window for her again and again, so anxiously that I began to wonder whether it was the *filet* after all. Why was I so anxious that this girl should come? Why was I feeling that, if she did not come, a spark would go out in my heart? I had not time to answer the questions, before she came. She had meant to be on the tick of time, but she had lost the way.[2]

Still, he kept to his plans. Once again they talked of Tchehov, till the floor was littered with little volumes of the Garnett translation. Then, at the appropriate moment, Richard's drawings were produced. Murry had hardly begun to expatiate on their merits, however, before his speech was cut short:

> Suddenly I heard her say, in her small calm voice: 'Mr Murry, I like these drawings, and I like your brother very much; but I can't love him, because you see I love *you*.' Instantly the speaking of the word whisked away the veil of illusion. The fact that I loved her stared me in the face. In vain I muttered that I was too old for her. She brushed that aside. 'The only question is: Do you love me?' 'I didn't know I did; but I do.'

I took her in my arms. It seemed to me very wonderful to be loved by one so young, for I did feel old. I felt that the kind of love she had for me, and which she had awakened in me, had passed out of my life thirteen years before, when I first fell in love with Katherine; and, even at that moment, it struck me as strange that precisely the same thing had happened again. Once again, I had been entirely ignorant that I was in love; once again, the woman had spoken, and only that had revealed it to me. I was too happy to do more than smile at myself for my own simplicity. It was really, I thought, an endearing kind of naivety. Still, it was strange. I had not changed so much as I imagined.[1]

By the time he and Richard set out on their Easter holiday, Murry was officially engaged. It was at Boxgrove, on the way, that he retrieved the little pearl ring he had once given to Katherine and posted it off to Violet.

After the stresses and strains of the winter, that holiday was joy from the start. It is celebrated in one of the gayest and tenderest of his essays – a marked contrast to its predecessors in *The Adelphi* – 'The Well at Cerne'. At Sullivan's suggestion, they exchanged their motor-bicycles for a Trojan car – unwieldy, but simple and reliable. In this they bore westward to Coleridge's Nether Stowey and Wordsworth's Quantoxhead; then, finding themselves unable to mount Porlock Hill, turned southward for Hardy's Dorset. Hardy himself – delighted by Murry's recent defence of his novels against 'that ludicrous blackguard George Moore' [3] – welcomed them both, and directed them on to the Chesil Beach. There they bathed; and there, facing the sea over a low line of tamarisks, Murry espied the house of his dreams – the long, squat, white-timbered, grey-slated Old Coastguard Station.

It was no part of his intention to buy a house, and only by chance that, as they were steaming back through Abbotsbury the following week, they caught sight of a notice in the estate-agent's window advertising this one for sale. But the temptation was irresistible. Though he had barely £200 in hand, he attended the auction, bid up to £925 – and the Old Coastguard Station was his. Then, while he was still wondering where the money was to be found, came the crowning stroke of luck – a cheque for £1,000, royalties on Katherine's books.

It was by far the biggest cheque I had ever received, and ten times as big as any Katherine had received for her own work. Even at that moment I was struck by the irony of it. On the other hand, in my half-superstitious way (of one who seeks meanings in all things) I felt that Katherine's blessing was on our marriage and our tamarisk-girted house by the sea, over which the swans came honking from the swannery every day. They were, at least, the next best birds to herons.[1]

Violet and he were married at Belsize Park on April 24 – in church, to please her parson uncle – and moved down to Dorset that summer. Murry's last effort in fiction, 'The Intruder' (published in the November *Adelphi*), commemorates their arrival.

Abbotsbury is an isolated spot, even today. The Old Coastguard Station, only to be reached from the village by a mile-long track by the shore, was remote and exposed indeed. Summer visitors were startled by the Murrys' indifference to bathing-costumes; in winter, the spray blew clean over the house, parching the garden behind – so that William Roper, the champion scytheman whom they engaged as gardener, chuckled at the sight of Murry importing a bunch of young fruit-trees. 'When you go,' he observed, 'be it in twenty years' time, you'll be taking those away with you just like that – under your arm,' as in fact he did. But the isolation did not trouble him at all. On the contrary, he loved it, and only for Violet's sake kept on a flat in Chelsea as well – No. 14a Whitehead's Grove – for use in the winter months. It was at Abbotsbury that he first made a practice of regular outdoor work – improving the track, constructing a tennis-court, bringing the garden into order (Roper still wistfully remembers picking fifty pounds of peas one June morning), and, taking shares in a boat, fulfilled his schoolboy dream of spending the long evenings afloat, seine-fishing.

The house being too large for themselves alone, they divided it into three, letting one part to the Tomlinsons, one to the Millers, and later to John Stewart Collis. This was all the company Murry wanted. If it was not a community, it was at least a congenial milieu. And, as always when he was at peace with himself and others, the fever went out of his writing. Violet's too 'began to take wings':

I printed a story of hers, 'A Queer Old Man', with full conviction of its quality, in *The Adelphi*, over the name of Mary Arden, which I chose for her; and no sooner had it appeared than Mr Edward O'Brien – that faithful champion of the short-story – wrote to ask if he might include it in his yearly anthology. And soon afterwards she wrote another story, 'A Casual Acquaintance', which was even better. There was no doubt at all of the authenticity of her gift. I, also, had my piece of luck. Out of the blue came an invitation to deliver the Clark Lectures at Cambridge, and that set me off on writing 'Keats and Shakespeare'. It was like the golden days at the Villa Pauline, when Katherine sat writing 'Prelude' on one side of the kitchen-table, while I wrote 'Dostoevsky' on the other. Truly, we stood on the top of happy hours.[1]

In point of fact, the next two years were among the most richly productive of Murry's life. They saw the genesis, not only of *Keats and Shakespeare*, but also of *The Life of Jesus* and all but two of the essays collected in *Things to Come* – still the best introduction to his thought. (When, in 1938, Queen Elizabeth expressed a desire to read some of Middleton Murry's work – which should she start with? – his friends unanimously recommended this.) All three books are, or deserve to be, classics.

In 1920, when *Aspects of Literature* was published, the blurb had announced 'a new theory of criticism, of which the essence is an emphasis on the intimate relation of literature to life'. That such a theory no longer sounds new is largely owing to Murry. But the phrase is vague and ambiguous. It could be, and has been, employed by those who require of the poet that he deal with 'questions of the day', valuing verse by its 'contemporaneity' (in effect, its ephemerality). The question to which Murry related poetry was the one real question, the same yesterday, today and tomorrow, 'What shall I do to be saved?'

This was so from the start. There is no breach of continuity in his criticism. It would take a very sharp eye indeed to detect which of the essays in *Discoveries* was written before, and which after, January 1923. 'The man who neglected his talents as a literary critic to indulge in a confused evangelism' [4] (even presuming that 'confused' means 'confusing') exists nowhere outside the imagination of fashionable reviewers. Because this was so, the poetry he valued most highly was always that which he called 'the spontaneous utterance of the un-divided being' [5] – in Romantic parlance, the poetry of Imagination. With the other sort, which is the deliberate construction of the divided being, he was never intimately concerned. He did not belittle it; within limits he admired it: but the least in the Kingdom of Shakespeare seemed to him superior in kind to the greatest in the Kingdom of Milton.

There was nothing mysterious about this 'undivided being'. It was the birthright, he believed, of every creature, including every child; and a few happy individuals retained it intact into manhood – Clare, for example, whom he had helped Edmund Blunden to resuscitate. Only, in most men it was disrupted with the advent of self-consciousness; and then, if they were poets, restored rarely in moments of 'inspiration', mysterious by reason of their rarity. So it had been with Collins, so with himself – 'they had poetic apprehension; they had not poetic comprehension'.[6] The problem confronting such men was to render it a permanent possession. Most had failed: but a few had succeeded, and of these few the greatest was Shakespeare – in whose tragedies we are conscious of no such disruption, whatever reality the mind presents being accepted and endorsed by the heart.

These few had been Murry's inspiration, consoling and confounding him with intimations of an attainable harmony:

> To struggle somehow to that point, to see life as it has been seen and can be seen, to know it as it has been known and can be known, has been my driving impulse as a critic. Somehow to make the secret my own so that I might live by it, not as the anguished memory of a departed ecstasy, but as a secure possession – this has been my incessant and at times only half-conscious purpose. And I have found myself turning away from those poets whose knowledge was but momentary and incomplete (as was the knowledge of most of those whom we call, and rightly call, great poets) to those who possessed it wholly. Always I found myself driven back to the pure poets – to Shakespeare pre-eminently, to Keats, and in our own day to Anton Tchehov.[7]

How insistently he had been driven back to Shakespeare, his 1922 lecture on 'The Nature of Poetry' shows. It had turned, in spite of himself, into a lecture on the development of Shakespeare's poetry: and this was what he was proposing to expand in his 1924 Clark Lectures. It was only when he re-read Keats's poems and letters for the purpose of an introduction, that he realized how perfectly these exemplified the stages of a poet's ascent, from the apprehension of beauty in some things to the comprehension of beauty in all – and took this for his theme instead.

It proved to be the theme he was born for. He had only to turn to the famous letter on the world as a Vale of Soul-Making to find his own faith expressed in an idiom more completely congenial, because more completely naturalistic, than any other. Of that letter he was to write towards the end of his life:

> When I first came to understand it, it was a pure revelation to me.

Truth and Beauty were stamped upon it. I took it into myself, and it has lived with me from that day. It has been incorporated into my life, it has been creative of my life. It has opened me to experience, and enabled me to assimilate and yet be shaped by experience. It has helped to expose me to experience, and helped me to receive the experience to which it exposed me. But for the endorsement which those words of Keats gave to my own dim perception of the truth which they contain, I would never have endured what I have endured or become what I am.[1]

Keats was a man with whom Murry could identify himself almost completely – which meant, of course, the very reverse of identifying Keats with himself. Assuredly his own personal vicissitudes, and Katherine's, stood him in good stead; but to say, as Collis once said, that he was 'really' writing about Katherine or himself is as preposterous as it is plausible. At no point in his exposition does he distort or depart from the text: his mind is as actively engaged as his heart. What he does is to lose himself in Keats, precisely as the great poet loses himself in the characters of his epic or drama. *Keats and Shakespeare* affords a superb illustration of its own thesis; the explicit is implicit throughout – even to that profound acquiescence in the tragedy of unmerited suffering which makes 'all disagreeables evaporate from their being in close relation with Beauty and Truth'. This is what makes it a great book – one of Murry's greatest, certainly his most nearly perfect.

It was not only the great poets, however, whom he could now comprehend in this way. The vital centre of his art having always been that of his ethics, he had always acknowledged an affinity between the self-abeyance of Imagination and of love; and the same experience which had brought him 'acceptance', and been the key to his presentation of Keats, had brought him also 'forgiveness', and opened the door to Eckhart. To him, therefore, the conclusion was unavoidable: 'The comprehension of the great artist is achieved by a process analogous to that by which the comprehension of the great saint is achieved.'[8] Keats's 'beauty in all things' was scarcely to be distinguished from Eckhart's 'sun in everything'; his 'dying into life' from 'losing your life to save it'. The undivided being, consubstantial with the universe, was precisely the mystic's Soul, consubstantial with God.

This is not to say that Murry imputed to Keats or Shakespeare, any more than to Katherine or Tchehov, a mystical experience like his own. That would be to confuse accidentals with essentials. What he did was to impute to the mystic a change of consciousness like theirs – a change from rebellion to acceptance. ('In some men the change may be sudden and dramatic, in others gradual and slow.')[9] It was not the poet whom he assimilated to the mystic so much as the mystic to the poet. But it did mean that all those 'bits of the New Testament' which had likewise haunted him for years, likewise 'put off their mystery: they became simple, familiar and true'.[10]

It appeared to him self-evident now that the 'rebirth' proclaimed by Jesus was nothing other than the reintegration achieved by the poets: the more so as Jesus himself was a poet, pre-eminently endowed with that gift of 'imaged speech which veritably does create within us a new vision, a new faculty and a new soul':

> If it can be put into a word, this is the fundamental distinction between the teaching of Jesus and all other religious wisdom that I know: that he taught not goodness, but *wholeness*: and this both in the inward man, and in the outward world. Wholeness in the man himself means that the soul is not a partial faculty of man; it is not something that can be opposed to and distinguished from mind and heart: it is a creation which includes both these within itself. The soul is simply the condition of the complete man. And to this completeness in the man, which is his soul, there corresponds a completeness and harmony of the world of his experience; it also, without abstraction or denial of any of its elements, suffers a like transformation, and becomes organic, harmonious – it becomes God.[11]

The essay on 'The Parables of Jesus' (from which these words are taken) is a worthy counterpart to 'Chapman's Homer'; *The Life of Jesus*, as Murry stated, a natural sequel to *Keats and Shakespeare*.

He himself, indeed, would go further, contending that the two books stood or fell together; but here he was mistaken. Not only is *The Life of Jesus* less well written (the reader is constantly jarred by the juxtaposition of Authorized and unauthorized translations), but it is, inevitably, less cogent. Although he availed himself freely of Schweitzer and Burkitt, his critical training did not extend to the Higher Criticism, nor, even if it had done, would the nature of the material have permitted an absolutely convincing interpretation. The most he could aim at was a more plausible one than the Liberal. Yet his contention was true in this sense, that by using the mystical experience as a key, he did succeed in eliciting a completely coherent and credible representation of Jesus, and that the Jesus so represented became, no less than Keats, part and parcel of his own life thence-forward. 'I love the man too much,' he wrote while at work on the book, 'more than I love Keats, more than I love Shakespeare – and that is saying everything.' [12] His words about the letter on Soul-making applied equally to the parable of the Prodigal Son.

Thus, by the summer of 1924 at latest (for *The Life of Jesus* was actually commissioned before *Keats and Shakespeare*), Murry found his subjective synthesis issuing in, and being steadily enriched by, an objective synthesis of literature and religion – further to explore and expound which was now his 'mission' as he conceived it. Not that he supposed his theory to be new – he was too familiar with the Romantics for that. It had been common ground to Coleridge and Shelley, Goethe and Novalis; whilst Carlyle, in critical essays closely resembling his own, had advanced it unequivocally. Nevertheless, his own talent being preponderantly critical rather than creative, he was able to submit it afresh, with a wealth of evidence which, defying refutation, invited ridicule.

Naturally, the ridicule was not long in coming. *Keats and Shakespeare* itself, though loudly acclaimed at first, was still more loudly abused. (One review, in *The Sunday Times*, headed 'Bombinations of a Chimera', he treasured for years as a curiosity.) He had taken Keats's greatness for granted: 'There is no danger that Keats's poetry will not be appreciated,' [13] he had written five years before. By the 1920s reaction against the Georgian poets was already extending to their models: and if Romantic poetry was falling into contempt, how much more so Romantic criticism? To the practitioners and exponents of an ever more sophisticated, ever more desiccated verse of intellectual construction, Murry's 'undivided being' could only mean what it meant to Eliot, 'the inner voice, which breathes the eternal message of vanity, fear and lust'; his Shakespeare could only sound like 'the messianic Shakespeare, bringing a new philosophy and a new system of Yoga'; while to the little people who troop in the fashion, the mere fact that Eliot himself had gone on to disclaim any first-hand acquaintance with the work proved it unworthy of acquaintance. Murry's star sank as Eliot's rose – rather ironically, since it was due to his own exertions, in the face of staunch opposition to an American, that Eliot was offered the next series of Clark Lectures.

It was much the same with *The Life of Jesus*. On its appearance, it was hailed by Dean Inge as 'a sort of *Ecce Homo* for our generation';

Evelyn Underhill was still more laudatory. Yet Murry was not a Christian – not even, therefore, what Eliot called him, 'a genuine Christian heretic'. That title, as he pointed out, applied better to Inge himself. If anything, he was a pantheist, treating the Christian dogmas simply, or obscurely, as metaphors: and this, to the less mystically minded, was bewildering. Eliot himself, for instance, to whom a rigid demarcation of the frontier between literature and religion was axiomatic, found it 'terribly hard to believe, with Mr Murry, that man is "the son of God" and also that he "must be God" '.[14] To which Murry could only reply (in a letter preceding the appearance of the review):

> You charge me with using the term 'Son of God' as though it had a precise meaning. No, I don't do that. I use it as though it had a *real* meaning. It had a real meaning for Jesus – sonship was the condition which supervened upon rebirth. Precise meaning it cannot have. I know you believe that there is no real meaning which is not precise. But you are mistaken . . .
>
> And so, when you make (perfectly legitimate) fun of me for saying that we must be sons of God, and we must be God, and say the metaphors cancel out, and that the 'idea is incomprehensible', I can only say that it is not an *idea* at all. If the wisdom of Jesus had been an 'idea' you would have absorbed it long ago: because it is not, it eludes you. But there is no contradiction between these two metaphors. (It is not the habit of metaphors to contradict, or cancel one another: metaphors, you know as well as I, are not logical statements.) To be son of God is simply an experience of a blessed and quasi-filial relation between ourselves and 'the power not ourselves which makes for righteousness' – 'to be God' is an experience of identification with that power. These two conditions are the same condition really. And Matt. Arnold's phrase will not really do. It should be: 'the power not ourselves, and yet ourselves, which makes for righteousness'. Not ourselves and yet ourselves. How incomprehensible! I am sorry. I would make it plainer if I could; but I can't. And if I seem to you to be maintaining 'the rosy tradition' of Rousseau and Wells, it doesn't matter.[15]

Actually, the paradox was typical. Murry is one of the most paradoxical writers in the language, and the style is the man. It was precisely because his 'truths' were grasped by the undivided being, that he could only express them intellectually in terms of thesis and antithesis, trusting his readers to reconstitute the synthesis. That was the inevitable liability of a poet reduced to prose; and that, no doubt, was why so many of his critics (not excluding admirers of Eliot) taxed him with obscurity. He acknowledged this, and bewailed it; but he could do nothing about it. And even when he tried to explain it, the attempt only landed him in yet further paradoxes:

> True knowledge being itself organic apprehends organically. It makes contact with that all-pervading and living reality which must needs be manifested to a knowledge that is not organic in antinomies and opposi-tions; it knows that these things must be thus and not otherwise; it watches the One flower into contradictions and dilemmas and mysteries; it watches, yet indeed it does not watch, for itself is such a One, flowering in the realm of discourse into contradictions and dilemmas and mysteries; yet indeed it is not such a One, it is itself that One . . .[16]

This, as it happens, is a passage which Murry himself cited as the sort of thing that came to him 'with a flowing pen, with the utmost ease',[16] and which, on reflection, he was forced to discard as unintelligible. But such passages could not always be discarded. Antinomies and oppositions (if not the related abuse of 'yet' and 'but', the most conspicuous vice of his style) really were unavoidable. The choice, as he said, was 'between contradictions and silence'.[17]

Perhaps, had he confined himself to the word 'life' or 'harmony' when writing about literature, and 'God' when writing about religion, he would have escaped some censure. As it was, like every synthetist, he laid himself open to attack from both sides at once. 'The Christian perspective is precious to me', we find him writing in January 1928, 'and I am not going to surrender my right to use and profit by it simply because I am told by one party that it is the only perspective and by the other that it does not exist.' At the same time, he had to add, 'You cannot be what I am and be fashionable. I am rather sorry about that, for I have my living to earn.'[18] Already by then, if he had not led his disciples 'into the wilderness', as Eliot put it, 'to the accompaniment of a titter of derision from civilised Europe'[19] (for his disciples, if any, were obscure, and the civilized do not ordinarily titter), he had gone far towards putting himself off the map in spirit as well as space.

INHUMAN?

───◆◆◆◆───

'IT MUST BE CONFESSED', wrote Murry's next-door neighbour, Tomlinson, 'that it is not usual to-day to find a journalist of Murry's reputation so lost in a re-examination of Keats – and lost for weeks and weeks – that he has completely forgotten the fact that he is the editor of a monthly review which is close to another publishing day.' [1] This incident had actually taken place, two months before; and it seems to have signalled the end of the 'Adelphi'. By October 1924, at all events, it had become plain that Murry's conception of the magazine was quite incompatible with the others'.

They had agreed that it was to be 'a thoroughfare for all thoughts', or, as Koteliansky put it, a magazine with 'a life of its own, irrespective of the views, beliefs and convictions of any one of its contributors'. [2] And so it was. Only, with the passage of time, the life had come to look uncommonly like Murry's. The difference arose over the explanation. According to Koteliansky (and most people, whether they liked it or not, agreed), it was because Murry was imposing his own pattern on it – and therefore betraying the original idea. According to Murry, it was because the paper was imposing its pattern on him – and therefore fulfilling it. After all, the whole point of a thoroughfare was that it should lead somewhere. If the conclusions it reached were his, that was not due to his excluding certain views, but simply to his growing to include them. But, whatever the explanation, one thing was obvious: either he must cease to be editor, or Koteliansky to be business manager. A review 'as big as a telephone-book' could not afford to alienate its subscribers; a venture in literary and religious synthesis could not afford £200 salaries.

Characteristically, Murry offered *The Adelphi* to Koteliansky, on terms which the latter called 'perfectly fair' [3] and promptly accepted, subject to the co-operation of the rest of the group. Equally characteristically, the rest of the group demurred – it was Murry's organ or nobody's, they said – and the exchange fell through. But Tomlinson, though he approved of Murry's procedure, deplored his mysticism; Sullivan, who approved of his mysticism, deplored his procedure; Lawrence pronounced both parties impartially 'Judases'; and Kotelianky retired in a dudgeon – to remain for the rest of his days Murry's most tireless traducer. From that time forward, *The Adelphi* became a one-man concern, destined within three months to disappear from the bookstalls.

The pattern was to be familiar in Murry's life; and no doubt it was still in Tomlinson's mind when he went on:

> For prompting sudden and even noisy petulance in those who know him and in those who don't, and won't, but always read him, Murry has a special gift. It comes easy to him, but he is blissfully unaware that it is his. It always astonishes him to observe so strange a consequence on his friends of one of his unimpassioned tussles with a literary problem. You can see the pain and wonder in his eyes. Anxious, absorbed, pale, and faintly smiling, the difficulty not exactly overcome, but maybe even increased – Murry has a native difficulty in claiming to have done more than to deepen to a profounder mystery any literary problem – he looks up confidingly, and discovers that we are swearing at him as heartily as though he had lost every train in the timetable for us. And he never knows why. For that matter, neither do we.[1]

It was true, and not only of literary circles. All his life long, Murry retained this singular gift for stirring up violent emotions in nearly everybody who came into touch with him. The emotions might not always be the same; his associates might dispute among themselves whether he was devil or saint; but the only ones to approach neutrality were those who concluded that he was both.

To these, for instance, seems to have belonged his other next-door neighbour, Collis, who wrote:

> He holds in himself some principle of division: it is – to be personal for a second – even outwardly visible: eyes of unexampled beauty – that cannot look at you; an occasional broad smile betraying the whole physic and psychic body, so that Mirth, quite possibly devilish, presides; a sneer that is wholly against his ideology. Not a man to sum up easily or to see through.[4]

It recalls Huxley's 'mixture of a card-sharping Lothario and a rapturous devotee', or Lawrence's 'faun on the Cross, with all the malice of the complication'. It even recalls the poor young man who, arriving one night, flung himself into Murry's bed – because, he explained, he could not be too near the Messiah – only to tell him a few weeks later that in certain lights he looked just like Mephistopheles (which was true) and soon afterwards hang himself.

The question arises: what was the root of these contradictory re-actions – of which the portraits are merely projections? And the answer, in all probability, is given in the word which Tomlinson used, when, quite rightly denying that Murry's absorption was a pose, he referred to it as a 'symptom of fanaticism'.[1] Provided we bear in mind what 'fanaticism' means – total devotion to a cause or a quest not our own – this accounts for a good deal, at any rate, of what people found enigmatic. For the essence of the fanatic is that he does not think of the cause or quest as his own either. On the contrary, he thinks of himself as the humble instrument of some supra-personal power, and is inclined to expect others to do likewise. Not only was this con-spicuously true of Murry, but it was demonstrably the cause of several of the major collisions punctuating his career.

In everything that concerned him personally, he was tolerant, courteous, diffident almost to a fault. Once, when Koteliansky had been pestering him with contributions to *The Athenaeum*, he wrote to Katherine:

> I've come to the conclusion that to be an editor and to try to do your friends a good turn is madness: your friends always try to impose on you. It's queer. But my impulse would, I think, be quite the other way. I should always be rather shy of even offering MS to an editor who was a friend; and try to make it particularly easy for him to send it back if he didn't care for it.[5]

That he was not mistaken in this, his behaviour in after years showed. Neither hard enough to push his own wares, however good, nor soft enough to push his friends', however bad, he lacked the first qualifica-tion for success in literary circles. On the other hand, the very condi-tion of his habitual modesty was his submission to a deeper self, whose purpose was to comprehend and grow; and, precisely because he never thought of this as his *own*, he could exercise a ruthlessness on its behalf that appeared 'wholly against his ideology'.

Thus, he was perfectly justified in his view of *The Adelphi* as 'a thoroughfare for all thoughts'. As a contributor, he observed the highway code conscientiously; and even as editor, he was no more, in his own eyes, than the policeman empowered to check the drivers' licences and see that they kept to the left (or the right, as the case might be). Hence his indignation when one of them charged him with arbitrary interference. *He* had not drawn up the code; the quarrel was not with *him* at all – but with the power not himself and yet himself which made for righteousness! The aspersion seemed to him no less unreasonable than it would to the constable at Hyde Park Corner – and he was capable of retorting with all the truculence of an outraged constable: '*The Adelphi* will have to change to suit me. I am convinced that I have a work to do, a function to perform, in the world: and *The Adelphi* is the instrument of that function. It is not, never has been, and never will be a thing in itself.' [6] No wonder Koteliansky was dismayed! Exactly what felt to Murry like the very nadir of humility could only have sounded to him like the very acme of arrogance. The incomprehension was mutual and complete.

What is more mysterious, at first sight, than the noisy petulance he provoked, is his own inability to understand it: for, though he gradually came to regard it as a 'law of nature', there is no evidence that he was any less baffled by it thirty years later than he was in 1924. But perhaps that, too, was a symptom of fanaticism. He once confessed that Koteliansky was never more than a 'pleasant piece of furniture' [7] to him. The very intensity of his absorption – not in himself, as some egotists presumed, but in whatever cause or quest engaged him – precluded an interest in people; and having so little interest in people, he could have little understanding of them either.

He himself, it is true, might have found that hard to admit, since in this respect, at least, he was unexceptional, that he thought himself an exceptional psychologist. He had his own account even of the idiosyncrasy noted by Huxley and Collis:

> I have an almost invincible reluctance to look people in the eyes. I can do it, *naturally*, only with people who are my close intimates. I can look anybody in the eyes: but it is with an effort, and often (perhaps generally) I safeguard myself by looking at them *blankly* – 'looking through them', I think it's called. And the reason? It's queer; but generally it is because I am ashamed *for* them. I am conscious of some humbug, hypocrisy, or meanness in them, and *I dare not look them in the eyes*. [8]

'But', he adds with typical candour, 'maybe, that's a too complimentary account of a real peculiarity of mine': and almost certainly it was. Had he really been so conscious of humbug, hypocrisy and meanness, he would not have been the ready prey he was to spongers, charlatans and designing women. His misjudgements of character were so numerous, naïve and notorious that one of his assistant editors confessed that he would have had the gravest doubts as to his own integrity, had Murry appointed him to the post.

If the truth were told, he wrote on another occasion, Jesus was a great deal more real to him than anybody he had known in the flesh – and coming from him, the remark was credible. With few exceptions, the people he knew in the flesh were scarcely real to him at all. Just as he could be ruthless in defence of toleration, so he could be blind in pursuit of vision; and no doubt this, too, was responsible for many collisions, since it was not everyone who could appreciate the compliment he paid them by crediting them with a devotion equal to his own: most expected some attention to themselves – and that was crying for the moon.

Murry wanted comrades – or at all events, the feeling of comradeship; he did not want friends, in any more personal sense:

> I have never, since the days of Gordon Campbell, felt the *need* of a friend. Then I did feel it, and something of the need remained with D. H. Lawrence; but by 1917 – when I was 28 – it had left me altogether. I have liked – perhaps loved is not too strong a word – the few friends I have had since those days, but I have not needed them – not personally, anyway. I have wanted them (as D. H. L. once said to me) to 'go along with me', in a common understanding and for a common purpose, but that's all.[9]

It followed from this that people either met Murry on the impersonal level, or they did not meet him at all.

Most people did not meet him at all. Finding no cause or quest in common, they found nothing in common; and, since his preoccupation rendered pose impossible, were soon made aware of the fact. For them, he 'just wasn't there', as Huxley used to complain – nor was there any *persona* to do duty in his absence. Of the things that meant everything to him, he could not speak with people to whom they meant nothing; of things that meant nothing to him, he could not speak anyway. Casual acquaintances would confront a wall of silence, which they and he strove vainly to surmount. Afterwards, he would justify himself in terms like these:

> Truly, I *have* very little to say. But it does seem to me that people talk far too much. They talk round *it* and about, say 'whatever comes into

their heads', and it's pretty trivial stuff. They don't wait to feel the whole of themselves, of their experience, behind what they say; they don't wait for the real 'spontaneity'. Or so it seems to me. In truth, I prefer real gossip to half-way intellectual talk. And, in general, I find grown-ups much *duller* than children.[10]

Once, after sitting speechless throughout a meal with some unemployed miners, Murry intimated to his hostess that, though nice, they had seemed to him rather 'constrained'. That he himself had anything to do with their constraint would never have crossed his mind. Some might attribute such behaviour to snobbery; nothing could be further from the truth. He was perfectly ill-at-ease in every walk of society.

By the same token, it followed that those who did find a cause or quest in common with him, found much else in common as well. Assured of that – and he was only too easily assured – he became a different man: animated, communicative, attentive, even entertaining (that Collis pronounced him devoid of humour proves their acquaintance superficial). But again – only as long as the assurance lasted. Let what he had taken for devotion to the cause turn out to be mere devotion to himself, or the cause itself change, as it often did, or they discover that it was not really theirs after all – and nothing remained but what he defined, in a letter to Sullivan, as 'affectionate tolerance'.[11] It was probably this, as much as anything else, that led to his being dubbed 'inhuman'.

Not only did he not need friends: he shrank from friendship. Inordinately shy as he was, he could not himself confide (except with the help of wine), and confidences from others made him shier than ever. He was afraid that, if involved at all, he would be involved entirely; and that, if involved entirely, he would be laying himself open to such wounds as he had taken at Lawrence's hands. Rather than run any such risk, he would freeze at the first touch of intimacy, or even of fellow-feeling – repelling it at times with a brusqueness bordering on brutality. It is not surprising that he occasioned resentment, and still less surprising that he was mystified by the resentment he occasioned. Had he been able to understand it, he would not have been able to provoke it.

That he was 'a man of the kindest instincts' (as one of his obituarists said), nobody who knew him would contest. His reluctance to hurt people wittingly amounted almost to a vice; whilst as often as he did so unwittingly, he was overwhelmed with contrition and embarrassingly eager to make amends. Kindness, however, is not imagination, and imaginative he was not – or rather, the imagination deployed to such effect in his writings was seldom apparent in his personal relations. Of that intuitive knowledge of what others are thinking and feeling, which women are often accredited with and men occasionally possess, he exhibited hardly a trace. What Katherine had written in 1914 – 'As long as one's mood isn't directed towards or against him, he's quite unconscious and unsuspicious'[12] – remained just as true ten years later. It was not long before Violet confirmed it.

One of the few to find their way to the Old Coastguard Station in the summer of 1926 was J. P. Hogan, the essayist. As a result of close and constant perusal of *The Adelphi* since its opening number, it had been borne in upon him that Murry had once had a wife, called Katherine Mansfield, and that she had died. 'I can still recall,' he says, 'how disconcerted I was when I found him sitting on the Chesil Beach alongside a young woman who looked astonishingly like K. M., and whose idiom, when she addressed him, evoked to an embarrassing degree the Wiggery-Tiggery idiom of K. M.'s. Journal and Letters. I lunched with them a couple of days later, and it did not ease my youthful diffidence to find the initials "K. M." neatly embroidered in a corner of my table napkin.' Hogan's confusion was pardonable. It took Murry himself three years to ascertain that Violet was not Katherine.

Assuredly, he had not 'changed so much as he imagined'. That is clear from his reminiscences. At the time of his marriage, he had still been in love with the idea of Katherine; and it was largely because Violet asked for nothing better than to step (almost literally) into Katherine's shoes, that their notes seemed to blend so perfectly. His friends might shake their heads over what they took for his overrating of her talent; her relatives grieve to see her adopting Katherine's dress, hair-style, handwriting and mannerisms: but it is an old saying that the man who marries must expect to shed most of his friends, and visits from the Le Maistres were not encouraged. Together, for the first few months, they lived the Heron dream. That by trying to be Katherine, Violet was being untrue to herself, and by being untrue to herself, being as unlike Katherine as possible, did not so much as enter Murry's head. He neither saw her as she was, nor helped her to become what she was. It took two mortal blows to open his eyes.

Katherine had longed for children – a girl and a boy. Because she had done so, Murry took it for granted that Violet must too. 'It never struck me for a moment that there was a great difference between Katherine when I first met her, and Violet now: that Katherine had had much, and some very bitter, experience of love, whereas Violet had had none.' Much less did it strike him that his own 'innocence' as a lover, which had enchanted Katherine, would awaken in Violet no desire for children – for he was still quite oblivious of his inhibition. 'I can see now, plainly enough, how great was my failure in imagination. I can see now that, had I been a wiser man, I should gently have initiated her into all the infinite delights of physical love between a man and woman who truly love one another, and waited patiently until the positive *desire* for children was kindled in her. But in those days I did not know how, and I did not understand the need':

Thus, it was a profound shock to me when, in the middle of her first pregnancy, which filled me with happiness, I began to be aware that she herself was unhappy. At first I had thought it nothing more than physical malaise. But one day she said she wanted to confess something to me, which she was afraid would hurt me. I said, quite truthfully, that I loved her in such sort that I did not believe that anything she could do or say would hurt me. It would be herself, and that would be enough. Then she said:

'Golly!' That was her name for me, transferred to me from a golliwog she had adored as a little girl. 'Golly! I don't really want this baby. I've tried to want it, but I can't. I only want you. And I'm afraid it will come between us. You won't love me so much. You will love her – I know you will.'

Hurt? No, I was not hurt; I was numbed, not so much by the shock of disappointment, though that was great, as by the sudden discovery of my utter ignorance of what she had been feeling. I was bewildered and lost, once more. What had seemed so simple and natural and lovely to me, the perfect juncture of the dream and the reality in which I had lived ever since it was revealed to me that I loved her, was now frayed and forlorn. I loved her for loving me so much; I loved her for her courage in telling me: but the blissful sense of complete union in love was torn away. I did my utmost to comfort her, and to implant in her my simple faith that when the baby came it would be to her, as it would be to me, our own bond of love made incarnate, which, so far from coming between us, would only unite us the more. I begged her to believe it, to trust me. 'I really do *know*', I said.

But the faint shadow that had fallen between us remained. The bloom of our love had been smutched. When the little girl was born in the Old Coastguard Station, it was not the blissful happening I had dreamed. It was marvellous indeed to me, but not blissful. The long waiting in the dark in the room below, listening to the murmur of voices above, then the sudden intense silence, like a lapse into the womb of all life, then out of the covering darkness, the tiny incredible cry, that sounded high and incommensurable above the steady boom of the great Atlantic waves: this was marvellous. And because it was marvellous, because of the kind of marvel that it was, there was bitterness in my heart when I learned that the baby was not to be fed at her mother's breast. That seemed to me all wrong, as it were to shut the door upon the angel.[13]

The baby was born on April 19, 1925; and what Violet had feared did happen – it came between them. Or rather, her own fear came between them – for she would have nothing whatever to do with it. For four months of ceaseless anxiety, while it hovered between life and death, the nursing fell entirely to Murry, absorbing his entire attention. It was only when, at long last, it began to put on weight that he was able to turn back to the mother: and by then, if the 'sense of complete union' had not been torn away, the illusion had. This was the first blow.

Happily, it was not final. He had hardly turned back to Violet before 'another miracle happened'. She, who had been so indifferent and resentful, grudging the devotion he lavished on the baby, 'for the first time saw it, and found it funny and delightful. She smiled on it with tender amusement, and to the scandal of its godparents nick-named it the Egg, because of its brown and shiny head' – a nickname which, soon softened to Weg, stuck ever after. Then, Murry writes, 'the happiness of which we had been disappointed, came in full measure, running over for the delay'.[13] For a few months, at least, the dream and the reality converged once more.

The little girl's real name was Katherine, of course – and Middleton, since he had not forgotten Katherine's wish that this should be their family name. The godparents were Thomas and Mrs Hardy. The christening, by the parson uncle, took place in the parish church of Abbotsbury; and, since Max Gate lay within easy reach, even by Trojan, the old couple saw much of their god-daughter. Years later, in a broadcast, Murry recalled Hardy's making her a handkerchief rabbit – it struck him as, in some quaint way, typical of his homely genius.

Now, indeed, life at the Old Coastguard Station seemed to him so good, his baby daughter so wonderful, that nobody could resist them – not even Lawrence. That autumn, hearing that Lawrence was back from New Mexico, he urged him to come and spend a few days in Dorset, believing that he had only to do so to 'succumb to it and England after all':[14] and although that was not to be, reconciliation must have been in the air. The two met in London, disputed amicably about Jesus (and Judas), and arranged to meet again the following January, when Murry would take his family out to Italy. It was only when this arrangement likewise fell through, and Lawrence, in a frenzy of irritation that left Murry 'sick inside for weeks',[15] refused to have any more truck with *The Adelphi*, that they gave up hope of each other finally.

By then, however, the halcyon days were already nearing their end. The second blow was already impending. For it was not through any want of good will on his own part or Violet's that they were unable to travel out to Italy. The doctor had peremptorily forbidden it. Violet was pregnant again: and when, on May 9, 1926, she gave birth to a son ('another John Middleton, ye gods!'[16] as Lawrence correctly recorded), there was still less cause for rejoicing. Not only was the baby delicate, but this time the mother herself seemed unable to recover strength. All that summer, Violet was tired and listless – a nurse had to be found for the children, while Murry attended to her – and with the onset of winter, anxieties thickened ominously.

Since Weg's arrival, they had exchanged their two rooms in White-head's Grove for a flat (No. 1a The Gables) in the Vale of Health, Hampstead – familiar terrain to Murry, overshadowed as it was by 'the Elephant'. There they repaired for Christmas; and there, almost at once, it became what it was always to remain in his memory, 'a Vale of Sickness'. Early in January, while the little boy went into hospital, Violet was taken to a nursing-home. (A third child was on the way, and the doctor had pronounced the risk too serious.) Immediately afterwards, Murry himself fell ill. He had been feeling 'very queer', he says, and, happening to have a thermometer, noticed that he was running a temperature of between 104° and 105°. 'I called in aid my next-door neighbour, Helen Thomas, rang up my friend, Dr James Young, made up some sort of bed in our little living room, so as to leave the big bed free for Violet on her return, and lay down with the feeling that not even the Last Trump could prevail to budge me.'[13]

The feeling was not unwarranted: he had just passed the crisis of double pneumonia.

But worse was to follow. Even before he was up, Young's attention was called back to Violet; and now there was no mistaking the symptoms: 'he suspected tubercle'.[13]

With that, Murry 'went down into the depths'.[13] Though a sputum analysis was necessary in order to confirm the diagnosis, 'what the result would be was a foregone conclusion. Though the idea of such a destiny had never been on the fringes of possibility, the moment it was put before me I recognized it as my own. This was what would happen. It was the most meaningful thing that could have happened.'

But *what* was the meaning?

With that problem I struggled. I reached back, for help, to Lawrence's conclusions in the Fantasia of the Unconscious. Was it love from the upper, the spiritual centres, once more? . . . But without agreement of soul, there was no possibility of love. Not even Lawrence could deny that. Or did he? Had I just taken what I needed from his doctrine and left the rest? But if I had, and if the rest which I rejected was that not only agreement of ideas but the meeting of souls was a false basis for love, then what could I do but reject it still?

But was *that* the meaning of what was happening? Had I to be taught, in this terrible fashion, that the love of the soul was indeed an illusion which led to death? I reacted against the thought with all my being, even to nausea. If that was the meaning, then to learn it would kill me. I scarcely even shaped the thought. I reacted away from the darkness and desolation out of which it would have arisen.

No, the meaning was utterly different from this, and it was plain. When I had, after my fashion, struggled for Katherine's life, I was impure. I had no faith in life. Having no faith in life, I did not, because I could not, give my all. Time and again, in little ways I failed her. Time and again, I had shrunk from insisting where I should have insisted, and in order not to hurt her, took the weaker line. As I had failed in courage, so I had failed in patience. Now, God helping me, I would fail in neither. My faith in life would give me courage and patience which would make my love a power. I had failed Katherine; Violet I would not fail. The very whole of me would be cast into the struggle for her life, and by the completeness of my dedication it would prevail. That was the meaning; that was the test.

I emerged from this long wrestling like a man renewed. I was now completely prepared for the verdict of the bacteriological analysis which was, of course, what James Young had feared. I was completely prepared to tell Violet the bad news: which I did. But I was completely unprepared for her reply.

'O I'm so *glad*!' she said. 'I wanted this to happen.'

I stared into her shining eyes. 'You wanted this to happen', I repeated, slowly and dully, while my world turned upside down.

'You see, Golly!' she explained. 'I wanted you to love me as much as you loved Katherine – and how could you, without this?'

Something within me turned to stone, or ice. A far-away voice, cold and crystal, seemed to be saying to me: 'Faith in life, my dear . . . Faith in life?' [13]

'I do not know whether I ever got over the shock of that revelation', Murry writes, 'or ever worked myself entirely free from the sense that a grim cosmic joke was being played on me.' [13] Violet and he had been 'playing at man and wife, and the game had turned dreadful. The child-wife greeted with ecstasy this romantic disease.' [13] Seven years before, Katherine had used like words of him: now her bitterness was his. It was only by looking upon Violet as a child that he could escape a feeling of resentment; and never thereafter could he feel assured of her will to recover. The dream had ended finally: the nightmare returned.

12. H. M. Tomlinson

13. J. W. N. Sullivan

14. J. M. M.: Portrait by William Rothe
stein in *Contemporary Portraits*, 19

15. Violet le Maistre, 1923

XII

RESURRECTION

---◆❀❀◆---

WHAT MURRY HAD RESOLVED to do, he did: the very whole of him was cast into the struggle for Violet's life. Ever since 1918, he had been reproaching himself for not sending Katherine to a sanatorium. This time there were to be no hesitations, no half-measures. He spoke to his child-wife seriously; tried to make her see that consumption was a deadly enemy, to be fought by every means at their command; assured her that if only they fought together they could, and would, prevail. In words, at least, she concurred. Then, on May 14, 1927 – as soon as she was strong enough to be moved – he placed her in the Edward VII Hospital at Midhurst.

A fortnight later, he himself returned to Abbotsbury. From there to Midhurst was a journey of seven hours by Trojan; but he would drive over every week-end, stopping from Friday to Monday with his friends, the Robinsons, at Yateley, in Berkshire. Marion Robinson, a woman of literary aspirations, was only too glad to be of service, and though her husband, a retired Indian Army officer, found the visits a strain ('They never stopped talking – about Keats, about Jesus, about Lawrence – and if you ask me, it was a lot of bosh!'), their hospitality made the separation bearable.

Even so, it had cost Murry 'a superhuman effort'[1] to enforce, and that summer was a miserable one for both. Alone at the Old Coast-guard Station, he sank once more into the depths. *Nessun maggior dolore* . . . Dante's line seems to have haunted him at this time. As for Violet, though she submitted implicitly to every prescription, never rebelled, never complained, seemed anxious for nothing but to be as little trouble as she could, her condition, instead of improving, deteriorated steadily.

By July, it was already clear that the treatment was unavailing; and when, at the end of three months, the Hospital Superintendent pronounced his verdict – the only thing to be done was to keep her as comfortable as possible – it came almost as a relief. 'Now we could start afresh, with simple love. I would nurse her now until I dropped, never leave her, do everything for her; and, above all, I would never do what I did to Katherine – never lose my faith.' [2] Within a few days of hearing the verdict, Murry drove Violet back to Abbotsbury; and there they spent the winter, alone.

> It was a queer timeless existence that winter. The Coastguard Station, at any rate in those days, was remote enough in the summer; but in the winter it was isolated indeed. The Atlantic breakers pounded incessantly against the beach at the bottom of the tamarisk garden, and a faint tremor seemed to shake the earth and the long low house continually. But, for the rest, I remember little, save the sense that we were totally withdrawn from the world – a tiny little community whose only contact with the life beyond was the postman, a handsome middle-aged man with a splendid white moustache, who battled his way along the coast road every morning. Every morning, the children would stagger off to meet him, and he would appear, carrying one or sometimes both of them. They adored him.[2]

The children apart, it was the life of Montana over again, with the same suspended sentence of death, the same precarious happiness – for 'in some strange way we were happy',[2] he writes. Violet's child-like doubt whether he loved her as much as he had Katherine was set at rest: and so was his own, whether he ought not to have sent Katherine to hospital. The treatment which had failed in the one case would, he was now convinced – illogically, but permanently – have failed in the other as well. Whatever hope he still cherished was staked on 'simple love'.

Not that medical attention was neglected; but 'it is impossible', he had written in *The Life of Jesus*, 'to set limits to the power of faith when there is an active human will to collaborate':[3] and for a time it looked as if his faith would indeed prevail. By the spring, at all events, he was able to tell Eliot that her condition had 'improved immensely since December, when it was zero. It is supposed to be a miracle – certainly is contrary to all prognosis – that she is now alive.' [4] Throughout those months he had tended her almost single-handed. From February to October 1928 he was never absent for a night, seldom for a day. If devotion alone could have turned the scales, Violet would surely have been saved.

Nevertheless, by the end of that summer it was apparent even to the eye of faith that the sentence was irrevocable. Honestly as Murry could say, 'I did not fail',[5] simple love had proved unavailing too. A further winter of such isolation was not to be faced; some spot within easier reach of doctors and nurses had to be found; and, with a heavy heart, he made up his mind to relinquish the Old Coastguard Station. Once again Marion Robinson came to the rescue, locating a bungalow on the outskirts of Yateley itself – a handsome, timbered building, newly built by an architect for his own home, and vacated because of his wife's death. It was secured for £1,137, and in October the Murrys moved. They were none too soon. The strain of those eighteen months had taken their toll of him too. Physically, mentally and emotionally, he was exhausted.

It is not to be wondered at that these years, 1927–8, were the least productive of his literary life. As soon as Violet's illness declared itself, he announced the ending of *The Adelphi* – and though, thanks to gifts from readers totalling £300, he was able to resume it after all, it was only as a quarterly, *The New Adelphi*. At Abbotsbury, as at Montana, he immersed himself in Shakespeare – but to no visible effect beyond the 'Notes on Shakespeare' which became a feature of the magazine, and a desultory correspondence with Wilson Knight, whom he was helping to launch on his career as a critic. The book on Shakespeare he had been projecting was deferred indefinitely. Apart from reviews and a selection from Katherine's *Journal*, his whole output was the handful of essays assembled in *Countries of the Mind* (2nd Series).

Luckily, his activity over the preceding years had been so great that he could afford to relax: for, though he never rid himself of the idea that he was poor, that was not the case. One man's Queer Street is another's Park Lane, and his standards were high – what he denoted by a 'wholesome frugality' amounting to little more than a distaste for ostentation and a lively horror of waste. The impulse of 1923 to give up everything and 'hide in a hole' had been purely momentary. By January 1927, when he was telling Eliot that he badly needed to make 'an extra £150–200 a year',[6] he was already in receipt of approximately £1,500, including dividends on investments and excluding Violet's annuity of £200. It cannot have been much less when, three months later, he appropriated £200 saved by the old *Adelphi* as a retrospective editorial salary. Moreover, during the succeeding winter,

Hardy procured him £250 from the Royal Literary Fund, and Gosse an equivalent grant. He would not have had to write very much, even if he had been in a position to do so.

It was not only his full-time attendance on Violet, however, that put writing almost out of the question. He was quite capable of turning out an article in circumstances that would deter most men from starting a letter: he was journalist enough for that. What he was not journalist enough for was to write merely for the sake of writing, or even of earning a living. 'There is that element in my nature, for better or worse, which listens in a cold and stony silence to the words I speak and write and asks, "Do you really *believe* that?" If I cannot answer, from the depths of my heart, "Yes, I do", then I am straightway dumb as the demon in the parable.' [7] If he was dumb at this time, it was primarily because he had nothing to say – nothing, that is, that could command the whole of his being.

'Faith in life, my dear . . . Faith in life?' How *could* he affirm such a faith, when life itself seemed bent on refuting it? When every day and in every way the conclusion stared him in the face that all things work together for ill to him who loves God? For four years he had followed faithfully the promptings of his undivided being, let the wind blow where it listed, and all that it had brought was public indifference and domestic disaster. If the touchstone of his religion was the quality of the marriage it sustained, then his religion was a mockery. He could no longer even believe in Violet's recovery as a test of faith. Though his heart might still cling to the assurance of 'belonging' conferred by the mystical experience, his mind pronounced 'even the memory of a mysticism a thing of scorn'. [8] By now, he was as divided inwardly as ever he had been in the past; and the very integrity which had brought him to this point forbade him to proclaim it any more.

It was the old, old story of the mystic:

> Where he has been he knows that the world of Good and Evil is a world of error; but where he has been he cannot remain and live, and when he returns the world of Good and Evil is there. It has been destroyed in him, but it has not been destroyed. It can be destroyed only in men; and men will not destroy it. And that slow realisation is a second death. Man who is God the Son will not *be* God the Son. Time after time God the Son has been destroyed by that realisation. The pain is too fearful, the loneliness too terrible. No power on earth can assuage that pain. 'My God, my God, why hast thou forsaken me?' [9]

The words belong to a later date – but this was the moment they referred to.

Inevitably, in this dark night of the soul, the Crucifixion became the focus of Murry's meditations, since there the problem was posed nakedly; there was veritably the crux. It is no accident that the words on his dumbness occur in an 'Apology for a Sermon' delivered on the theme of the Cross. His heart could no more deny that the life of Jesus himself had ended in utter dereliction than his mind could affirm that a life so perfect had stemmed from a pure illusion. Furthermore, just as often as he plucked up courage to re-imagine that life to the end, so often, he found, his own sense of unity was restored, and with it 'some high and certain knowledge that in the utter disaster of the bravest and most beautiful soul that has visited this earth, is the supreme revelation of the beauty and purpose of life':

> To such a one the life and death of Jesus of Nazareth is the arche-type of all tragedy: and the experience which comes through the unflinch-ing contemplation of that life and death, is the experience in which all tragic experience culminates. What we know when we read *King Lear* to the bitter end, that we know, more fully and deeply, when we have followed Jesus of Nazareth to His last despairing cry.[7]

But how to account for this experience? For the first time since his illumination, Murry was being forced to call it in question – to ask whether it was not, after all, 'communion with a loving and ineffable God'.[10] Hitherto, he had been too busy obeying and explicating the unity it conferred to analyse the experience itself. Now the question confronted him inescapably – and there were months when, as his 'Notes and Comments' in *The New Adelphi* show, he 'trembled on the brink of Orthodoxy'.[10] The fullest account of his struggle is con-tained in a letter to Du Bos, who had suffered a similar temptation and succumbed:

> Two years ago I was trembling on the very verge of Catholicism. My sheer isolation had become unbearable. As you know I had married again. Within two years of my marriage, my wife was struck down with pul-monary tuberculosis. This repetition of my destiny preyed upon me, and working together with my intellectual and spiritual isolation, pro-duced in me a hunger for communion such as I had not known before. At that precise time I was reading Bossuet, very patiently. The magni-ficent comprehensiveness – the utter cogency of his refutation of Pro-testantism – enthralled me; but what chiefly tugged at my soul was the

sudden realisation (in reading some of Bossuet's prayers) that 'belief' was, for him, a mighty and continual *effort*. Suddenly he, and catholicism, became intimate and human. Why (I asked myself) should I not make the same effort? Was it only spiritual pride that held me back? Then began a fearful struggle. It was crucial. It presents itself to me now as one prolonged temptation. How I overcame it, I can hardly say. But my resistance focussed to the single point: Ought I, J. M. M. make the effort, or not? I knew I *could* make it, which I had never known before. Gradually, I reached a kind of peace. I learned that I ought not to make this effort: – that, for *me*, it would be a self-violation from which I should never recover. And, as that became clear, and more and more confirmed by the events of my life, I came to love Catholicism more and more deeply. Its fearful compulsive power had vanished, and I was free to love. Just as a son can only truly love his mother when the anguish of breaking free from her is overpast.[11]

This revealing letter (Du Bos was the only man in whom Murry confided so unreservedly) was written in July 1929. Meanwhile, what actually withheld him was the impossibility of denying that the self-same experience which came to him from the tragedy of the Cross – the self-same assurance 'that, in the last resort, all is well' [7] – came to him from the tragedy of Keats. And had it not come to him originally from the tragedy of Katherine herself? That was the shock which had sensitized him, as nothing else could, to tragedy in all its forms. 'Orthodoxy required me to sacrifice Keats to Jesus, to believe that the life and death of Jesus was *the* revelation.' [10] No such sacrifice was conceivable without a self-violation.

But if he could not sacrifice Keats to Jesus, still less could he bring himself to believe in the bodily resurrection. That the disciples had felt the 'presence' of Jesus after his death, he would freely admit, seeing that he himself had felt the 'presence' of Katherine at the time of his mystical experience. Even so, the only 'resurrection' of which he was fully convinced, either then or later, was this very assurance itself, that love is reborn out of its own defeat. If explanation for the experience there was, therefore, it had to be sought for outside Catholic Orthodoxy.

This was the conclusion inferred in his essay 'Towards a Synthesis', which attracted so much attention in *The Criterion* of June 1927: an important essay biographically, since it signifies Murry's realization that what he was really in quest of was a world-view, as satisfying to 'intelligence' and 'intuition' as Thomism had been to Reason and

Faith. With this, he discards his demand that everyone should face an isolation akin to his own, as a pre-condition of rebirth. The very function of such a world-view would be to forestall the conflict of heart and mind out of which Romanticism is born, and so make possible once more a genuine Classicism.

The *Summa Theologica*, he submits here, represents 'a complete objective synthesis of experienced reality, based upon, or correspond- ing to, a complete subjective synthesis of the experiencing soul'. Since the Renaissance, no such synthesis has existed, let alone been generally accepted as it was in Dante's day. Intuition ('the faculty of apprehend- ing a whole as a whole, and not as the sum of its parts') and intelligence ('the faculty of cognition that operates through concept and abstrac- tion') have gone their separate ways, the one finding expression chiefly through art, the other through science:

> While the scientific mind pressed forward to complete its exploration of reality, on assumptions which were to take three hundred years to reveal their own nature, the artistic mind of Shakespeare was busy with the effort towards a new subjective synthesis. The effort must have been in the main unconscious and spontaneous, taking its rise from a fullness of concrete experience which could not be denied: somehow this concrete experience had at once to be mastered, and obeyed. There was no philo- sophical, no religious system which could be applied to it: no philo- sophical or religious system existed any more.

The 'symbol and touchstone' of any future objective synthesis, there- fore, will have to be Shakespearian tragedy. In other words, it will represent a translation of the tragic into the philosophical *pathos*.

When he wrote this essay, Murry evidently hoped that it might pave the way towards a synthesis of Classicism and Romanticism themselves – of Eliot's views and his own. He was, of course, dis- appointed. In subsequent numbers of *The Criterion*, M. C. D'Arcy contended (no doubt correctly) that the activities he had labelled 'intuition' were subsumed in the Thomist 'Reason'; Ramon Fernandez, that 'intuition' had an intellectual component; Charles Mauron, that science did not rely exclusively on concept and abstraction; and Eliot that '*Nessun maggior dolore* . . .' was a disputable proposition. None of these critics, right or wrong, touched the crux of his argument; none of them shared his problem sufficiently to do so. The only effect of their rejoinders was to deepen his sense of isolation. 'All my hopeful feeling when I undertook that frightful essay has evaporated,' he wrote to Eliot, after reading them: 'It seems that there really is some sort of abyss between us – not humanly thank goodness – but in respect of our ideas and convictions.' [12]

By then, indeed, the only man with whom he still had any 'sense of a common quest' [13] was Young: who, so unlike him in most respects – in his robust humour, his violent tantrums, his unblushing addiction to 'the good things of life' – yet resembled him in this at least, that his theories, whatever they might be, were never merely theories, to be toyed with in thought and subordinated in practice to the continuity and respectability of a career. By common consent of his associates a psychiatrist of genius, Young might, like Murry, have won the highest awards of his profession, but for this passion for truth (combined with a hearty contempt for wealthy hypochondriacs). As it was, his submission to the discipline of the Gurdjieff Institute had been as characteristic as his later commitment to the doctrines of Jung, Adler, Nietzsche and Matrinovic in turn.

Since Katherine's death, and still more since Violet's illness, he and Murry had become close friends. His own friend, Sir Richard Rees, having taken a cottage at Yateley, he would come down from London for week-ends, and there all three would engage in fervid discussions lasting far into the night. It was in the course of these discussions, no doubt, that he familiarized Murry with some of Jung's and Nietzsche's ideas.

Not even Young, however, could shed much light on the problem most exercising him, especially as he could neither share nor sympathize with his impassioned contemplation of the Cross. In fact, it was beginning to be obvious to all Murry's acquaintance, if not to himself as well, that he was becoming 'obsessed with the contemplation of suffering'.[14] Even Marion Robinson, now his secretary and general factotum, plucked up courage to remonstrate, urging him to consult Young professionally, and telling him frankly that parts of the book he was writing were 'hardly sane'.

This was a book on Christ and Christianity, begun in the winter of 1928–9, for which he had taken as a text Goethe's maxim, '*Dass man gerade nur denkt, wenn, das worüber man denkt, man gar nicht ausdenken kann.*' (Goethe, too, was much in his thoughts at this moment – he, too, had groped towards a new synthesis.) By struggling with this, he was hoping, as usual, to clarify his mind: for, whereas most authors write in order to set out ideas they have reached, Murry only set out to write in order to reach his ideas – he rarely knew beforehand what they would be. But, try as he might, it merely 'lost itself in the sands of the old inconclusiveness',[15] adding to his despondency; and at last, in response to Marion's exhortations, he agreed to lay it aside. He had already arranged to submit to an operation on the septum, as a cure for his endless colds: he would go into a nursing home forthwith, and see if he could not do better afterwards.

He could. The operation, though it made no difference whatever to his colds, had another, quite unexpected and far more radical effect, which he detailed a few weeks later:

> I went into the nursing home; I went under a full anaesthetic for the first time in my life, and experienced something which was for me quite indistinguishable from the mystical experience. Strangely enough, though the struggle back to consciousness was prolonged and peculiar, I was only mildly interested in my experience. It seems that I should have been immensely excited by it; but at the moment I felt simply like one who had revisited a country where he had been before. A familiar thing had happened again.
>
> I returned home, and took up the book again. I was as discontented with it as ever. But one small thing was now clear to me. It was interlarded with autobiography. Either I must cut away the autobiography altogether; or I must gather the fragments together, face what I was doing honestly, and write it as a whole. So I sat down and wrote the first section as it now stands. Quite unexpectedly, when I had reached the end of it, I felt that I could go straight ahead. With a strange feeling of relief I put the old manuscript in the waste-paper basket, and began.
>
> Then I realised that my insoluble problem had been solved. The mystical experience and the anaesthetic experience were indeed the same. That identification which had seemed to me, as to others, so degrading, was the key to the real unity of man and the universe. It was all perfectly simple. The last irrational surd had been eliminated.[16]

This was at the end of March 1929. From then until May 5, he worked on steadily and rapidly, the amanuensis, once more, of a book that wrote itself: *God: an Introduction to the Science of Metabiology.*

It might be thought that this discovery would have been disconcerting, to say the least. Although, thanks to Huxley's experiments with mescalin, the identity of the mystical and the narcotic experience is more familiar today than it used to be, adherents of the 'Perennial Philosophy' still commonly avoid the term, preferring to speak of 'similarity' or 'analogy'. Why, then, was it so welcome to Murry?

First, because his own being a 'mysticism of descent', the significance of the experience, for him, lay entirely in the psychological unity it conferred; and secondly, because he had only to acknowledge that a 'relapse of the organism into a condition prior to the differentiation of consciousness' [17] would make manifest the consubstantiality of life with life, to complete a naturalistic interpretation of religion, which, far from impugning that unity, ratified it.

It is this that he proceeds to do in *God*: claiming that 'metabiological' (i.e. psychological) unity represents the latest stage of evolution – evolution being regarded as a progressive realization of wholes; that the individual who attains it, therefore, is veritably a new species of man; and, most vital of all, that this unity is self-perpetuating. For, he submits, even though it spell disaster to the individual concerned, that very disaster, by setting up an inward conflict in the sympathetic spectator, will precipitate a like relapse of the organism, and consequently a like reintegration: 'This is the secret of all great tragedy.' [18] The nature of the universe, in short, is on the side of metabiological unity – all things work together for good! And a universe so conceived is 'harmonious'. It evokes the same awe, the same peace, the same sense of dedication, as used to be evoked by God. It is, indeed, equivalent to God – *deus sive natura* – and being equivalent, renders God Himself redundant.

Thus, from one point of view, *God* represents Murry's attempt to provide that 'complete objective synthesis of experienced reality' which he had already declared to be necessary. That 'every essential element in the great whole of Catholic Christianity has its equivalent somewhere in the system outlined here',[19] that 'in it, conscious Science and conscious Religion become absolutely identical',[20] are among the claims he advances explicitly. He even hopes that, by resolving or forestalling the conflict of heart and mind, it may serve as a 'prophylactic' against mystical experience: 'Modern man must achieve his resolution into metabiological unity less violently, by ways less fraught with the possibility of illusion.' [21] And, granted the validity of the holistic premise which he borrowed from Smuts and Whitehead, the claims are not unwarranted. Considered simply as a world-view, his 'system' deserves a more adequate presentation than he gave it.

His own, unfortunately, was deplorable. Seldom has even an existentialist displayed such contempt for definitions (the key-word itself, 'organic', is used in a variety of senses) or betrayed his ignorance of physical, biological, psychological and anthropological tenets so blatantly by the very terms in which he dismisses them. The inspissated prose-style, the maddening repetitions, the intemperate *obiter dicta*, make *God* a philosopher's nightmare. With so many faults, it is astonishing that it remains a seminal work.

The book, however, does more than present an 'objective synthesis of experienced reality'. It also records a 'subjective synthesis of the experiencing soul': and this is not, as may appear at first sight, of purely biographical interest, since the implicit is once again explicit. When Murry forbore to revise it, he knew quite well what he was about. He did so in order to demonstrate that 'even the most abstract speculations of the mind are as integral a part of their author's organism as the fingers of his hand'.[22] That is actually its main contention, and by any criterion its most important.

Of course it was not altogether new, even for Murry. As long ago as 1925, he had written: 'The philosopher who attains to a vision of the universe which, with his whole being, he can accept for true – and these alone are the philosophers whose work makes an indelible impression upon us – becomes a poet. It is the complete acceptance by the philosopher of his own vision which matters: it is this which excites and fascinates us in our turn.' [23] Such philosophers, in his view, were Plato, Lucretius and Spinoza. Fundamental to 'Towards a Synthesis' was his claim that 'objective synthesis is nugatory unless it rests upon a subjective synthesis of which it is the harmonious and orderly projection'. Indeed, it was just this claim that Eliot, for one, found exasperating: being unable to distinguish it from irrationalism, although no system could satisfy the 'whole being' that failed to satisfy the intellect, nor from pragmatism, although, as Murry pointed out, 'the harmonious correlation of all the truths known at a given time' [24] is as near as we can get to Truth. In reality, it is pure Nietzscheanism.

But to apply the contention to others is one thing, to apply it to oneself quite another: and when, in the Epilogue to *God*, Murry applied it to himself, the effect was overpowering – for it spelt a total detachment, not only from the objective synthesis of which the book was a confused presentation, but equally from the subjective synthesis of which it was a clear projection, that is, from the 'soul' itself. It spelt, in other words, nothing less than the restoration of his vision of six years before; and with that, deliverance and peace.

Now, seeing even his own world-view as but one 'perspective' among many, he could freely acknowledge that 'final truth' was a will-o'-the-wisp, any claim to possess it a fantasy. Hence, among other things, the abrupt disappearance of Metabiology from his writings henceforward. Not that he repudiated his theory, but, in the very act of propounding, he transcended it. As he explained in 'The Detachment of Naturalism', his last important contribution to *The Criterion*:

> No doubt a given individual may make his acquaintance with Detachment by means of one particular natural philosophy, but if the acquaintance be authentic, he must needs end by kicking away the ladder by which he climbed. He will see that a thousand other ladders might have been as efficacious, and that his particular ladder is unique only because it shares the evident uniqueness of his individual history.[25]

Now, moreover, seeing even his own soul as a portion of existence in time, he could calmly acknowledge, not only that the conflicts it underwent were incident to its nature, but that they were the appointed means to its enrichment – and more, that no such conflicts could ever impugn this seeing itself. Hence the abrupt appearance in his writings of the new distinction between 'soul' and 'spirit', 'existence' and 'being', 'time' and 'eternity', which he adopted from Santayana. The very essence of *God*, he was to write a few years later, is that 'the secret of deliverance and peace is to regard oneself impersonally, to be able to acknowledge that one is simply a vehicle or nucleus of Life, where conflicting forces strain after a resolution':

> In this flux and surge of Existence our personal lives are totally immersed, but there is a vision, or the potentiality of a vision, in ourselves which can acknowledge this total immersion. This vision, to which the whole of our personal being – our most secret and precious ideals no less than our animal desires – is an object, must necessarily be impersonal, or supra-personal. I call it pure Spirit; it is the *species aeternitatis* of which Spinoza spoke with authority; it is, I believe, implicit in Jesus' teaching of the Fatherhood of God; and above all, it is 'beyond Good and Evil'.[26]

That supra-personal vision is actually Murry's most precious gift to those who persevere with his works. Whoever makes that his own will, sooner or later, become what he himself is – which (need it be said?) will be something quite unlike Murry.

XIII

SON OF WOMAN

———◆◇◆◇◆———

IF HE WAS EXTRAORDINARY at all, Murry used to say, it was by reason of his ordinariness. In a sense, that was true. There was no literary genius to distract him (or his critics) from his laborious, single-minded quest for 'deliverance and peace': perhaps that was what Lawrence meant when he called his effort 'purer' than his own. And the deliverance and peace he was in quest of were always such as the ordinary man could share: like Rousseau's, his 'mind was central; it never wandered far from the simple, profound and permanent problems of humanity'.[1] The search for a credible religion, which engrossed him down to 1929, was as representative as the search for a way of life to match, which was to engross him for the next twenty years.

Extraordinary he was, none the less, and not least by reason of this belief in his ordinariness. That the integrity he brought to his problems was proportionate to the extremity (if not the eccentricity) of the experience that posed them, he found so hard to admit that, long after his millenarian enthusiasm had dwindled, he still expected his solutions to command an immediate response. This was the case even with *God*. This book had meant so much to him, indeed, that he awaited its reception with more than his usual keenness – and suffered more than his usual disappointment.

Recalling that 'metabiology' was a favourite word with Shaw, he sent a copy to him, reminding him of their past exchanges and, with the deference he always adopted towards older writers, entreating him to read it:

> I think you will understand, if you will read the book, why I am anxious that you should read it. There aren't many people who will understand what I am driving at; you will. I have never made any exertions on behalf of a work of mine before; but this time I must. My conclusions are terribly

[157]

important to me, and if they appear to others who are capable of judging, either crankiness or moonshine, it is equally important for me to know.[2]

Shaw's answer, as usual, is scribbled across the foot of this letter:

> The subject is hackneyed; but if the book is readable I'll read it. But I warn you that if you show the faintest symptom of sentimentality, the book will knock the bottom out of the waste paper basket. Your conclusions about God don't matter a solitary damn to Him (or It) and therefore cannot be terribly important to you or anyone else. So buck up; and carry your convictions lightly and gaily.[3]

Presumably, since the correspondence ends there, *God* did knock the bottom out of the basket.

'That attractive man G. K. Chesterton'[4] was more sympathetic. Not content with reviewing the book, he remonstrated with Murry privately over his 'prejudice against the supernatural', arguing that this was 'merely a mental habit inherited from the mechanical cosmos which nineteenth-century Science established – and which Twentieth Century Science is already beginning to undermine'.[5] But, since Murry's prejudice, though undeniable, amounted to no more than a refusal to have recourse to the supernatural as long as the natural would suffice, the argument made little impression. He was more amused than instructed by Chesterton's epigram:

> *Murry, on finding* le bon Dieu
> Chose difficile à croire,
> *Illogically said 'Adieu'*
> *But God said 'Au Revoir'.*[6]

Of the men whose opinions he respected, Du Bos and Santayana alone were genuinely appreciative, albeit with serious reservations. For the rest, the reception was almost uniformly hostile. The religious – even those who had accompanied him so far – recoiled from meta-biology; the scientific could hardly be expected to welcome a theory couched in such terms; as for the literary, the mere idea of a book with that title beginning with an autobiography was enough to set them tittering for months on behalf of civilized Europe.

This particular reaction, as it happened, Murry *had* foreseen – and not only foreseen, but courted, in a mood of contemptuous defiance provoked by *Point Counter Point*. Soon after receiving Huxley's novel, he had written to Rees:

I couldn't resist looking out the passages about Birlap. I don't know whether A. H. intended him as a caricature of me; but he's certainly too generally intelligent not to know it would be taken by others as a caricature of me. And that, I suppose, is rather disgusting of him.

But oddly enough, it doesn't seem to touch me personally (I may be deluding myself about this, of course; if I am, at some future time I shall surprise myself by feeling an intense hatred of A. H. But it doesn't *seem* possible.) I have been hurt in this way, by D. H. Lawrence, once – made to squirm – by a short-story about myself: but the difference is, I suspect, that I have a pretty deep admiration for Lawrence, and I haven't for A. H. In other terms: D. H. L. can stick the barb deep, and A. H. can't.

And that's about all I can say. I think I know myself well enough to be positive that my only valuable reaction is a feeling that A. H. has rather beautifully confirmed my own strong impression that he hasn't very much notion of what I *am* driving at. I have thought that any time during the last six or seven years; and that, rather oddly – here perhaps is some corroboration of the feeling of yourself and others about him – because I have felt that if he really had a notion he would be on my side . . .

And – one thing more. A. H. has settled it. I must call my blessed book 'God'. It would be monstrous in me to try to safeguard myself against that kind of misinterpretation. One is frightfully tempted to: but it's weakness. So I'm grateful to Birlap for making me realise this clearly.[7]

Though Murry could turn even an insult to advantage, however, he must have known how damaging it would be. In fact, he had been more outraged by Burlap than he cared to admit. His first impulse had been to challenge Huxley to a duel (a vision to which Max Beerbohm alone could do justice); and it speaks highly for his critical integrity that when, in after years, they did find themselves on the same side, he was among the first to praise *Science, Liberty and Peace, The Genius and the Goddess* and *Adonis and the Alphabet*. By the end of 1929, what with *God* and *Point Counter Point*, his fortunes were approaching a nadir.

He followed the book up that winter with *Studies in Keats*, completed just before Christmas, and a series of public lectures at the Mary Ward Settlement, Bloomsbury, on 'A Modern Religion'. The *Studies* were a natural sequel. *God*, after all, could be treated as an extended commentary on the Vale of Soul-Making; the detachment he had achieved at the end was of the same kind as Keats had achieved, when he saw himself with the eye of 'a Superior Being'; and, just as this had made possible the self-forgetful contemplation of the Odes, so it made possible his own contemplation of Keats. 'When I wrote *Keats and Shakespeare*', he explained later on, 'it had never occurred to me to use the word "Spirit" for that which supervenes upon a total detachment from the organic or animal self, and contemplates that Self':

> For that, in *Keats and Shakespeare*, I used 'Soul'. But Soul is not quite the same as Spirit: otherwise I should never have had recourse to the 'new' word. Spirit, so to speak, is the self-awareness of the achievement, or birth of Soul. The psychology that fits my experience most exactly is that of Blake – a fourfold psychology. In *Keats and Shakespeare* I taxed a threefold psychology almost to breaking-point, and I was conscious of the strain at the time.[8]

It was this four-fold psychology that he brought to the elucidation of Keats's experience in 1819, with memorable results. It was to the exposition of this that he also devoted his lectures – in which, for the first time, he adapted a trinitarian formula to his purpose, equating Father and Son with Nature and Soul, and Spirit with the Holy Ghost, aware of their consubstantiality. This was a usage in which Blake was to confirm him.*

* In an illuminating letter to Mr Colin Dawson, dated April 12, 1943 (which reached me after this book had gone to press), Murry wrote:

I still stand by *God*. Indeed, it has never occurred to me to question its findings, so much are they a part of myself. But I understand that the use of the word 'God' in some of my subsequent writings is liable to cause confusion. Actually, I have used and do use it in a sense which I call Christian – but is very closely related to the book *God*. God in this subsequent sense, I use to describe or convey the mode of working of the Power which produces significant variations in individuals, when their obedience to their destiny compels them to endure suffering. I regard Jesus of Nazareth as the prototype in which this working of the power is manifest – the vehicle through whom 'the laws of God' have been made manifest.

I admit, as I say, that this is liable to cause confusion. But the difficulty is to find the language to express myself at all. I do tend to fall back on the traditional Christian idiom, which I use as a language to make myself comprehensible to folks who jib at the language of *God*.

I have had to accept the fact that that book, which I think is the most important I ever wrote, has found far fewer readers than any other. So that I have come to take it for granted that its importance was mainly subjective. It cleared things up for me – and for a few hundred others like yourself – . Consequently, I have had to try other modes of expression. But, as I say, you can take it that, if ever I use the word 'God' in a more seemingly orthodox

16. J. M. M.'s parents with Weg and Col

17. The Old Coastguard Station: the Murrys' quarters

18. Violet with Weg

19. J. M. M. with Violet, Weg and Col

20. James Young with Weg and Col

The *Studies in Keats* prove that his critical powers were never keener; and the lectures were followed by an invitation to contribute regularly and profitably to the newly founded *Aryan Path*. Yet, valuable as these contributions were, he never troubled to collect them: who would have wanted to buy them? Elsewhere, the demand for his work fell off steadily; and his confinement to the organ of an esoteric sect made an ironical commentary on a life-long struggle to 'belong'.

As public reverses multiplied, so did private griefs. Just before starting *God*, he had been 'ominously impressed' [9] by a letter of Lawrence's, written from the Hotel Beau Rivage, Bandol – where Katherine had suffered her first severe haemorrhage. He had hardly finished the book when Sullivan brought news from Huxley of Lawrence's fatal illness. The longing for reconciliation stifling every other consideration, he would have travelled out to Mallorca then and there, but for Lawrence's own prohibition: 'It is no good our meeting – even when we are immortal spirits, we shall dwell in different Hades. Why not accept it. But I do hope your wife is getting better and the children are well and gay.' [10]

Even that must have sounded ironic. Not only was Violet, of course, far from getting better, but the younger child, 'Col', was now suspected of tuberculosis; whilst Murry himself was tortured by sinister pains in the chest, brought on, perhaps, by sympathy. It must have seemed as though the disease pursued him. He had need of all his detachment. 'Don't be depressed', we find him writing to a neighbour, Clare Farr, herself consumptive:

> Try to let the waves go over you. There comes a moment when it's a mistake to fight against things. Ultimately we all have to say, 'Nevertheless not my will, but Thine be done'. The whole point is not to say it until we *have* to. Then we can at least be sure we haven't taken a short cut – to salvation, or whatever it is we all need. When we are stripped naked, we know that most comfort is only words; but the difference is that we know that that is a good thing to know – in some way it's a privilege. I stick up for it to the end: yes, the *privilege* of suffering. It puts people apart: there's a gap across which you can't talk to people who don't know it – and yet, after all, after all, one would rather be on this side than on that. That's what I've found. It doesn't sound much. But it lasts.[11]

---

sense, it always means the Power – call it nature, life, or God, – whose mode of working I expounded to my satisfaction and permanent peace of mind in the book *God*.

To 'let the waves go over' was as near as he could get to 'welcome joy and welcome sorrow'.

Clare Farr, in spite of her illness, was a hospitable neighbour. She had written to Murry à propos Katherine's *Journal*, and been surprised to learn that he was living near by. She remembers him calling one afternoon, 'looking very neglected, in a threadbare grey flannel suit conspicuously mended with braid'. Thereafter he would drop in often, sometimes to chat, sometimes just to sit and smoke or enjoy her cherry jam ('the best outside Russia'). Once he brought Violet with him: 'They were like two children together' – Violet delighted with a pair of Woolworth's ear-drops he had bought her. At other times, Weg and Col would dress up and play in her house – on one occasion adorning their father with a garland of cotton-reels, which he went on wearing all the way home.

He had other neighbours, too – Violet's doctor, for one, who found his conversation so congenial that he was with difficulty prevailed on to take a fee; and Marion Robinson's acquaintance, most of whom sympathized with his predicament, and some of whom, like Mary Horsfall, became devoted friends. Yateley being only thirty-five miles from London, he was by no means so companionless as in Dorset. He would travel up every Wednesday to attend to *The Adelphi*, and longer journeys were not entirely excluded. It was in November 1929, for instance, that Sarah Gertrude Millin arranged a meeting in Oxford with Smuts, who had been nearly as impressed by his review of *Holism and Evolution* as he himself had been by the book – and was by the man. It was then too that he became acquainted with Max Plowman.

Nevertheless, these consolations were hardly sufficient to lighten the sense of failure, public and private, that weighed on him continually. He could not help contrasting his situation with that of other writers he had known, who, at so much less cost, had won so much greater recognition; nor would he have been human had he not, at times, cursed the day on which he had married Violet. '*How* many years have I been doing this sort of thing?' he burst out once, with inexpressible bitterness, at the end of a day's nursing. The answer was: eight out of twelve. Mary Horsfall thought that his 'black moods' must weigh on Violet herself, and it is all too likely. They cannot have been concealed from her entirely. 'What's required of me', he confessed, 'is to look back on our life together and see that it was "good" as the Lord saw that creation was very good. There are moments when I can do this; but it can be done only by a detachment so absolute (and so ecstatic) that it leaves me quite powerless on the plane of existence.' [12]

One is reminded of the ecstasies which had visited him during Katherine's illness: and there were other parallels between his reactions then and now. Just as in 1919 and 1920 he had sought diversion in tennis, so at Yateley he began using golf 'as another man might use whisky' [13] to stop himself thinking – to such purpose that within a year he had reduced his handicap to 12. The children, equipped with miniature golf-clubs, would go with him daily to the East Berks Golf Club, while Young 'blasphemed his way round the course' [14] at weekends. Again, he would spend days on end tending his garden, for the same reason that he had once made a practice of buying furniture – less because either was necessary than because it symbolized solidity and security. The coincidence of the economic Depression with Violet's decline, following that of the War with Katherine's, had so enhanced his sense of the precariousness of existence that the notion of some occult 'correlation between my personal condition and that of the world' [15] was to shape, or distort, his thinking for the rest of his life.

As time went on, moreover, although he continued to wait on Violet as solicitously as ever, his nursing became lifeless and clumsy: 'The primitive physical vitality from which our power to love is nourished was failing within me.' [16] Once more, he was in need of a 'blood-transfusion', and, as in Katherine's day, 'travailed by a longing for physical love':

It always meant very, very much to me, whose life from the beginning has been lived under an immense sense of strain. Physical love, lying with the beloved in my arms, was my repose. It's always been taken away from me. If I went into the wilderness, I could overcome the longing. But the burden of existence makes me long for this release.[12]

The 'truth to life' [17] of the situation portrayed in *The Genius and the Goddess* was one of the things he was to praise in that book.

In Katherine's day, Murry had restrained this longing – indeed, repressed it as 'callous and heartless'.[18] By now, he was less 'idealistic', in the scathing Lawrencian sense of the word. 'True spirituality shrinks from no fact,' he had written in *God*, 'rather, it delights in all facts.' [19] Not only had he learned, at last, to accept his instinctive nature, but he had acknowledged the part played by sexual privation in promoting mystical experience. And since he had no wish for such experience, he saw no reason for restraint. On the contrary, early in 1929 he had been within an inch of trying to contact Marguéritte through an advertisement in a French paper; he had actually written to Mrs Miller; and when, that summer, a wealthy supporter of *The Adelphi*, in whose presence he had broken down completely, insisted on his taking a holiday, put his own wife in charge of Violet, and carried him off on a luxury tour of Brittany, he once more slept with a *petite femme*. It was only because this lapse reminded him that, try as he might to humanize the relation, sexual intercourse without a 'meeting of souls' was as comfortless as sexual abstinence, that he never sought to repeat it.

But if that was the case, what was the 'meaning' of his experience – of the disastrous failure of both his marriages? For no more now than three years before could he bring himself to believe that physiological causes alone were responsible for Violet's succumbing to the same fate as Katherine: 'Physiology can only tell us that pthisis is due to the operation of the tubercle bacillus; as to why and when it operates it can tell us nothing.' [20] Three years before, he had persuaded himself that the fatal element of his 'spiritual' love had been the want of any purpose beyond itself. That was no longer possible. Faith in life had availed Violet as little as unfaith had Katherine. Her doctor had told him that an unwanted pregnancy was often a contributory factor – and that fitted the facts too well to be dismissed: but why was the pregnancy unwanted? These were the questions agitating him all through the winter of 1929–30.

Once again he reached back for help to Lawrence's *Fantasia of the Unconscious*; and this time the conclusion, which had repelled him so violently before, seemed to stare him in the face inescapably: 'The love of the soul was indeed an illusion which led to death'. He seemed to himself, indeed, the man appointed by destiny to prove it; and even if he could not go all the way with Lawrence, even if he could still not 'assert the biological at the cost of the metabiological',[21] this, at least, must be taken as datum. What, then, was the alternative? – 'Just a sort of fondness and loyalty', such as he had once proposed to Vere? . . . It was while he was still wrestling with this problem that the news broke of Lawrence's death.

He died on March 2, 1930. Murry was overwhelmed. Not all their bitter disputes had sufficed to stifle his personal affection; and more than once, during the dark years preceding the illumination of *God*, he had repented his refusal to go along with him to Mexico. It had taken that illumination to convince him finally that he had done right to stand by *The Adelphi*. He was still unconvinced that he had done all that he might have done to spare Lawrence his loneliness, though where and how he had failed he had no idea. Since their exchange at the Café Royal, he had tried not to think on the matter too closely. Now, just when he was being forced to do so as never before, the bond was severed. 'I can't tell quite what my feeling is', he wrote to Plowman four days later, 'but it is something deep, vague, and sickening – *fear* . . . And some vague instinct tells me that I must go away alone':

> Everything that I had to do in these 7 years seems to be done – all suddenly, and at once. The last publication of Katherine's MSS is over; my second book on Keats done – everything done. That sounds tragic. Don't suspect me of suicide. I'm merely registering – like a clerk – a sudden realisation that Destiny has closed a chapter: and that I'm *afraid* of the new one.[22]

Of course he did not go away alone. It was impossible to 'leave, desert, a sick wife and two little children'.[22] Instead, he sped to the South of France to pay his last respects to Lawrence. There, however, he met Frieda: and this time, there was no holding back. 'With her, and with her for the first time in my life, I knew what fulfilment in love really meant.' [23] When he returned after that, it was with 'a clue'.

During the next six months, he wrote the *Reminiscences of D. H. Lawrence*, published by instalments in *The Adelphi*. These were meant to be, and for the most part were, purely personal recollections of the man – of his charm and perversity, the good times and bad they had spent together. As such, they rank high in the legion of Lawrence memoirs. But for Murry it was impossible to stick to that level long. The issues involved in their relationship were the very issues that had been travailing him for six months past; and before even the *Reminiscences* were completed, he was immersed in a full-length book, trying to make up his mind about Lawrence in the same way as he had made it up about Dostoevsky and Jesus.

Son of Woman, despite its subtitle, 'The Story of D. H. Lawrence', was not a biography. The material for a biography was not available, and even regarding the order of the novels, Murry was sometimes at fault. Much less was it literary criticism. He had affirmed Lawrence's superiority as a writer so often, been derided by *The New Statesman* so recently for likening his 'power of dynamic utterance' [24] to Jesus's, that he thought 'his significance as an artist' [25] could be taken for granted. The one and only purpose of his book was to expound and evaluate Lawrence's 'message', on the basis of what he afterwards called 'a dogma of my own making (though Lessing said something to the same effect long before), namely, that the most fruitful way of approaching the doctrines of creative thinkers . . . is to approach them along the path of the process of their own formation: genetically, or historically'. [26]

Lawrence, he stated in the book itself, 'conceived it as his mission to teach us the way to sexual regeneration, and he claimed to give the world the ultimate truth about sex. If we take him seriously, we must take his message seriously.' [27] It was because he himself took Lawrence so seriously that he did not shrink from 'laying bare the physical secrets of a dead man' [27] – or rather, that he overcame his shrinking; and because he overcame it, *Son of Woman* still holds a place apart in the literature under which Lawrence is being buried. Although, undoubtedly, Murry interpreted the message too narrowly, he alone, so far, has tried to evaluate it existentially.

It does not follow, of course, that his interpretation is correct: he himself was to adjust it repeatedly, in the light both of fresh material and of further experience. Nor does it follow that *Son of Woman* is a work of art: it is not. For all his protestations to the contrary, it lacks the objectivity of *Keats and Shakespeare* or *The Life of Jesus*. Like most of his writings of this time, it bears too evident traces of the strain under which he was living – there is far too much tranquillity recollected in emotion; and the last third, at least, might have been profitably curtailed. But it does follow that 'Murry, that prime denigrator and misinterpreter of Lawrence', [28] is a chimera of the academic brain. One need not even have recourse to his letters and journals to show how unfailingly, at every crucial turning-point of his life, his eyes were fastened upon Lawrence. Keats and Jesus alone had a deeper hold. 'We have to complete Lawrence: to round out his message and destiny in ourselves,' he concluded: 'That is what a great man is for.' [29] And that is what he himself did.

Hence his scorn for the many who, without ever having attempted

to put Lawrence's precepts into practice, charged him with traducing
Lawrence; and his amusement at the expression on the faces of
American visitors, *soi-disant* disciples of Lawrence, who expected to
find a mud-worm. Only his own surprise is surprising. After all, he
had long before written of Hazlitt:

> As Lamb said of him, 'he hath a demon'. The 'Liber Amoris' shows
> the nature of one demon that possessed him; another, still more urgent,
> compelled him to utter in public his convictions about men who had been
> his friends. He was, in this as in most things, utterly sincere but a little
> inhuman. Apparently it never occurred to him to make a distinction
> between the public and the private word . . . No wonder, then, that we
> find him . . . asking naively: 'I want to know why everyone has such a
> dislike to me.' [30]

But what were, in point of fact, Murry's conclusions in *Son of
Woman*? Briefly, that the *Fantasia* was right – and therefore, from
the standpoint he was adopting, Lawrence's 'greatest book';[31] that
Lawrence was wrong, in so far as he failed to live by its teaching;
and yet, that a 'failure' so sublime was worth more than any 'success',
save only that of Jesus himself.

The *Fantasia* was right, because it reaffirmed and completed the
wisdom of Keats:

> Keats, in his letter on Soul-Making, accepts the traditional distinction
> of man into Body, Heart, and Mind. Body corresponds to Lawrence's
> sensual centres, Heart to his spiritual centres. 'The Heart', says Keats,
> 'is the Mind's Bible, the teat from which it sucks its identity', and by this
> profound submission the Mind becomes a Soul. 'Yes', Lawrence would
> reply, 'that is true, but only half the truth. Body no less than Heart
> is the Mind's Bible; the sensual centres no less than the spiritual.' And
> Keats would have agreed and been grateful to him for this new clarity
> which did not deny, but only completed, his own insight. Both saw
> clearly that Mind was only an instrument. It was the means by which –
> in this matter of individual self-achievement – Body and Heart, the
> sensual and the spiritual centres, attained to their own self-expression;
> the means by which the true equilibrium of the fourfold being could be
> attained and know itself as existing.[32]

Consciously to attain and maintain such an equilibrium was to become
a nucleus of Life, where conflicting forces strain after a resolution.

Lawrence was wrong because, sensitized as he was to an extremity
of suffering by the exploitation of his 'spiritual love' as a child, and

simultaneously deprived of the chance of fulfilment in marriage, he had sought release from 'the burden of existence' in a 'physical love' which could only spell humiliation and hatred. In other words, whereas, in the *Fantasia*, he had implicitly accepted his own inability to reconcile Body with Heart and Mind, thereby realizing a unity of Heart and Mind at least, elsewhere he had immolated both Heart and Mind to Body, explicitly denying the possibility of such a reconciliation:

> He was far more spiritual, far more capable of love, than other men: he had far more reluctances to reconcile with his animal self than most men have. He was doomed from the first to a lonely struggle, having for the crown of achievement an exceeding great reward. If he had been able to attain his own point of integrity, then he would have been the fore-runner of a new kind of man; he would have been himself the first of a new race of men. But the burden of that destiny he could not bear. He shrank from it; his strength failed him. He became, not the forerunner of the integration of a new man, but the perfect paradigm of the disinte-gration of an old one. In him was manifest the last extremity of the con-flict between animal and spiritual in man; the final abandonment of all hope of unity.[33]

That was Lawrence's fatality. His error was to universalize it, exalting his personal necessity into a gospel for mankind at large.

Nevertheless, because he continued to set himself on record to the end, 'no man in these latter days has given to men so marvellous or so terrible a picture of Man'.[34] It was Murry's intention, by refuting the error, to reveal the fatality, and so to draw all men to that picture. 'It seems like, feels like tragedy', he wrote just after *Son of Woman* was published, to one of the few who understood: 'So does the life and death of Jesus, the life and death of Keats – but it is something far different, of which the shallow-minded have no inkling.' [35] As he saw it, he was performing for Lawrence the service that Judas had performed for Jesus: betraying his secret, in order that he should be 'lifted up'. That Lawrence was 'the Jesus of our times' remained his life-long conviction. It is possible that he overrated Lawrence.

XIV

BREAK-UP

————◦❊◦————

*T*he *Adelphi* for June–August 1930 was a Lawrence memorial number, and with it Murry's editorship ended. 'I began with the hope of Lawrence, and L's approaching death must have knocked it out of my hands.' [1] He entrusted it thankfully to two men who, from this time forward, shift in and out of his life like the figures in a weather-gauge, Max Plowman and Sir Richard Rees. They were the only men to whom he would or could have entrusted it, being the only two who, between them, comprehended his philosophy entirely – whatever part the one disapproved, the other approving. It must have been an uneasy partnership.

Rees, eleven years younger than Murry, had started out on a political career, lecturing for the W.E.A. and standing as a candidate for the Labour Party, only to realize (in his own words) that he 'was not the stuff of which Tribunes of the People are made'. What stuff he *was* made of seems, at this date, to have puzzled him – and not only him. 'So far as I know', Murry recorded, 'R. R. is the man who most exactly agrees with me: yet he has little or no direct experience. This is strange.' [2] Still, a magazine neither party-political nor academic presented obvious attractions to a cultured, modest, well-to-do baronet, still uncertain of his real vocation; and 'he is, indeed, the very man to take charge of *The Adelphi*',[2] Murry concluded.

Plowman was a very different personality. Five years older than Murry, he had been engaged in journalism quite as long as he – by sight and name, indeed, they had been known to each other since *Rhythm* days – and there had been enough similarity in their courses to make it a wonder to both that they had not converged sooner than they did. Plowman too had drunk deep of the Romantics, though Shelley meant more to him than Keats; he too had endured the War, though as a front-line infantryman, not as a 'back-room boy'; he too

[169]

had emerged with a 'faith in life' – so revolutionary as to carry him clean out of the trenches as a conscientious objector; and, above all, he too had undergone a mystical experience – at the bedside of his eleven-year-old son, who had died in 1928. It was this experience which had drawn him to Murry, when, soon after their first meeting the following February, he had learned that Col was seriously ill.

To win Murry's friendship at that time had proved no easy assignment. Bruised and bewildered, he was wincing from every contact, even the gentlest. It was months before Plowman could elicit more than a perfunctory response to his inquiries, not till the end of the year that he secured an invitation to Yateley. Yet, if the two were alike in 'direct experience', their virtues were complementary. All the imagination, devotion and zeal that Murry poured into his books, to the impoverishment of his personal relations, Plowman poured into his relations – to the impoverishment of his books, which amounted in the end to little more than a prolegomenon to his *Letters*. Plowman, in short, had a genius for friendship: and it was this that not only won the day eventually, but made him, for the next twelve months, the dominant influence in Murry's life.

His readiness to join with Rees in taking over *The Adelphi* was only one of innumerable services. As soon as they had seen how the land lay, he and his wife, Dorothy, laid themselves out to lighten Murry's domestic burden too. No task was too trivial for their attention. Was it the children's nurse who had suddenly given him a month's notice? – They found an acquaintance of their own, Maud Hogben, to take her place. Was it the woman he had engaged to wait on Violet whose drunkenness and too evident designs were growing insupportable? – Dorothy interviewed applicants, and promptly secured a girl so competent and cheerful that, from the day of her arrival, his 'little house of the dying grew suddenly warm with life':

> Such laughter as I had not heard for years came echoing every day from Violet's room. There was the same dull hammering of her cough upon my spine. But it was now only the undertone – forgotten in laughter. And Betty's life seemed to pour into Violet's veins. She worked the live-long day gaily; she never went out and never complained: she was happy. And she loved Violet with a careless, living love; whereas my love was the careful, anguished love that is death.[3]

Betty Cockbayne's arrival, in May 1930, coincided with the departure of *The Adelphi*. No wonder Murry could find himself saying of Plowman that he had entered his life at 'a critical moment'! [4]

Meanwhile, their community of thought and experience was also coming to light. While Plowman persuaded Jonathan Cape to reissue *Discoveries*, Murry was discovering in *The Right to Live* and *An Introduction to the Study of Blake* an author who spoke his own language as a native – an author, therefore, to whom he could explain his problems (how to expose Lawrence's errors, for instance, without seeming to claim parity with him), and submit his manuscripts with an invitation to 'criticise them *ruthlessly*'.[5] And Plowman would take him at his word, for 'peers, *peers* are what you need', he realized, 'not girlish admirers who would hang about your neck like garlands'.[6] As his *Letters* prove, he could take sides loyally, not only against Murry's detractors, but equally against Murry himself; and more than once his greater knowledge of men forestalled needless misconception and ridicule.

Even so, it was always as a personality, rather than a critic, that Murry esteemed Plowman most: and that not only because what he had to say mattered more than how he said it. Despite all their community of outlook, there remained one sharp divergence. Plowman, whose illumination had occurred before his son's death, was convinced, not merely that the love it had released in him had helped to prolong the boy's life, but that 'the life of the body is in the Spirit, and if the body can be brought into harmony with the Spirit, health results', in no matter what extremity of sickness. He was still, in other words, convinced that 'it is impossible to set limits to the power of faith when there is an active human will to collaborate'; and for this reason, much of Murry's work since *The Life of Jesus* was bound to appear to him retrograde. Since Murry had neither wish nor will to 're-intoxicate' himself – since he could not go back on *God* – the gulf between them on this issue was impassable. And it was no academic issue.

If disinterested love were really all-powerful, then even Violet's life might be saved! Plowman believed that implicitly. It was the *raison d'être* of his activities. 'I've only one thing I really want to give you', he had written in November 1929, 'and that's an immense belief in miracles.' [7] Ever since Col (thanks to Young's skill) had been put out of danger, his attention had been focused upon Violet. Guessing that her submersion in Murry, with all the dependence and unconscious resentment it engendered, had been partially responsible for her illness, he was persuaded that, if only this could be rectified, she might still be restored to health: and he was prepared to put his faith to the proof.

To Murry, this was just as incredible as Katherine's similar persuasion had been. 'False religion denies the fact of death,' he was writing in *Son of Woman*: 'True religion accepts it, and in that act of acceptance, the soul of man dies and is reborn into the Spirit.' [8] His own faith of three years before, in the efficacy of 'simple love', could, he now knew, like the despair it had brought him to, have arisen only from the confusion of 'soul' with 'spirit'. The 'good' of the soul, as much as its 'truth', was a phenomenon in the realm of time, whose failure or success could neither impugn nor substantiate the 'very good' of total detachment. *Sub specie aeternitatis omnis existentia perfectio est*: it was just this realization that had delivered him from his despair.

He was not fatalistic: the philosophy of *God* is not fatalism, whatever Plowman may have thought. Still less was he resigned, as a man, to Violet's death: the journal which he began to keep in the autumn of 1930 (it had grown, significantly, out of his meditations on Spinoza) makes heartrending reading. But already at the beginning of that December, her doctor was warning him that the end was near; and, though Violet herself did not know it, every witness was on his side:

At 10 o'clock, V. called me in. She said: 'You won't be cross because I called you, Golly?' It's an aching bruise to think that there have been times when I have been cross: but there it is. 'Did Wingfield say anything about my chest?'

'He said it was the old cavity causing the sputum.'

'That's a good thing, isn't it? I don't mind about that. I know it's all rotten up there. What would be awful would be if the good part were getting active.'

'Yes, that would be bad. He says that as soon as the temperature goes down, he's going on with Sanakrisin.'

'Yes, he told me that.'

'How beautiful your little lamp is,' I said. 'It has a little halo.' It looked lovely, and so peaceful, as I sat facing it on the bed, and she looked lovely and happy. There had been just a tremor of fear when she asked: 'Did Wingfield say anything about my chest?' but it was light like a thistledown, easily blown away. Now she was happy, with me there holding her hand.

'It makes just the right light,' she said.

Oh, my sweetheart! Sweetheart – that is the only word. Oh, you who come after me, don't let a woman become your sweetheart. It's unbearable – unbearable: just unbearable. For she will die, and the world will stand still, and your heart will burst. I have had two sweethearts.

And my heart is breaking again, but oh more terribly. Katherine had her life, but Violet has had nothing – nothing: and I have known the end from the beginning. But when the end comes, you know only that you haven't known it, that you can't know it. It is all new, all unbearable.

There is *nothing* to save you – nothing at all.

Why should *you* be saved? Of course, you don't want to be saved. If I could die now, this instant, I would refuse. I must be there, quiet and calm, to the end: to *help*, to love, to help by being there to be loved. Then, afterwards, to die.

Oh help me, Powers, to help – to be stronger than my love, to ignore the anguish. To be *strong*. To be *strong*. TO BE STRONG.[9]

To be strong in this sense was the limit of Murry's hope. To be strong in hope itself was beyond his power.

Yet what man, faced with even the remotest possibility of refutation on such an issue, would refuse to avail himself of it? If Plowman still felt in himself 'an active power to drive back the onset of the disease',[10] could Murry do less than make way for him? To pretend to a confidence he did not share – that was impossible. But to tell Violet about it, and persuade her to give it a trial – that was only right. So, at least, he concluded. And towards the end of the month it was agreed that he should go to Margate with Young for a few days' rest, while the Plowmans took charge of Violet.

The effect was 'magical'. Though he was absent only from December 30 to January 4, Murry came back to a different woman, her 'confidence in herself completely restored'.[11] For a moment, at least, it looked as if Plowman's faith might be vindicated. '*If* a psychological regeneration can cause a physical regeneration, then the miracle will happen. And then my universe will have to be reconstructed again from its foundations.'[11] After this, the Plowmans came every weekend, stopping at The Noah's Ark in Yateley and visiting Violet, for whom they both had a genuine affection. 'She was', Plowman wrote later, 'the most beautifully spontaneous woman I've ever met.'[12]

The treatment, however, had had another, more immediate consequence, not unfamiliar to psychologists, and not wholly unforeseen by Murry himself:

> What I knew she would say, she said. 'Golly', she said to me one day. 'I don't want to tell you this. I know it will hurt you. But I must tell you – because I love you. I don't love you any more. I am in love with Max.' [3]

Hurt? Not, perhaps, as Violet had expected. What little possessiveness he ever had had long since been burned out of his system, and jealousy could find no entry. But the pattern, Murry felt, was repeating itself to the end. Just as Katherine had turned away from him at the last to Orage and Ouspensky, so Violet had turned away from him to Plowman. And for the same reason: because he had shrunk from his duty of reconciling her to death. True, there was 'one *mighty* difference – that whereas I mistrusted Orage and Ouspensky, I trust Max implicitly'.[13] Without that trust in the man, he would never have deferred to the philosophy. But to defer is not to endorse. The issue, he now foresaw, would be one and the same; and at heart he was bitter indeed – not against Violet and not against Plowman, but against himself, for his failure:

> I must simply focus on the fact that she is being made happy – being cheated into happiness. Does one really want the being one loves to be cheated into happiness? At this moment it seems impossible that one can: simply because one does love. I love V. absolutely, therefore I cannot bear that she should be cheated into happiness. Because I love her, I want her to accept what I believe to be the truth, even though it costs her pain. It would be still more pain to me, but none the less that is what I want. And now I feel I have connived at the cheating: succumbed to a terribly insidious temptation to spare myself – an incredibly insidious temptation. And in love it's not possible to spare yourself: the attempt means a heavier burden. And the temptation was overwhelming, because it looked like an effort to spare *her* . . . But it is wrong to mingle Being and Existence: even though it requires superhuman strength not to do so.[14]

Wrong though it might be, there could be no going back at this stage. Violet was now as dependent on Plowman as ever she had been on Murry – and Plowman himself, of course, was still confident of her recovery. It had been arranged that he should give her a room in his own house at Golders Green, where he and his wife could look after her uninterruptedly. 'Either Max's universe must crumble or mine will', Murry wrote that February: 'And it's *better* that mine should.' [15]

Naturally, he did not believe that his own would; nor was he sure that Plowman's would either. If the treatment failed, he foresaw, the latter would lay the blame, not on his philosophy, but on himself or Murry – as in fact he did. But for the time being he kept silent about his doubts, fearing – once again – to give pain. It was only when Violet was on the point of departure that he finally forced himself to confess the 'added sadness and isolation' [16] the arrangement had brought him: and only then, when the insidious temptation was overcome, that he realized how close his very fear of estrangement had come to estranging them. Then, however, sadness and isolation alike dissolved in the joyful acknowledgement: 'Whatever the difference between your belief and mine, we hold one in common: namely, that "sorrows bring faith", are alone truly creative' [16] – and that no power on earth could impugn that fundamental identity.

Then everything 'dove-tailed together'. Suddenly a line from The Marriage of Heaven and Hell that I had been reading a little while before took on all its depth of meaning. 'Everything possible to be believed is an image of truth.' It was the key – the link between us. It was completely satisfying. Then the phrase 'a joyful clarity' came into my head: Now I saw the whole situation, and the rightness of the whole situation, I said, with a sort of joyful clarity. It was now as clear as day to me that two men, like Max and me, each wholly *permeated* by his own belief, which was the same belief differently manifested according to the individual, in what they did together, or in what resulted from their meeting, *could not make mistakes*.

'That's good enough for me, John', said Max, with love and pain and joy in his blue eyes. Then we shook hands.

And with that, which is and will be abiding, we sat still for a while. Then I said:

'That joyful clarity of which I spoke – I suppose that's what you mean by your old joy, Max?'

'That, and nothing else,' he said: and then he quoted:

'For Man cannot unite with Man but by their Emanations
which stand both Male and Female at the Gates of each Humanity . . .
When Souls mingle and join through all the Fibres of Brotherhood
Can there be any secret joy on Earth greater than this?' [16]

This moment of illumination, memorable to both men alike, occurred on February 13. Three weeks later, in a letter to Orgill MacKenzie, Plowman was announcing 'A great event: Murry has been seduced into reading Blake. The old beggar has *got* him. I've been

waiting years for this to happen. The result will be beyond expectation.' [17] With that, the bond was sealed.

Meanwhile, nevertheless, Violet had taken leave of Yateley. And,
in all but words, Murry had taken leave of her. For, though he went
up to visit her weekly, or whenever the situation became critical, and
found her, on at least one occasion, 'radiantly happy' [18] – happier, he
believed, than he had ever seen her before – he himself no longer bore
any part in her life. 'Wittingly or no, Max has done what he wanted
to do – taken the burden from me – the burden, and also the love.
It's not to be regretted, only to be recognised.' [19] That Plowman was
striving might and main to restore her affection to him, he did not
realize; nor did Plowman realize that he, far from collaborating, was
already looking beyond her death.

He was not the only one. Although he was forty-one now, and, with
his monkish tonsure and heavy lines, looked (according to Plowman)
'a good deal older',[20] suffering had not diminished his romantic appeal.
It may rather have increased it. Such stigmata, after all, befitted one
whom, even seven years before, his Cambridge audience had likened
to Hamlet. Violet had hardly reached Golders Green before he was
being abashed by a declaration of love from one of his neighbours at
Yateley – a well-to-do, idealistic, emancipated young woman whom
he had never once thought of in this light.

That was not hard to repulse, even for him. The last thing on earth
he wanted now was idealistic, 'spiritual' love: his whole nature was in
revulsion against it. In *Son of Woman* he had repudiated it once and
for all, affirming his faith that 'the new Jerusalem must be built on
a basis of true sexual fulfilment between achieved individual men and
women',[21] and that such fulfilment was at least as much a matter of
Body as of Heart. To be sure, this was not much more than an
affirmation of faith, since, on the very day that he finished the book,
October 30, he had confided in his journal:

> Probably I couldn't love anyone but a girl. Katherine was a girl. I
> don't know what a Woman is: and never shall. Not that I have avoided
> Woman. It is simply that I can't see, can't make contact with, Woman.
> She doesn't exist for me: a sort of Bogy of whom I hear report. Not in
> my destiny. In my destiny only Love, and the inevitable disaster of Love.

But rather than court that disaster a third time, he would have surrendered his lot in the New Jerusalem.

Even so, the gods must have rubbed their hands when Murry opened his journal with that entry – the journal he was to keep uninterruptedly for the next eleven years. For, though he might be proof against 'spiritual' love, he himself cannot really have believed, except in a moment of despair, that he was 'incapable of anything else'. Had he not still the 'clue' of March 1930 to follow? Moreover, the very extremity of his revulsion laid him open to the contrary temptation, especially when reinforced by gratitude on the one hand, and weariness to the point of impotence on the other.

As early as January 13, 1931, he had been noting the contrast between the 'corruption' of the nurse he had dismissed and the 'warmth', the incapacity for resentment, of her successor. A week later, he had found himself 'according to the law, rather too glad' [22] to see Betty Cockbayne come back from a holiday; and, a few days later still, rather too sorry to hear her announce that she was leaving in March to get married:

> Hell! Absolutely nothing will stay put in this accursed life. It's disappointing of C. 'Never depend on anyone: you will *always* be let down' is all the wisdom I've learned from life. Consider seriously, if V. dies, living entirely alone with the children in a little house. Life as it is becomes more and more utterly burdensome. [23]

Now the projected marriage had come to nothing; and here were he and Betty left alone at South Acre with the children. And the children, however much they might tease her, chanting 'old Ada Cockbayne' in chorus for hours on end, were fond of her too. To them, too, she seemed an improvement on her predecessor, who had only been prevented from beating them by their nurse's hiding the stick. 'You people', said Betty one day, after Plowman had left, 'take life too seriously, too damn seriously' – and her insouciance was medicine to Murry. The upshot was a foregone conclusion.

Violet never knew. She died at 3.30 on the morning of March 30, 1931, in the Plowmans' house at Golders Green. Murry went up that day, and, as he took the ring from her finger – Katherine's ring, which was now to be Weg's* – broke down once more. But only momentarily: 'The agony was overpast long ago: the final pang was when

---

* In a letter dated Sept. 9, 1919, delivered to Murry after her death, Katherine had written: 'I think you ought to marry again. If you do give your little girl the pearl ring.'

she went up to Max.' [24] Next evening, perching the children one on each knee, he broke the news to them:

> Weg thought a little while, and said: 'It's a good thing you didn't die, Dadda. Then we should only have had Maud and Miss Cockbayne. And Col, as usual going to extremes, said 'If Maud and Miss Cockbayne had died too . . .' 'I expect', said Weg, 'that we should have found another house to go in.' [24]

It was not their universe which had crumbled – nor his.

The funeral was held at Golders Green Crematorium on April 2, Violet's parents and Murry's attending. Then, while Rees took charge of the children, Young accompanied Murry back to Yateley. For a few days he seemed to be on the brink of a nervous breakdown; but that passed, and on the 12th he resumed his journal:

> And now I feel that the second great chapter in my strange life is at an end. There will be no repercussions. In or about Christmas time and January I had endured the worst, and though there were terrible moments afterwards, the essential pang was over. I have a duty to V. which I must fulfil – to make a beautiful book out of her little books. I am at peace. Whereas, when Katherine died, my conscience smote me that I had failed her, with regard to Violet I feel, simply, that I did all that I could. At times I failed her, but only in little ways and never essentially. Essentially, I laid down my life for her, as indeed I would gladly have done in the flesh if it had been possible. If there is a place where Katherine and Violet meet, they will be at peace with one another and about me. I have learned what few men have ever learned about life from those two lovely women; I know that there is something for which my soul was hungry which cannot be. Yet to know that does not involve my denying that thing. It wasn't wrong; it needs to be differently sought.

The next day, *Son of Woman* was published, and letters of condolence mingled with hoots of derision from the Press.

PART III

1931–1939

XV

REVIVAL

<hr/>

'A N ORIGINAL MAN IS another name for an experimental man':
the saying happens to be Carlyle's, but Murry would have subscribed to it heartily. His own life was experimental through and
through: not in the vulgar sense, in which 'experimental' is synony-
mous with 'unconventional', but in the strictly scientific. Charles
Mauron once pointed out that the account of 'the effort of living' in
'Towards a Synthesis' applied word for word to the effort of experimental science. It was no coincidence. Like other existential thinkers,
Murry was a thoroughgoing empiricist.

Unconsciously at first, consciously from 1929 onwards, he was in
search of a way of life that should satisfy his entire nature – Mind,
Heart and Body. Consequently, the only 'truths' that were true to him
were such as commanded his entire nature. Yet even these he treated as
working hypotheses, to be tested by the experience they prompted, and,
since experience invariably exposed their partiality, corrected and completed by their contraries. 'The only truth I know which does possess a
real finality', he declared, 'is that which, in one idiom or another, impresses upon men the necessity of a continual self-annihilation: that is
to say, a continual surrender of the finality of one's own truth.' [1]

The paradox was inescapable. Equally inescapable, and for precisely
the same reason, was the seemingly wilful inconsistency that typifies
his work as a whole. What his paradoxy is to the tissue, this inconsistency is to the *corpus*. The one reflects his 'organic' thinking, the
other its organic development. In other words, what Tomlinson, in a
moment of understandable exasperation, labelled the 'Murry-go-round'
represents, in reality, an unbroken dialectical progression.

Unless we apprehend this – unless, that is to say, we ourselves can so
far think organically as to reconstitute the synthesis of which these contradictions are an expression – Murry is bound to remain unintelligible.

The moment we do apprehend it, on the other hand, everything falls into place. It is not only that to see him as a developing organism and his work as 'the involuntary biography of a soul', is to see him as he saw himself – and thus to glimpse that very detachment which, 'in one idiom or another', is the elusive essence of his philosophy; but to glimpse that detachment is furthermore to see that it was, itself, the condition of this development. It was just because, in the last resort, he was not identified with his experiencing self, or the truths consubstantial with it, that he was able to surrender his self to experience, and his truths to the test it incurred.

Such an experimental man (or 'experiencing nature', as he called it) is bound to make headlong mistakes; and Murry made more than his fair share. There were times when he himself ruefully regretted his inability to learn except by experience – especially when, as not seldom happened, the conclusions he reached at such cost were taken for granted by everybody else. Rees once said to him:

> You are an astonishing man, John. I shall *never* understand you. You walk straight on, straight into a brick wall that I can see miles ahead of you. You don't listen to anybody who tells you 'There's a brick wall ahead.' You look, with your eyes apparently open, and you don't see it. And then comes the crash. You run your head into the brick wall. And you pick yourself up and walk on into another. And for some strange reason I admire you for it.[2]

All Murry's friends, at one time or another, felt like that about him – and there is no denying that his hypotheses were often adopted precipitately and uncritically. Yet Rees did right to admire. It would not be to belittle his contributions either to literature or to religion or to sociology to say that, added together, they are of less importance than the way in which he made them. One could dissent from nearly all, and still find that instructive. Which, no doubt, was what Plowman meant when he wrote, 'Though he's never right, he'll never be wrong. – Murry is the most valuable man alive.'[3] He was not only paradoxical himself, but a cause of paradox in others.

What Rees was to discover four years later, Plowman discovered in April 1931, when, to his dismay, Murry broke the news of his forthcoming marriage to Betty Cockbayne:

> His reply is interesting. 'Well, John, you are an enigma. I believe in you, all right, but I'm blest if I understand you.' Then, after a pause in

which I told him I didn't expect it would be all plain-sailing, and that precisely because I didn't expect that, I felt it was right. I had to learn to live differently, to grow roots, to put (as it were) my head in the earth. 'Well, I'm not one to put myself at a gate.' [4]

Actually, Plowman was deeply shocked – as were most of Murry's acquaintance. Even to those who could not be suspected of snobbery or 'idealism', it seemed only too plain that he was, in Jack Common's words, 'laying up another Hell for himself'. But, as always when his mind and heart were made up, he would listen to nobody.

That he was being false to the memory of Violet, he naturally would not admit for a moment. 'I am sorry that you should have to think that of me', he wrote to Plowman: 'But since you must, you must':

Because I do not act in the way you would act, or the way you think you would act, if you were me, you doubt the reality of my love: and the world would think as you do, quote Hamlet as you do –

> The funeral baked meats
> Did coldly furnish forth the marriage-tables –

and the world, like you, would be wrong. Because I do not believe in living on the memories of those I loved and love, I do not love them the less. They are me, part of the inmost fibre of my being, and I owe to them to live out my life till the signal comes. Had I, when Katherine died, followed your inclining, do you think that Violet would ever have been in my life at all? I lived through Katherine's death to the last bitter drop, and followed the sign: Live and learn what I have to teach you. Likewise, I lived through Violet's death to the last, far bitterer drop. You do not think so. But I *know*. Months ago the agony was over. And once again, I follow the sign. You do not like the path it leads me. Neither did my friends when I chose Violet. They were 'right' with the same 'rightness' with which you are 'right', now. I was 'wrong': but I rejoice in my 'wrongness' – in every unbearable pang it cost me.[5]

Many years later, Murry would still cite Goethe's 'Forward over graves' as one of his 'texts for living'.[6]

Betty was a fair thirty-five, a cheerful housekeeper, an excellent cook; she appeared fond of the children, and they of her; above all, she was spontaneous, overflowing with health and unashamedly sensual. What matter that he was not 'in love'? If the Body was in truth the Mind's Bible, no lesson could be less equivocal:

There *is* a simpler kind of love, and it has nothing whatever to do with Annable's heresy. There is the love of simple affection, possible now to

[183]

me because I have entered what is to me the veritable world of spirit. Of old spirit and flesh made up the total man in my belief. Now I know differently. True Spirit is utterly impersonal – that which comes after a final self-annihilation. The individual man remains – the 'creature' of the mystics. That creature loves, with a real love, and with a commitment of its total self, but what is not-self (the true Spirit) it cannot commit. Believe me, I love Betty with such a total self-commitment of the creature. I have brought no violence to bear upon my life – only applied to it a new patience.[7]

Murry's working hypothesis was formed: experience alone could verify or refute it.

The marriage was committed at Odiham registry office on May 23: and from that day forward, he and Plowman began to move apart. Though the personal bond remained unbroken, the cleavage between their philosophies had deepened to a chasm, making further discussion futile – how futile may be seen from Plowman's uncomprehending strictures on *God* in the June *Adelphi*, and the replies by Murry and Rees. 'Murry and I have reached a point of complete disagreement and perfect amity', he told Hugh I'Anson Fausset that month:

It has been frightfully painful getting there for I love the beggar too much for my own comfort. I've an intense regard for him which has only increased with intimate knowledge. But our paths converged only to part and each knows now, I think, that his direction is opposite. Just what it means in regard to *The Adelphi* I haven't the least idea, but at present I can't see myself staying on.[8]

What it meant was that Plowman resigned soon afterwards, as Murry had intended that he should, the editorship passing to Rees, who, needless to say, approved of both *God* and Betty.

Meanwhile, Murry was becoming impatient to be rid of South Acre, with all its 'grinding memories'. 'I feel almost inclined to give it away',[9] he wrote, though in the end it fetched £800. His old dream of a community of friends was in full flower again. He wanted a house big enough to provide a 'retreat' for his brother, Young and Rees; grounds in which the children could run wild; above all, a garden that would render them as nearly as possible self-supporting. On May 1, he and Betty had set out on a tour of Norfolk and Suffolk – the most likely area – and alighted on the very place: The Old Rectory at Larling, on the edge of the Norfolk breckland – a substantial, sunny Georgian building, complete with wall-garden and meadow, which had won their hearts at sight. He had secured it, like the Old Coastguard Station, for £1,000. On July 27 they were off.

Larling was nearly as isolated as Abbotsbury, and itself consisted only of a church, an inn and a post-office, serving the neighbouring farms. To Murry this was one of its attractions. A friendly vicar, whom they had met on their first visit, recommended a first-rate gardener; Betty engaged a maid for £20 a year; they had brought with them, as governess for the children, Tomlinson's sister, Emily. Other company neither of them needed; nor did he regret the Wednesday trips to London. On the contrary, he was delighted at shedding his 'senti-mental admirers' [10] and looking forward to becoming 'the complete bucolic recluse'.[11] At the back of his mind, he may already have fancied himself as 'local big-wig and patriarch, school-manager and J.P.' [12]

In fact, he arrived full of good resolutions: to learn the names of the birds and wild flowers (by the end of the summer he could actually distinguish a thrush), to remedy the shortcomings as a mechanic which had made him ignominiously dependent on Major Robinson whenever the car broke down, and, of course, to resume his interrupted literary work – for, apart from reviews, he had scarcely put pen to paper since *Son of Woman*. The book on Shakespeare was still to be written – it would take, he estimated, three years – and Liverpool University had just awarded him the William Noble Fellowship for a study of 'Blake and Keats'. (He had also accepted a lectureship at the University of Peking, to take effect in 1932, but that was forgotten all about.)

However, it was not until well on in August that the painting and carpentering, scything and felling, were done with, the library recon-stituted – in short, the decks cleared for action. And by then the sharp edge of his confidence was already blunted. Already there were ominous signs that the experiment was not going to work out as intended. Any-way, it was proving harder than he had thought to gather together the broken threads of his life. Throughout the journal entries of that summer and autumn, there sounds a faint but unmistakable elegiac undertone.

Whatever he might say against living on the memories of those he had loved, Murry was too human really to dispense with a ritual grounded in an older, and surer, knowledge of human nature – the ritual of mourning. One of his first acts on occupying his new study was to place Violet's photograph by the desk: 'I couldn't bear the thought of the darling not being near me.' [13] Again and again, in the weeks that followed, we find him reverting to the past. The entry of October 11 is typical:

> Put some Mozart and Beethoven on the gramophone yesterday evening. It brought back Violet, and the gramophone played to her in the cloudy room at Max's house. Those were, without a doubt, the most agonising moments in my life. Yet for some reason when I stare back into them I can't see her face clearly – not as it was then, with the pain and strain of death upon it. Whenever I think of her, I think: What does anything matter? What the *hell* does anything matter?
>
> It seems that now all that concerns me really is simply living from day to day – to shoot things and eat them, to plant things and watch them grow. There remains the world of spirit, which I can enter – the great, calm, impersonal world, where all things are, and nothing cares. Between that world and the world in which I live is a great gulf fixed. In the world in which I live, I have neither ideal nor ambition; it is as though all the vital energy of illusion had been taken away from me. Perhaps I should find content were I to withdraw altogether: but I can't hand Weg and Col over to others, I can't simply say Goodbye to Betty and her unborn baby. No, no: life must be lived.

Again, whatever he might say about the total commitment of the creature, could he ever be really content with a Spirit unmediated by love – or a love that was no medium for Spirit? The evidence speaks for itself. From the moment that Violet had turned away from him, his journal had begun to abound in anecdotes about his small daughter. 'I'm afraid she is terribly fond of me', he writes at the end of one of these: 'As indeed I am terribly fond of her: how can it, as things are, be otherwise? I reared her as a tiny mite, fed her, watched over her: she is named after Katherine, and is the image of Violet, who came to adore her. A great many ideals are focussed in Weg.' [14] How could it be otherwise? Though he had learned the lesson of the *Fantasia* too well to exploit the child's affection, even had he been inclined, his devotion was too obvious to be hidden even from her little brother. There were times when even he showed symptoms of jealousy – and he was not the only one to do so.

No doubt an exceptionally understanding and well-balanced woman could have waited patiently for this elegiac note to subside, as in the fullness of time it would have done. But Betty was neither the one nor the other. Her temper had been a by-word in her family long before Murry entered her life; and if she was simple and passionate, she was also blindly possessive. Probably she was aware of his dissatisfaction even before he was – for, though incapable and contemptuous of reasoning, she was not devoid of feeling – and the sense of something eluding her worked in her blood like a fever. Before they had been at Larling three months,

> She came to me, quite unexpectedly, one day, and staggered me by asking me to let her go away – for ever. If I would give her twenty pounds, that would be enough. She would get a room, and go to work as soon as her baby was born. She besought me to say 'Yes!' 'Let me go out of your life – for ever. Please! Please!' She stood before me like a slave before her master, and pleaded. She was never to plead to me again. I was equally horrified and bewildered. What on earth had come over her? What she wanted was fantastic – impossible. We were not unhappy. And anyhow the baby was mine as much as hers. It would be our baby. It was our duty to make a home for it together. We had made a home for it. 'This lovely house' – and it was a lovely house – 'we chose together for our life together. I just don't understand.' And I just didn't. The whole thing was incomprehensible. I couldn't even believe she was really serious. She was. The next day she tried to run away, and had got half-way to the railway-station before I knew she was gone. I overtook her, and persuaded her to come back. She came neither willingly nor reluctantly, as one submitting to Fate.[15]

The Fate was not only to be hers. Long before the end of that year, a pattern was beginning to establish itself which was to confirm his friends' worst forebodings. 'This looks like being my baptism into direct knowledge of the Female – the thing that I have always eluded,' he is writing early in September; and already the ominous question has posed itself: 'Am I attracted only by two kinds of women – one that I kill, the other that kills me?' [16] It has posed itself, indeed, only to be dismissed as better befitting a Stavrogin: but sooner or later, clearly, the working hypothesis will call for amendment.

Thus, it is not surprising that Murry should have found himself 'still far removed from the working vein' [17] – that he should have been faced, in fact, with what he would call, in mystical terminology, one of his 'periods of dryness'. Though he continued to turn out reviews for the *Literary Supplement*, and to immerse himself in Goethe and Blake, his writing itself only added to the sense of futility. What, after all, was the object of saying things that nobody understood? Why labour to communicate conclusions to be lived, when the most that his readers wanted was opinions to discuss? The little *rapport* he had ever had with the literary world was by this time completely dissolved. As Peter Quennell was to jeer a year or two later: 'Did not his posthumous attack on D. H. Lawrence "Son of Woman", that queer essay in "destructive hagiology", as Aldous Huxley aptly entitled it, knock the last nail into the coffin of a never very brilliant literary reputation?' Not for the first time or the last, he was beginning to wonder whether his right place was not in the Church.

On June 7, after reading Mauriac's *Vigile*, he had confided in his journal:

> It came over me again that the only 'society of awareness', the only possibility of communication on a basis of tacitly accepted spiritual discriminations, is still to be found in the Christian Church. Christians, like Altermann and Claudel – even like Maritain – can say things with the consciousness of an understanding audience, which when I say them outside the specifically Christian frame of reference – and that is not essential – seem to drop unregarded into an abyss of silence and incomprehension. Perhaps this is appearance merely and the reality is different: but that is what I feel.
>
> And then I begin to wonder, once again, whether it is not the duty of one who has so intimate a sense of the 'truth' and significance of the Christian religion as I, to enter this society, as being one of
>
> > the best that speak this language
> > Were I but where 'tis spoken.
>
> And then the old, old question rears its head: 'Is it just spiritual pride that holds me back?' And the old, old reply. 'No, you are tired, and flinching from the harder path. The accusation of spiritual pride is only a temptation, for you – a siren-call to comfort and safety and friends. You are weary of your own loneliness, and long to be understood.'
>
> This is a moment of the supreme wavering – supreme, in the sense that is a flickering of the most secret me, the finest point of my soul. And when it came to me again this evening I found some comfort in the thought that even this almost sickening flux and reflux is to be *endured*, truly endured, accepted as a positive destiny, as something of worth, as my own particular service to God.

The conclusion affords a beautiful example of Murry's 'Negative Capability'. Always, rather than take a decision which his whole being could not endorse, he would resign himself to 'uncertainties, mysteries, doubts', until circumstances presented the clue.

Now, for a moment, it looked as if the clue were to hand: for not only was his house an old rectory (a fact that secretly pleased him) and the Vicar his personal friend, but, in a hamlet like Larling, to cut oneself off from the church would be to cut oneself off from the community. Soon he found himself, almost instinctively, attending the Harvest Festival – and shocking Rees with the notion of taking Orders.

In the remote countryside, one realises what a focus of 'light' the parish church has been and potentially is; how tawdry and superficial the school is by comparison: what a wonderful basis for true education the English Church might be – true education being the awakening of the awareness of 'spirit'. In church, we do for the moment if not actually 'stand apart' (which is always an individual achievement) at least make a space in our lives – symbolic of that spiritual space which we must create and enter. And, God knows, symbols are too rare in this polypus of modern life for the richest of them to be cast away and lost.[18]

Nevertheless, to attend church on Sundays was one thing; to employ in public what he still regarded as the metaphors of Christianity, quite another. Besides, was anything substantial to be gained from the compromise, in England anyway? Did professing Christians really share his concerns any more intimately than others? 'If Christianity were real, if the values and discriminations explicit in Christianity were really understood and shared to-day, no-one would be shocked by "Son of Woman".' [19] Did Christians even share what was rapidly becoming his deepest concern of all – to achieve a measure of social justice?

In after years, Murry came to believe that it was his frustration of spirit at home as much as anything else that diverted his thought at this time from religious to social problems: and probably that was true. It is significant that this 'social solicitude' [20] dated from the previous winter, when, after a fervent perusal of R. H. Tawney's *Equality*, he had confessed to Plowman, 'I suppose it's because I have failed that I begin to turn with longing towards building the Kingdom of Heaven on earth.' [21] At the same time, as he told Rees, 'the moment the pressure of my individual life and circumstances was removed by Violet's death, I was bound to take up the fiery cross again'.[11] It was also a quite natural sequel to the establishment of his personal philosophy, indeed to that philosophy itself.

Moreover, as always in his case, objective factors interacted with subjective. By now the Depression was at its deepest. That February, lecturing on Lawrence in South Wales, he had seen for himself, and been appalled by, the condition of the unemployed miners. A few months later, he had to write off his entire capital of £3,000, which, from idealistic motives, he had invested in German reconstruction. These sharp reminders of the nature of capitalism were quite enough of themselves to pose the Condition of England Question.

Like many others, anyway, he began to look with new eyes towards Soviet Russia. Not that Russian Communism bore much resemblance to Tawney's Christian Socialism, least of all after Stalin had abruptly ended the experiment in economic equality, turning 'a possible swan into an unmistakable goose'.[22] Unlike many others', Murry's were critical eyes. But, undeniably, there was some truth in what Rees submitted, 'that materialistic communism is, in a way, the physical and political counterpart of the thing that you represent in the realm of ideas and mind'. What, after all, had he been expounding ever since 'Towards a Synthesis' but a 'complete materialism' (or naturalism) as the ideology of a new social organism, to which the arts could be as integral as they were to that of the Middle Ages? 'We have to work for a new orthodoxy,' he had written as long ago as 1929, 'a Catholicism without God.'[23]

Leninism – an incomplete materialism, reducing man to a function of his economic activities – clearly provided no such orthodoxy. 'Russian Communism', he wrote in the September *Adelphi*, 'is a symbol, not an example, to the West':

> It is a symbol because it is based on a complete denial of transcendentalism; it is not an example, because it is based on an incomplete and palpably false materialism. The philosophy of Russian Communism, as Canon Quick truly says, is a biological pragmatism. And that is disastrous: so humanly disastrous that I take it upon me to prophesy that Russian Communism will not survive for very long in its present form.

What Leninism failed to provide, however, Marxism might. Within a few days of writing these words, Murry was deep in *Das Kapital*.

The result was electric. 'I do not suppose', he was to surmise a few years later, 'that many men of to-day, and certainly not many Christians, know the experience of being consumed even to tears by the reading of *Das Kapital*.'[24] It does seem unlikely. Yet he himself had hardly laid it down, and begun, hesitantly, gropingly, to clarify his ideas on paper, before his pen took wings – before, in such a state of inspiration as he had not been possessed by since *God*, he was writing *The*

Necessity of Communism. And the reason? It is given in the book itself, a better title for which would have been: 'What Marxism Means to Me'. He took as his motto the words of *The Communist Manifesto*:

> Just as in former days part of the nobility went over to the bourgeoisie, so now part of the bourgeoisie goes over to the proletariat. *Especially does this happen in the case of some of the bourgeois ideologues, who have achieved a theoretical understanding of the historical movement as a whole.*

Both Marx and he were such bourgeois ideologues; and what fascinated Murry in *Das Kapital* was precisely that vision of the historical movement as a whole. He had long been accustomed to interpret history dialectically: only by so doing could he invest it with a 'meaning' that satisfied heart and mind. To that extent, he was prepared for what he saw. But his own interpretation had been confined to the realm of ideas and mind. To see it now extended to the realm of economics was, for him, simultaneously humbling and exalting.

It was humbling, because it exposed the magnitude of his own 'idealism'. Consciously engaged in promoting the brotherhood of man, he had all the while been unconsciously participating in a system of economic relations that not merely stultified his efforts, but made crisis and catastrophe inevitable: 'I was appalled by the revelation of my own self-ignorance, and by the thought of my own long dream-existence ... It was almost nightmarish that one who really did believe in the possibility of a decent human relation between men should suddenly discover that nine-tenths of him was unconsciously working to prevent that decent relation.' [25] That the 'reality' of contemporary man was social remained always, in Murry's eyes, Marx's greatest and most durable contribution to twentieth-century enlightenment.

On the other hand, this vision was exalting, because, at the same time as it accounted for his ineffectiveness in the past, it pointed the way towards completely effective action for the future. By demonstrating that there was 'in existence a great body of men ... whose interests make the same demand upon society as our disinterestedness',[26] it proved that 'the hour had struck when disinterestedness could become completely active, when its action was no longer condemned to incompatibility and inefficacy'.[27] This was the crucial revelation, which spelt for Murry a new reintegration. Once again, his heart's desire was ratified by the finding of his mind; once again, he was 'whole'.

Furthermore, to the eye of detachment, it was apparent that just such wholeness would be the decisive factor: for, while the revolution was inevitable, only such a combination of 'ethical passion' with 'intellectual objectivity' [28] could evoke from the bourgeois ideologue a readiness to sacrifice his all; and only such a readiness on his part could convert the event from 'a thing of terror' into 'a thing of joy'.[29] *The Necessity of Communism* presents a dialectical materialism complete enough to include the dialectical man; and it was to the bourgeois, first and foremost, that it was addressed.

Yet, when Murry himself thought of the possible sacrifice entailed, of 'houses and lands, wife and children' – when he thought that he might have to give up Weg! – he 'simply collapsed'.[30] The period of dryness ended in a torrent of tears.

Mr Middleton Murry embraces Communism

21. Cartoon by Thomas Derrick in *The Bookman*, April 1932

22. J. M. M., 1935

XVI

SOCIALIST AT SEA

————◆◇◆◇◆————

HAD MURRY LIVED IN the seventeenth century, there can be no doubt whatever that he would have taken his place beside Fox and Harrison as the founder of some dissident, millenarian sect. Even as it was, his cry was the same as theirs: Repent, and flee from the wrath to come! Only, the wrath he predicted was secular – the 'unimaginable catastrophe and horror' [1] of war; and the repentance he preached, social – the supersession of capitalist individualism by the equalitarian 'economics of Jesus'.[2]

In *Das Kapital*, he more than once said, he heard the voice of a modern Baptist: and he owed it to Marx that he was able, at last, to enter fully into the eschatological expectation of primitive Christianity. From 1931 onwards, the apocalyptic note is seldom far absent from his writings. It is one of the things that gives them their unique air of realism. Has not 'that remote and to us fantastic belief of the Jews of the time of Jesus . . . the belief that the world was on the brink of a universal cataclysm . . . suddenly become the conviction, or the fear, of every thinking and imaginative man to-day?' [3] One sometimes gains the impression that, while the generals were preparing for the war before, he was preparing for the one-after-next.

The religious individualist of 1923 had re-emerged as a religious socialist, in the fullest sense of the words. He saw now that all the traditional truths of Christianity, once they were applied to the real, the social man, took on a new relevance and urgency; and it seemed to him, as he finished *The Necessity of Communism*, as if everything he had lived through hitherto had been merely a preparation for this hour: he was being 'tempered to make a Socialist without illusions'.[4]

The book had taken a fortnight to write. On the day he finished it, November 9, he wrote to Plowman:

Ah, you don't know – yes, *you* do – how profoundly happy I am. The old impersonal act of faith in founding The Adelphi is justified. – all the bitter, bitter struggle justified. – all the pangs – the awful rendings from Katherine, from Lawrence, from Violet, even from you – justified. The dead live. Blessed be the unutterable name of the Lord.

The same ecstasy pervades all his correspondence and journal-entries of that month. He was living in 'a fever of zeal' [5] – his old preoccupations become suddenly so unreal that the very idea of reviewing seemed farcical, though his living depended on it.

Here in Marxism, truly understood, was a cause in which Christian and non-Christian, supernaturalist and naturalist, could unite. The idiom was immaterial – or rather, a matter of pure expediency. If he himself favoured the materialist, that was mainly because it was less compromised than the religious in the ears of the working man. 'Communism is a world-philosophy – the equal and inevitable successor of Catholic Christianity. It has to be as dogmatic *and* as catholic as Catholicism – only more so, in both respects. And this it is. We can be all things to all men.' [2] So much and more he explained in letter after letter to Plowman and Rees, to both of whom he sent the manuscript of his book, and both of whom objected to the 'Postscript to Christians' – the one for its hostility, the other for its indulgence, to the Church (in the end he discarded this). He had written, he believed, 'our English Communist Manifesto'.[6]

'If ever there was a bloke who knew what it was to be "converted", I am he.' [7] It was true – and no Fox or Harrison outstripped him in missionary fervour. Now it was his friends and neighbours who were the objects of his evangelism; now the leaders of the New Party (to which he had previously promised his vote) – Sir Oswald Mosley, John Strachey and Harold Nicolson. 'I am sure that I can convert these people. You may think me over-confident: but we'll see.' [8]

We did. The first-fruits of his proselytism were not conspicuously blooming. The Vicar, for one, proved obdurate. His only response to Murry's exhortations was 'an hour's inconsequent diatribe on the theme that the unemployment allowance, which enabled those who didn't want to work not to do so, was the cause of all our discontents. If only the unemployed had "the right spirit", all would be well.' [9] Thereupon, Murry discontinued his church-going.

Equally obdurate, and far more disappointing, was Plowman, who, after reading *The Communist Manifesto* and actually seeming to agree, abruptly drew in his horns, refusing to commit himself to any line of action whatever. Marx, he averred, was merely an analyst; a movement based on negations could never achieve anything constructive; and anyway, he himself was not a materialist. In vain for Murry to contend that *his* materialism was 'not the materialism which Marx held *consciously*', but a 'delighted acceptance of "the minute particulars" ',[10] and that such men as they, who owed their very insight to their privilege, had no right to demand altruism of the workers: Plowman would not budge. The correspondence, extending over four months, concluded in mutual exasperation, a 'final' farewell – and, a few weeks later, in agreement henceforward to confine their discussions to Blake.

Rees, on the other hand, became Engels to Murry's Marx; and, at the psychological moment, 'Marxist Providence' [2] itself stepped in with a coincidence hardly less encouraging than the arrival of the *Fantasia* eight years before. Murry describes this in a letter to Clare Farr:

A queer thing happened when I arrived here. A man came to deliver petrol and oil. I had to sign a chit. He looked at the signature and said: 'You're not *the* Mr Murry!' At which I couldn't help laughing. 'I've never been called *the* Mr Murry before. But I daresay I am.' 'Well', he said, 'I've just finished reading one of your books for the seventh time – "God".' Naturally, we became very friendly: and slowly (on his weekly visits) he told me all his life. He had been a revolutionary Socialist since he was a boy. His father was an old Anarchist-Communist. He had been all through the war, and finished up in 1918 as a bad case of 'shell-shock'. Suddenly, after a time during which he was the leader of the revolutionary organisation of discharged soldiers and sailors, which failed, he had had a mystical experience. In trying to find out what to make of it, he had run across my books. Then he had given up revolutionary socialism, feeling that it was no use unless men were 'converted'.

So I had to convert him back again into becoming an active Communist once more. It wasn't difficult: he was just waiting for the hint. Now, he and I are sort of blood-brothers. He is the finest revolutionary leader – of the pure working-class – I have met; and we are working hard to build the beginnings of a new party in Norwich. And I feel in my heart that we are going to succeed, though it's hard work.[11]

He and A. W. Votier had joined the Norwich branch of the Independent Labour Party in December.

Having committed himself to the Marxist hypothesis of the 'historical mission' of the proletariat to establish a classless society, Murry had no thought of remaining merely a theorist. He had to identify himself with one or other of the working-class parties, and this seemed the best available. The Communist Party was ruled out, as both intellectually and instinctively out of touch with English conditions. Leninism might be right for Russia, where revolutionary passion could be taken for granted and violence had been unavoidable; just because it was right for Russia, it was wrong for England, where democracy was taken for granted and such passion conspicuous by its absence. 'An English Lenin doesn't, can't look like Lenin. I don't mean he looks like Max. But he must combine – in a living dynamic unity – Max and Marx.' [2] The Labour Party, on the other hand, was discredited by its sorry performance the previous summer. If an English Lenin could not look like Max, still less could he look like MacDonald. He might conceivably look like James Maxton. As an instrument for revitalizing what was left of it, therefore, only the I.L.P. remained.

Needless to say, neither Murry nor the I.L.P. welcomed the other unreservedly. Whilst he 'took to Maxton rather violently' [12] at their first meeting, in February 1932, he viewed the rest of the leaders askance; and whilst Tawney greeted *The Necessity of Communism* warmly, pronouncing it in a letter, 'the best book on the foundations, as distinct from the methods, of Socialism, which has appeared in England', most of the Party theorists were dubious about its 'ethical passion'. And when Murry went on to contend that Marxism, since it proved the system and not individuals at fault, was a doctrine of forgiveness, not hatred, dubiety turned to downright distrust. He was not more 'bewildered at first by the lack of theory' [13] than they were by the theory he proffered. To them, he seemed to be emasculating the movement; to him, they seemed to have emasculated it already – especially the Pacifist element, which, he told Geoffrey Sainsbury, ought to be 'extirpated'. (His prejudice against Pacifists dated from Garsington days.) Having capped his reading of all Marx's works with an intensive study of Lenin's – he was soon in a position to bandy texts with any Party fundamentalist – he was looking for a resolute, disciplined, revolutionary party, quite unlike the existing I.L.P., 'a sect without sectarianism'.[2]

Thus it is no shock to find him, at the very outset of his political career, projecting 'an independent organisation':

> The kind of organisation I have in mind, would be very small – and consist of men sustained by an absolutely 'religious' conviction of the necessity of complete self-sacrifice. They would be bound to one another, and also bound in the case of the better-off, like myself, to live with the

utmost economy and devote the whole of their surplus of money to the movement. It would be a sort of 'religious' brotherhood. The poorer members would contribute a minimum of a penny a week: but everywhere there would be most stringent conditions of admission. It would simply be a fighting nucleus everywhere – of men whose principles were so deep within them that they *could* not fail.[14]

So he wrote in January to Votier, who had reported that the Norwich comrades were wondering what his 'little game' was. It was only when Rees prudently nipped this proposal in the bud that he agreed, for the time being at least, to stick to his last – on the one hand, to go on trying to convert the bourgeoisie, on the other, to take simply such steps as the Party required of him. 'I really am a terrible novice, politically,'[15] he admitted.

However, it was not long before the Party was requiring a good deal. He had followed up *The Necessity of Communism* with a pamphlet, *The Fallacy of Economics*, and, with Rees's concurrence, turned *The Adelphi* into a theoretical organ of the movement. Soon he was in continual demand, not only as a contributor to Socialist papers, but as a speaker on Socialist platforms. That February, being booked to lecture on Blake at Liverpool University, he took the occasion to address a Labour meeting also, on 'The Religion of Communism'. There was standing-room only. At the end, 'They gave me a really wonderful "ovation". And one old fellow got up and sang out that all who could must go and hear what I was saying about Blake: so they turned up in a body and again in the evening – as a sort of bodyguard.'[12] Both the meeting and the reception were typical of scores to follow – in Lancashire, the Midlands, London, Scotland, South Wales. Days at a stretch were devoted to arduous tours: and as a propagandist, Murry excelled.

However dubious the Party intelligentsia might be about his ethical passion, the workers both understood and appreciated it. Indeed, they and he found common ground in their mistrust of the intelligentsia. If it was a relief to him to face an audience that wanted to learn, and to learn for the sake of living, it was a still greater relief to them to find a speaker with something to say, and no other object than to say it. And Murry could be a captivating speaker. On the platform, his self-evident sincerity and fervour dispensed with any need for oratorical tricks, making them look foolish in others. Off it, his unaffected simplicity and modesty (he charged himself with being rather too deferential to old-time Socialists), his readiness to listen and learn in his turn, recommended him immediately to men inured to professional politicians.

Moreover, he practised what he preached. 'Our money, our energies – all are required of us,' [16] he declared: and his own money, equally with his energies, went to the cause unstintingly. All the royalties on *The Necessity of Communism* were ploughed back into further advertisement. A Socialist printer, whose equipment was threatened with sequestration, got £100; the I.L.P. itself another. He rarely accepted payment for lectures or articles; continually, in unobtrusive ways, assisted his unemployed friends – some of whom hardly deserved it. His expenses were such that he could not have afforded, even had he thought it proper, to send his children elsewhere than to the village school. For the time being, all desire to be a local big-wig was suspended. In fact, since rediscovering his grandfather's world, he had grown rather proud of his proletarian origins: and there was something appropriate to the moment in a letter he received from his father (who, as he never read a line of his books, must have come across a review), castigating this latest relapse: 'You stick at nothing. You have denied God; now you will deny your country . . .'

All in all, it was not without reason that, within twelve months of his enrolment, he had become a force to be reckoned with, not merely in the Norwich branch, but also in the I.L.P. at large. And for once, things seemed to be moving his way: for naturally he supported wholeheartedly the mounting demand for disaffiliation from the Labour Party, which came to a head at the Bradford Conference of 1932. The decision taken that August to reconstitute the Party on a basis which, rightly or wrongly, he believed himself to have been 'the chief influence in shaping',[17] marked, indeed, the apogee of his enthusiasm. It was then that he bestowed on Maxton the highest compliment in his vocabulary, pronouncing him 'quite as remarkable as D. H. L.'; then that he divined in Fenner Brockway 'an English Stalin'.[18] The dictatorship of the proletariat – by which he understood a parliamentary majority pledged to suspend the two-party system and silence all opposition, until collectivization had been accomplished and economic equality secured – seemed to him just round the corner. Within three years at most, he foretold, the Party would be 'a great power once more'.[19]

Then came the check. Inspiring all Murry's activities, his strategy no less than his propaganda, had been that familiar Marxist hypothesis of the 'historical mission' of the proletariat. That there existed a great body of men whose interests made the same demand on society as his disinterestedness, was the very foundation of his politics. It was in conformity with this that he had laid himself out to create an incorruptible, avowedly equalitarian leadership, 'around which the working-classes may reform their ranks when they have learned by bitter experience of further defeat that the policy of the Labour Party means nothing for the workers, but a slow process of economic impoverishment and spiritual starvation';[20] in pursuance of this, that he had urged disaffiliation. And the result was calamitous. Cut off from its rank and file, clinging obstinately to their traditional loyalties, the I.L.P. found itself, for the first time in its history, condemned to ineffectuality. The split, he had written, might prove as historic as the Bolshevik-Menshevik schism of 1905 – and so, in a sense, it did. It signalled the beginning of the end of the Party.

As usual, he was prompt to draw the lesson. That he had some of the qualities required of a Marxist revolutionary cannot be doubted. It was just by virtue of that Marxist readiness to revise theory in the light of practice, which he carried over from his personal life into his political, that he became something totally different. The countless literary Bolsheviks of the '30s, who found out ten years later what they had derided him for telling them then, might do well to bear that in mind. Already by the following spring, he was recommending reaffiliation, on terms proposed by the Socialist League; and himself refusing to stand as an I.L.P. candidate for his native constituency of Peckham, where he stood every chance of election.

But the lesson, driven home as it was, not only by the ineffectiveness of the I.L.P. at home, but by the ominous effectiveness of the Nazis abroad, cut deeper than that. For if, in truth, the working class was so little enamoured of Socialism that it would exchange its political freedom for the economic security of State Capitalism – then, State Capitalism, not Socialism, was inevitable. Instead of collapsing, as every Marxist had presumed that it must, the system would go on and on adjusting itself, by means of massive rearmament, till further adjustment became impossible, and it exploded in war. The 'proletariat' was a fiction, its 'historical mission' a myth.

Was brotherhood, then, not practical politics after all? That Murry was loth to admit. Week after week, as his journals show, he brooded over the problem; and eventually, partly in consequence of an ardent perusal of Reinhold Niebuhr's *Moral Man and Immoral Society* (which he wrote up in such terms as he had not used 'about any book since *Fantasia of the Unconscious*'),[21] a possible solution did present itself. Since war was the life of Capitalism, he argued, the death of it could only be – peace. In other words, 'If, *by any means*, that "inevitable" expression of the capitalistic contradiction in war is aborted for twenty years, then there is bound to be a revolutionary change in the economic structure.' The moral, therefore, was plain: 'The main long-view policy of Revolutionary Socialism in the proximate future is to organise resistance against war.' It was all the plainer because 'for some time to come there is likely to be far more general sympathy for active war-resistance than for revolutionary Socialism'.[22]

This conclusion, or rather 'provisional diagnosis' reached 'on January 18 1933 at 10.15 p.m. after a tiring fortnight',[23] immediately set in train the process Murry called 'convergence' – convergence, that is, between the findings of his intellect and the promptings of his heart. For already three months before, in the course of his study of Blake, he had discovered that non-violence was a moral imperative. He had written to tell Plowman so:

> I discover that my antipathy to violence in the cause of Socialism is absolute. It contravenes the very realisation which made me a Socialist – namely, the realisation of Eternity. How it contravenes it is very hard to say. But I can best express it by saying that, since the realisation of Eternity is potential in every living man, it is a crime against Eternity to take a man's life. The realisation of Eternity is the highest joy. It was in order that others should have the opportunity of that joy, in order that the crass obstacles which the human selfhood interposes between men and the attainment of that joy [be removed], that I became a Socialist. For a little while, it is clear to me, I lost the end in the means.[24]

The same moment of discovery is commemorated in his journal, in letters to Rees and Votier, and in his book on Blake. Now that it coincided so exactly with the demands of the objective situation, he lost no time in submitting his diagnosis to Maxton.

By this time, however, it was too late. Conscious of its electoral impotence, yet unwilling to discard its dogmas, the Party was fast inclining in the very opposite direction – towards a united front with the Communists and romantic insurrectionary tactics. And Maxton himself was unsympathetic. Instead of examining Murry's thesis on its merits – which was all that he had hoped – he brushed it aside with the remark that 'the English working man would not be inclined to "turn the other cheek" '; while Murry himself, 'too shy, too modest with these politicians', forbore to press the issue. 'I contented myself with saying that people didn't understand the difference between non-resistance and non-violent resistance (which he didn't, himself).' [25]

Thenceforward his disenchantment proceeded apace. Though Hitler's advent to power dispelled his Pacifist sympathies, it did not restore his faith in the I.L.P. Whatever else that might be, it was no 'experiencing nature', prepared continually to surrender the finality of its own 'truth'. Within a matter of months, the English Lenin had become 'a man who dabbles in revolutionism merely in order to be certain of being returned in Glasgow to be the star-turn of that very congenial club in Westminster';* [26] the English Stalin – but there is no need to say what the English Stalin became. By July 1933, 'I think that as a practical proposition . . . Socialism is almost hopeless', Murry was writing: 'The working-classes do not want it, and never will want it. To be a Socialist demands a degree of intellectual emancipation and imaginative understanding that is, alas, very rare, whether in the working-class or any other.' [27] A sense of proportion had descended upon him.

Brotherhood, after all, was not practical politics; after all there was no short-cut to the millennium. For the second time in ten years, he was finding himself back where he had started: and, exactly as ten years before, when his hopes of revolutionizing the world were thwarted, he was beginning to dream of 'a community whose force shall be measured not by the numbers of its professed adherents, but by the intensity and spontaneity of their devotion to the work before them: work on themselves, and work on the world without, shaping some small fragment of it into harmony with the world within'. It was during that August that, yielding to his recurrent desire to establish a more personal relationship with his readers than was possible now through *The Adelphi*, he announced a new periodical, *The Wanderer* – like Johnson's *Rambler* to be written entirely by himself and issued to private subscribers. Almost the first article, 'On Marriage', concluded with a meditation on Lawrence's New Mexico project and his own refusal to support it.

That project, he still maintained, had been misconceived: 'There is no possibility of such escape from the existing order as Lawrence

* Murry's final, much fairer, estimate of James Maxton is to be found in *The Free Society*, p. 291.

dreamed.' None the less, 'the desire to create "the nucleus of a new community" is deep and deeply justified':

> It is not, nor can it be, enough to work through 'politics' (or through 'religion') to bring the new order into being. It is not enough, subjectively: for the man who intuits the necessity of 'a new community' must needs demand that its nucleus shall actually exist. It is a new mode of living for which he is prepared; and he must demand that it shall begin now, not because of any 'Utopian' impatience, but because the new mode is actually being born in him, and clamours for embodiment, lacking which the vision itself must fade and become instead of an imaginative reality, conjunct to life, an intellectual conception divorced from life. Nor is it enough objectively: for action towards a new order must be continually re-inspired and purified by its own part-realisation . . . Unless we already half-become members of the new community, no matter with what intellectual clarity our politics are directed towards its realisation, we shall find our action fatally confined within the limits and practice of the old order. We shall have 'new community' on our lips and on our flags: but we shall belong to the old one . . . The creation of the nucleus of the new community is the sole guarantee of the integrity and vitality of the politics that is aimed at the creation of the new community itself.[28]

A fresh 'convergence' was already under way.

Over the ensuing months, this was reinforced by his reading of history, particularly seventeenth-century history: for 'I comforted myself with the thought that there had once been an English revolution – a real one; and I turned to that'.[29] As he immersed himself in the documents of the Great Rebellion, it became clear, first that the decisive factor had been the conviction of Cromwell's Ironsides, who 'knew what they fought for, and loved what they knew'; and secondly, that if they knew it, it was because the freedom of worship they were demanding was actually practised in their ranks – because, in the words of Henri de Man, their end was implicit in their means.

It was this reading also, as much as current events, that convinced him, once and for all, of the preciousness and precariousness of parliamentary democracy. What had been won at such cost must not be abandoned. Socialism, he began to insist with ever-increasing emphasis, must present itself as the completion, not the negation, of democracy: and that not merely because there was no other way, in England, of 'having the biggest battalions on the revolutionary side';[30] but, still more, because 'democratic political rights, however specious in regard to the underlying economic reality, are still the symbol and expression of an individual freedom which we cannot afford to sacrifice without disaster'.[31] The fashionable Marxist dismissal of these rights as 'super-structure' or 'sham' exasperated him:

> Even a small advance, democratically won, won that is to say by the conscious and determined exercise of their individual political freedom by the people, is worth more than a spectacular advance achieved by the surrender or the abrogation of those freedoms. It is the same with the nation at large as it is with the individual man: what he learns by his own effort, by the painful struggle of his own mind, is of far more enduring worth than any conclusion he learns at second hand.[32]

There speaks Murry's inmost mind.

But it was to no purpose, so far as the I.L.P. was concerned – well and truly infiltrated as that was by the Communist Party. At the York Conference of March 1934, the unanimous resolution of the Norwich branch, which he had helped to draft – 'This Conference asserts that in a country where the industrial working-class is in a majority, a Socialist regime can only be firmly based on the enlightened democratic assent of the majority of the people' – was heavily defeated, along with that of the Lancashire Division, whose delegate he was, and out of loyalty to which alone he had forborne to resign:

> It was, indeed, an honour that had befallen me: to be deputed by the Lancashire I.L.P. to move their resolution – an honour of which I was deeply sensible, but a responsibility to which I felt myself unequal. When I stood on the rostrum and turned to Maxton to ask how long time I might be given, my heart was thumping. When I heard the sentence, 'Ten minutes', knowing that speaker after speaker would be given twice and three times so long to move meaningless resolutions on sympathetic, or hostile, or circumspect, affiliation to the Comintern, I knew my time was over with the I.L.P. I was overwhelmed by the sudden realisation that there was not one among the leaders of this party of 'Marxist Socialists' who had a glimpse of the inward meaning of this crisis in the Lancashire Division of the I.L.P. I have written somewhere that Marxism is a triumph of the imaginative vision. And at that moment, on that rostrum, at the last conference of the I.L.P. at which I shall ever be present as a member and a delegate, a touch of the Marxist imaginative vision visited me. The great historical Socialist party of Britain celebrating its triumph-ant metamorphosis into a party of Marxist Socialists by alienating its Lancashire Division! It was too grotesque, too sinister! I could have

turned upon the leaders behind me with the solemn word of Oliver Cromwell: 'I beseech you, think it possible that you may be mistaken!' [33] Instead, he resigned directly afterwards.

So that was that. Not only he, but the Socialist movement itself seemed to be back where it had started – where William Morris had left it with the warning, 'The only practical or possible task of a Socialist movement was "to make Socialists".' [33] Murry's disillusionment both in politics and in politicians was complete. Though the Lancashire dissidents duly reconstituted themselves as an Independent Socialist Party, on the lines he had proposed to Votier two and a half years before, and he himself duly paid his subscription, it was no longer as a party that he envisaged it, rather as 'a non-political movement with a political aspect'. [34] In fact he soon afterwards rejoined, as an individual member, the South Norfolk Divisional Labour Party. 'The way out is plain', he mused on the evening of Dollfuss's assassination: 'But the world will not take it, and men will not believe it.' [35]

However, 'I've felt down and out like this many times before in my life', he resumed, 'And I shall emerge again, I don't doubt, with a new hope and a new conviction.' [35] And of course he did. There could be no real return to the starting-point, for himself any more than for the movement. If Socialism had proved harder than either had foreseen in the first flush of their enthusiasm – well, that was the lesson to be learned; and even if no short-term policy was practicable, even if catastrophe was inevitable, still something could be done to keep the flame of fraternity alight through 'the grim time coming'. [36]

That summer, at the suggestion of an unemployed miner, an Adelphi Summer School was held at Glossop, in Derbyshire, to give the Independent Socialists a chance to meet and discuss their future. Some fifty to a hundred were present, proletarian and bourgeois in approximately equal numbers; and 'that experience of mutual discovery', Murry was to write a couple of years later, 'is, and always will be, vivid in my memory'. [37] It was vivid not only in his. N. A. Holdaway, the Marxist theorist, and Plowman, the Pacifist idealist, were no less impressed: so much so, indeed, that he could not resist reminding the latter that it was 'a justification of precisely the path you wouldn't agree to go with me', since 'where, but in the rough and tumble of the working-class Socialist movement, should I have gathered together such a sample of "proletarians"?' [38] But for Murry, at least, it was more than a blessed respite from the acrimonious controversies of the I.L.P. 'Our brief fraternity was to me veritably the evidence of the human possibility of the classless society. Community among Socialists was itself a religious experience. I came away renewed; and I felt that I had a clue.' [37]

That Summer School was decisive. What was needed, he was now convinced finally, was a community – or better, a multitude of such communities – where men whose Socialist idealism was in danger of dissipation or corruption by the exigencies of the day-to-day struggle could renew their failing inspiration. This, and this alone, could safe-guard the Labour movement against a repetition *ad nauseam* of the sorry history of the past forty years. It was in the exaltation produced by this discovery – he was moved once again to tears – that he com-posed the magnificent essay on Cromwell, 'From the Lamb to the Bull', with which *The Wanderer* ended.

Before he could do anything further to put theory into practice, however, he was faced with a two-months' lecture-tour of the United States, commissioned earlier in the year. On December 23, accordingly, he was embarking at Southampton on the *Vollendam*; and New Year's Day 1935 saw a bewildered New York audience, assembled to hear the uproarious Liam O'Flaherty on 'The Art of Enjoying Life', being treated, instead, to a very sea-sick John Middleton Murry on 'The Agony of John Keats'.

XVII

LARLING HARVEST

————✦◉✦————

MURRY'S CONVERSION TO COMMUNISM did not shatter all the good resolutions with which he had arrived at Larling. Little by little, as the reverberations died away, his life gathered itself together according to the original pattern. Conferences and lectures, after all, took up only a small part of the year; most of his writing was done at home; and between writing much of his time was devoted to work of a practical nature, which, while providing a useful counterpoise, also helped to bind him to the neighbourhood and neighbours.

It would hardly be correct to speak of Murry as a 'low-brow': yet he had never been altogether a 'high'. As long ago as 1917, D. L. Murray had noticed his fellow-feeling for 'ordinary people' and the tastes he shared with them – his enthusiasm for old-time music-halls, for example, or the cup-ties he attended with Katherine (they were both keen supporters of Tottenham Hotspurs), or the first Chaplin films. Although all but crushed under weightier concerns, these tastes had persisted; and, however chequered his relations with intellectuals, the bonds of affection and trust he established with the simpler people who worked with and for him only strengthened with time. With them he was at ease, as they were with him. He himself often doubted whether his choice of literature as a profession had ever been more than a *faute de mieux*; in no other, it is certain, would he have felt so completely cut off. The very recurrence of the words 'simple', 'simplicity', 'quite simply', in the most tortuous passages of his books, reflect his incessant striving to overcome his imposed intellectualism. Literature, for him, was a means to an end that was not literary at all – and he was already on the way to achieving it:

> Very gradually, in the country a sense of community returned to me. I now had real neighbours. And slowly, my religious faith, which had been real, but private and ecstatic, passed out of my consciousness into

[206]

my being. At the same time my work and my living became continuous: the impatience of the intellectual dissolved away. There ceased to be any essential difference between my work at the desk, at the carpenter's bench, in the garden or the woods; or between my work and my wife's, my maidservant's or my man's.[1]

By the end of three years, he could truthfully claim that, wherever his head might be, his roots were firmly stuck in the earth.

He was always a creature of routine. Life at The Old Rectory began sharply at 7.15 a.m., winter or summer, when the one servant, Ruby Batley, rang a bell in the hall. By 8 o'clock he was already at his desk, answering letters if the post had come (it was brought on foot by a woman from the village, as at Lark Rise). From breakfast till lunch, and tea till supper at 7.30, he wrote. He usually slept for half an hour after lunch, never retired later than 10.30 p.m. The afternoons were consecrated to the carpenter's bench, the garden or the woods. Though he himself had a poor opinion of his craftsmanship, that was not generally shared. 'He was no cack-handed fumbler,' says J. H. Watson, who knew good work when he saw it: 'When digging a garden he had a clean style, and the finished plot was of professional standard . . . The spade went into the ground the full depth of the blade, with great economy of effort, the hall-mark of good digging . . . He could hive a swarm of bees as to the manner born, without fuss or bother.' [2] Bee-keeping, like book-binding, was one of the hobbies he took up soon after arriving at Larling.

Rees had his own rooms in a wing of the house, which he would sometimes occupy for months at a stretch; Young, having married soon after Murry (they were witnesses at each other's weddings), took another Old Rectory hard by; Richard Murry came down at week-ends. Otherwise visitors were few, and not much encouraged. Murry was happier exchanging gossip and practical information with Mr Hewetson, the poultry-farmer next door, or his wife, who ran the village school, than entertaining literary or political acquaintances. He was happiest of all working silently side by side with Mr Hewit, the gardener – 'Bodge' to all the family – with his children just in or out of earshot. Then, and perhaps then alone, he enjoyed hours of such 'quiet and brimming self-abeyance' [3] that it was harder to disbelieve than believe in the reality of the classless society.

To Clare Farr he wrote in July 1933, when his Socialism seemed to have reached a dead end:

[207]

It's pretty depressing to realise that Socialist politics is no cleaner than any other. Personal vanity, personal self-interest, the cheap desire to have applause rather than speak the truth – it's all there. And there come moments when it seems unfair to have to struggle against it all. Then I go to bed, as I'm going to in a few minutes, and wake up to hear my dumpling of a baby daughter talking thirteen to the dozen, and everything seems possible once more. By heaven, life could be a good thing if people would only let it be, instead of trampling one another in the mud.

That's how things are with me! Up and down, up and down. I have to fight sometimes to resist the desire to go right away and live on two-pence a day. And then I feel thankful that I have children. They chain one to the earth. One is always brought back to the point that one must struggle to make it a little better world for their sakes and the hundreds of thousands like them. It would be awful to think that they should get to 44 – I shall be that in a fortnight – and find the world even more night-marish than it is! Still more awful if they had to look back and say: At this point my Father wilted. So politics it must be. But one needs to be disinfected night and morning.[4]

When the professional politician discourses of that little homestead to which he would so gladly retire, but for his duty to his country etc., constituents are tempted to smile. In Murry's case it was the truth. 'Life could be a good thing if people would only let it be' – it is the refrain of his journals too.

That little phrase, 'to let be' meant much to him. All that he understood by 'detachment' was implied in it. For there was nothing forced, or stoical, or self-watchful about this detachment (as even Plowman imagined). On the contrary, to see oneself simply as a thinking, feeling, developing organism, which could no more take responsibility for its virtues or failings than the cherry-tree for its blossom, meant, for him, to see others in exactly the same light – 'as his equals', therefore, 'or his brothers: leaves of the same Tree';[5] and, just as it endowed him with the 'will to pure self-emergence',[6] enabling him to develop freely, so it endowed him with the will to *their* emergence, enabling them to develop freely as well. 'To let be' was a positive thing: 'first, not to demand, not to interfere, not to possess – to *let* be; second, to cherish, to liberate, to suffer to unfold – to let *be*'.[7] A society in which each, surrendering possessiveness if not possessions, the better enabled the others to *be*, was what he really denoted by Socialism. A better name for it might have been the Kingdom of Heaven on earth.

It was also what he denoted by the family. Indeed, it would not be

23. The Old Rectory

24. Max Plowman

25. Sir Richard Rees with Betty and Mary

26. J. M. M. with David, 1939

27. J. M. M. with James Maxton (front), Joseph Kruk and Dick Wallhead, I.L.P. Summer School, Caerleon, 1932

28. J. M. M. with H. R. L. Sheppard (centre front), P.P.U. Camp, Swanwick, 1937

going too far to say that he looked on the family as a miniature common-wealth – or Kingdom of Heaven. After all, he observed in an essay 'On Equality', written at the same time as the letter, what Jesus meant by 'love' is 'plainly revealed by his utterly new and repeated comparison of the condition of man in respect to God with the condition of little children in respect to their parents':

> It is a pity that theologians do not generally know much about children. Theology and celibacy have always gone together. But, as D. H. Lawrence was the first to point out vehemently, children do not 'love' their parents; they are too sound, too living to do that. Their attitude to their parents is that of the leaves to the tree, the kittens to the cat. They rely on them, treat them as the main part of the solid old furniture of life. To make them start 'loving' their parents is an abuse and a disaster. The egoism of the parent enslaves the child-nature to its service. 'He who loves God', said Spinoza, 'cannot endeavour that God should love him in return.' Like-wise, he who loves his children cannot endeavour that they should love him in return. It is a violation of the nature of love.[5]

He would even go so far as to say that 'Socialism was Socialists – individual men and women, who knew the necessity of letting their children be.' [8] And judged by this unusual criterion, he himself was a pretty good Socialist. Although, like most religious reformers who take to politics – like Shelley, like Godwin, like Gandhi – he sometimes made the best the enemy of the good, he seldom ran the opposite risk of losing sight of the end in the means.

Not that he was the ideal father, supposing such a monster to exist. In this as in other connexions, his total absorption could make him distant and cold: he was oblivious to a surprising amount of what was going on around him. But if he was rarely demonstrative, he was never demanding. One of the strongest and purest motives of his life was the determination (which he recognized in Coleridge) that his children should not be cheated of their birthright as he had been; and throughout these years of political embroilment, the relationship he enjoyed with his daughters was the best he knew. Had his relationship with Betty been one half as good, life at Larling would have been idyllic.

Alas, it was not only in the commonwealth at large that people would not let life be. The acquisitive spirit, as he so often said, was ubiquitous. What went far towards spoiling everything – what may have impelled him into politics in the first place, and what his politics certainly exacerbated – was the stark incompatibility between himself and his wife. It was not for nothing that he spoke to Clare Farr of going 'right away'.

Their baby daughter, Mary, was born on January 27, 1932. For months before then there had been scenes. Emily Tomlinson had been driven out of the house; so had Marion Robinson, who had taken her place. Altogether three governesses had found the situation unbearable, to say nothing of servants and visitors. Now, instead of drawing them together, the child herself became a bone of contention.

> We fought over everything, the servants, the neighbours, the children. I would have her treat them as human beings, as individuals with their own inalienable right to be. We fought, above all, over Mary – I fought, desperately, for Mary – simply that she might be. 'Mary is mine', Betty would cry. 'She came out of me: she is part of me.' And to me it seemed terribly true, and terribly false.[8]

Not only to prevent Betty becoming the stepmother of legend, but to prevent her 'possessing' Mary, was now Murry's thankless task.

Of course there were lucid intervals, otherwise neither of them could have endured as long as they did. And with every fresh reconciliation, his hopes bloomed afresh. Reading his journals, one can but marvel at his inextinguishable optimism, or obtuseness. Long afterwards, he marvelled himself, concluding that he must have been 'one-third part hero (or saint) and two-thirds sheer bloody fool' [9] – which was the opinion of most of his friends at the time. Even after three and a half years, on the eve of his departure for America, he was still persuading himself that they had 'come through', and, in his homesickness there, indulging dreams of an idyllic homecoming.

It was all illusion. That very detachment which was the breath of life to him, was death to her. If, after one of her outbreaks, he withdrew, emptied his mind of all thought, and waited immobile until what he called 'the peace of God' flooded into his heart, then indeed, 'with it there came a sense of absolute renewal, of complete immersion in the cleansing water of Forgiveness, and a cool and beatific knowledge that I had been given the strength to build up again what had been destroy-ed':[10] but what was this but a further manifestation of the spirituality she hated and feared? If, on the other hand, goaded beyond endurance, he struck her – then, of course, she was content, and more than content: but he himself felt degraded. The only thing these two had in common was their incapacity or contempt for dissimulation. Had either been of the sort to 'make the best of it', for the children's sake or merely for appearance', they would never have married in the first place. As it was, The Old Rectory became the scene of a struggle so elemental that Lawrence alone could have depicted it.

This was the struggle which underlay his *William Blake*: for, though Blake meant many things to Murry, he came to mean, first and foremost, the prophet of 'the Regeneration of Generation' – that is to say, the man who had striven most consistently to bring marriage into harmony with the spiritual life, to realize a relationship equally satisfying to Heart, Mind and Body. It was because this was now, and henceforward always to be, one of his own main preoccupations, that he turned so avidly to the Prophetic Books. No more than *Son of Woman* is *William Blake* literary criticism. One might call it a psychological study, had the word not been largely pre-empted by psychopathologists. Whatever the correct description, it is a powerful battery of 'life-wisdom' for those with the incentive to tap it.

At an early stage in his research, he had discerned the analogy between Blake's progression from *The Marriage of Heaven and Hell* to *Milton* and his own from *Keats and Shakespeare* to *God*. This was the golden string which he seized on to thread the labyrinth. There is no mistaking the personal accent of a passage such as the following:

> Not the defeat of the ignoble desires of the human heart gives birth to the doubt that is Doubt indeed; but the disappointment of its noble longings, when all that is most precious to the individual soul is seen to be irrelevant to the inscrutable purpose, or the blind process of the universe. Then, it seems, the inward fire is quenched, the inward light put out. What the individual man knew within himself as the very pulse of life is suddenly still. He dies; as surely as he will die when his fleshly heart beats no more, so surely now, when his spiritual heart has ceased to beat, he dies. And that condition, of veritable death in life, is Doubt indeed.
>
> From that condition, if a man emerges, he can emerge only by one way. He must see, with direct and simple certainty, that the desire in him which bruised itself to death against the bars of experience, was a desire of the Self. He had sought, though he knew it not, to impose his own terms upon Life, and to make it conform to his pattern. But he is in Life not to command, but to obey; not to form, but to be formed. And this liberation from the Self is the essential realisation of all true religion.[11]

This was the liberation he himself had undergone in *God* – the Felpham might have been the Yateley 'moment' – and this alone would have been enough to illuminate the symbols from within.

Nevertheless, it is clear that as time went on his attention became more and more closely riveted on those 'torments of love and jealousy' chronicled in *Vala*, as well it might. Not only had Blake identified the apparent resistance of Time to Eternity with the antagonism of the old social order to the new, but he had personified this antagonism in his wife. For him, therefore, the liberation had taken the form of an over-whelming experience of Forgiveness, issuing in reconciliation and con-summated in the act of love. 'There is a point at which, for Blake, the emotion of Eternity becomes absolutely identical with the perfection of human tenderness. That would have been, I think, the point of illusion for Goethe, whereas for Blake it was the pinnacle of reality.' [12]

Thus, in Blake Murry found what he needed most – a ratification of his own conviction, or faith, that the 'man-woman struggle', far from being sterile or deathly, might itself be made 'the means to a rare spiritual achievement':[13]

> The doctrine of true marriage, of which Blake and his wife offered so memorable an example, is instinctively held by many simple people. They know the experience which Blake described as the destruction of the Negation and the redemption of the Contraries, although his language would be meaningless to them. The passing from sullen and embittered hostility between man and wife into a condition of mutual recognition of the Identity (although that positive condition is, in the nature of things, no more secure or undisturbed by relapse, than any other condition of grace) is the true potentiality of marriage. Achieved, it is completely invulnerable to the efforts of modern iconoclasts to persuade mankind that marriage is an obsolescent institution. It is now, what it has been, a sacrament, an outward and visible sign of an inward and spiritual grace. Whether the man and woman can proceed from the outward and visible sign to the slow conquest of the inward and spiritual grace, depends on them, and chiefly on the man. But that the steadfast relation of marriage is the path to a truly human perfection of the spiritual life admits of no doubt whatever.[14]

The motto of his book might have been that 'casual equivalence' [15] which he picked out of *Jerusalem* and treasured: 'The Minute Particulars, the Mutual Forgivenesses'.

William Blake was completed in December 1932 – the fruits of two years' intensive study, in the course of which Murry had brought almost all his experience, past and present, to bear on the elucidation of the Prophetic Books. Plowman, an authority here, hailed it immediately as 'the best book on the subject so far',[16] and his verdict is likely to stand, since even those who repudiate mysticism must allow that it takes one mystic fully to understand another. 'John has the greatest insight of any man living,' he declared roundly: 'How he has understood so much of Blake in the time at his disposal I simply can't imagine.' [17]

It is difficult for anybody to imagine, conversant with Murry's political and domestic entanglements. That the books he wrote during these years are uneven in quality is less surprising than that they were written at all, especially as he was no rapid writer and did all his own typing in addition. The same frustration that lent zeal to his politics, however, must have stimulated his productivity: for, since Katherine's works could be relied on to bring in £500 a year, his need for money was not really urgent, and certainly the reception of his own gave little encouragement.

By 1933, his reputation had touched bottom. Now that both the clericalism of the '20s and the Communism of the '30s have fallen out of fashion with the intelligentsia, it is not easy to realize the extent of the prejudice against him; but Rayner Heppenstall probably did not exaggerate when he called him 'the best-hated man of letters in the country'. Though the eructations over *Son of Woman* had begun to subside (outside America), the stench still lingered; and *The Necessity of Communism* had done nothing to dispel it. On the contrary, there was little to distinguish between its treatment by the Communist *Daily Worker* and the Catholic *Colosseum*. It actually pre-supposed some independence, on the part of a young and unknown aspirant to letters, to produce such a sympathetic examination of his thought as Heppenstall's *John Middleton Murry: a Study in Excellent Normality*. One of the reviews of this book is worth quoting, not because it was exceptional in its references to Murry, 'than whom surely no more discredited square-peg-in-a-round-hole ever rattled in a Bloomsbury hat-rack', but because it was typical:

> From the Old Rectory, his integrity-factory, Mr Murry continues like a renegade free-lance vicar to preach his lugubrious apostatical sermons and in the intellectual underworld he still enjoys the support evidently of a small fan following. Before the public he feels compelled at rather frequent intervals to 'change his mind' and 'bare his soul' and in general to luxuriate in the role of the very ill-used but at all costs really 'sincere'

man, ever eager to endure fresh spasms of martyrdom . . . As to Mr
Murry it is difficult to see how anything of a wide and durable value can
emerge from the labours of such an indiscriminate, submissive and parasitic
patient. Although, of course, after tunnelling through the collected works
of Shakespeare, Keats, D. H. Lawrence and Marx, even a worm would
inevitably expel, in its cast, a few till then unventilated novelties . . .

This happens to be a Mr Hugh Gordon Porteous in *Time and Tide*, but
it could equally well have been any one of two dozen others.

Murry himself, needless to say, knew what value to attach to such
vulgarities (his friends were commonly more indignant than he); and,
owing partly to the irritation involved, partly to his reliance on time to
set matters right, he made a principle of not replying to personal
criticism. But he was not made of steel; he was far from luxuriating in
ill-use; and even a worm may turn. Catherine Carswell's fictitious
account of his relations with Lawrence was too much even for him.
'Good God!' he burst out in his journal, after a belated reading of *The
Savage Pilgrimage*, 'I have acquiesced in so much slander that I almost
begin to believe that there is something in all this. I have to shake myself to remember the truth . . . It is time to lance that imposthume' [18]
– and lance it he did: not only getting the book withdrawn and corrected,
but, since it had already gained wide publicity, reissuing his own
Reminiscences, with as many of his reviews of Lawrence's books as he
could remember (he overlooked the most laudatory of all, that of the
Fantasia in *The Nation and Athenaeum*) and a point-by-point refutation
of Mrs Carswell's allegations.

It may be doubted, however, whether this served any useful purpose.
True, Frieda, who had been among the loudest in her protests against
Son of Woman, was appeased. It was soon after this, in November 1932,
that Murry stood witness in court on her behalf in the dispute over
Lawrence's will, and she spent an amicable week-end at Larling. But
the general reaction is epitomized in the story told by Harry T. Moore
concerning 'a well-known British woman novelist', who, without even
waiting to hear Murry's case, told Mrs Carswell, 'I have only a few
pounds to my name in the world, but they're all yours if you'll use
them to fight Murry to the wall.'

Besides, Murry was habitually at his worst defending himself, even
when one hand was not tied behind his back by consideration for
Frieda or others. The stronger his case, the weaker he made it appear.
Those emotional lapses into archaism – 'Ah me!' 'verily', 'passing

strange', 'exceeding great' – were the despair of his most ardent well-
wishers ('John's done a weep', the sigh would go round the *Adelphi*
office); while, as Rees once told him, he neglected the virtue – for he
did not lack the gift – of 'irony and understatement'. The absurdities of
The Savage Pilgrimage could have been more effectively disposed of in
a few well chosen sentences than in all the heated pages he devoted to
them. And what could be more inept, in a public defence, than a preface which 'perchance only one living soul will understand'? *Reminiscences of D. H. Lawrence* contains many good things, but they were
not of the kind to raise his standing with the public. *William Blake* sold
fewer copies than any of his books since *Dostoevsky*; *Between Two
Worlds* was generally spat upon (only Havelock Ellis went out of his
way to uphold it); it was not until the publication of *Shakespeare* in
1936 that his prestige began to revive.

Between Two Worlds itself, like *The Wanderer*, was a product of his
political relaxation in July 1933: and its purpose was much the same –
'(1) to get a fuller understanding of my own life – its "pattern" and
(2) to help other people in the same way as I have been helped by the
self-revelation of people before me'.[19] But it may more properly be regarded as a delayed result of his 'conversion' two years before, since it
is noticeable that each of his other major reorientations (of 1923, 1929,
1936 and 1947) was either accompanied or shortly succeeded by an out-
burst of autobiography. To this was due, no doubt, his reputation for
'baring his soul'. *Between Two Worlds* differs only by its wealth of docu-
mentation and episode, the passages of vivid, often humorous narrative
and the unforgettable pen-portraits of contemporaries, which combine
to make it something more than a 'spiritual autobiography' – a fas-
cinating 'tract for the times', comparable to Rousseau's *Confessions* or
Goethe's *Dichtung und Wahrheit*.

It was in an essay on Goethe, as it happens, written early in 1932 (an
essay which Lowes Dickinson thought the best on the subject in English), that Murry shed most light on this autobiographical propensity.
It was an expression of what he there called 'a true process of evolution:
of subjective growth through objective experience . . . On the one side
a continuous opening of the whole receptivity of the subject to all experience, a constant submission of the self to the "pure phenomenon";
and on the other side, an equally constant relegation of the self enlarged
by experience to the status of the "pure phenomenon".'[20] Such, he
indicated, was 'the dialectical process of human growth as Goethe

experienced and conceived it'; such, undoubtedly, was the process as he did. In *Between Two Worlds*, as in *God*, he turns the same eye upon his own development as he has turned upon Dostoevsky's and Lawrence's, comprehending it in such a way that the comprehension itself confers a new unity on him, and hence a new motive to action.

In his case as in Goethe's, this was intimately associated with what he called his 'fundamental Spinozism':[21] for, though he had neither inclination nor aptitude for metaphysics, and was content to leave the husk of the *Ethics* to the mathematicians and linguists, he rejoiced in the detachment at its core, 'and by the simplicity and directness with which he grasped it he became a truer Spinozist than many who were better able than he to explore Spinoza's subtle distinctions between substance and mode'.[20] It was not for nothing that he called Spinoza 'after Jesus, the greatest Jew',[22] reverting to him again and again to the end of his life. His epitaph might have been Samuel Alexander's: *Erravit cum Spinoza*.

Unfortunately, the narrative of *Between Two Worlds* stops short with the War. Whilst he achieved his object (2) successfully, the nearest he came to (1) was in the long collateral essay in *The Wanderer*, 'The End of an Egotist'. The book turned out longer than either he or his publishers had anticipated; and before they had settled the question whether one work meant one book or one volume, other things had put it out of his mind – among them, 'a kind of desperation, a determination to get something said about Shakespeare before I became incapable of saying anything about him at all'.[23]

For this determination there can be few regrets, *Shakespeare* being by common consent a major contribution to criticism. The issue of fifteen years saturation, not only in the poems and plays themselves, but in the literature concerning them, it takes its place among Murry's most stimulating and scholarly works – a durable proof of how great a literary critic he would have been, had the very qualities that made for greatness not compelled him to be something else.

Essentially, his Shakespeare is Coleridge's, 'the Spinozistic deity – an omnipresent creativeness'. (Some years later, he copied out the passage from *Table Talk* containing this definition, with evident approval.) But he had the advantage over Coleridge both of a century's historical research and of having been a working journalist, accustomed to making a virtue of the necessity of writing under stringent conditions. It was probably this, more than anything, that saved him from the

Romantic temptation of picturing Shakespeare a free agent, with all the conundrums that leads to; though he may well have learned something also from the example of Hardy, a poet by inclination, a novelist by resignation, whose own greatest felicities were attained precisely through the 'humanization of melodrama'.[24] As it was, his profound understanding alike of the process of poetic creation and of the psychological evolution reflected in the plays was reinforced, replenished and enriched by 'the conception of Shakespeare as primarily an Elizabethan playwright dependent on the theatre for a livelihood'.[25]

Yet Murry could not have achieved so much where Coleridge and Goethe failed, had he not himself been endowed with a measure of 'the Shakespearean character', which his saturation in the plays had expanded; and because he was so endowed, his *Shakespeare* is far from being the book he had once projected. If it was due to his own capacity for adopting many 'perspectives', employing many idioms, being 'all things to all men', that he was able to enter into them so intimately, it was due to this also that he had learned not 'to impose his own terms upon Life, and make it conform to his pattern', but to look for a pattern in Life to which he could conform himself. And, regrettably or not, just because he had learned that lesson so well, he was forced to leave the book as it stands – an assemblage of lectures and articles, loosely strung together, rather than a rounded achievement.

'Of Shakespeare', he writes, 'it was as true as it was of another great Englishman a generation later: that he went so far because he did not know where he was going' – adding that in Oncken's view, Cromwell's saying reflects 'an idiosyncrasy of the English character'.[26] Perhaps it does, since the principle of growth is likewise the empirical principle. Be that as it may, it was by virtue of this idiosyncrasy that Shakespeare grew as he did, that Cromwell grew – and that Murry grew out of *Shakespeare*:

> Religion is still the simplest speech of Imagination, and the attitude of Imagination is humility, real humility, an emptying of one's self that that which is greater may take possession. Of this Imagination I believe that Shakespeare was one of the most perfect vehicles humanity has known. The humility of Imagination will not, because it cannot, utter itself in comparable forms to-day. If it could, this book of glimpses and half-lights might have been a little nearer to the book on Shakespeare I once proposed to write. It is very far from that dream. But it is no use deluding myself any longer with the hope that one day I shall be free to write it

as I once desired. I know, quite well, that I have no longer even the desire to write it: because what grains and germs of Imagination are included in my substance insist on uttering themselves in something more like an Act than my book on Shakespeare could ever have been. That was, indeed, for many years, what my Imagination conceived to be its proper Act. But something happened, and I changed; and the book is nothing more than the record of some tentative gestures towards an Act that could not be.[27]

That is the conclusion of a discarded preface to *Shakespeare*. The something that had happened, of course, was his conversion to Communism; the Act towards which he was being impelled, the creation of that nucleus of a new society which, only now with the twentieth century, had become a practical possibility and necessity.

XVIII

ALL-TOO-HUMAN

————◆◆◆◆◆◆————

K ATHERINE USED SOMETIMES TO call Murry 'very English'. His reaction to America certainly was. A fortnight's impromptu lecturing in New York, Toledo, Pittsburgh, Grand Rapids, Fond du Lac, Milwaukee, Albana, St Louis and Iowa City was sufficient to convince him that England was far in advance politically. By the end of a further six weeks in Chicago, Cleveland and Buffalo, he was sure that the same applied socially. Aboard the *Majestic*, on March 2, 1935, he summed up his impressions as follows:

I see, by comparison with the other great English-speaking democracy, how wonderful is our instinctive political wisdom, our elasticity, our capacity to 'muddle through' i.e. to retain as much as we possibly can of what is valuable in the old while yielding to the new. I think the U.S.A. is a great and (in spite of all) a lovable country, with an incalculable future. I think the kind-heartedness of the Middle Westerner is really *beautiful*: restorative of one's faith in simple human *nature*. It's certainly not by be-littling the U.S.A. that I came to have this renewed confidence in my own country: it's simply that I see how precious are those capacities which hitherto I have taken for granted, or even been inclined to regard as vices: e.g. (1) 'muddling through' is a very poor name for the capacity it conceals; and (2) 'hypocrisy' is a very poor name for the social conscience which will not tolerate such an exhibition as the 'strip act' I saw in the 14th St. Burlesque.[1]

America bewildered Murry even more than it attracted him: he did not profess to 'understand' it. New York, so beautiful from the sea, so concentrated at close quarters, seemed hardly real; Chicago, too real by half – 'full of nice people, but then I suppose so is Hell'.[2] He made a number of friends and met some congenial writers – Thornton Wilder, warm in praise of *Keats and Shakespeare*; Reinhold Niebuhr, whom he had found two years before 'an attractive fellow, American

[219]

in energy and keenness, but with something more';[3] above all, Waldo Frank – but this did not prevent him becoming 'acutely conscious . . . of the extent of my own isolation'.[4] It was, he surmised, 'entirely due to the fact that I never did put on much "side" '[5] that he himself attracted even more than he bewildered the Americans and was persuaded, before he left, to sign on for a further four months the following year.

The immediate result of this tour was to give him what he called 'a sense of proportion that will last me for years to come'.[5] Never again would he meddle in British politics – they were quite capable of muddling through without any assistance from him. 'With a long distance perspective', he told Rees that January, 'I incline more and more to Tawney's position';[6] and again, 'I am more than ever convinced by my experience out here that I can be chiefly helpful to Socialism in indirect ways. Our business is first to create *awareness* – complete social awareness – and to foment a sort of loose unity on that basis.'[7] He would take no responsibility for the I.S.P.: 'If the I.S.P. doesn't want to become a simple Socialist Society, well and good: but I don't intend to belong to anything else . . . And I've a good mind to exorcise my repressions by doing nothing but literary work for the *Adelphi* for a year or two.'[5] It was in conformity with this resolution that, directly on his return, he settled down to *Shakespeare*.

Not unnaturally, Rees was upset, as were Holdaway and other I.S.P. spokesmen, who remonstrated with him over his 'don'tcarishness'. It was all very well for him to nurse a picturesque vision of himself 'walking at the tail of a tiny party of working-class Socialists from Lancashire, in the simple faith that they are the salt of the earth':[8] the working-class Socialists from Lancashire expected him to walk at their head. He had led them into the wilderness: it was up to him to lead them out of it again. Had he not expatiated for years on the irrelevance of art at the present juncture?

Murry was unrepentant – or rather, he was quite unaware of the extent to which the movement depended on him, and the trouble the others had had to hold it together in his absence. 'The Adelphi, the Summer School, the I.S.P.,' Rees tried to impress upon him, 'all the enterprises in which you and I are associated – are far more of what is called in France, I believe, a *mouvement personnaliste* than you care to recognize. A mouvement personnaliste is a perfectly good and desirable thing, but the personne has to be aware of what he is doing . . .

For fully two years I have felt that you were walking head-in-air and that I, so to speak, was running round averting obstacles.' If *that* was what the movement was, Murry retorted, then the sooner he got out of it the better: he was 'congenitally incapable' of thinking of himself as 'an "important" person' [9] and not interested in an organization without roots of its own. That such modesty was incompatible with objectivity, he does not appear to have acknowledged.

All the same, his indifference was more apparent than real. He might be disqualified for a politician or propagandist by his inability to say the same thing again and again: 'My Socialism requires too much the excitement of discovery. I can't change my spots. My Socialism is just as personal as my criticism; and *is* my criticism in a new manifestation.' [10] But, for that very reason, he could not go back on his Socialism. He might apply for a Leverhulme Research Fellowship, in order to write a three-volume history of the Great Rebellion: but his interest in Cromwell itself was anything but academic, otherwise he would probably have been granted it. The months following his return from the States were simply a period of 'gestation'.[11] The project of a Socialist community, conceived the autumn before, was not merely still alive, but on the point of delivery.

It was delivered that August, in the shape of a lecture to the Adelphi Summer School at Caerleon: 'Socialism, 1935' – a lecture which, even today, makes stimulating reading. Indeed, one cannot read either this or the succession of articles with which he followed it up – 'Creative Socialism', 'Russia and the West', 'The Adelphi Centre' – without sensing a new vitality in his writing. Not that their substance was new. That in England there no longer existed a proletariat in the Marxist sense; that the working-class as such was as little concerned for equality as the bourgeoisie; that a Socialist Society, therefore, could only consist of an *élite* of all classes, consciously dedicated to the supersession of individualism, economic and social – all this he had propounded before. His optimism, moreover, may provoke a wry smile today, especially where Russia was the theme. Yet how little political journalism of the '30s has worn so well!

If he found reasons for justifying the Soviet dictatorship, in a country which had never known freedom and was newly emerged from a violent upheaval, he never denied that it was a dictatorship, much less held it up as a model, as was then the fashion of the Left Book Club. The only organ to compare with *The Adelphi* of those days was Emmanuel Mounier's *Esprit*; and Murry's commentaries, like Mounier's, were informed by an historical understanding to which his Marxism was instrumental. Even the terms in which, at the end of his lecture, he broached his own particular project, have not lost all their relevance:

> To put what is in my mind as concretely as I can, or as I dare, I believe that for a period of the year we ought to make, and persevere with, the experiment not merely of being and talking together, but of doing things together. I want to see a beginning made in some country place of a settlement to which we could go, each of us for some part of the year, to renew our Socialist inspiration and our faith in one another, by working together concretely, creatively, simply, blunderingly – a place where we resolved to live with the utmost simplicity and frugality, whither we could continually invite our unemployed comrades, not as a charity, a condescension or a panacea, but as men who understand, perhaps better than any of us, our aim of keeping ourselves fit for the real battle of Life against Death, which is what I mean by Socialism. It would be, I know, a quasi-return to monasticism and retreat: I like it none the less for that. In my own way, I know what profound renewal of energy comes to a man from working at a simple practical job in silent understanding with another man. The comradeship we need to-day is not of the head, not primarily of the heart even, but of something deeper and simpler still.
>
> I do not believe this simple plan of mine is Utopian. But I beg, once again, not to be misunderstood. I am not pretending that this is complete Socialism. I am merely contending that this may be the best way to solve a problem which no one has solved, and which very few even see must be solved – the problem of constantly renewing the morale of Socialism and Socialists, and of combating the insidious degeneration by which the Socialist movement under political democracy is continually being undermined.
>
> I believe that this essential part of Socialist work is in danger of being completely neglected, and that it is a part of that work which such people as we are are chiefly fitted to perform. Here is something which we can do, and something which, without us, will never be done.[12]

The proposal was not received enthusiastically. Some of the Lancashire Socialists were hostile, most were circumspect, very few were favourably disposed. The only whole-hearted support came from a wealthy lady, Miss Gill, who offered £100 there and then to the venture, and from Plowman, who evidently saw it as a step in the right direction – that is, away from the 'dictatorship of the proletariat'.

By the end of the Summer School it was clear that if anything was going to be done, it would have to be done by Murry.

He, however, convinced that this was the only way forward, was not to be daunted now. 'I am determined to make a beginning,' he told Miss Gill: 'It takes me always a very long while to get my mind and heart in unison – and anyway *I* can't do anything about it: I simply have to wait – but when the moment comes and my mind and heart are in unison, then something has to be done. Hence my determination.' [13] He had been hoping to see the settlement established in Derbyshire, within easy reach of the Lancashire comrades; since the responsibility had all fallen on him, it would have to be in East Anglia. But the Summer School had scarcely dispersed before he was scouring the country in quest of a suitable site; and on September 10, he found it – The Oaks, Langham, near Colchester.

As he envisaged it, The Adelphi Centre was to consist of a house and grounds manned by a staff of a dozen men and women, half of them recruited from the unemployed, whose functions would be, first to make themselves as nearly as possible self-supporting by the establishment of various workshops, and secondly to maintain a guesthouse and conference centre for Socialists of all denominations. 'Everybody at the Centre will be expected to make himself useful, either in the work for which he is best fitted or of which his life stands in most need. For it follows naturally from the aim of education into community that it should be equally an education into individuality.' [14] *The Adelphi*, he hoped, would one day be printed as well as published on the premises; the Summer Schools would be held there of course. The Oaks, a commodious late Victorian mansion, erected by a retired courtesan and more recently distinguished by a stirring *crime passionel*, seemed admirably fitted for the purpose.

The price of the house, together with an adjoining cottage, Little Oaks, and two pasture fields, was £2,475. Murry himself invested £1,000 at 4½ per cent.; subscriptions, including his own, totalled another £1,800. By the middle of November, a limited liability company, The Adelphi School Co., had been set up to conduct the enterprise; by Christmas, the transaction was complete. The Directors, apart from the Permanent Chairman, were Richard Murry, Rees, Holdaway and G. C. Adeney; the objectives as defined in the Articles of Association, 'to promote the education of children and adults of any age, whether male or female, and whether separately or by way of co-education in accordance with the philosophy, principles and methods heretofore set forth or hereafter to be set forth in the published writings of John Middleton Murry and Professor John MacMurray with such modifications thereof (if any) as may from time to time be determined'. The final provision was prudent.

All that remained, then, was to find the right personnel – and that, Murry thought, would not prove difficult. 'I have an instinct for the kind of people I want, and against the kind of people I don't want,' he assured Rees (who may have had his doubts): 'Proletarian scroungers certainly won't be in the least attracted by anything I shall ever have to offer; and I don't believe bourgeois escapers will be either.' [11] Meanwhile the more active members of the Chelsea I.S.P., constituting a 'flying squad' under his brother's direction, were descending on The Oaks at week-ends with paint, brushes, hammers, files and card-indexes. Whatever happened the stage would be set for the 1936 Summer School. 'It's the founding of *The Adelphi* all over again – in a new order of existence,' he exclaimed to Plowman: 'And just as I was then *possessed*, so am I now.' [15]

Unluckily, it was not only Rees who had his doubts. Once again, when it came to the point, Plowman himself drew in his horns. He would accept no responsibility for 'a home for stray dogs', he declared: something more 'personal' was required. Useless to contend that 'the authentic spirit of community and communion arises only when we are no longer trying to capture it directly,' [15] only through work on a common task – this time he actually broke off the correspondence. And that was a bitter disappointment. The prospect of being reunited with Plowman in a truly 'impersonal' cause had been one of Murry's main incentives.

Nor was that all. Though his head and his heart might be in unison, his body was playing an air on its own. Plowman's resistance, in other words, was as nothing compared to Betty's. For the dream of an idyllic homecoming which he had nursed in America (and which may have had something to do with his momentary dissociation from politics) had collapsed at the first touch of reality. Throughout the summer and autumn of 1935, Murry's journal is a record of deepening despondency over his marriage, touching downright despair at the time of the purchase of The Oaks. There were moments when Forgiveness itself – 'the one thing in which I have believed' [16] – now began to look to him like weakness: 'I ought to have fought, and fought, and fought, till my legs were broken, as Aaron Sisson said.'[17]

He was caught in a vicious circle indeed. The more his craving for domestic peace was frustrated, the more intense his concern for the 'nucleus of a new community'; the more intense this concern, the more persistent the frustration. It is not by chance that the passage on the 'new community' in *The Wanderer* comes at the end of an essay 'On Marriage' – in which, turning to Lawrence once more, he tries to relate his struggle with Frieda, 'the substantial theme of nearly all his work',[18] to the social background of an age of transition. The same experience that underlay *William Blake* had enabled him, far better than before, to enter into Lawrence's feelings. There were actually occasions when he wondered whether he too might not 'begin dreaming of Teresa's – *à la* Lawrence – and priestesses of Isis'.[19]

That essay, a minor masterpiece of imaginative dialectical materialism, had ended by endorsing the conclusion of the *Fantasia*, that only men committed to 'disinterested, non-domestic male action' could, or should, enlist the spontaneous loyalty of their womenfolk. It was the conclusion he had never tired of impressing upon Young, who, at the time, had been involved in domestic collisions as spectacular as his own. (A novelist attracted by Lawrence's recipe, 'Take two couples and work out their relationship', could find matter of volumes in the chronicle of those two Old Rectories.)

Now he was not so sure. 'Let the men do their duty, and the women will be such wonders', Blake had said. He was doing what he took to be his duty – and at every step the saying was falsified. 'For his highest, man is responsible to God alone', Lawrence had declaimed: 'He may not pause to remember that he has a life to lose, or a wife and children to leave. He must carry forward the banner of life, though seven worlds perish, with all the wives and mothers and children in them.' It was beginning to look as if it might come to that. When, at any rate, Betty finally gave him to understand that she would wreck the Centre within a fortnight (and this was no empty threat) Murry foresaw his premonition of 1931 being fulfilled – that Communism would require of him the sacrifice of houses and lands, wife and children.

This was on the eve of his second departure for the United States, in December 1935; and the breach was still unclosed when he embarked. No wonder he dreaded that tour. It was bad enough having to leave his 'beloved Centre only half-born' – although, as he confessed to Hogan, 'perhaps it is as well, for assuredly if I go on as I have been going these last few months, my family will be in the workhouse; or may be we shall get the A.C. going just in time to take on the founder thereof'.[20] It was still worse having to take leave of his family with 'nothing to cling to, to set against America'.[21] He had actually tried to escape the commitment, by applying for a Chair of English Literature at London University; but professorships, pressed on him five years before, were hard to come by now when he wanted one. In the event, 'I left England', he recalled, 'with the despairing conviction that if I was to carry the job at the Centre through, it meant that I should have to part from my wife.'[22]

Happily, at New York on December 28, there was a friendly face to greet him – Nehale (as he called her), a former neighbour in Norfolk, who, having parted from her husband, had returned to her native country. Knowing Larling, she could understand his feelings. She persuaded him to relax for once before setting out on his tour, even taking him to dancing-classes – where the question stole into his mind, supposing he had taken Betty dancing, would everything have turned out all right? Before he had had time to answer this, however, and long before he had mastered the first steps, he was being whirled away again the length and breadth of New England.

Professor Clarence Thorpe, author of *The Mind of John Keats* (which Murry had read and admired in Abbotsbury days), remembers him arriving at the University of Michigan towards the end of January – already tired, and troubled by a sore throat. In spite of which, he writes, 'He was all eagerness to see our campus':

> At home in the afternoon preceding his lecture we had tea and some rest. Murry got on famously with my wife; he praised her tea, 'just like home'. He was the perfect guest, with indeed a British restraint that we had learned to know and respect in trips to England. He and I curiously enough talked very little about Keats. But again why should we? I had read all he had written on Keats, and he had reviewed my book. He had not, however, seen my then new edition of the Poems and Selected Letters, but he took the copy I gave him to bed with him, and I found out later, scanned the text, notes and all, before he went to sleep. (He wrote a card a day later saying he had done this; the edition was fine, he said, but why had I inserted such and such a note? It was wrong, of course.) The subject of his lecture here, in response to the vote of our com-

mittee on the list submitted, was Katherine Mansfield, and he talked of her with understanding and brilliance, but with a sort of diffidence and withdrawal, I thought. He told me afterwards he never gave that lecture without deep pain. His attitude was a fine blend of affection and objectivity. The matter was a well-supported analysis of Miss Mansfield's unique artistic endowment, beautifully leavened as it was by her warm human quality, her artistic integrity, her method and accomplishment. Most of his audience left the room, I believe, impressed with the fact that they had been offered a rare first-hand, close-up view of a great artist at work. Others were disappointed. One of my most distinguished colleagues was so disturbed that he cancelled his reservation for the faculty dinner with Murry that evening. How could a literary man discuss his wife in such a way in a public lecture?

This one recollection will stand for many. In America, Murry departed from his life-long rule, never to discuss, but only to present, Katherine's work. It was not till after his death that the text of this lecture was published – so that the reader may now judge for himself whether the distinguished colleague's reaction was justified. Nearly everywhere, the impression he made, both in public and private, was favourable: as he said, he never did put on much 'side'. All the same, as he wrote to Thorpe afterwards, he would have much preferred to visit fewer colleges and stay long enough at each to have proper discussions with the students. As it was, there was barely time even for proper introductions. He never forgot being presented to an enormous audience by the President of the University of Minnesota, 'after a long and well deserved eulogium, as the internationally famous Doctor Gilbert Murray'.[23]

The strain of such a tour is heavy at the best of times. This time it was magnified tenfold by 'nightmarish' weather. His arrival in Chicago that February coincided with the coldest spell for thirty years, his departure with the most violent blizzard. 'The trains are never on time – because there's always a fresh blizzard – so I find myself stranded at wayside stations at 3 a.m., having neatly missed the connection,' he wrote to Victor Cooley, 'becalmed, somewhere in Minnesota.'[24] In Minneapolis he caught a cold in the thaw, which turned to double influenza in Toledo. By the time he had struggled on, conscientiously but imprudently, to Cincinnati, he was feeling so near death that he actually scribbled a will, to be delivered to his brother Richard. 'It's hard, as Katherine used to say, to imagine a grimmer break than lying feverish night after night in one of these strange and horrible modern American hotels. You can go out beautifully alone in such a place.' [25]

However, by then salvation was in sight. What might have been expected to happen, had happened. 'Tired and beaten',[26] he was in the very state to take the singing in his ears for the voice, if not of a captive princess, at least of a fairy godmother. Almost from the day of his leaving New York, he had been followed by letters from Nehale – variations on a familiar theme. '*Ma décision est prise*', he had recorded in his journal, relapsing abruptly into the privacy of French, '*de ne point refuser le bonheur qui m'est offert.*' [27] A tryst had been arranged for the end of March, and only another fortnight's blizzards lay between.

However slow it might be to dissolve, Murry's romanticism was always astonishingly quick to precipitate. The least speck of hope would do. It had taken five years to demolish his faith in the possibility of a love both physical and spiritual; it took as many days to restore it. Though he had known Nehale well in the past – pitied her, indeed, for a 'neurosis so profound as to be quite unmanageable'[28] – they had not been together a week now before the 'miracle' was worked: 'Somewhere, somehow, a new, divinely simple love was being born':

> I did not know there was such a condition. It seemed to me that the pattern of my life was there to demonstrate that what I mean by Love was unattainable in this life. Complete mutual surrender, complete acceptance, complete simplicity, complete faith – what has this been all my life long but a dream – in which I had ceased to believe, because I *dared* not believe in it. I have struggled with a marriage that denied the dream; I have had the strength to struggle only because I would not, could not believe in the dream. And the struggle ended because there was nothing left to struggle with. And then – and then only – did my heart open again – [26]

and so on, page after page. The date was April 1.

Only this had been wanting to clinch Murry's half-formed determination to bring the misery of Larling to an end. Time and again he had been on the point of doing so; all that had withheld him had been the thought of Mary – on to whom, as on to Weg, so much of his love had been diverted. He could bear neither to leave her nor to have her exploited as a weapon against him, as she certainly would be.

But now, he was sure, he had a 'clue', which he must follow at no matter what cost.

Heart and mind had found a body to match. If he belonged to the Centre, he belonged no less to Nehale. Sooner or later she would join him there as his wife. Meanwhile, he would be 'like a knight going away to perform his vigil'.[29] By April 15, when he boarded the *Aquitania* in New York Harbour, a 'final resolution, completely unchangeable',[30] had been communicated to all concerned. It remained only to carry it into effect.

And this time he did carry it into effect, though the cost proved even heavier than he had anticipated. The journal entry for May 28, 1936, is headed, 'LEFT LARLING':

> After five years the end, the bitter end, of a chapter. The men came to take my furniture in the morning; by lunch-time they had loaded. All the morning my darling Mary helped me. After lunch she went to rest. At 2.30 I went up to say Good-bye. She was still awake. She said to me: 'You won't be gone long.' I should have answered 'No', but I had to say: 'Darling, you won't see me again for a long while.' She said, 'The days go quick.' I said 'Think of me, won't you?' And that was the end.
>
> Ah God, I never knew what agony I should feel at parting from my darling. Houses and lands and wife and children. It has come to pass as I foreknew it would. And nothing will ever take this pain away. Nor God nor demon can undo the done. What has life to offer me compared with the love and trust of my darling? Beside that, everything seems dust and ashes. My baby, my sweetheart! Oh Christ, Christ. Jésus sera en agonie jusqu'à la fin du monde.

The same evening saw Murry installed in 'a place where men and women loved one another without possessiveness – the Adelphi Centre'.[31]

XIX

RENOVATION

❧⟐❧

I T IS NEITHER DESIRABLE, nor necessary, nor even possible, to
unwind the entire tangled skein of Murry's private life in the six
months following his return from America. The curious may consult Gissing's novel, *The Year of Jubilee*, in which he himself found the
closest parallel. On the other hand, neither can it be ignored, if only
because there was so little that was private about it. Suffice it then to
say that his break with Larling was by no means so final as intended.
Although he had taken advantage of his wife's absence on a cruise to
transfer his indispensable belongings to Langham, where the two
elder children spent their summer holidays, and Nehale was to join
him in the autumn, Betty would hear nothing of a separation, much
less consent to a divorce. The result was a phantasmagoria of comings
and goings, negotiations, altercations, raids, kidnappings and settle-
ments that settled nothing. It was not till the middle of October that
the situation came to a head.

Meanwhile, the Centre was taking shape. Richard had thrown himself into the work with a will; and out of the other volunteers a more
or less coherent team had emerged, which, it was tacitly assumed,
would constitute the 'permanent nucleus'. It comprised an unemployed architect, whom Marxist Providence had led to camp in the
meadow at Larling; a Chelsea sculptor; a young writer, in whom Murry
had divined a vocation – unsuspected by himself or anyone else – for
cookery; and two or three practical men. There were also a number of
women, including the sculptor's consort, an artist; a housekeeper,
appointed, apparently, for her knowledge of bookselling; and a
Scottish secretary, who, having followed the fortunes of *The Adelphi*
from the start, felt that she had reached her bourne. Although
Lancashire was well represented, the proletariat was conspicuous by
its absence.

It does not sound a very promising team; and Murry's own domestic plight was hardly calculated to make for stability. At one time or another, he recalled later, every one of the women had come to warn him against the others' designs; and it may be doubted whether anyone else in his position would have been tolerated, at least by him. True, he had left houses and lands, wife and child – but only when another house and lands, wife and children, were waiting to receive him. Voices were not lacking, even then, to infer that the real purpose of The Oaks was to provide him with an alternative establishment – and if him, why not them as well? After all, the one principle upon which they were all agreed was that the day of the celibate community was over. By night, the sound of music and dancing, echoing up the uncarpeted staircase, must have fluttered the ghostly heart of the house's original occupant; while the villagers, who had always maintained that it was 'built of bad bricks', saw no reason to alter their opinion.

Still, as Murry said, had he waited till he was perfectly sure of having the right personnel, he would have waited for ever. Nobody yet knew what 'living in community' meant; and this community had been conceived for so novel a purpose that no precedent would have helped much. Whatever there was to be learned about qualifications and conditions would be learned from the experiment itself:

> The genius of Socialism must work out its own salvation in men: it cannot be matured by law and precept, but by sensation and watchfulness in itself. That which is creative must create itself. In the Centre, we leaped headlong into the sea, and thereby have become better acquainted with the soundings, the quicksands and the rocks, than if we had stayed on the green shore and piped a silly pipe and took tea and comfortable advice.[1]

So he was to write that autumn, paraphrasing Keats. He had a healthy distrust of blue-prints. In this, as in every other venture to which he committed himself, his approach was empirical first and last. He expected the community itself to constitute an 'experiencing nature'.

Furthermore, when all is said and done, the method of selection was probably as sound as any, since there is no more exacting test of character than voluntary team-work. During those months of intensive preparation for the Summer School, the members came to know one another's strength and weakness as they could never have done otherwise – and strength predominated. The day's work proceeded smoothly; the evening discussions were informed by a spirit of genuine comradeship. To all concerned, those were memorable months; to Murry himself, a revelation. Unused as he was to 'working with men', he felt that only now did he fully understand what Lawrence had meant by 'the sense of touch': while the ceaseless activity, of course, provided him with a much-needed distraction. 'It made me insensitive to things that would have destroyed me . . . And I was utterly ruthless to the few who worked with me, save only to my brother who was ruthless to himself.' [2]

The extravagance of the phrasing is typical of this moment. One feels that Murry was screwing himself into an unnatural posture; doing what hurt him most *because* it hurt, and wringing all the consolation he could from self-dramatization. Yet the word 'ruthless' was not out of place. It had become, for the time being, his key-word. Being 'all of a piece', he could not harden his heart against Betty and Mary without hardening it altogether. His politics themselves were affected. That July saw the outbreak of the Spanish Civil War – the dress-rehearsal for World War II. On August 20, he was writing in his journal:

> My personal destiny fits absolutely with the abominable horrors of the Fascist counter-revolution in Spain, sanctified by the Catholic Church – the mass-murder at Badajoz. The two together convince me, as I have never been convinced before, and could never have been convinced otherwise, that one must fight: we shall never achieve it without a bloody struggle for which we must be prepared – that it is pure self-deception to believe that violence will not take us, cannot take us, to a Socialist society. That may be true: it will not and cannot. But violence will take us to a society that may become a Socialist society – and *that* is what we are fighting for.

The sense of being 'a man of destiny, in a small way',[3] dating from the coincidence of Katherine's illness with World War I, was by now continuous.

He spoke in the same strain at the Summer School itself, which opened in August. 'I personally', he averred in a lecture on 'Socialism, the State and Violence', 'find it difficult to be ruthless: but I think I understand the necessity, and, whatever it might cost me personally, I should be prepared to obey it.' [4] Ever since the Italian invasion of Abyssinia the year before, he had been advocating 'collective security' as the only rational short-term policy; in the discussion following a lecture by Plowman, now General Secretary of the Peace Pledge Union, he came out vehemently against Pacifism.

Feeling was running high in Left Wing circles that summer over the question of intervention in Spain – so high that it speaks a great deal for the virtue of the Centre that the School was an overwhelming success. Though it lasted a month, so seldom did controversy even verge upon acrimony that Plowman himself, by the end, was forced to admit that the experiment had justified itself. Every shade of Socialist opinion was represented, the speakers including such contrasted figures as John MacMurray (the dominant influence), John Strachey, Herbert Read, Sam. Higgenbottam, Karl Polanyi, John Hampden Jackson and George Orwell. The participants, numbering several hundreds, were drawn from every quarter and class, bourgeois paying for proletarian and all, clerks, schoolmasters, professors and miners, taking a share in the practical work. (Murry himself was in particular demand as a *plongeur*, his expertise in this department being exceeded only by Orwell's.) Nobody left without feeling that the 'classless society' had been brought, if not nearer, at least within sight.

Murry summed up his own impressions in the October *Adelphi*:

To the new and intenser reality of Socialist thinking which was achieved at the Summer School I can honestly bear witness. It had its ups and downs: there were moments when the spell was broken; but it re-asserted itself and became steadily more dominant. This spell consisted simply (I think) in a communal exercise of imagination. There was, in the main, no effort to enforce a personal or egoistic point of view: what attempt there was in this kind seemed gradually to become submissive to the demands of a disinterested search for truth. This was to me a revelation, a revolutionary realisation, despite the fact that there had been moments, months ago, when I had an inkling that it might be so. But to be confirmed in a surmise, to see an experiment succeed, is a totally different experience from entertaining the surmise or forming the hypothesis.

Again, the experience is hard to formulate; but it may perhaps be expressed in these simple terms: that an attempt at Socialist living is the necessary basis for Socialist thinking. Only those who have learned, or are trying to learn, to overcome their egoism in the practical business of living, are able to overcome the subtler egoism which substitutes for the disinterested search for truth the vindication of one's own 'truth' as an exclusive possession. In other words, the Socialist search for truth is a new, communal and corporate manifestation of the poetic search for truth as described by Keats . . . The mind of the Summer School became 'a thoroughfare for all thoughts – not a select party'.

That this was no purely individual impression was proved by the numerous letters received from participants afterwards, a selection of which featured in the same number of *The Adelphi*. The Centre had proved its capacity for re-creating Socialist idealism.

Nevertheless, by the end of the month Murry was exhausted: not without cause. Since the previous August, when he had taken the family to Barmouth for a fortnight (and that had been spoiled by quarrels) he had been working uninterruptedly; his domestic crisis alone would have prostrated a normal man; while the Summer School itself had demanded every ounce of his energy. Indeed, it had probably demanded more than he knew, for, often as Lawrence had chidden him in the past for his want of elementary care for his health, he had never acquired it; he never even realized how exorbitantly he taxed his strength – it was others who struck him as lazy – and was invariably astonished afresh by the miraculous effects of a holiday.

So it was now – since, luckily, the Plowmans were wiser. Knowing his position, they had arranged that as soon as the School was over he and Col should join them for a week's sailing on the Norfolk Broads: and 'you wouldn't believe how revived J. M. M. was', Plowman reported afterwards: 'He came back like a plant that drinks up moisture while you wait and he said that nothing so renovating had ever happened to him in a single week.' [5] His gratitude was such that he fell on their necks and kissed them, pronouncing himself a new man. It was as though the contentions of the past twelve months had never been.

And really they never had. The contentions between these two were never more, or less, than what Blake called (in one of their favourite phrases) 'the severe contentions of friendship'. If Murry had been gratified by Plowman's sudden reappearance at the Centre, he had not been greatly surprised; and if Plowman was disturbed by Murry's vehement onslaught on Pacifism, he was not deceived. Not only did he know quite well who was kicking against the pricks: he had already decided that it was up to him to 'tip J. M. M. over the line',[5] and it was as much for this reason as any that he had planned their week together. Although 'little or nothing was said about positions or attitudes except those that applied to sailing, mooring, quanting or fishing',[5] that was merely his tact. At parting, he took care to present

Murry with a copy of his book, *The Faith Called Pacifism* – leaving the leaven to work. 'I think things – good things will happen',[6] he was writing on September 10.

Perhaps they did. At any rate, Murry read the book during the next day or two with as much pleasure as *The Right to Live* six years before. For the moment, however, politics had taken second place in his mind. The immediate effect of his 'renovation' was to set him yearning more ardently than ever for Nehale. She had come over for a week in May, to whet his almost blunted purpose; since then, as he recorded (with evident surprise at his fortitude) he had 'lived a life of complete chastity for four months'.[7] Now, the children's future was settled: Col was to go to a boarding-school, Weg to friends in Belgium for a year, Mary to a kindergarten in London, where the Plowmans could keep an eye on her. Little Oaks was all appointed for the honeymoon, and he was due to meet the *Bremen* at Southampton on the 28th. 'I am just simply "in love"', he was soliloquizing, 'with a youthful, incredible love, such as I had twenty-five years ago . . . Yet she is a woman with a grown-up daughter, and I am a man of 47!'[8]

Nehale's was the 'star'[2] by which he had steered over these months; the spar he had clung to, to prevent himself being carried away by his longing for Mary, his compassion for Betty, or vice versa. For 'there is only one way to abandon dead life, – by yielding to a new life', he had written: 'The only thing that can drive out "love" is Love.'[9] The Centre alone would never have upheld him so long. Whatever his devotion to a cause, it always took second place at heart to his quest for the perfect marriage. In fact, he scarcely distinguished between them, the perfect marriage being his touchstone of the perfect society. Hence his rejection, from the start, of the idea of a celibate community. If Nietzsche's words on the married philosopher occasionally stole into his mind, it was only in moments of despair. His own vocation was to realize a way of life appropriate, not to the philosopher, the artist or the saint, but to the common man.

But was his star a true one, or merely a distress-signal? Even at this moment of yearning, he himself had his doubts: 'Of course I can't help "touching wood" about all this.'[8] His faith had been shaken more than once – had Nehale not written, 'This Jesus stuff simply nauseates me'? His resolution was correspondingly vulnerable. He had only to meet Betty in London on a matter of business to set it pitching and tossing dangerously:

> I used to have contempt and aversion for the man who had a wife and a mistress: and there is no doubt that by inclination and experience I am monogamous. Whether the situations for which I had an aversion were essentially like my own, I cannot say. If so, I am sorry for my presumption in judging. But, somehow, this situation of mine seems all of a piece with all that I am trying to do – part and parcel of that 'taking of responsibility' which is necessary during the breaking-up of bourgeois society, of which this strange love-relation of mine is a part.[7]

This was on the eve of Nehale's arrival. Clearly, she would need to be the pole-star itself, if there was to be no turning back at this stage.

She was not. They had not been together a week before the illusion began to show through. It was Jimmy and the Desperate Woman over again: and, as in 1923, so now, he began to behave 'like a lunatic, or like a rat trying to escape from a trap'.[10] He himself was reminded of Mansfield. By October 2, 'I feel that I am in an *impossible* situation', he was wailing; and indeed he was. The journal, at this point, becomes such a farago of spiritual dialectics, of frenzied attempts to discover a 'pattern', a 'meaning', in the event, that one is divided between wonder that he did not have a nervous breakdown and wonder whether, in point of fact, he did.

One thing, at any rate, was certain: Nehale was 'out'. The only real choice, therefore, lay between Betty and the Centre – and Murry being Murry, there could not be much doubt of the outcome. If all that was needed now to reconcile mind, heart and body, was some assurance that Betty had 'changed', the assurance would be forthcoming. Even if it had to take the fabulous form of Betty's 'accepting' Nehale – still it would be forthcoming. Murry would believe what he wanted to believe, provided only the knot was cut. And cut it was, vigorously.

Poor Nehale! She lingered on at Langham a little longer, but her star had set; and it was not many weeks before – with a parting prediction that 'the next few years will be a bloodier Hell than anything I ever saw at Larling' – she followed it west. Murry paid for the voyage.

He, on the other hand, was by this time in the throes of a renovation – or relapse – more convulsive than even Plowman had foreseen. October 14 found him back at The Old Rectory with Betty. The same evening he was writing to Plowman:

> Wonderful (isn't it) that the day I go back to Larling is Katherine's birth-day.

Ah, dear Max, darling Max, these last days have been terrible and wonderful. And it is all simple, and utterly joyful. Joy, joy, joy. I wrote these words just now, because I could write no others: for a fire seemed to burn through all my physical being, consuming and creating it, melting it, softening it, till it was just one steady flame of life and love – that, I knew in my heart, must one day consume the world. Nor will it be long. The harvest is ready: the reaper, who is Love, will put in his sickle. Nay, it is already put in.

Oh, Max darling, I feel that I can't bear it. I am for ever dissolving into tears of joy, as I am now. (Such a big tear on the end of my nose!) And more strangely still a big tear of sweat running down my side, and now another. My very body weeping tears of joy. Now another. So my body really was consumed. It's frighteningly, joyfully simple.

Nehale is through. Last night she gave me up: sent me back to Betty with *joy*. Love has conquered. I have – we have – been through the last Hell. Henceforward there is nothing but Love and Joy.

And there's no impatience. The speed just happens: it is, and will be, the swiftness of absolute calm. Do nothing, do everything – it's all the same. Love is, and is everything. Time and Eternity are one: simply Life. And the wonder is that I feel I shall not die, but live. Not die yet, anyhow. It's marvellous – just to be, and to know that being is doing. One is, and one loves.

In this singular condition – 'half mysticism, half hysteria',[11] as he recognized later – Murry passed the ensuing fortnight: confident that neither principalities nor powers not even Betty herself could prevail against his new love; 'filled with the sense of fulfilling D. H. L.';[12] intent on begetting a son – to be christened after Lawrence, David – as the pledge of their reconciliation. 'Nothing matters, because everything matters,'[2] he was writing: and nothing was too trivial to be pressed into the service of his idea. Was it not of profound significance that he and Betty should catch a cold-in-the-head on precisely the same day? Or that the architect should write to him from No. 24 Adamson Road, Swiss Cottage? 'Adamson. Son of Adam. Sons of Adam. Sons of God. 24. 2–4–8. 2–4–8–16. 2–4–8–16–32. 64. 128. 512. 1024. Adelphi. 2 Brothers. Who knows? Who knows anything?'[2]

On October 18, he began to write, at break-neck speed. Three days later, he was telling William Wordsworth, the young composer whom he had met at the Summer School, 'Something – yes, God – is using me now to write a book, – and I know myself to be merely the piano – the voice.' The things God does get credited with! The book in question was an autobiography, ostensibly a sequel to *Between Two Worlds*, but as unlike that as anything could be: unplanned (he was relying on 'inspiration'), meandering, maudlin, rising every few pages to an execrable *vers libre* or descending to excruciating archness, it resembles nothing so much as a vicious parody of his style. Four months afterwards, he pronounced it the best thing he had ever done; ten years afterwards, the worst. The second verdict was correct.

Happily, this appalling document was never submitted to a publisher. Plowman saw to that. The only symptom of delirium in his published writings of the time was a certain inflation in the currency of deaths and annihilations; and by November even that was subsiding. The hysteria had discharged itself harmlessly, and only the mysticism remained.

But, of course, just as his former ruthlessness had extended to all his activities, so did his recoil from it now. He could not soften his heart towards Betty and Mary without softening it altogether. As he explained to Wordsworth (while the inflation was still at its height):

At the Summer School I was in the final extremity of impending annihilation. In the awful struggle with my wife, I had gone hard. Verily, there *was* nothing else for me to do. I was utterly weary. I had worked to prepare the Centre beyond human capacity; nor do I believe that I could have done it if I had not sought in the work release from my extremity of suffering at parting with my little daughter . . . And since I am all of a piece – my only merit – my Socialism went hard, too. I felt that there was something utterly cruel in the world, which we *must* fight: if we did not kill it, it would kill us. We must fight it, suffering tortures at the violation of our love: but we must fight. The final sacrifice demanded of us Socialists was the sacrifice of our love.

That was where I was when I took the chair for Max. Then I found that if I stayed there I should die. And if I did not stay there I should die: for that meant I must love my wife, who would destroy me. At last I chose the latter – and I was destroyed. And I am re-born, into the knowledge that there is no power, no life, no future, no anything except Love.[13]

'Love at all costs' was therefore the key-word now. On the very day of his return to Larling, he had joined the Peace Pledge Union.

Here was a *volte face*. Plowman, needless to say, was overjoyed. 'John has discovered his Pacifism,' he exulted: 'And there I think you

have the fellow who must experience everything on his pulses . . .
To me, it's like the dawn of a new era.' [5] Canon 'Dick' Sheppard, the
founder and Chairman of the Union, was hardly less gratified: it
was 'the best thing that ever happened to the movement', he said.
But to most of Murry's other associates, the announcement was a
bewildering shock. Holdaway and Votier vanished, never to reappear.
Rees, who had been watching his gyrations over the past six months
with deepening dismay, saw his worst forebodings realized. Murry
was mad, he assured him, and he himself had been mad to think otherwise. He would neither edit nor subsidize *The Adelphi* any longer;
and January 1937 saw the magazine reduced to a meagre thirty-two
pages, supplied by post to some seven hundred subscribers. 'Go Not
to Spain!' was the title of an article by Plowman – but Rees had
already gone.

Supporters of the Centre were no less upset; for, though Murry had
neither suggested nor intended that it should be anything other than
it had been, a meeting-place for Socialists of all persuasions, it was
foreseen that his would be the dominant influence. Not only at
Langham, but in London and Lancashire, I.S.P. meetings were convened to discuss the situation; and a movement was set on foot to oust
him. After all, his critics could point out, their donations alone had
made possible the purchase of The Oaks; they were in a majority; and
he himself had consistently referred to the venture as 'democratic':
ought he not, then, to withdraw? Murry did not think so at all – naturally enough. He had sunk £1,000 in the place; but for his exertions it
would never have existed; and anyway his position by the Articles of
Association was impregnable. Unedifying scenes ensued.

'I went down to Langham yesterday,' Plowman told Geoffrey West
on October 23: 'He was not here – but it was like following in the
wake of a whale in a harbour of canoes':

> In my present mood I've small hope of what may eventuate from the
> conference at Langham tomorrow. They won't understand him, because
> he'll only be able to speak subjectively at the very moment when the
> clearest objectivity is essential . . . And the silly ones will enjoy the
> sensation of the 'great man', and the rest will diffuse among themselves
> a sense of indeterminate dissatisfaction. And so follow, I suppose, months
> of imperfect personal self-explication. – Damn it!

It was exactly as he had foreseen – Murry trouncing his critics with all the ineptitude that typified his public defences. 'How dictatorial we true democrats become!' [14] he exclaimed in a letter to Plowman soon afterwards: and many must have echoed the exclamation. The upshot was a schism which virtually ended the Centre.

Not that it closed down at once. Replacements were found for some of the seceding personnel – a German refugee, a young Welshman, a Scotswoman amiably convinced that she was about to give birth to the Lord; two or three more small conferences were held; a printing-press was installed; and Murry himself made a point of attending every week-end. But his heart was no longer in the venture – he was too preoccupied with his domestic evangelism – and without his presence on the spot, the rest relapsed into an indolence so perfect that it remained a byword in the village for years. 'The Centre is dithering,' he observed glumly on November 16, 'flapping and flopping about, not knowing what it is doing . . . It seems in danger of turning into a place where people disintegrate, instead of reintegrating.' [15] Only a few more months were required to convince him that all the members, past and present, with the exception of his brother and himself, were either bourgeois escapers or proletarian scroungers; and by May 1937 he was thankful to hand it over to the P.P.U. as a home for Basque refugee children. The last Adelphi Summer School, a small one, was held at Larling.

The whole crisis bore more than a casual resemblance to that of twelve years before. Indeed, it struck Murry as more than a coincidence that he should receive letters just at this juncture from both Koteliansky and Sullivan, the one asking permission to publish some of Katherine's letters, the other to stay at The Oaks (both requests which he readily granted). It may have been this that reminded him, in the January *Adelphi*, of the meaning of its title, 'The Brothers'. Fundamentally, the issues were identical, as were the misunderstandings. He would never have acted so autocratically, had he not been disinterestedly bent on maintaining that 'thoroughfare for all thoughts' which was what he understood by a democracy; and he would never have been called upon to do so, had he explained what he understood by it beforehand, instead of blindly crediting his colleagues with clairvoyance. As it was, he could only look to them like a self-appointed dictator, the more reprehensible for cloaking his dark designs in the language of humility and love. Always it was just what prompted his sillier disciples to worship that provoked his pettier opponents to blaspheme – the perennial difficulty of telling where Murry ended and God began.

However, by 1937 he was growing used to being denounced as a Judas in one quarter while being hailed as Messiah in another. Besides, the more dearly he paid for his conclusions, the more store he set by them. Consequently, instead of being discouraged by this bathetic end to his endeavours, 'I feel rather exhilarated,' he confessed in the same editorial, his first since 1930: 'We are at rock-bottom in size, in circulation, and – in conviction. Or, at any rate, I am.' And this was the mood in which, a week or two later, he began *The Necessity of Pacifism*.

Some such book had been in his mind for months, setting forth the conclusions he had reached after 'five years more or less continuously spent in an effort to answer to the satisfaction alike of my instinct, my intellect and my imagination the question that has lived with me by day and vexed me by night of how the social revolution may be achieved in England'.[16] It was to have been called 'Creative Socialism', and no doubt would have followed closely the lines of the lecture of that name. For the most part, *The Necessity of Pacifism* does this. It is what he called it, a sequel to *The Necessity of Communism*, and, at the time of its appearance, provided the sole case for Pacifism calculated to appeal to a Marxist.

Capitalism, it claims, will give way only if deprived of its outlet in war; and only for resistance to war can the sympathy of the 'mass-man' be enlisted:

> That may be illogical; but it is because creative life is always illogical. That motion to repudiate Capitalism, in the form of war, which stirs in the mass-man who acquiesces in Capitalism, in the form of peace, is nothing other than the repudiation by his individual consciousness of the act of his unconscious social being. This repudiation is of the very essence of Socialism. This is what Socialism is – a dawning of imagination in the social man, and an impulse to translate imagination into act.[17]

As, in the seventeenth century, the demand of a minority for freedom of worship coincided with that of a class for economic freedom, so now 'the physical reluctance of the instinctive man to be murdered' coincides with 'the spiritual reluctance of the imaginative man to do murder'[18] – for murder, and nothing else, would be the destruction of that highly integrated economy of which the modern mass-man is the creature. Such a convergence of interest and disinterestedness is the hall-mark of a revolutionary situation. Only let the Socialist be prepared for it, therefore, and brotherhood may yet become politics.

Substantially, this was the same argument that Murry had submitted to Maxton in 1933. What new factors, then, had arisen to make him revert to it? The book itself names two: the first, and more objectively important, being the undeniable popularity of Pacifism. By now his surmise had, to all appearances, been confirmed. What Maxton had brushed aside as utopian, Sheppard had shown to be practical. Thousands had already signed the P.P.U. pledge, 'I renounce war, and I will never support or sanction another'; dozens more were being enrolled daily. Thus 'from a decreasing participation in a dwindling movement', the Socialist turned Pacifist 'passes to increasing participation in a growing movement; from seeking, in vain, the dynamic of change in economic necessities, he advances to finding it in a human necessity; and, above all, he becomes a member of a movement which has something quite simple to say: "Refuse all complicity in war, and take the consequences" '.[19] This it was that led him to adopt as a motto for *The Adelphi* Blake's proverb, 'Religion is Politics and Politics is Brotherhood'.

The second factor named was the experience of the Centre:

> One simple and important thing has been proved by actual experiment: namely, that the kind of comradeship that is necessary to any Socialist movement that seriously seeks to maintain itself as a Socialist movement in the peculiar conditions of English capitalist democracy is intrinsically, and psychologically, incompatible with the imagination of violence as a means of establishing Socialism in this country. I hold it as demonstrated that it is impossible to persevere to the end with the effort to create a body of truly realistic Socialists in this country without their becoming Pacifists in the process.[20]

This was untrue. Few if any of the members of the community had become Pacifists; some had joined the Communist Party. It was an unwarranted generalization from Murry's personal experience.

Nevertheless, it should be pointed out, first, that he may have been right in believing such a corporate effort to overcome egoism incompatible with the imagination of violence; secondly, that he may also have been right in treating his domestic struggle as 'part and parcel of that "taking of responsibility" ', as of more than purely personal significance therefore; and thirdly, that whether he was right or wrong, the personal equation by no means invalidates the other arguments he advanced for Pacifism. On the contrary, although he may well have been deceived, he was not deceiving himself. *The Necessity of Pacifism* represents a genuine synthesis of instinct and intellect. Hence its continued power, even after twenty-five years, to compel 'that willing suspension of disbelief for the moment which constitutes poetic faith'.

XX

SON OF MAN

———❧❀❧———

'I AM VERY RELUCTANT to change my idea', Murry confessed in
May 1937, 'but when I do change, I turn very thoroughly over to
the new one.' [1] That was certainly true. His brilliant skit on
dogmatic Marxism in the April *Adelphi*, 'Freud and Marx, or Super-
Ego and Super-Structure', recalls earlier roundings on the Georgians,
the Bloomsburies and the transcendentalists; whilst his sudden return
to Christianity, or the Christian idiom, at the end of *The Necessity of
Pacifism* contrasts signally with the calls of six years before for the
'abolition of religion'.

Yet his *volte faces* are always more apparent than real. If we look
closely, we shall invariably find the new idea anticipated months or
years beforehand. Even in 1934, for instance, in a sermon which he
called the best he had ever given, 'The Agony of Christianity', he had
affirmed that 'To the consciousness of the ordinary Western man the
essential revolutionary demand made by Communism will present
itself in terms of his own highest religious and ethical tradition' [2] – 'Be
Christian or perish', not 'Be Communist or perish'. It is not so much
the 'new' idea itself as Murry's very reluctance to entertain it (for –
pace Robert Lynd – he did not 'love to recant') that, by leading first
to an exaggerated emphasis on the old and then to a proportionately
sharp recoil, gives his 'line of life' the semblance of a zig-zag.

Its continuity is much more impressive. From *The Evolution of an
Intellectual* onwards, whatever the variations, the one theme persists
unbroken: the imperative necessity of a new kind of consciousness, if
the catastrophe of 1914–18 is not to be repeated on a still more
devastating scale. Early in 1938, while preparing a new edition of
Things to Come, he himself remarked with surprise, 'That first essay,
"The Need of a New Psychology", is as appropriate to-day as when
it was written. I seem to have been hammering away at the same old

tack for years: and I must say, I don't seem to make much headway.' [3]
And that too was true. Only a month before, in an article, 'The
Purgation of Christianity', he had been writing:

> In the last hundred years the 'natural man' has veritably changed his
> nature a thousand-fold for the worse, not because he is as an individual
> morally or religiously more depraved than he was, but because he is
> become hardly an individual at all. The physical and productive power
> with which a mechanised society endows him collectively, diminishes his
> individual reality almost to zero point. Hence the apparently superhuman
> demand that, if the 'natural man' is to remain even approximately at the
> level of 'natural' decency, the mechanism of society should be under
> such spiritual control as none but the Christian saint has been accustomed
> to exercise over himself. Now, the seeing and promulgation of this truth –
> the actual situation of Man to-day – is the function of the religious im-
> agination; pre-eminently of the Christian imagination which *should* be
> prepared for it. It is here that the Church has failed, and failed terribly.
> So that it has been left for eccentric Christians like myself to do the work
> of the Church. And all that has happened so far is that I have scared the
> Christians and exasperated the Marxists.[4]

Substantially, this was what had been contending, not only in 'The
Need of a New Psychology' (1925), but in 'The Nature of Civilisation' (1919).

In twenty years he had learned much indeed concerning both the
need and the nature of the new psychology – but nothing that obviated
either. Marx, he would continue to affirm, had taught 'the truth of
the great Christian doctrine of "original sin" in a new and terribly
urgent form';[4] and if he now turned his back on the Marxists, it was
mainly because of their refusal to admit this – because of their inveterate habit of projecting all the evils of the system on to an abstraction,
'the boss class', ignoring their own individualism. Likewise, if he
turned towards the religious, it was because 'The Christian knows
that the seeds of all these horrors are in *himself*. He is free from the
diabolical illusion of righteousness; and he knows that the way of the
Christian who would dedicate himself to the struggle against the
mystery of iniquity in its contemporary form, is likely to be the way
of the Cross.' [5]

As usual, he was generalizing from his personal experience: 'sound-
ing *himself* to know the destiny of man'. The chief cause of this
reorientation was his experience of community living, inseparable as

that was in his mind from his bitter domestic struggle and the Pacifism in which both together had issued. 'I as an individual', he had told the rump of the Centre on February 21, 1937, 'could never have endured the strains of the last 4–5 months here except for the presence in my mind – the real presence in my imaginative being – of our Lord; I could not have gone on without that; I don't think this is an idiosyncrasy.'

If a Christian inspiration was called for even in those conditions, how much more would it be in the event of war, or even a threat of war, when, as was only too likely, Pacifists would be driven underground and their families victimized? This consideration alone would have been enough to persuade him that nothing was to be lost, and much to be gained, by an open profession of Christianity; and already at that date he had been proposing that they erect a chapel at Langham, where 'we could more or less, as free spirits – as those who are not and are never likely to be, involved in the equivocation of the secular institution of the Church – make our own, quite legitimately our own, something of the great Catholic tradition – the ritual and worship of the Catholic Church'.

Nothing had come of that, naturally; but the need for ritual and worship persisted. At Larling, resuming his church-going, he realized anew what a 'focus of light' the parish church must have been in its day. All that the Centre lacked, it was borne in upon him now, the medieval commune had possessed – the discipline imposed by unremitting agricultural labour, the symbol of a common allegiance. More and more, as he steeped himself in the history of the period, the disintegration of the commune emerged as *the* tragedy of English history since the Reformation; and he was resolved that, if ever he embarked on a fresh community venture, it should be based on the land and have, for one of its objectives, the reinvigoration of the village itself. And could not even the Church be reinvigorated? As was practically inevitable, now that the Socialist movement had proved a *pis aller*, that question also was returning to his mind; and it had hardly begun to do so before it was powerfully reinforced by the example of various churchmen with whom his Pacifism brought him into contact – first and foremost, 'Dick' Sheppard.

Sheppard had wanted to meet Murry ever since *The Life of Jesus* appeared, though *Son of Woman* had damped his ardour. It was Murry who had shrunk from the acquaintance of one whom he took for a popular sentimentalist. Consequently, it was not until March 5, 1937, that Plowman succeeded in bringing them together. But Plowman's hopes were not disappointed. Unlike as the two men were by temperament and training – the witty, sociable, enormously popular Canon of St Paul's, and the earnest, withdrawn, derided author – they warmed to each other at sight.

Sheppard read *The Necessity of Pacifism* three times over with glowing approval, donated £25 to the Centre and helped to publicize *The Adelphi*. At a P.P.U. camp held at Swanwick that summer, he hailed Murry's lecture, 'God or the Nation', as 'the finest speech he had ever heard'; while Murry, for his part, observing the other closely, was 'admitting with astonishment and gratitude that the thing I had despaired of ever seeing was there before my eyes: laughing at me and I at him – a great democratic and Christian *leader*'.[6] It was Sheppard, oddly enough, who convinced him finally that it was easier to inspire Christians with a social understanding than Socialists with a Christian.

Oddly enough – because ostensibly it was the other way round. At the time of their meeting, Sheppard himself was feeling, not for the first time, ill-at-ease in the secular institution of the Church. Almost his first question to Murry was 'Should he come out of it?' And it was Murry's telling him of his own unobtrusive return to the Anglican communion that determined him not to. Not that Murry brought any persuasion to bear – his response was very characteristic: 'I answered (1) "That's for *you* to decide" (2) "The fact that you ask me means that the moment for decision is not come" (3) "That means you must wait. Don't do anything about it now." '[7] But that was sufficient. 'It is easy, in the case of Dick, to exaggerate one's personal influence upon him: but I did have the feeling that, after this, leaving the Church ceased to be an urgent problem for him. And this feeling of mine was confirmed by Charles Raven who said to me . . . that he believed I had more influence on Dick than anybody, and that I had kept him in the Church.'[7]

For Murry, however, the significant fact was not that Sheppard should be thinking of leaving the Church, but that he should be thinking of staying in it. This was what made him believe that his own inclination was of more than 'merely personal'[7] significance, that it was truly the inclination of 'the average, representative Son of Man',[8] which was what he wanted to be. For in Sheppard he discovered something over and above a leader. 'Recalcitrant to intimacy' though he was, he found himself, in his turn, confiding as he would never have done in 'any other man of comparable popularity and influence'.[9] They shared one problem, and one 'clue':

> We were talking about Faith; and I had been trying to convey to him the intolerable complexity and incredible simplicity of my own. Then he said, 'I don't think I know *anything* about Faith. The only clue I've got is Love; and I *hang* on to that.' And there was silence. There was indeed no more to say. For in my own way I too had learned that we hang on to that, or to nothing at all. There is no other clue: there and there alone is the gleam of light in darkness, the spark of life in death, that burns in us until we are consumed.[10]

A Church that was good enough for Sheppard, Murry felt, was more than good enough for himself.

This particular conversation took place at Windlesham that September, where they had met with some friends to draw up a 'Pacifist Manifesto'. John Barclay, the P.P.U. organizer, remembers the occasion as one of the few on which Murry lost his shyness, keeping the whole company entertained with anecdotes of his American tours. But it was memorable to Murry as well. It was then that Sheppard gave him a copy of Bernanos' *Diary of a Country Priest* – at the same time suggesting that they two should take a caravan and tour the country together, addressing the villagers wherever they happened to alight; then also, or shortly afterwards, that Murry resolved to become a country priest himself, to give Sheppard moral support.

It was too late for that. Though they met once again for the Glasgow Rectorial Election campaign – on October 31, within a few hours of the announcement of his triumphant defeat of Winston Churchill and J. B. S. Haldane, Sheppard was dead. Murry had barely had time to communicate his resolution.

This, nevertheless, persisted. Attending the two memorial services, at St Paul's Cathedral and the Albert Hall, he was struck by the contrast between them – the traditional Anglican and the deliberately secular commemoration designed by the P.P.U. 'I do not think that the P.P.U. can simply make Dick Sheppard the symbol of its unity and remain at that point,' [11] he wrote directly afterwards – loyalty to Sheppard himself entailed loyalty to Sheppard's Master. And then, going further still: 'I think that, if I could do, or help to do, one simple thing I should be a happy man. And that simple thing is to convince all pacifists that their place to-day is within the Church.' [12] He had already taken the first steps towards ordination.

There were, of course, some difficulties. For one thing, he was not an orthodox Christian. He had retracted none of the conclusions set forth in *The Life of Jesus*. Not only did he think the Virgin Birth a blasphemy and the Bodily Resurrection a blunder, but he was still unconvinced of any resurrection at all beyond 'the real presence in my imaginative being' of Jesus, Keats and Katherine. If he had any theology it was Blake's. 'I daresay I'm a good deal of the heretic still,' [13] he admitted to Eliot in January 1938. That was an understatement.

On the other hand, he had ceased to rebel against the notion of a personal God. In fact, he acknowledged its cogency. 'I cannot love God (as I believe I do) without by the very act declaring him to be a person: an incomprehensible Person, indeed, who is comprehended only in the act of love. But is not every person whom we love incomprehensible save by love?' [14] Furthermore – and it was over this that he joined issue with Huxley, another P.P.U. Sponsor, whose latest book, *Ends and Means*, had popularized some of his own views of ten years before – he had been accustomed since *William Blake* to identify detachment with 'the perfection of human tenderness':

> Perhaps I am a mystic of a different kind from Mr Huxley. Certainly I am very shy of calling myself a mystic at all. Nevertheless, I have to recognise that I have been the recipient of some at least of the experiences of which Mr Huxley speaks at a certain distance; moreover, I believe I have struggled against the acceptance of Christianity as stubbornly and as advisedly as any man of my time. If I have surrendered, it has been because I had to surrender. I have fought, to the utmost of my integrity, every inch of the way; but my conviction is that there is no rest for a mystic of my race save in Christianity. The struggle of the Western man is not (in my experience) simply to be 'non-attached', which is Mr Huxley's favourite phrase; the struggle of the Western man is to *love*. That love cannot pass from human to divine except by the road of 'non-attachment' is true, and perhaps it is the truth which has been most forgotten, or most lost, in contemporary Christianity. But 'non-attachment' is not the end; 'non-attachment' is the purification which human love must pass through in order that it may be irradiated, alchemised, and made eternal by divine love . . .
> I suppose I am as adept in 'non-attachment' as most Englishmen. And I also know the complete surrender of the self which is implicit in the simple Christian's simple devotion to Christ is just as valuable as the

mystic's arduous separation of himself from 'all that is creaturely':
nay more, it is the same thing. I know further that the man who will
exercise himself day by day in the simple practice of Christian love –
or let us call it love – 'hanging on' to love, as he will have to 'hang on'
to it, has nothing to learn from all the esoteric mysticism in the world.
His self will be destroyed, again and again. He will not need a technique
for destroying it. Let him but love, and love will see to it.[15]

To hang on to love meant, for Murry, to 'hang on to the Man who
was Love, who hung on to Love, and was God';[10] and in order simply
to express the experience supervening upon the shock of the Crucifixion – the transmutation of 'human love' into 'divine' – he found a
trinitarian formula indispensable. The dogmas of Pauline Christianity
fitted his experience, because (he believed) they had been cut to fit.
Thus it would have taken an exacting orthodoxy to deny him the
right to profess and call himself a Christian – and the orthodoxy of
the Church of England is not of that exacting kind.

Towards the end of October 1937, he talked the matter over with
an old Oxford acquaintance, F. R. Barry, then Canon of Westminster
– who, like Sheppard, had been influenced by *The Life of Jesus*. Barry
saw no insuperable objection to his taking Orders. Neither did Canon
Raven, whom he visited at Cambridge on his way home. He too had
been affected by Murry's writing – in particular by a review of his
autobiography, *Wanderer's Way* – and made a point of commending
God to his theological students, as a viewpoint they should take into
account. He still remembers this interview: 'I can see J. M. M. now,
slumped in a deck-chair, head bent, as though all the cares of the world
were on his shoulders: and the poignancy of his suffering moved me.'
Murry spoke of the charm of the Norfolk breckland, where he had
spent an afternoon lately, of the potentialities of a country parish, of
the failure of the Centre, and his own vocation. Raven arranged that
he should receive special consideration as a candidate for ordination
at Westcott House, 'one of the broadest and humanest of theological
colleges' – though inwardly wondering how he and his fellow-candi-
dates would take to one another.

It was soon after this that Murry was invited to join a group of
religious and social thinkers assembled by Dr J. H. Oldham, which
may also have strengthened his determination – the 'Moot', as it was
called, including such distinguished personalities as A. R. Vidler,
Karl Mannheim, Adolf Loewe, Christopher Dawson, M. A. Hodges,

Sir Walter Moberly, Sir Frederick Clarke, Hector Hetherington, William Paton, T. S. Eliot, Gilbert Shaw, John Bailey and Eric Fenn. Its purpose being to give men and women already influential in their own walks of life an opportunity to exchange ideas, stimulate one another and, perhaps, jointly exert some influence on the ecclesiastical hierarchy, he threw himself into it keenly – impressing the others, according to Vidler, not only by his theoretical contributions, but also by that unity of theory and practice, that total commitment, which ruled out any such security or standing as they themselves had achieved.

At the same time, he was impressed in his turn, especially by the two refugees, Mannheim and Loewe, whose thought seemed to him more intimately related to their experience, their experience to the realities of the time. 'These men have been through the hoop,' he remarked: 'They can start thinking again from zero. Until we have known what it is to be spied upon by secret police and to work under a terror, we can't be completely realistic about what is going to happen in Europe. I consider myself a pretty realistic thinker, yet even I am conscious of being, in comparison with them, up in the air.' [16] The beneficial results of this renewed intercourse with thinkers of his own intellectual calibre are very apparent in his works of the next ten years, during which the Moot met quarterly; and it is probable that it confirmed him in the belief that, heretic though he was, his heresies counted for little compared with a common allegiance. When, at any rate, 'The Purgation of Christianity' brought appreciative letters from men of such widely different backgrounds as J. H. Oldham and J. H. Watson, he took it as a sign that he was on the right lines.

Finally, in February 1938, he spent a couple of days with the Bishop of Chichester, George Bell: who, understanding and approving of his wish to combine parochial with literary work, intimated that he might, if ordained, act as assistant to the vicar of some country benefice where two neighbouring parishes had been joined together. One of these, he added, might be Larling itself: and that clinched the matter. After that Murry looked forward confidently to attending Westcott House in the autumn – and beyond, to the security of a living which, without precluding, would put an end to his dependence upon, writing.

In the meantime, however, scarcely a month was going by without some fresh literary project exciting him. Now it was to be a detailed exegesis of Blake's *Milton*, now a book on St Paul, now a study of

Wordsworth and Coleridge, or of Coleridge's influence on nineteenth-century thought. The three-volume history of the Commonwealth was not forgotten, a critique of Marxism was begun. It was as if his pen could not keep pace with his ideas – and his actual output was imposing. During the twelve months succeeding *The Necessity of Pacifism* it comprised, apart from weekly reviews and monthly articles, all the essays collected in *The Pledge of Peace*, the substantial addition to *Studies in Keats, New and Old*, and – richest harvest of all – *Heaven – and Earth*.

Of the twelve studies composing *Heaven – and Earth*, only those of Chaucer, Milton and Wordsworth were entirely new. Earlier versions of 'Goethe' and 'Morris' had appeared in 1932, of 'Montaigne' in 1933, 'Rousseau', 'Godwin', 'Shelley' and 'Marx' in 1934, 'Shakespeare' in 1936. Originally, in fact, it was conceived as a sequel to *Countries of the Mind* – and individually these studies are at least as penetrating as any in the earlier volumes. But, by selecting only such figures as had been more or less consciously involved in the social changes of their day, Murry was able to achieve something more than a series of individual portraits. His purpose, in drastically rehandling the earlier material, was not merely to throw fresh light on the men by setting them in their historical context, but to throw fresh light on the context by showing how it had been actually experienced by men of prophetic insight.

The result was a work that gave the utmost scope to his distinctive gift – a work which, whether classified as biography or history, is as impressive as it is original. For no one but he could have made so intimately his own the contrasting viewpoints of Marx and Godwin, Morris and Goethe; and only a mind thereby 'habituated to work simultaneously on many different levels – on three, certainly – on the economic, on the political and on the moral; and I am impelled to add a fourth – namely the religious',[17] could have acquired so comprehensive a vision of the period.

What is implicit, moreover, is as usual explicit. For instance, 'There is more than one revelation of the truth,' he writes: 'My own conviction is that we need, above all to-day, the imagination to see how and where the different revelations correct, complete and fructify one another.'[18] And the emergence of such an imagination – contemplative in Shakespeare, 'the prophetic soul of the wide world dreaming on things to come'; militant in Cromwell, the soldier of toleration;

speculative in Rousseau, the philosopher of democracy – is the actual theme of the book. This, and its steady endeavour to embody itself in a society, constituted, in Murry's eyes, the 'meaning' of the past four centuries, of Renaissance, Reformation and Revolution.

Heaven – and Earth challenges comparison with *Heroes and Hero-Worship*. It is not merely that several of Murry's heroes – Shakespeare, Goethe, Cromwell, Rousseau – happen to be the same as Carlyle's. Like Carlyle, he is keenly conscious of what has been lost, as well as gained, in these centuries: the sense of collective responsibility fostered by the village commune, the personal relationship between men, the communion of a common faith – all sacrificed to individualism, economic, political and religious. Like Carlyle, he foretells the nemesis of individualism; and, like him, he looks forward to a new ecumenical society combining freedom of conscience with social responsibility. Yet, of the two books, *Heaven – and Earth* is the richer. More lines of thought are gathered together, more vistas opened up by it. And what it lacks in literary genius it makes up for in political insight, since, unlike Carlyle, Murry really understood Rousseau, and understanding him, could see in democracy itself the germ of the new society.

He himself thought the study of Rousseau the best in the book. Certainly one has only to set it beside the essay in *Aspects of Literature* to realize how greatly his political preoccupation had deepened his understanding. Though he had a native sympathy with Rousseau – the first writer after Dostoevsky in whom he had sensed 'an intimate, personal possibility' – in 1918 he had been unable to see in the *Contrat Social* more than 'a parable of the soul of man, like the *Republic* of Plato',[19] whereas now he could present it as *also* 'after Plato's *Republic*, the greatest attempt of the European mind to create a consciousness of the social whole – and so to bring the social whole into being'.[20]

In Rousseau he recognized the creative counterpart to Marx. As Marx had shown what disaster must overtake a society whose economic activity was abandoned to the play of self-interest, Rousseau had shown what was needed if that disaster was to be forestalled: namely, a voluntary acceptance, by every citizen, of such restraints as were necessary to promote the well-being of each – in other words, a conscious endeavour to convert the secular collective into a 'religious' brotherhood. This being Murry's own central idea, the persistent theme of his life, it is not surprising that he bit straight to the core of the *Contrat Social*, as few political philosophers have done. His

'Rousseau' may be regarded as the germ of both his succeeding books, *The Price of Leadership* and *The Defence of Democracy*.

These, like *Heaven – and Earth*, incorporated earlier material: lectures and articles (including 'The Purgation of Christianity') in the one case, the critique of Marxism in the other. But both grew under his hands into expositions of this 'Idea' of democracy as 'a Christian political society'.[21] *The Price of Leadership* is Murry's *Emile*, its point of departure being a consideration of the role of education in such a society. Like other Socialists, he was opposed to the dual educational system, more rigid then than now, which resulted in a ruling-class recruited on a basis of wealth and inherently biassed against any Left Wing legislation. Where he differed from many others was in clearly acknowledging the necessity of a functional ruling-class, and of its being reared in an ethos of responsibility to society as a whole. Product as he himself was alike of Rolles Road and Christ's Hospital, he whole-heartedly approved of the precedence accorded in the English public schools to 'character', rather than learning. The failure of Socialists to reaffirm this was a long-standing grievance of his. What was new was his insistence on the need for an explicitly Christian ethos and on the vocation of the Church to provide it.

In both books, the 'Idea' is developed with a wealth of historical illustration and practical proposals (some of which have since been adopted); in both, of course, he dwells lovingly on the opportunities confronting the country parson as 'the instructed guardian of a system of social relations which are concrete and personal instead of abstract and impersonal'.[22] Essential to his standpoint was the view that the secular institution of the Church and the religious institution of democracy, to the extent that they realized their common aim of constituting fraternal societies, were destined to converge and finally amalgamate. If 'many lines of real creative thinking – the thinking, not of the mere intelligence, but of the total being, which is the prerogative of creative and prophetic genius – converged to bring *The Social Contract* to birth',[23] hardly less can be said of *The Defence of Democracy*. Indeed, re-reading these books after an interval of twenty years, one finds it hard to believe that, even at that date, there were still pundits who thought of Murry, if they thought of him at all, as a literary critic who had missed his way. Give a dog a *good* name and hang it.

Even so, it may be admitted that the best parts of *The Price of Leadership* itself are those devoted to the elucidation of Coleridge and Arnold – Murry's two earliest heroes, with whom, by virtue of a genuine affinity, he had now linked hands again. However much we may regret that other literary critics do not miss their way to the same good purpose as these three, there is no doubt that it was as an interpreter that his talent approximated to genius. Neither *The Price of Leadership* nor *The Defence of Democracy* is as fine or fertile a work as *Heaven – and Earth*. This is Murry's greatest work, and intrinsically it is great. If he had written nothing else but this, he would still have deserved well of the Commonwealth.

XXI

BREAK-DOWN

◄━━━◄❂❂❂◙❂❂❂►━━━►

O N MAY 8, 1938, Murry had to go into hospital for a month. The autumn before, during the Glasgow Rectorial Election campaign, he had noticed a numbness and cramp in his right leg, which had come back since whenever he walked more than a few hundred yards. His doctor, nonplussed, had sent him to an orthopaedic surgeon, who, diagnosing Burger's Disease ('*endoteritis obliterans* with *intermittent claudication*'), had recommended diathermy and massage as 'the first line of attack'. With Young's approval, he had agreed to submit to the treatment, realizing that if it proved unsuccessful – and success was rare – a major operation would be called for.

To him, the event was a 'sign' – a sign, first and foremost, that he was not to enter the Church. After all, 'since my one desire, if I became a priest was to be a country parson, of whose function in the community I had a very definite conception, I was already out of the running. What was the use of a country parson who could not walk?' [1] Already before this he had been hesitating, conscious that his decision had been tainted by a 'tiny effort of will'.[1] Now the issue was taken out of his hands: and at heart he was relieved.

It was not merely that he still had theological qualms. All along, at the back of his mind, there had been lurking the question, 'What could a country parson hope to do with a domestic life like mine?' [1] For by 1938, the confidence which had carried him back to Larling had long since subsided. If he had, in his own words, discovered Christianity through marriage, he was further than ever from discovering 'the secret of Christian marriage';[2] and just this, he had come to believe, was his 'appointed task'.[1] In a way, the priesthood would have been an escape:

> How could I honestly become a priest when I had made so absolute a failure of Christian marriage? I wanted to run away from my marriage

into the priesthood. But nothing I could ever do, as a priest, could surpass what I had done already, to make my marriage Christian. I should never again be visited in such plenitude by the peace of God as I had been, or have the same spiritual power of forgiveness. However truly I might become the instrument of absolution to others, I could never hope to be it to her. For me to become a priest meant a final divorce from her. Yet the one thing I had struggled for all my life was the transfiguration of sex by religion. Was I to surrender that? Still worse, was I to surrender it in reality and pretend not to have surrendered it in fact?[1]

It was characteristic of Murry that he had never been able to voice these misgivings to any of the clergy he had met, except Sheppard. Kind as they were, they had seemed too naïve, too inexperienced, really to understand. Indeed, what he called, in a letter to Susan Miles, his 'unbelievable marriage struggle' [3] had cut him off utterly from all but a handful of friends. It was equally, though differently, characteristic that he never communicated his change of intention, even to those who had taken most trouble to smooth the way to his ordination. Hearing no more, they were left to draw their own conclusions.

If his disease was a sign that he was debarred from the Church, however, it was a still more evident sign that he could not go on leading the life of the last two years. The doctor had only to mention the cause – prolonged nervous strain – for him to realize how aptly it applied. 'That strain actually reached a maximum since we lost touch with one another,' he wrote to Young: 'It was (as you know) bad enough before: but the last $2\frac{1}{2}$ years have been *terrific*, judged even by my standards.' [4] He had veritably fought, and fought, and fought, till his legs were broken (as Aaron Sisson said): and there was a bitter irony in the birth of his second son, David – he who was to have been the pledge of domestic reconciliation – on May 25, 1938, while he was still in hospital.

Unless he relaxed, he was told, he could not expect to live many more years. He must, at the very least, reduce his work to the minimum necessary to earn a living. And this he did: engaging a part-time secretary, handing over *The Adelphi* to Plowman, and firmly refusing any longer to read, revise or recommend the manuscripts constantly sent him by aspiring poets and authors. This last item alone meant a pretty considerable reduction, since a full list of those he had helped, especially during Edward Garnett's lifetime, would be far more imposing than their public acknowledgements might suggest.

Even so, no real relaxation was possible at The Old Rectory, Larling.

On the contrary, as Europe, over the ensuing nine months, rocked steadily on towards disaster, so did his 'diabolical mockery of Christian marriage' [1] – and he was possessed, once again, by the sense of some occult correlation. Once again it seemed to him as if 'there was something utterly cruel in the world'. It was partly for this reason that he attached such significance to the 'visible Church': even lip-service to the traditional Christian values was better than no service at all.

All his life he had taken it for granted that men and women, however vilely they might behave, in their heart of hearts 'believed in God': that is to say, acknowledged that love and truth were better than hatred and falsity (for 'no-one can acknowledge a supra-personal loyalty to Truth or to Love without believing in God').[1] Now he had come to doubt it. At all events, he could no longer say, as he had once said to Sheppard, that evil as such was unknown to him. The question, Could love prevail? was not simply, as he had hitherto presumed, Could love awaken love? – but, Could love call love into being? And it was the same question abroad and at home.

Thus, his 'mission', as he now began to see it, was to put this question to the proof – by trying to make one person at least 'who did not believe in God, believe in Him':

I do not think I set about it clumsily or condescendingly. I began quite simply as I should have done with a backward child. I tried to interest her in improving her own handwriting and spelling, which was that of an illiterate; I persuaded her to learn a few good but simple poems and to copy them out carefully in a handsome leather book which I bought for her; I began to read a Psalm every day before breakfast, even at the risk of boring my own children, in the hope that the meaning or the beauty of the words might awaken some chord in her; I began to say my own prayers every night at my bedside, though it is not a natural practice for me, and I would murmur the Lord's Prayer aloud in the hope that she would join me. I knew that I must have infinite patience.

For a time it seemed to be succeeding. For a time she seemed to be really trying to improve her writing and to remember her poetry, at least. During this time she was strangely docile. The terrible explosions began to grow somewhat rarer; and once at least after an explosion she amazed and touched me deeply by reproaching herself bitterly, and asking to be forgiven. That was the only time she ever used that word. It made me a happy man. But a few days later after another explosion she amazed me no less, but for some reason disheartened me, by turning on herself as it seemed with the same fury of hatred. 'I'm bad, bad, bad, I'm all bad, altogether bad. It's no use. Why did you marry me? Why couldn't you let me go? I had all I wanted – your baby. I should have been happy. Why did you come after me? Why did you make me come back? I knew what it would be. I knew. I knew'. And she burst into a paroxysm of passionate tears. Then she turned on me and said with a strange vindictiveness: 'You're a fool – a fool. Don't you know that women are all bitches – *all* of them?' A doom closed down on my heart . . .

I played my last clumsy and desperate card. 'Why don't you say your prayers, sometimes?' I felt her shy away, like a scared horse. The plunge was audible to the spirit. And suddenly I knew something else. It was not true that she did not believe in God at all. She did. She was mortally afraid of Him. She was terrified of the very idea of God; it was utterly unbearable by her. Then I knew that there was indeed an impassable gulf between us . . .

I had the deep and overwhelming knowledge that what I had hoped and laboured to achieve was absolutely impossible. Tell a man to lift a hundredweight, says Georges Duhamel; he will try – and succeed. Tell him to lift two hundredweight; he will try – and succeed. Tell him to lift a railway-engine; his heart will faint within him. So it was with me and her. By a kind of mutual consent in a common despair, our efforts petered away. The leather copy-book was abandoned, the Psalms were silent, I ceased to pray by my bedside. What had seemed a hope had become a provocation to her. I went to sleep in another room. That brought me one fitful happiness. Often, I would steal, unknown to her, into my elder daughter's bedroom, where she lay silently weeping in the dark. We hardly ever spoke. There was nothing to say. But we held each other tight; and we comforted each other – she in her suffering, I in my despair . . .

From that moment onward, we moved towards Death. Our mutual negation was absolute. My extremest Love aroused in her the absolute of Fear. So long as my love was spontaneous, unthinking, natural; so long as it had in it those elements of physical desire, of bodily worship, which human love between a man and a woman must have or be but a shadow of itself: so long she could avoid its impact and its meaning. It was an animal motion. That was real to her. It was the only reality. All that my love for her contained beyond that was nothing, worse than nothing, a vague presence that disturbed and bewildered her, of which she was half-scornful, half-afraid. Now that, by her own intensity of animal hatred of me she had burned away those elements in my love that seemed to her, but were not, the same, so that the love in me became, perforce, a purely spiritual power, it moved as inexorably towards her destruction as she had moved towards mine. As she had driven me into an ecstasy of spiritual love which, blessed though it was, was not truly me or mine, so in turn that power drove her into an ecstasy of Fear. We could but hound each other into the abyss.[1]

This account was written eight years later, and episodes of different dates have got telescoped. In a life that consisted of little but horrors, Murry confessed, he found it difficult to distinguish between one and another. But the horrors were real enough. The atmosphere of the Old Rectory during these months defies description. Between the extremes of spiritual exaltation and animal fury, universal benevolence and particular, unremitting malevolence, all ordinary human inter-course was suspended. The children alone, unhappy though they were, preserved some semblance to normality – they, and the little maid, Ruby, who hung on through thick and thin out of devotion to them and to Murry. Of 'the Hell that was Larling', Col writes:

> Even now, nearly twenty years later, I can still be drawn back in dreams to those appalling scenes and awake in the grip of the old familiar terror. It was as though we were all under some terrible sentence – so terrible in fact that we hardly dared to speak of it even among ourselves. Fear crept into us like a cold fog and the form it took was the belief that a 'row' was about to break. We read the message in each other's eyes, conscious that we were engaged in a never-ending conspiracy whose sole aim was to preserve, by any means, the uneasy peace. Betty must be propitiated – but how? Gradually it dawned on all of us that there was *no* way out. This was to be our life and we must make the best of it. Even our games took on a slightly hysterical tinge. Yet much of the time I was away at School and my sister assures me that during my absence I either contrived to forget what life was like at home or, by some mysterious mental process, managed to persuade myself that it was not as I had remembered it. Such illusions rarely survived for more than a few days. Sooner or later I would wake to hear that terrible voice screeching abuse at my father; the sound of feet running along the landing; fists pounding on a locked door; the hysterical wailing of my small step-sister and brother. No illusion could long survive the nightmare of that reality.

Powerless to help his children either by staying with them or leaving, Murry himself used to say in after years that only his carpentry and gardening kept him sane: and that was probably the truth. For, in spite of his illness, he would still spend the afternoons at his bench, or deep in the grounds 'digging', as Katherine had once put it, 'as though he were exhuming a dead body or making a hole for a loved one';[5] and visitors would still be surprised to find, in place of the intellectual they expected, a skilful countryman. But visitors were rarer than ever. Not many could stand the strain of that household. Apart from a young man in Rees's old quarters, writing a book about Shelley, the only regular ones were Richard, who continued to travel down at week-ends, with a sinking heart, to give his brother moral support; an elderly convict, who spent the intervals between sentences imbibing methylated spirits in an out-house; and a mild, silver-bearded old gentleman who would turn up from time to time to announce the end of the world. And even they must have left with relief, wondering how, despite his long hours, Murry contrived to write as much as he did.

It certainly gave cause for wonder: for, while *The Price of Leadership* and *The Defence of Democracy* demanded most of his energy, there was no falling-off in his contributions to periodicals. In the ordinary way he kept no record of these – nor, after a few weeks or months, could he even distinguish his own – but from June 1938 to March 1939 his secretary filed such as came her way, and they include between thirty and forty reviews from the *Literary Supplement* alone, of which one each month, on an average, constituted a full-page article. Their quality, moreover, is no less remarkable than their quantity. 'The Contradictions of D. H. Lawrence' (June), 'Coleridge on Politics' (July), 'Chateaubriand' (November), 'Hölderlin' (December), Maritain's *True Humanism* (February), 'Wordsworth's Last Letters', 'Matthew Arnold Today' and R. W. Chambers's *Man's Unconquerable Mind* (March) would, had they ever been collected, have made a worthy successor to *Countries of the Mind*. 'I can work hard enough to say something which I feel ought to be said', he told Plowman, 'but not otherwise.' [6] It speaks much for Sir Bruce Richmond's perspicacity that he, at least, had kept pace with Murry's changing interests, continuing to send him such books as were calculated to call forth his best.

The *Literary Supplement* for November 5, 1938, contains also a moving article, 'Peace at Christmas', expressing the relief, gratitude and hope which Murry, like most other Englishmen, felt after war had been averted at Munich (and which, like most other Englishmen, he later affected not to have felt). 'Perhaps nothing will come of it at all', he wrote, 'but I hardly believe it. It seems to me rather that one day, far hence, the world will realize that through the fidelity of one Statesman to the instincts of the common man there was a miraculous birth of a new awareness of common things.' How pathetic it sounds in retrospect!

Before Christmas it was clear to all but politicians and journalists that the Munich Agreement had only postponed the day of reckoning. In the January *Adelphi* he was already exposing the specious idea of an 'understanding' with Nazi Germany. By February, when he put the finishing touches to *The Defence of Democracy*, his last hopes of peace had evaporated. Europe, too, was moving towards Death.

If his output during these months was surprising, however, his failure to recover was not. With all its merits, *The Defence of Democracy* itself witnesses to his ebbing vitality. It is the work of a weary man, unable to master his material or impose any unity upon it. One could guess, without knowing, that it was taken up and abandoned time after time, and sent to the publishers at last more in desperation than satisfaction. By February, in fact, he had need to get it off his hands, the 'first line of attack' on his disease having definitely failed. If his leg was not slowly to mortify until an amputation became necessary, an operation could no longer be postponed. In April 1939, he went into hospital again.

And again, the sequel is best told in the words of the fragmentary autobiography, written eight years later:

So it was done. Unfortunately – or fortunately, perhaps – I had not realised that this particular surgeon, though his diagnosis had been quick and convincing, was not primarily a neurologist but an orthopaedist; and I eventually came to the conclusion that he was interested in doing an operation outside his own line of country. He got the ganglion right enough; but (as I learned when six years later a neurologist did the same operation for the other leg) he had upset something in the process which a neurologist wouldn't have upset. In consequence when, after a month, I emerged from hospital, it was to endure a further six weeks of fantastic pain . . . The outer world became quite unreal. I walked, or sat, in it as though in a transparent cage of pain. No dope – or none that I was given – had the faintest effect upon it. My recollection is that for those six weeks I never slept at all.

Quite suddenly, it ceased. Timidly, incredulously, I entered into life again like a baby fifty years old. And I went off, almost immediately, to a friend's house in Wales where I had been invited to convalesce. I stood on the station platform one mid-May morning and marvelled that the sun shone warm on me, and I was alive: weak, almost imbecile, but undubitably alive. I made the long journey in a quiet ecstasy of painlessness. To prove that I was alive, and that the operation had done its work, I went next morning for a long, but slow and steady walk, of nearly six miles;

then in a motor-boat down the river towards Milford Haven; then out to tea with some friends of my friend.

It began in the middle of tea-time. Suddenly, I felt very queer indeed. Not with pain – it had nothing to do with pain. As my consciousness translated the extraordinary and terrible sensation, it was that I was certainly going mad. Since I have been told that people who think they are going mad, never do; while those who do, never think they are (which I can well believe), and, anyhow, I did not go mad, my consciousness was all wrong. What it was doing was to describe this utterly intolerable sensation in the only terms that seemed appropriate to it. But certainly it seemed to me that I was on the brink of a spiritual abyss, some vast internal void. I tried to behave like a normal person till the unending tea-party was ended. I clutched my chair, to give me confidence, and answered questions as best I could, astonished that the replies were not gibberish. I got away safely into the car. 'I'm feeling queer', I said to my friend. 'Hellishly queer!'

I cannot really remember what happened then, for the next few hours. Somehow, I think, I must have got through dinner and the night. I remember another walk, in the morning, during which, as I walked slowly up the tree-lined road, I knew it was only a question of minutes. I was overwhelmed by the longing to get home, to get into the warm safety of my wife's arms, even while I loathed and despised myself for the longing. But the Terror beside me, within me, waiting for me, was too awful. My fear – or the fear that was me – was such that it would have blotted out all the past. My friend, I knew, would willingly have sent me home post-haste in a fast car across England. But it would be in vain. I should be mad before I got there. The thought and the longing left me.

That night, at dinner, my teeth began to chatter – to my inward ear like castanets. As good fortune would have it, a doctor, who was an old friend of mine, was in temporary practice some twenty-five miles away. I rang him up and tried to explain what had happened. He said I was to come immediately; he would have a bed ready for me. I was there within three-quarters of an hour. Within two minutes he had given me a powerful shot of adrenalin, tucked me up in bed with a big cup of hot tea at my side. Almost instantly the drowsy magic worked. The terror was gone, and a feeling of warm fatigue rose up within me like life itself. I passed the night somewhere between wake and sleep, absolutely happy.

But those six weeks of physical pain, followed by those three days of unspeakable Fear were the grimmest of my life. Their grimness lay in the fact that they did not belong to life at all. They were outside the range of permissible experience. I have never been able to incorporate them into my own history. The pattern was, for the time being, absolutely broken. But the difference between this rupture, and the rupture of

[263]

anaesthesia, was absolute, because there was no interruption of consciousness itself. Where 'I' had got to, God alone knows: but the consciousness, of pain, of terror, was there all the while.

It took me another fortnight, mainly in bed, to get rid of my terror completely; and for a few days I was haunted by the fear that it would return. But copious draughts of a black medicine that seemed like the elixir of life to me, and the reassuring explanations of my doctor friend, gradually expelled the Fear. 'You were completely exhausted when you came to Cresselly. You had undergone a major mutilation, from which you had been prevented from recovering by your pain.' At this point he burst into a diatribe, well-deserved, against his professional colleagues who will not make a proper use of drugs. 'You monstrously overtaxed your strength by that fantastic walk, when you should have been in bed, or at most in a deck-chair. No wonder the whole show collapsed. No wonder all the suppressed dread of the last six years of your damnable life came out and engulfed you – in a classical example of the Nervous Breakdown.' [1]

The doctor, of course, was Young, whom a merciful Providence seems always to have placed in Murry's reach at critical moments. But this was more critical than most. For, though he was unaware of it until he got back to Larling at the end of May, it had released him once and for all from the thraldom of those six years:

The last tenuous and forlorn wisps of the aura of affection that had once united me to the woman to whom I was married had completely disappeared. I saw her in a hard clear light, with not a trace of warmth or radiance in it. I felt an immense pity for her, but no love. That had been finally killed. And the reason why I pitied her was that she had killed my love for her. It must have taken an almost superhuman will to do that. I looked at her now as a creature from another place. I said to her quietly, soon after my return, when for some trivial and indeed unreal offence she was storming at me in a violent passion: 'Please take this seriously. I don't love you any more.'

Of course, she did not take it seriously. Had she been capable of doing so, that part of my life which was now ending would have been quite different. But it was true. And it seems clear to me in retrospect that the last tie had been broken when I had resigned myself to the impossibility of fleeing from the Terror into her arms. Then, in the very depths of my psyche (or my psycho-somatic being) the severance was made. . . .

I find it in the last degree illuminating. The condition to which it put an end was a life of spiritual torment which was so exhausting to my bodily energies that the life had begun to withdraw from my body. My six years of spiritual mortification had culminated in the declared and obvious beginnings of physical mortification. The gangrene of my soul had become the gangrene of my body. To check this purely physical mortification I underwent a severe operation, and a subsequent extremity of physical pain, which so weakened my total being that, under the strain of a fresh physical exertion, I sank down into a condition of absolute terror. That terror created its myth: the myth that I was on the brink of a spiritual abyss, which I called 'madness'. Any other name would have done: not-Being, *le néant*, nothingness. And that very nameless Terror held me back from returning to that condition which was the first cause of the Terror itself – that soul-destroying persistence of a physical bond between a man and a woman when the spiritual bond of Love has been worn away. From that the Terror saved me; and its salvation of myself was final. In that strange paroxysm of my psycho-somatic being, the last remnants of the animal bond between the woman and myself were dissolved completely away. The Terror had extirpated its own root.[1]

The experience fascinated Murry, as well it might – for 'it was quite decisive for my life. It ended one pattern and began another. It ended a progress towards spiritual and physical inanition and death, and began another process towards spiritual and physical life.' [1]

PART IV

1939 – 1957

PART IV

1939 – 1947

XXII

LIFE IN DEATH

⬦⬦⬦⬦⬦⬦⬦

LOOKING BACK IN 1947, Murry was struck by the contrast between his personal experience of the years 1914–23 and 1939–47. Upon him as upon most of his generation, the First World War had descended like a bolt from the blue. A man of twenty-five (and young for his age), rootless, faithless, he had been as unprepared spiritually as materially. If he had avoided it as long as he could, that was not because he had any conviction to oppose to it, but simply because he had none to endorse it; and little by little it had thrust him into a condition of isolation from the mass of his countrymen which the sordid armistice of 1918 could only exacerbate. 'During that my misery and despair steadily increased, until at the end I was a dreamer who had "venom'd all his days". I was (or felt myself to be) cut off completely from all life-giving contact with my fellow-men; I was "a fever of myself". All that remained spiritually alive in me was the agony of my love for Katherine Mansfield, whom yet I felt, with a sick foreboding, was doomed to die.' [1]

During the Second World War and its aftermath, for all that it found him, a man of fifty (and old for his age), isolated already by his convictions and prepared for the worst, he was to know 'a steadily growing sense of inward security, a day-by-day growing wonder of simple human happiness in love, an ever closer return to what seem to me the fundamental simplicities of life – as farmer, as gardener, as thinker, as writer': until, the yet more sordid victory of 1945 notwithstanding, his feeling of identification with his countrymen was such that 'I have come to love the free society of Britain with a calm passion which is to me a new experience: I love it, not indeed for what it is – though even that, compared to other countries is something great – but for what it may be: for the "idea" which is partly, and may be fully, realized in it.' [1]

[269]

That the one experience was thus the 'strange counterpart and opposite' [1] of the other was due to a single event, which, for this reason, he sometimes called the most important of his life – his *liaison*, on the eve of the War, with the woman who was to restore him to health, revive his faith, fulfil the dream he had never been able wholly to relinquish, and in due course become his fourth wife – Mary Gamble.

Mary was ten years younger than Murry, and by birth, upbringing and temperament very unlike him. The daughter of a well-to-do architect in Lincoln, she had enjoyed a sheltered, comfortable childhood, and embarked on a public career with all the advantages of material security, robust health and buoyant optimism. Before being invited by Sheppard to address public meetings for the P.P.U., she had published two or three small volumes of verse, been prospective Labour candidate for a Midland constituency and played an active part in the Christian Industrial Fellowship. But she was no career-woman, much less a bluestocking. Had she been either, she would have steered clear of Murry, and he of her. Instead, she not only read and admired him, but allowed others to know that she did.

Her admiration dated from 1932, when she had heard him lecture for the I.L.P. Since then they had exchanged a desultory correspondence. But it was not until 1938 that they actually met, on a P.P.U. platform in Oxford ('I seem to have made a convert,' he remarked, on hearing from her a day or two afterwards); and not until towards the end of that year that they found themselves lunching together in London before a committee meeting. 'I was very shy on arrival', Mary writes, recalling this occasion, 'and so was he':

> Then, when we went into lunch, he began to talk. There was cold chicken to start with and he served me with some of that, but, utterly absorbed in what he was saying, forgot to offer me anything else. He helped himself liberally to apple tart, followed by cheese and biscuits and coffee and I, far too nervous to draw attention to my plight, sat and listened hungry but enthralled. Only later, during the meeting, when I began to feel rather faint – I had had a very early breakfast – did I realise what had actually happened. [2]

It was as well that Mary had a sense of humour, and also that Murry's absorption was such that he never realized the *contretemps* at all. Even so, it was not so complete as to prevent his heart beating faster afterwards at the sight of her handwriting on an envelope.

Not that he had any thought at this time of repeating the ill-fated venture of two years before. On the contrary, the same 'single, total and natural change' [3] that had carried him into the P.P.U. was also that which had taken him back to Larling, in the Wordsworthian belief that 'Duty was the fulfilment of Love'.[3] If he had given up the idea of ordination and dropped his domestic crusade, it was only to resign himself bleakly to the inevitable. That venture had convinced him that, come what might, he could never tear himself away from the family; and he was rather fearing than hoping that he and Mary would be thrown together more often. It was not until after his breakdown in May 1939 that he dared even confront, let alone confess, his feelings.

Nevertheless, she had only to write to him that July, for advice on a personal problem, for all the accumulated misery and longing of his 'damnable life' to burst into words:

It's no good: I cannot be a father-confessor to you in these matters: my own heart is too much involved. I don't want to fall in love with you. I am old, and terribly tired: I shall be fifty in another fortnight. And my experience of love has been heart-breaking. Two women I loved with all my heart, mind and soul: they simply died under it. And it was to break away from this awful intensity of love that I married my wife – an utterly simple girl who doesn't understand any of the things that I have struggled for. She loves me after her fashion, passionately; but the form her love takes is a terrible jealousy – an almost murderous jealousy. I have lived through eight years of this; and I marvel that I am alive. I left her once, and returned to her because I *knew* that I could not let our little daughter suffer . . . I shall never leave her again. It cannot be: grown-ups may suffer – it is their privilege – but children must not. But it is no use my pretending; my hunger for a woman who will be gentle towards me grows month by month. And destiny has determined that the woman is you. I don't know what I want of you. I think no more than to be with you for a day now and then – to be assured that my dream of *love* between a man and woman is not only a dream . . . As far as I know, I don't want to be your lover. If I were younger I should desire this tenderly, passionately. But I think that that is gone from me. Maybe it's only that I am tired, tired, tired. But that is what I want from you – rest from my weariness: the beating of my heart tells me that you are capable of the tenderness of love, and that you have this wonderful and precious thing to give me – and that you will. I want you to take me in your arms, to let me sleep in peace with you, to reassure me of the eternity of human love. I want, I need terribly, to believe in love between a man and woman again. Now that I know you have suffered the anguish of love, I am not afraid to speak.

But, my dear, whatever you do, don't do this out of pity for me. I desire no-one's pity. If there is no upspringing of the tenderness of love – the love that may be required to give all and receive nothing and loves the more tenderly for that knowledge – in your heart, say 'No'. Believe me, it will not *hurt*. A man of my bitter experience is not hurt by knowing that a way is closed to him. He learns that he may not dream a dream. Whatever happens, our friendship will endure.[4]

Although, having never been repulsed, Murry disbelieved in the possibility of unrequited love, he wrote this letter, he confessed, in fear and trembling. It was the first time since 1911 that he had taken the initiative himself. Yet it would have been an unusual woman who could have resisted such an appeal: and Mary had only to read it to know that this was the letter she had been waiting for all her life. After all, 'for years he had been my hero. His words had meant more to me than those of any other living writer. For years past all my ideas on socialism – on living – on a religion based on love had been inspired by him.'[5] Before the middle of August, he was writing again:

The idea that this sweet and steady, generous and tender love awaited me after all touches me to the quick. I had truly ceased even to dream of it. I never tried for it so deep was my disillusion. And now – in a short afternoon, in some for ever indefinable way, you have convinced me of the reality of the love that 'seeketh not its own'. I had almost persuaded myself that I was a childish fool in ever having believed that a woman was capable of this; and equally that I was guilty of some colossal self-deception in imagining that I was capable of it myself. In an afternoon you have swept all this distrust away. Quite simply, I trust you utterly.[6]

It was the story of Nehale over again, only with one all-transforming difference – that this time his star never faltered. Although he was too weary even to make love; although he made it clear to Mary from the start that he had no intention of leaving his family, and might, on the contrary, leave her, if ever there were a 'visible and certain change in Betty'[7] – this time there was no disillusionment. And it was due to this, beyond doubt, that he was able, not merely to recover from his break-down, but to face the outbreak of War with a new and unlooked-for access of determination and energy.

To be sure, the fateful September 3, 1939, found him in near-despair. Like every other house in the country, The Old Rectory was being draped in funereal black; Betty was preparing accommodation for ten evacuee children; he himself had just returned from a conference of

Modern Churchmen at Cambridge, as hopeless now of the Church as he was of the Pacifist movement – which, he predicted, would 'just melt away'. 'It is so ghastly,' he moaned that evening, head sunk between his hands: 'I feel that I just cannot live through another war. The last one destroyed all my friends. Those whom it did not kill physically, it killed in the spirit. Lawrence and Katherine – they were *broken* by it; and I only crawled out of it, spiritually maimed. Now to see the same thing performed on an even greater scale, on a younger generation – it's more than I can bear.' [8]

Yet, as week followed week without any large-scale offensive opening in the west, his hopes revived. After all, 'If once Pacifists succumb to the view that the validity and value of their movement depends upon its success in preventing war, they have surrendered everything,' he had written in *The Pledge of Peace*: 'The real business of a Pacifist movement is to bear its witness against the total dehumanization of humanity that is necessitated by modern war.' [9] Even supposing that the Phoney War could not be protracted indefinitely, still something of value might be preserved through the grim time coming.

To the majority of the 140,000 P.P.U. members, this attitude of Murry's was incomprehensible. They drew no distinction between preventing war and abolishing it; and, in his view, had a very inadequate idea of what abolishing it entailed – namely, the creation of an entirely new social order. This was one reason why, since Sheppard's death, he had had little to do with the P.P.U. – had, indeed, more than once been on the point of resigning from it. The weekly *Peace News*, he confessed, made him ashamed; and most of his own contributions had been directed towards dispelling the facile illusion that peace could be had without personal sacrifice or social revolution. They would not have been published, had Plowman not paid for them personally.

He, on the other hand, had always been concerned first and foremost with that new social order – and was therefore, as he told Plowman, 'only incidentally a Pacifist':

Anyway, my whole bias is towards doing what I can to establish a truer *mode of life*. That is my real concern; and, of course, intimately connected therewith, is the desire to propagate imaginative comprehension – the understanding of how radically irreligious is the prevalent life-mode. In a sense, I'm back with Lawrence, though of course with a rich nuance of difference. But I shall never be content, never be able to say my Nunc dimittis, until I have established a core of simple, natural and religious living among a few people who trust one another completely.[10]

Such an effort as this, he had learned, involved the renunciation of war; but equally, the renunciation of war involved such an effort as this, if it was not to amount merely to non-combatant service. This, accordingly, was what he began to enjoin upon Pacifists as soon as it became clear that no mass-revulsion, culminating in a general strike against war, was to be looked for.

The question was, What could he do about it himself? That autumn, Plowman enlisted a group of young volunteers to restore The Oaks, at Langham, now that the Basque children were leaving, and to re-establish a community there. Had Murry been a free agent, he would have joined him. As it was, being unable to move from Larling without precipitating a domestic crisis, he had no option but to go on propagating 'imaginative comprehension': and this, he knew, would not be easy. Signs were not wanting already that journalism, for such as he, was liable to become a hazardous business.

True, *The Price of Leadership*, adopted by the Religious Book Club, had proved unexpectedly successful – so successful that he was beginning, at last, to command the attention due to him as a social thinker. Even the B.B.C. had awoken to his existence, commissioning a broadcast for Armistice Day; while D. L. Murray, who now replaced his old patron, Sir Bruce Richmond, as editor of the *Literary Supplement*, lost no time in proposing a series of articles on 'Democracy and War'. But war had hardly been declared before the broadcast was cancelled; and, for the first time since 1913, his articles were returned – with the unintentionally ironical request that he should so reconstruct them 'as to make their theme the necessity of rallying all the forces of the spirit to resist Hitler until he and his system are finally overthrown, no matter what has to be inflicted on the German people in the doing of it'.[11] Since he was unable to do this, it was the end of his connexion with the *Literary Supplement*.

Still, other opportunities did present themselves. For one thing, although he could not comply with Murray's request, he could so far moderate the articles as to admit of their being published, first in the *Literary Supplement* itself, and then as a pamphlet. For another, this had the surprising result that the B.B.C. turned to him after all, and not for one, but for a series of talks along the same lines. Moreover, a new and enterprising publisher, Andrew Dakers, was eager to add a book to his list with the title, *The Betrayal of Christ by the Churches*: so that as long as the Phoney War lasted, his hands were full. And he made the most of his chances.

He had only broadcast once before, from Glasgow in 1926; and used though he was to addressing large audiences, was 'petrified with terror' [12] by the microphone. Yet no one who listened in to the series, *Europe in Travail*, in the winter of 1939–40 would ever have guessed it. Manner matched matter – and that was masterly. Into those five short talks he distilled the essence of a decade's social thinking, presenting his unfamiliar and unpopular thesis so lucidly and arrestingly that the simplest could grasp it, the most knowledgeable not forget.

The thesis itself was one that he was to reiterate *ad nauseam* over the ensuing years: namely, that the root-cause of the War was man's failure to master the machine. Instead of couching it in those abstract terms, however, he concentrated on the single, concrete and crucial issue of unemployment – the standing army of unemployed in every country being at once the most palpable witness to that failure and the direct agent of Hitler's ascendancy. There is an echo of one of his recent conversations with the Durham blastfurnaceman, Watson, in the memorable passage:

> Remember the word of the unemployed man: 'For us your peace is war, and your war is peace.' Think of the grim paradox that lurks behind those words: That modern society has found no way of keeping its machines running, and its members at work, save by preparing for war. Ultimately, for one simple reason: that a machine-economy can work to capacity only if its products are given away. And in this civilisation we dare not give things away, because we should knock the bottom out of it if we did. Here is a civilisation which its very machines would compel to be Christian, but the nature of men rebels. Give away it must. Give away in love it will not, it dare not. Give away in hate, therefore. Give away to each other as enemies – destruction and death beyond the dreams of avarice. The charity of this civilisation is war – total war.[13]

The moral was twofold: explicitly, that the sole alternative to the compulsory and brutal collectivism of the totalitarian States was a voluntary and humane collectivism, informed by a 'conception of social discipline and social responsibility' [14] such as no nation had yet achieved; implicitly, that just because no nation had yet achieved such a thing, there was neither cause nor excuse for national self-righteousness.

To Murry himself, convinced as he was that unless the temptation to self-righteousness were resisted there would be no chance of the self-discipline emerging, the implicit moral was the more important. It was in order to forestall the 'moral savagery' that would make a better social order inconceivable, that he strove to present the War as 'primarily not a crisis in the fortunes of the British nation, but a crisis in the history of mankind at large'.[15] It was for the same reason that he appealed to the Government again and again that winter to proclaim as its goal the establishment of a society of nations: 'It is folly and crime to wait. Once the swinish descent of recrimination and reprisal has begun, the thought of world community will fade in a mist of blood. We need to grave it on stone like the Ten Commandments now – that we may never forget.' [15]

Early in 1940, he was addressing a packed meeting at the Central Hall, Westminster, convened by the National Peace Council – C. E. M. Joad in the Chair, S. de Madariaga and H. G. Wells the other speakers. 'A terrible sinking of heart came over me,' he confessed from the platform, 'when I heard both Dr Joad and Mr Wells speak of the new world order *after* the war':

> It would be wrong in me to dwell on a subject so controversial, and I do not wish to do so, but I should be lacking in common honesty if I did not confess my conviction in this matter, because after all, the crucial experience in my life was living through the last war. Then I came to the bitter conclusion that at the end of a modern war humanity is so exhausted that it is incapable of implementing its first idealistic purposes. It can't implement them; it is too tired to do so. If a vastly more destructive war is carried on to the bitter end and until one side is more exhausted than the other and one side capitulates to the other, I see no hope at all of a better world order being constructed out of that exhausted state.[16]

This particular meeting had been called to debate the possibility of a negotiated peace with Germany. It seems strange, in retrospect, that so many people, even at that date, should have thought such a thing feasible – a peace that would have left only a little less of Europe under totalitarian rule than today. But could Britain and France alone stand up to Germany and Russia? Would the offer of an armistice, on terms that included a Czech Bohemia and a Polish Poland, strengthen the German cause, even if it were rejected? Of the speakers that evening, it was indisputably Murry who carried the audience, 'his profound understanding and that hesitant moving eloquence of his', as one of them recalls, 'making H. G. Wells' and Senor Madariaga's contributions seem almost trivial'.[17]

It is clear, not only from his lectures and articles, but also from his letters and conversations of this time, that Murry was possessed as never before by the sense of having a duty to discharge towards the 'lost generation' of 1914–18, 'our friends who died as dedicated men'.[18] In *The Betrayal of Christ by the Churches*, he actually cites his own words from *The Evolution of an Intellectual* arraigning the 'old men' of Versailles and predicting the nemesis on their treatment of defeated Germany. 'For me it was a purely moral issue. I felt simply that if the democracies did not implement their professions, and fulfil their pledges a terrible retribution was inevitable. Unless Germany was converted to democracy by the justice and generosity of our treatment of her, democracy in Europe was doomed.' [19]

It was the gravamen of his charge against the Churches that neither then nor since had they shown any awareness of that crime, let alone summoned the nation to repentance; and that now, when the retribution had come, they looked on Hitlerism as 'an uncaused malignancy',[20] a *deus* – or rather, *diabolus* – *ex machina*:

> It is not as a pacifist that I criticise the Christian leaders, but simply as a very humble and utterly imperfect Christian, who is only a little less convinced that there is a true Christian case for the stubborn prosecution of the war than he is convinced that there is a true Christian case for renouncing war completely. My criticism is that the Christian case for prosecuting the war, as put forward by Christian leaders, is unworthy of Christianity. It is shallow and self-righteous; it lacks depth and humility . . . It is the absolute duty of our Christian leaders – ecclesiastical and political alike – to acknowledge that we are chiefly responsible for the appalling aberration of Nazi Germany. Only if we create among ourselves the clear consciousness that we, equally though not contemporaneously with Nazi Germany, bear the guilt of the present condition of internecine warfare in Europe, and only if we retain that consciousness undimmed, can there be any true hope of arresting the swift process of moral degeneration which has raged on unchecked in Europe since 1914. If such a lively consciousness of our own partnership in guilt with Germany were to be created, then it would be possible – indeed, it would be inevitable – that our statesmen should conceive this unholy struggle as the common tragedy of European man. And that way of conceiving the struggle is necessary to salvation . . . On the prevalence of this fundamental conception depends the possibility of establishing any kind of just international order.[21]

Alas, by the time *The Betrayal of Christ* was published, the bombs were raining on London; and 'retribution' already ranked high on the Prime Minister's list of war-aims, approved by Oldham's *Christian News-Letter*.

The Betrayal of Christ was a labour of unrequited love. It was because Murry himself had cherished such hopes of the Church that he now turned on it so bitterly – and only a man who realized so keenly what it might have been could have exposed it so penetratingly for what it was. It signified his final disenchantment with institutional Christianity. Although, the following January, he was to electrify the Archbishop of York's Malvern Conference with his impassioned peroration – 'The Church fails in leadership, because it shows no sign of having known despair; no evidence of having been *terrified* by its own impotence' [20] – he alone of his closest associates there, such as Eliot and Vidler, was not disappointed by the occasion, having expected nothing.

It is none the less certain that his characteristic reaction carried him away. The brilliant exposure of the 'Christian Statesman', Lord Halifax, which excited Lloyd George's admiration, was salutary and sound; but his revulsion against the pharisaism of parliament, pulpit and press caused him to lean over backwards, almost as much as his opponents mistaking a half-truth for the whole. For once, his capacity for adopting a variety of viewpoints forsook him. *The Betrayal of Christ* is a polemic, and like all polemics, one-sided. It did not deserve to sell better than any other of his books.

The very clarity with which he saw the economic predicament common to all the belligerents blinded him to the political and ideological cleavage. 'It would betray a grave defect in our imagination', he wrote in the June *Adelphi*, 'if we were to allow ourselves to be misled by an abstract and rational pacifism into blurring the deep moral distinction between Hitlerism and our imperfect democracy' – adding that he had listened to utterances from Pacifist platforms which did blur it, and could 'hardly fail to be deeply shocking to the consciences of our fellows'. Yet he himself was the worst offender, elsewhere dismissing this very distinction as of no 'great or lasting significance',[22] and asseverating time after time, 'If Hitler represents the perverted future, we represent the decadent past.' In private, he would go further still, pronouncing the Nazi social system, 'taken on the whole, better than ours: less corrupt, more truly communal and creative'.[23] He had little real reason to complain of being 'a pacifist pariah',[24] because, pre-

sumably, he was refused a Civil List pension and banned from the
air.

Europe in Travail had proved extraordinarily popular, as did his concluding talk in a subsequent series, 'A Christian Looks at the World'.
Never before had such a fan-mail inundated The Old Rectory. By
May 1940 the danger seemed real that he might even yet become a
national figure – and questions were asked in the House.

Why, demanded Mr H. G. Strauss, the Conservative member for
Norwich, had such a person as Mr Middleton Murry been permitted to
broadcast? 'Facts known about this gentleman were that he was a
Communist, a Pacifist and one of the leading members of the Peace
Pledge Union.' It struck him as 'very strange', as indeed it was; nor
was he reassured by Harold Nicolson's reply: 'Mr. Middleton Murry
was an extremely cultured critic with a very sensitive mind and great
knowledge.' [25]

Perhaps Mr Strauss had dark recollections of subversive activities in
his own constituency. He certainly possessed a copy of *The Necessity of
Communism*, for when, three days later, Murry wrote to *The Times*
denying that he had ever been a Communist, the retort came swift and
sharp – a volley of quotations that could hardly fail to establish his
guilt in the eyes of anyone who did not possess one. And that was con-
clusive. Even when, some fourteen months later, the Communists
became Mr Strauss's glorious allies, Murry was not required to broadcast again.

XXIII

'PEACE NEWS'

◄◄◄═══❖═══►►►

JUNE 1940 – Britain's Finest Hour. Plans to take over Norway had been forestalled by the German occupation; Belgium and Holland had surrendered; France was cracking. The Minister of Information was calling for a 'sixth column' of private informers; spies were suspected everywhere. At Langham, a posse of detectives descended on The Adelphi Centre, bearing away Murry's article, 'The Anti-Pacifism of Reinhold Niebuhr' (obviously a teutonic title). At Larling, another ransacked The Old Rectory, while the village constable kept Murry under surveillance:

> He sat, with his helmet in his hands, patiently watching me at my carpentry, keeping up official dignity for a while. Then the situation became too much for him. He suddenly grinned from ear to ear. 'The silly buggers!' he said. And I knew with relief that the heart of England was sound. And I felt that, even if Hitler did win the Battle of Britain, Nazism could never subjugate the spirit of the people.[1]

All the same, the outlook was bleak – and not only from a national standpoint. It had been declared a criminal offence to disseminate any opinion that might cause 'alarm and despondency' – any opinion, in effect, that reflected the true situation. *Peace News* was banned by the wholesalers, printers refused to handle it; even Murry's contribution to *The Adelphi*, 'Good-bye Europe', could not be set up without being submitted to the Ministry of Information. 'My occupation is gone', he was mourning, 'and I am not fit for any other.' [2]

For a season it really looked as if his worst predictions were to be fulfilled – as if Britain, in the fight against Fascism, would turn semi-Fascist herself; and he heartily repented his failure to act on them betimes, by investing in a farm. As it was, though he had just finished *The Betrayal of Christ*, it was doubtful whether it would ever be published; and though he had entered into partnership with a neighbouring bee-keeper, doubling the number of his hives, he could hardly hope to support his family from that source alone. 'Probably the best thing I could do', he wrote to Mary, 'would be to tackle some subject entirely remote from the war. But so far I find it quite impossible. When your "line of life" has been to turn, more and more, from "literature" to "religion" and from "religion" to "politics", you can't suddenly put the machine into reverse.' [3]

To make matters worse, hostilities had reopened on the domestic front. For nearly six months, he had managed to conceal his *liaison* with Mary, the result being an unprecedented lull – proving, as he realized at the time, that his own frustration of spirit had had something to do with his wife's paroxysms. But secrecy was not Murry's *forte*. His natural trustfulness, his absent-mindedness, his inability to keep order among his papers, all militated against it. It had only been a question of time before one of the letters he and Mary exchanged almost daily fell into Betty's hands: and then the fat was in the fire.

'Since December, when B. discovered that I loved Mary Gamble, I have suffered more than ever in my life,' he told Wordsworth on June 7, in a long explanatory letter:

> But the irony of it is rather overpowering. I, a sort of apostle of peace and understanding and love and I don't know what, have never known what peace is in my own home for nine years, except on one occasion when I was too ill to appreciate it. Your question, 'If one can't create peace in one's personal life, what right has one to pretend that one can't take part in war?' hits me *terribly* hard: but it's not new. It's a kind of mystery that gnaws at my life – upheaves my whole faith. If after nine years I have been utterly unable to convert B. to a modicum of kindness and decency, must there not be something radically wrong in me? Or, if there isn't anything radically wrong in me, isn't my faith mistaken? Well, I suppose it depends on what my faith is. And again I suppose that my faith is that, if you hang on to the truth, you are crucified – but I would vastly prefer a less domestic kind of crucifixion.

Unfortunately, the crucified are rarely given much choice in the matter; and anyway, Murry was not the stuff of which martyrs are made. A faith that demanded martyrdom was no faith for the ordinary man; and what was not for the ordinary man was not, in the last resort, for him.

His own Pacifism having been bound up from the start with his domestic struggle, he was uncomfortably aware that his principles required him to hold out at home until he collapsed once more – until 'jealous, deathly, possessive love capitulates to non-possessive love at my death-bed, or over my dead body'.[4] But, as he confessed in his journal, that was 'much too romantic'[4] for him. When it came to the point, it was only because he 'could not face for a second time the sheer agony of parting from the children'[5] that he hung on through thick and thin, practising *ahimsa* to the best of his ability; and an *ahimsa* which had failed so conspicuously even when there was no Mary to inspire it, was unlikely to prevail when there was. An arrest for espionage would have created a sensation in the village; an arrest for murder would not. Altogether, life at The Old Rectory was such that he could not have done very much work, even if there had been work to be done.

As luck would have it, however, the very difficulties accumulating for Pacifists proved his salvation: for it was at this point that the P.P.U. National Council, deciding that the best hope of saving *Peace News* was to put an influential journalist in charge, offered him the editorship. He seemed to them the obvious man – had he not once been Chief Censor? And to him, in his present predicament, the opening came as a godsend. It would mean a platform for his convictions, a salary of £7 (plus fares) for a three-day week, and, not least, an opportunity to meet Mary regularly. If there was any risk involved, it was no greater than he had bargained for when he joined the Union. By the second week of July, he was installed once more in a London editorial office.

It was a far cry from the sober, sedate *Athenaeum* to the twopenny four-page *Peace News*; from Adelphi Terrace to the lugubrious staircase winding up from a stationer's entrance to the first floor of No. 3 Blackstock Road, Finsbury Park. And Murry could hardly have chosen a worse time to return to a city he loathed. His arrival practically coincided with the 'Blitz'. Yet, had the contrast occurred to him, he would probably have preferred his existence in 1940 to that of 1920. Mary, having moved from Lincoln to Dedham, in Suffolk, in order to be within reach of the Centre, could join him every Monday and Tuesday evening at their *pied-à-terre* in Oakley Street, Chelsea. When that became untenable, she found another room closer to the office, at No. 755 Seven Sisters Road: and, she writes, 'we were incredibly happy there'.[6] His letters prove it.

Physically, he was fearless. Once, during the First World War, he had astonished his brother and Katherine by arresting a runaway horse in full career down the Fulham Road; while in those days he had rather courted than avoided the bombs. Now, though he did not court them, neither was he at all disturbed by them. But for her, Mary says, he would have been out of doors, watching and helping where he could. As it was, he slept through all but the loudest explosions – when, noticing her fear, he would get up and start making tea, that typical Englishman's remedy for every emergency. 'He was quite convinced, that he would not be killed . . . I remember him saying, with a smile, "the play in which J. M. M. has been cast for the leading role has not been played out yet" '.[7] So fortified, by her devotion on the one hand, his sense of destiny on the other, he could, and did, throw himself into the P.P.U. with all his old fanaticism.

Since the outbreak of serious hostilities, the membership had declined precipitately, several even of its foremost sponsors, like Bertrand Russell, abruptly renouncing their Pacifism. This in itself was encouraging. It was what Murry had been expecting; and only with the departure of those who had joined to prevent war, he believed, could the remainder get down to their proper business of abolishing it. 'I am one of those who consider that the actual outbreak of war changed the very nature of relevant pacifist action,' he wrote: 'One chapter closed; another opened: and thenceforward the true concern of pacifists was to help to build a religious political movement which could endure the incalculable moral and material stresses of a total war':

> I see in the pacifist movement the raw material of a new Christian Church, which would be created under the shadow of the end of an epoch; much as the original Christian Church, which was created under the shadow of 'the end of the world'. The pacifist community (and I use the word community in the widest sense) is to me the analogue of the Christian community nineteen hundred years ago. I look to it for a revivification of the Christian religion, and new effort to realise – in the light of centuries of historical experience – the life of brotherhood without which Christianity is an empty form. Such a view of the pacifist movement cannot anticipate in the near future a large-scale 'revolution' of which it is the instrument; it is much rather the leaven that will leaven the lump of the new civilisation which must come, for assuredly we are in the death-throes of this one. Therefore, when I am asked 'what are we to do now?' I can only answer: 'Strengthen the bond of brotherhood in the movement, by every possible means. Let us not waste our energies now in trying to stop the war. The time for that is past. Let us

concentrate on trying to form a new community to operate amid the wreckage of the old one.' [8]

Such a view of the Pacifist movement, naturally, did not commend itself to all: yet there was enough to warrant Murry's optimism. The new leadership now emerging constituted as fine a body as could be found in the country at that date. Max Plowman, Eric Gill, Laurence Housman, Charles Raven, Alex. Wood, the Cambridge scientist, Wilfred Wellock and George M. Ll. Davies, the social reformers, were all men he could love or respect. In Gill, in particular, he found a man who 'came nearer than anyone else I have known to being what a modern saint ought to be'.[9] And the response of the rank and file was no less heartening. For his broadcasts had impressed Pacifists too, and they appreciated his loyalty the more for the defection of so many of their spokesmen. Within eight months of his appointment as editor, he was able to report: 'By the devoted and incessant efforts of the staff, by the equally devoted and incessant efforts of group-members of the P.P.U., a new organization for distribution has been created, and slowly and steadily the circulation has risen from 9000 to 18000. The Peace News Fighting Fund is well past £1500, and the financial situation of the paper is sound.' [10]

This was no small achievement. It is not easy, even in peace-time, to keep an unpopular paper afloat; in the circumstances of 1940, it argued a devotion and discretion which few but Murry could have combined. Clearly his War Office training stood him in good stead now, when his purpose was to search out the truth behind the official communiqués and estimate how much could be divulged without causing 'alarm and despondency'. As a matter of fact, the acute, incisive and often entertaining political commentary which he wrote every week for the next seven years, over the name of 'Observer', was studied with evident attention far beyond Pacifist circles; and if some (unhappily not all) of his gloomier prognostications were falsified, it is possible, at least, that he himself was partly responsible.

To present an honest picture of events was especially difficult during the early months, when no objective observer believed that Britain could preserve her independence, let alone reconquer the Continent. (It is sometimes forgotten, by the British, that Britain could not have won the war without Russia and America, any more than with them she could have lost it.) Murry himself was persuaded that the chance to make Europe safe for democracy, which had been missed in 1918, would not be offered a second time. 'Hitler is the instrument by which certain inevitable economic and political changes are being effected,' he insisted: 'They are being effected brutally, because we had not the courage or vision to effect them humanly.' [11] Once effected, he thought, they would prove irrevocable; and since the supersession of nationalist anarchy and competitive capitalism was desirable in itself, the concern of the true democrat should be, not to disrupt, but to liberalize, the Nazi-imposed 'new order'.

That it was susceptible to liberalization, he was confident: men could not be 'conditioned into helotry for ever'.[12] 'In course of time it will lose many of its objectionable features, and will develop into a kind of federation . . . And the more various are the national elements included within its orbit, the less is a mechanical and arbitrary *Gleichschaltung* capable of enduring . . . The idea that it will be a permanent and universal European tyranny is the romanticism of impotent democracy.' [13]

The worst way to promote this aim was to prolong the economic blockade: that could only play into Hitler's hands, consolidating the peoples of Europe behind him in hatred of Britain and provoking the invasion he appeared reluctant to launch. The best would be to use British-American sea-power 'instead, creatively: as a basis of negotiations – as a means, a powerful means, of assuring that Germany undertakes her rightful task of organizing Europe in a humane and decent spirit'.[14]

The German attack on Russia in July 1941, although it took 'Observer' as much by surprise as it did the Russians themselves, only strengthened him in this belief, by reducing still further the likelihood of invasion and increasing Britain's bargaining power. Since the Soviet annexation of the Baltic States, he had lost all sympathy for Russia; and the sudden reversal of the Party Line – not only Communist, but Labour and Conservative – sickened him. Between Communism and Nazism, he affirmed, there was nothing to choose:

> Both creeds inculcate the utmost use of violence in achieving their ends. The Communist makes no bones about his intention to extirpate the capitalist everywhere; the Nazi is equally forthright about his determination to extirpate the Jew. Both these intentions seem to us morally abominable. And it does not appear in fact that the Nazis have behaved any worse to the Jews than the Communists have behaved to the unfortunate *Kulaks*. Both systems violate the fundamental axioms of

Christianity and democracy. No moral issue at all is involved in the struggle between them.[15]

This being so, Britain was under no moral obligation to rescue Russia, let alone exhaust her vitality and jeopardize her traditions 'in order to hand Europe over to the re-ordering of Russia'.[16] From the democratic standpoint, she would do better to ensure that 'some sort of equipoise should be reached between Russia and Germany';[17] and meantime, 'while remaining on an impregnable defensive',[18] concentrate on evolving a pattern of society superior to either the Communist or the Nazi. In that way she might, even yet, save herself by her exertions and Europe by her example.

This was the dialectic which Murry developed that autumn in a series of lectures at Manchester College, Oxford, on 'The Impact of Total War on Society'. It was the dialectic which, by ratifying his aversion both to the decadent past and to the perverted future, satisfied his whole being, conferred a new unity upon him, and prescribed a course of action that would reconcile the positive contributions of democracy and totalitarianism, freedom and order. His main endeavour as a commentator, in fact, was to elicit a 'pattern' from the seeming chaos of current events, of the same kind as the 'pattern' he was accustomed to elicit from his personal experience and from history at large. A kindred endeavour was what he had admired in Cromwell – and, like Cromwell, he was not averse to proclaiming the prescription of his undivided being, arrived at through such 'wrestlings of the spirit',[19] the 'will of God'.

It was, of course, nothing of the sort. It was the will of Murry. And it would have been better for all concerned if he had acknowledged that – if, like Nietzsche, he had had the candour to say, not *Gott will*, but *Ich will*. It might have exposed him (as it did Nietzsche) to the charge of arrogance; but it would have saved him from the temptation of postulating the desirable as the inevitable:

> I am quite certain – and I give this plum of prophecy to the investigators of the files of *Peace News* fifty years hence – that the peace which will come when the German hegemony of Europe is recognised as inevitable will be the beginning of the decay and downfall of the evil of Hitlerism.[20]

In actual fact, his fanaticism could hardly fail to engender a certain sympathy for Hitler (his exact contemporary, whose early struggle with his father to escape a civil service career so closely resembled his own), his sense of 'destiny' predisposing him to attach deep significance to the Führer's disquisitions on his 'mission'. He was certainly fascinated as well as repelled; he no less certainly sentimentalized the Nazi 'new order'. And that was the flaw in his 'pattern'.

It was one thing to see Hitler as the Scourge of God, quite another to credit him with the intention and ability to reconcile the conquered nations; one thing to rebut (as Murry was the first to do) that 'puerile pot-pourri of faked history',[9] Sir Robert Vansittart's *Black Record*, and the vicious notion it disseminated that Germans were inherently incapable of creative achievement, quite another to speak of Europe (even the Scandinavians?) as deliberately rejecting democracy, and to dismiss the idea that 'the people everywhere are straining at the leash for the opportunity to eject the German oppressor and welcome the British liberator' as 'the opium-dream of an obsolete statesmanship'.[21]

For all his insistence that to predict is not to approve, Murry himself was not guiltless of wishful thinking; while his honourable determination to 'set down nought in malice'[22] could mislead him nearly as seriously as the professional hate-mongers of Fleet Street. Amid the spate of atrocity-stories, he rejected the true with the false, remaining sceptical even towards the reports, released in 1943, of the mass-extermination of European Jewry. He simply could not believe that, if these were true, the British and American Governments would use them merely to whip up hatred, and do nothing to save the victims.

In general, however, his judgement of the Allied leadership was soberer than of the German. Churchill he sized up from the start as 'the strong, short-sighted man',[23] who, however capable in an emergency, required to be 'subordinated to some statesman who sees the necessity of community by peace and community for peace, who boldly takes the historical initiative from Hitler, instead of following his with a mere military reaction'.[24] The Prime Minister's stubborn refusal to proclaim any goal beyond 'extirpating Hitlerism'; his contemptuous rejection of Indian national aspirations; his appeasement of Russia over Poland; his eventual emergence from a six years' struggle with nothing more constructive to offer than the preposterous 'Morgenthau Plan' for the 'pastoralization' of Germany, all incurred Murry's forthright criticism, confirming his initial foreboding that no better issue was to be looked for than a super-Versailles, setting the stage for one more holocaust.*

From the moment America's entry into the war made military victory feasible, he devoted his commentary incessantly to emphasizing the 'barrenness of "unconditional surrender" ' [25] and the need to proclaim, as the Western goal, a society of nations which could command the enthusiasm of the European peoples, Germans included. 'Unconditional surrender', he reiterated, was 'the utterance of a blank in the mind, produced by the conception of your enemy as totally evil';[25] it was morally retrograde and politically disastrous; it made 'nonsense of all high-flown pretensions to be fighting for a world of justice and peace',[26] prolonged the struggle, played into Stalin's hands. The unquestioning acceptance of this slogan, by a Parliament reduced to a caucus of adulous yes-men, brought him near despair of democracy.

To him, it was axiomatic that if the 'survival' for which Britain was said to be fighting meant anything that deserved to survive, it meant 'democracy with civic liberty to defend us from its abuses; and the possibility of peaceful progress which both together contain': that the preservation of these, therefore, 'must absolutely condition the nature of our war-effort'.[27] If the war was not to be totally irrational – if it was to be a continuation of politics by other means – then this should be the limiting conception within which every decision should be taken, every measure scrutinized. 'Parliament should have its own strategy of the war: a strategy compatible with its own continued existence as an effective organ of sovereignty. A Parliament that is content to gobble up the crumbs of enlightenment which fall from the map-strewn table of a romantic and "war-minded" politician is preposterous at this moment of crisis in world-history; when it is Parliament's function to keep the "war-minded" man in his place.' [28] The nature of such a strategy, not only foreign but domestic, was the theme of his book, *Christocracy*, completed in 1941.

Earlier than most critics, Murry foresaw that the enormously increased powers of the State could not be discarded after the War without precipitating economic chaos and political violence; consequently, that there would be 'no escape from the necessity of planned production for peace':[29] and, like most Socialists, he looked forward to the oppor-

---

* Towards the end of his life, Murry came to admire Churchill after all – mainly, it appears, on the strength of *The Life of Marlborough*, which he studied in connexion with Swift.

tunity this would afford to bring the machine under control 'by peaceful and legal means'. Had the Beveridge Report been made law in 1931, he was to write a couple of years later, 'the Nazis would have failed to establish their grip on Germany. Britain would have had a pattern to offer a Germany frantic with despair.' [30]

At the same time, unlike most Socialists, he foresaw the dangers of centralized planning – dangers that would not be diminished, but rather increased, by 'full employment'. Full employment in mass-production was stultifying: 'We need the machine: but we cannot do with the machine-minder: the man so vitally exhausted by the life-destroying monotony of the job that he can think of nothing better to do than fill up pool-coupons or crawl into the cinema.' [31] Such a man might find relief from his frustration in the excitement of rallies and war; he could never make a responsible citizen. 'Not merely the right to work, but the right to be trained for the work for which the citizen has a vocation, is implied in a valid conception of social security.' [32]

Again, the State was too remote an abstraction to evoke the loyalty, as distinct from the idolatry, of the average man. Rousseau had been right to maintain that democracy was real only in small communities – 'communities of such a size that men can grasp and understand them as a whole, and be continually conscious of their obligations to one another within them'.[33] However necessary it might be to remedy the anarchy of capitalism, centralized planning as such must sap those very qualities, of corporate, as well as personal, responsibility, upon which the avoidance of totalitarianism depended.

'The only genuine solution to this profound impasse of our modern society', he submitted therefore, lay 'in the revivification of the national society from below' [33] – by the multiplication of voluntary associations and regional and local communities; in other words, by 'a steady effort towards decentralization'.[34] He had already advanced this thesis in *The Defence of Democracy*: and no doubt it had been reinforced both by his reading of Gandhi and by his intercourse with Mannheim, Wellock and Gill.

That such a policy of decentralization was practicable, he saw no reason to doubt. Electrical power and motor transport had rendered industrial concentration superfluous:

> It will be said that such a distribution of industrial enterprise comes into conflict with fundamental economic necessities. Coal-mines must be on

coal-seams; ironworks near iron-ore, or in places to which it can conveniently be shipped. We do not deny it. Some basic industries are immovable. But, in the first place, these basic industries are nothing like so important to the national economy as they used to be, except in the incurably vicious conditions of war; and in the second place, their immobility need not prevent us from drastically redistributing those which are mobile. Further, it will be said that by decentralisation we lose all the benefits of rationalisation – of mass-production and the conveyor-belt. If we want cheap motor-cars, we can have them only from factories that employ ten or twenty thousand men. I am not so certain that we do need cheap motor-cars as badly as all that: I sometimes think they have become a necessity because men are so eager to get quickly away from the kind of places in which they live. But there is no real difficulty about drastically decentralising the manufacture of the innumerable components of your standardised car. Some of it is decentralised already. Decentralise it to the maximum, remembering that your real concern is not the production of the cheapest motor-car possible, but the cheapest compatible with a regeneration of the social life of the country.

It is this sense of the supremacy of the social end that is so hard to get into men's heads. 'Man's life consisteth not in the abundance of goods he possesseth.' Not that abundance of goods is not a good. It is. But it is a good which must, in any sound or Christian social philosophy, be reckoned entirely subordinate to the quality of life men live. Who, having really known the former, would exchange a life of £5 a week in the countryside for a life of £10 a week in the town, even as things are, when the country community is but a shadow of its former self and a shadow of what it might become? We might cheerfully forego twenty-five per cent of the maximum production and consumption of manufactured goods for the sake of universal decentralisation of industry, well knowing that the loss would be repaid tenfold in the quality, the quiet happiness, the human interest, of life that would be gained.[35]

Murry, needless to say, had never known life in the countryside on £5 a week; and thousands who have would exchange it without hesitation for £10 a week in the town. But that does not invalidate the thesis, which, when propounded later by Huxley and Russell, was to attract a good deal of favourable notice – from himself among others.

Ideally, he thought, the State itself should initiate such a policy. Even in the incurably vicious conditions of war, it could do something. It could, at least, create a propitious climate of opinion by adopting it as a long-term objective and promoting the political education of the troops. 'The enforced idleness of the British Army is, if rightly considered, the preordained opportunity for preparing citizens worthy of the British tradition.'[36] In his mind's eye, he saw an army of Ironsides, stimulated by the discussion, enthused by the vision, of 'a democracy of democracies, or, as we prefer to call it, a community of communities'.[37] Did he also see *Christocracy* itself taken up as an army text-book? It is not impossible. Asked how he managed to retain so much optimism, at any rate, he replied that there was always a one-in-a-hundred chance of Sir Stafford Cripps reading the book – and Cripps he was hailing at this time as a possible alternative Premier, 'capable of some creative response to events'.[38]

However, not even Murry was so optimistic as to bank on the initiative of the State. On the contrary, that would have meant succumbing to the very inertia he feared. It would be enough, to begin with, if the State remained benevolently neutral towards the initiative of societies and groups. It was for them to pioneer the way. And there existed one group, even now, with not merely the opportunity, but the obligation, to do so – namely, the conscientious objectors. These, directed as most of them were being to work on the land, were duty-bound, he maintained, to make a virtue of necessity by discovering and demonstrating in practice 'a new pattern of social living'.[39] Yet once more, now that 'large-scale "revolution"' was ruled out, the old community dream was reviving.

XXIV

HOME IS THE SAILOR

MURRY'S CONCERN FOR PACIFIST agricultural communities was not merely academic, nor was the idea advanced in *Christocracy* a new one. Already by the summer of 1940, wherever land was neglected, sodden or sterile enough to be cheap, groups of young men and women, as liberally endowed with energy and idealism as they were deficient in funds and experience, were diligently establishing 'new patterns of social living' – and very odd some of them were. If these were not swiftly to go the way of their Christian, Socialist, Anarchist and Distributist forerunners, something more than propaganda was needed. That autumn, a Community Land Training Association was formed to acquire a 300-acre farm in Lincolnshire, where conscientious objectors with a vocation for agriculture could be trained as community leaders. Through *Peace News* and its monthly supplement, 'Community', Murry was mainly responsible for raising the initial £10,000; and to his other commitments was added that of a Governor.

He was also, of course, Permanent Chairman of the Adelphi School Co., and, though unable to make Langham his headquarters as he would have liked to do, kept in touch with developments there. Mary and her friend Ruth Baker, who shared her cottage at Dedham, spent much of their time at the Centre; his brother and co-Director, Richard, was a frequent visitor, till the Navy claimed him; he himself paid a flying visit as often as possible. Plowman and his team of C.O.s having finished restoring The Oaks, and converted the grounds into something resembling a market-garden, it was owing to Murry's intervention that the house was given up to some seventy aged evacuees from the East End of London, whilst a dozen of the keenest youngsters, ten men and two girls, moved into a cottage down the road to reclaim a derelict farm.

Plowman himself was not in favour of this departure. In business matters alone less down-to-earth, he did not share Murry's anxiety to see the Centre made a paying proposition, by expanding production and reducing costs to a minimum; nor did he trust the leader of the Farm Group, a twenty-four-year-old Quaker, Walter, whose practical ability and zeal were matched by his overweening self-assurance. Murry, however, was enthusiastic. Always prone to admiration for a craftsman, he would listen to no criticism of Walter – even rejecting a proposal, supported by the other members, that they should retain the services of an experienced farm labourer. Thus it was to him rather than Plowman that the Group came to look for advice: and before long Adelphi Farm had become one of his principal interests.

This would probably have happened anyway, since he could not propound a theory without wanting to put it into practice: and the attraction of Langham was irresistible. His closing down of the Centre in 1937 appeared to him now a retrogression. Nothing had given him more pleasure than Plowman's decision to reopen it, nothing more regret than his own inability to help more. Sooner or later he would have found himself involved again, even if everything had gone smoothly. As it was, events in 1941 – two in particular – left him with little option.

The first of these occurred early in the summer – by which time his experiment in community by remote control was already showing signs of strain. The Farm Group, not unnaturally perhaps, resenting a ukase from Larling dismissing three of their number on Walter's recommendation, he had been forced to pay a visit to Langham in order to set matters right. After the meeting as they were strolling back arm-in-arm to The Oaks, Plowman remarked, 'John, I wish we saw more of each other – just now. Just to be together, and nothing said.' To which Murry could only rejoin, 'I wish that too, with all my heart. But Providence has decided against it.' 'Well', was the reply, 'that's all that really matters: that we both wish it. It's the same thing as if it were really so,' [1] and with that they parted. Three weeks later, on the afternoon of June 3, Plowman died.

His illness, pneumonia, was too sudden and short for them to meet again. Murry arrived an hour after his death. When, having paid his last respects, he proceeded to address the Farm Group, he was still in tears: no wonder! 'The man who has just died', he began, 'was my intimate friend for sixteen years . . . And of all the men I have ever known, Max was the most warm-hearted, the most understanding, the most loving':

If ever there was a power in a man to bear another's burdens, it was there in Max. When all the world was reeling about me, when all the things and all the people I had believed in fell away and I had to perform acts which I knew to be absolutely mad in the eyes of the world – Max stayed still, and accepted, and understood. 'He was he, and I was I.' Not once, nor twice, nor three times, nor four times, nor five, he was there ready to take over when I was . . . tired. In all the crucial events of my life during those sixteen years, he was crucially involved. In fact, it sometimes seemed as though he were more crucially involved in them than I was myself.

Max spent himself recklessly (I use the word advisedly) for others. You all know that he killed himself here. But that's no matter: he would have spent himself just the same, somewhere, in the service of something he believed in, whatever had happened. He had that kind of devotion and courage. Of all the men I have ever known, Max experienced the last war most deeply. He took it into himself; he came to his decision, and he stuck to it. And through all the years before that war which, he knew, was coming twenty years afterwards, what Max said was the right thing to do – that *was* the right thing. He was a prophetic man.

The star by which Max steered was one absolutely fixed in the heavens. This is not a matter of opinion with me; nor do I say it simply because his opinions and mine were often the same, and we were at one in the service of what he and I were content to call Imagination. It is *true*. Now that he is gone, if we try to imagine what Max would have wished for and what he would have approved, that, we may be quite sure, is the thing to aim at.

The Langham that exists here is not all that he wished to see, or all that I or you wished to see either. But I don't believe that any of you, even the most rebellious, when you leave here will ever forget the experience of Langham. You will every one leave some part of your heart behind: and the reason for that is, quite simply – Max. And this work which he took over has got to go on. I am as certain as I am of my own existence that it will go on; that Max's Langham will develop and grow into something beautiful and valuable.

I can see him, and feel and know him, now that I am detached from him, more completely than ever I knew him before . . . Yes, I am detached now . . . There are many people who will be more talked of than Max will be; but none, I believe, who will be the object of such loving, and happy, memory. I say 'happy', and I mean it. No, I am not sad now – even though I am blubbering . . . I am happy . . .

And, in some strange way, he was. A week later, 'I hope I'm not a kind of inhuman monster,' he wrote to Mary: 'But I just don't feel it in the way I am apparently expected to feel it. About Max as a person I feel quite happy; my concern is quite "impersonal" – about his loss to the movement and to Langham.' [2] This, even better than his published tributes, testifies to the depth of their friendship.

Soon after Plowman's death, J. H. Watson was invited to take his place as Warden of the Centre, and two assistant editors were appointed to run *The Adelphi* in Murry's name. But the loss, both to the movement and to Langham, was severe. Now that Gill too was dead, Murry found himself in a minority among the Pacifist leaders – only Wellock shared his concern for communities whole-heartedly – and reduced more and more to doing for himself whatever he thought necessary to be done; in addition, he felt obliged, for the time being at least, to visit the Centre fortnightly. The strain of so many commitments would have been too much for most men even in normal circumstances: in his own, it was killing. For, far from easing his domestic struggle, they contributed towards bringing it to a climax: and that, so far as he was concerned, was the second decisive event of 1941.

He still could not tear himself away from Larling. For one thing, even if he took the two elder children away, he would continue to be tormented by anxiety for the younger; for another, as he had explained in one of his last letters to Plowman, 'The children here, through a common suffering, have learned to live a strange and wonderful close-knit life of their own. They are more faithfully attached to one another, and to Ruby, than one has any conception. To them the one disaster is that they should be separated.' [3] Weg in particular – now, at fifteen, 'old and wise' [4] – would not leave little Mary and David as long as she could do anything to spare them; and her father, though he could not even talk to her without exposing her to cruel reprisals (they had to separate on the train that took them both from Thetford to Larling, before being met at the station) neither could nor would leave her. The refrain of his letters, she says, was always the same: 'I will never desert you.'

At the same time, it was growing more obvious with every week that his presence, instead of lightening their burden, increased it. The grotesque and revolting scenes attending his arrival at The Old Rectory alarmed even grown-up neighbours – who, more than once, had to be called in to save the situation. It was impossible to go on like that. 'Assuredly, I can say with Paul: "I die daily",' [5] he wrote to a friend that summer, and it sounded nothing less than the truth. Even physically he appeared to have shrunk, to have turned small and hard-drawn, like a mummy. If he was not to break down for a second time, and so become useless to anyone, he would be forced to tear himself away.

In September, he decided to do so. 'It seems an odd and fantastic thing to ask one's friends to *pray* that one's heart may be hardened,' he wrote then: 'Yet that, it occurs, is the one thing I must ask of my friends now.' [6] Warned by some instinct that if he gave way to his feelings on one front, he would give way on all, he told Mary Gamble that they too must separate until the 'dreadful thing' [7] was done. Once again, as in 1936, he was 'like a knight going away to perform his vigil' (the comparison was Lawrence's). And – once again – his resolution collapsed. Within a week, he was not only making one last effort to reconcile Betty to a dual arrangement, but rejoining Mary at Dedham, 'completely exhausted, and with the horrid fear that I was on the brink of a nervous breakdown'.[8] Even at this stage it looked as if the 1936 crisis might repeat itself.

But this time the relapse did prove momentary. It was, as he had said earlier, 'a *clarified* version of the situation with Nehale'.[9] The loftiest optimism has limits. On October 1, in response to a further telegram, Mary met him once more at Ipswich, and, 'as he walked out of the station he said simply: "That's over, I shall never go back again." ' [10] Nor did he. In fact though not in name, this was the end of his third, most disastrous marriage.

Thereafter, things moved quickly. Although there were still desperate moments when he felt that he could never resign himself to parting from the children unless Mary herself bore him a child, he had 'crossed the Rubicon',[11] as he put it, and it was not long before the rightness of the step was confirmed on every hand. By December, he was writing in his journal:

Mary has been with me since last Saturday; and she returns again tomorrow. This is as it should be. By a slow and sometimes very painful process we have become completely united. We *have* to be together: and though I have no idea what will finally happen about the children and Larling, I must stick to the one certainty I have. That has become more and more clear to me; I have become less and less *troubled* about it: and deep down I am happier – more steadily and undisturbedly happy than I have been for years. There *is* a divinity that shapes our ends. My love for Mary began at the moment when the war became inevitable; it has grown and grown, insisting, like a slow force of nature, on making its own conditions; and now, at the moment that the war is become a world-wide, global war, Mary and I have to be completely together – the tiniest, most infinitesimal assertion of individual love against the surrounding chaos. Without Mary (I sincerely believe) I should not have been able to stand the war. Undermined at home, – my home-life being the extremity of war as it is experienced in an individual life – I should simply have succumbed to the influence of the war outside, having nothing to put up against it. Now I have: there is the fact of Mary and me.[12]

A month later, of her own accord – for he had left the decision to her – Weg also left Larling, she and Col joining their father. 'The "family" – which B. had prevented from being the family it so longed to be – was breaking up,' he recorded: 'And somehow, deep down, I believe that everything will come right: that *all* my children will be gathered round Mary and me – in happiness.' [13]

And with that, Murry's regular entries in the journal ended. Though he would still take it up from time to time – sometimes for months at a stretch – the urge to confide night by night in its pages, as he had done for eleven years past, was gone for good. 'To keep a journal one needs to lead a lonely life.' [13]

The old Flemish cottage at Dedham, which he had been sharing with Mary and Ruth Baker, was now too small for their purposes. Not only would Weg and Col need a home for the holidays, but there could be no question of Ruth's being allowed to leave them – or rather, when the question did arise, neither Murry nor Mary would hear of it. She had been Mary's almost life-long companion; she had won his heart by the grace and understanding with which she had accepted their relation; and the children took to her warmly. Early in the new year, accordingly, they exchanged Dedham for Langham itself. A couple of buildings, re-named Adelphi Cottages, were knocked together: and these, for the next nine months, became their home.

Thus, the 'retrogression' of 1937 was atoned for. Heart, mind and body were reunited at last – and very soon, as a consequence, Murry's physical health revived likewise. Though he could not walk more than a few hundred yards without pain, the farm lay at his door; and, methodically bringing the new garden into order, adding brick-laying to his other accomplishments, he seemed to shed a month or two weekly. There at Langham, in more senses than one, he was back where he had longed to be. It was at this time that he adopted Stevenson's 'lovely lines':[14]

> *Home is the sailor, home from sea;*
> *And the hunter home from the hill.*

Nevertheless, he seems never to have thought of this as a permanent arrangement, if only because he could not afford to support two households by his pen alone. Dakers, indeed, were eager to publish whatever books he might write – they had just reissued *Cinnamon and Angelica** – but *Peace News* took up most of his time, and there was no knowing how much longer that would be permitted to circulate. Already in February, before they had been at Langham two months, he was asking Mary, 'How would you like it if we bought a farm?' – And together they began picturing the details.

It would have to be in East Anglia, of course – the country he knew best. It should be stocked with a herd of red polls, the local breed, and a flock of the black-faced Suffolk sheep; the horses, too, should be Suffolk. Murry had definite ideas on the subject of balanced husbandry: he would like a farm which had been allowed to run down, so as to have the satisfaction of making two ears of corn grow where one grew before. In a world given over to destruction – a world, moreover, in which the results of one's actions could so rarely be calculated – this at least would be 'a *certain* good'.[15] And he was still only fifty-two – not too old to make a fresh start . . .

It was while they were actually talking this over, Mary recalls, that the telephone rang to communicate an announcement from the Air Ministry – that the fields outside their windows, the miry fields which the Farm Group were trying to reclaim, were to be commandeered for an aerodrome. Not many minutes were needed to interpret that 'sign'. If Langham would have to be evacuated, and quickly, why, here was the very opportunity to reconstitute the Centre itself as a farming co-operative!

Here, indeed, was the very goal upon which his thoughts had been converging ever since the original Centre was disbanded. In *Christocracy* he had stressed the need for producer co-operatives; in article

---

* Murry had a soft spot for this play. The reviewer in *Peace News*, having described the characterization as 'surprisingly felicitous', was still more surprised to find 'surprisingly' altered to 'memorably'.

after article in *The Adelphi* – 'Community Blue-Print', 'Community and Totalitarianism', 'Educating for Chaos' – he had sketched the long-term objective, a multiform village-community embracing a variety of industries, and likewise the 'one essential foundation: cultivation of the land in community, both for subsistence and "export" '.[16] Now, overnight as it seemed, subjective and objective necessity had conspired to render it feasible. He lost no time in submitting his proposal to the Centre's Executive Committee.

The reception was something of a shock. Characteristically, he had never thought of discussing his ideas with the Warden. In fact, since his arrival at Langham, they had barely exchanged a word. He had just taken it for granted that they saw eye-to-eye. Watson, on the other hand, had taken it for granted that the Centre was intended, now as in 1935, to be primarily a conference-house, a place where men and women from all walks of life were 'educated into community'. It was for this that he had taken Plowman's place, for this that he had already, in his nine months' tenure of office, built up a substantial outside connexion. The farm, in his view, had never been more than ancillary – for which reason he objected as much as Plowman to Walter's unco-operativeness. To him, therefore, the proposal could only sound like a sudden repudiation of all that Murry had stood for in the past, and all that he himself had been attempting. He would hear nothing of it.

Murry was completely taken aback. His habit of assuming that others knew what he expected of them, without their having ever been told, was one that all his colleagues and subordinates noticed. Indeed, the whole episode is illustrative of his impercipience: for, had he only talked to Watson as man to man, eliciting his viewpoint and explaining his own, the misunderstanding could have been remedied. That Watson was open to conviction was shown soon afterwards, when he, in his turn, initiated a co-operative farm. Instead, whether from shyness or impatience, Murry made matters worse by communicating his intentions in a succession of *billets doux*, conveyed by industrious female hands from one side of Langham to the other – and, without further consultation, setting out with Walter in search of a farm. It was like adding insult to injury.

To be fair, when the truth at length dawned on him, he did try to make amends, offering to equip Watson with another conference-house from the funds of the Adelphi School Co. and do all in his power to support it. But by then the damage was done. Though the breach between the two was smoothed over, it was never healed. To Watson, it meant a sad disillusionment in a man he had trusted and admired; to Murry, yet one more instance of the incomprehensible perversity of mankind. From any point of view, it was an inauspicious start to his venture.

By the spring, however, he had found the farm of his dreams: Lodge Farm, Thelnetham, on the border of Norfolk and Suffolk. It was in the country he knew – the country he and Betty had scoured eleven years before, when they alighted on Larling. The farmhouse itself, 'a roomy old stud and plaster affair with a thatched roof facing north-west',[17] was big enough to accommodate the Farm Group as well as the family; the 180 acres were suitably run down; it was to be had for £3,325. On April 13, 1942, he paid the deposit. 'I suppose it's a great risk', he wrote in his journal that evening – the occasion deserved an entry – 'But in my bones I feel it is a wise and good thing to do':

> It gives me a purpose in life, or rather commits me to the attempt practically to realise a scheme which I have long been convinced theo- retically is the creative thing to do, to-day. My one regret is that I am 52, nearly 53, and a semi-invalid. I would give a good deal for a sound pair of legs. But one can't have everything: and if I last out 10 more years – having had a hand in creating one of the elements of a new society – I shan't have done badly.

The risk was not as great as all that. To Watson, who knew what poverty meant and had sacrificed his livelihood to the Centre, it seemed trivial – and he resented the funds of the Adelphi School Co. being appropriated to a purpose seemingly so remote from the original. The purchase and equipment of Lodge Farm called, indeed, upon all Murry's capital (except what was locked up in Larling) and loans of £2,500 in addition. It was then that, having at last taken his M.A. degree *in absentia*, he asked for his name to be removed from the Brasenose College books, 'for the simple reason that, being a mere writer, I find it impossible to make ends meet nowadays'[18] – which meant a saving of 32s. a year. But land was an excellent investment, and he was still drawing, on an average, £500 in royalties on Kather- ine's books, as well as Violet's annuity. 'It is Katherine who has bought this farm for us, and Violet who has stocked it,'[19] he reflected.

The move was accomplished at Michaelmas. On October 6, four days after his arrival, he was writing to his brother: 'I feel that I have found my place and my way of life and of course my woman. All that I once hoped for at Larling – indeed the purpose for which I took Larling, is being realised here in Thelnetham.' [20] And for once his optimism was justified. Difficulties there would be, as he knew, but none to compare with those of the past. Verily, it was 'passing strange' so to find oneself 'in the midst of a hopeless world-war, yet happy, happy, with a simple fulness of happiness that I have never known before'.[21] The book he had begun writing at Langham, and finished in his first months at Thelnetham, communicates the quality, as it does the cause, of that happiness. He himself thought it one of his most important – a '*pièce justificative*'. However that may be, it commemorates the fulfilment of a life-long quest.

It is in *Adam and Eve* that Murry arrives at that perfect definition of himself, 'a cleric without a Church';[22] here that he realizes, for the first time clearly, the nature and origin of his quest. Before all else, he is the representative figure of an age of breakneck social transition: the man who, by descent and upbringing, has been exposed most nakedly to 'the gradual disruption of the life-pattern of society, made absolute by the revolutionary development of power-production in the last hundred years';[23] and who, because of this, has been 'condemned to spend a life-time in the attempt' [23] to discover a new one. His significance lies in his being 'the scientifically perfect product of that period of extreme social dislocation' [23] – first clinging to love as the one self-evident good; then creating for himself a religion that ratified love; finally, seeking a way of life congruous with this religion: a way of life which, if widely adopted, would render impossible and unnecessary such a course of trials and errors as his own.

For one extraordinary by reason of his ordinariness, it could, of course, only be a way of married life. Marriage, therefore, becomes once again the haunt and main region of his song; and once again, as might have been predicted, he turns to Lawrence – only not, this time, for guidance. 'In my utter perplexity,' he confesses, 'I was prepared to take the plunge after Lawrence; and I did. And I discovered, on my pulses, that he was wrong.' [24] Lawrence was wrong in pronouncing physical love incompatible with spiritual. Not only are these compatible, but they are indispensable one to another. If spiritual love requires physical for its incarnation, physical requires spiritual for its redemption. Only where both are present and at one is 'the Regeneration of Generation' a reality.

To be sure, there was nothing new in this. Murry had affirmed as much in *Son of Woman*. His error had lain in giving body priority, not in denying soul. There was nothing new even in his conception of the act of love as a sacrament; while his further claim, that 'sexual life is not only not inimical to the religious life, but in reality the only full and satisfying form of the religious life',[25] was one of those sweeping generalizations which he would later on have to retract. But, as he had said in another context, 'to be confirmed in a surmise, to see an experiment succeed, is a totally different experience from entertaining the surmise or forming the hypothesis'. The synthesis enounced in *Adam and Eve* is the synthesis in which the book had its origin.

Moreover, this and nothing else, he now submits, must be the foundation of any stable Christian society; and it is to their equivocation over this that he attributes the failure of the historic Churches. For no religion will either deserve or secure the undivided allegiance of the ordinary man that does not sanctify and reinforce every instinctive motion of self-abeyance; and in the experience of the vast majority, the motion of sexual love itself is the strongest. 'The total relation between man and woman is the chief of all the human relations wherein we learn to surpass the Selfhood and enter into possession of our own Identities.'[26] A Church that denies, disputes or disregards this is a Church divorced from life; only a Church that endorses it can make for life, and life more abundant.

This was the main theme of *Adam and Eve*, and the theme that was to dominate Murry's thought for the rest of his life. To a prominent Quaker, who objected to his theory or practice or both, he wrote just after the book was finished:

I am sorry to have caused you sadness, or concern. But this is a matter in which my whole religious belief, my whole integrity as a man, is utterly involved. If there is tragedy to come (as you surmise) well, so it must be. But I do not feel that there is tragedy to come. The tragedy is in the past.

I will not go into details of my personal history. It is sufficient to say that my experience of the man-woman relation is strange, and (I make bold to say) significant. My old mother, whom I visited a week ago, said she had always thought of me as Anthony Adverse. Anyhow, here is the bare record: my first wife, Katherine Mansfield, whom I loved passionately, died of T.B. at 33; my second wife, whom I also loved passionately, died of T.B. at 26, leaving two baby children; my third wife treated me and – for this was the crux – my children very cruelly. I stuck it for ten years, during which two more children were born: until finally I was warned, in no uncertain fashion, that I was being killed – literally killed. That was in 1939. When I recovered from the consequent operation on my nervous system, I had a complete psychological break-down, in the course of which it was made clear to me that I must, at all costs, leave my home and my wife. Had it not been for the disinterested love, and fearless courage of Mary Gamble, I should never have had the strength to do this. Mary Gamble, by her love, saved my life.

That is the experience out of which I prophesy. If I were to deny it in any way I should, quite simply, cease to be myself. *Adam and Eve* is the fruits of my experience.

> What is the price of experience? Do men buy it for a song
> Or Wisdom for a dance in the street? No it is bought with
> the price of all that a man hath.

I have paid the price. And I want – above all things else – that young men such as I was – and young women – should not have to go through what I have been through. There is no need: and, so far as I can, I am determined to teach them.[27]

So far as he could, he did.

Second only in importance to self-forgetful love, in the foundations of a Christian society, however, Murry presented self-forgetful work. 'However clearly I see that "there is no going back", it still seems evident to me that no Christian, or religious, or human society is possible unless the common man finds fulfilment in his daily work.' [28] It was not by accident that puritanism and industrialism had gone hand in hand – sexual frustration promoting inventiveness, inventive-ness vocational frustration; or that those same Reformers who had ousted Woman from the Godhead had exalted the Saviour to the exclusion of the Carpenter. As Gill had so often stressed, an ecstatic Sunday religion was the corollary of an irreligious week-day drudgery. Consequently, 'whether the reconciliation between the machine and man's desire for fulfilment in his daily work be achieved in the near future by the effort of the many, or in the remoter future by the effort of the few, it is here, I insist, that the real problem lies'.[29]

And here, of course, was the problem which he had now set himself to solve, in the only way in which it *could* be solved, by experiment – that is to say, by trial and error, on the part of men and women who had already a criterion of fulfilment, who had, as he liked to put it, 'the root of the matter' in them:

In terms of agriculture the problem becomes quite practical. Thus: given a mixed farm of 185 acres, on fairly good soil, to find how many families it will support at a modest but adequate level of subsistence, while making a modest but adequate return on the capital employed? The aim is not to make the largest possible profit, but to support the greatest number of men fulfilled in their work, because it is axiomatic that agriculture is an intrinsically good way of life. How far does the use of the power-machine facilitate this aim, how far does it militate against it? Is there a point at which the machine ceases to be beneficent and becomes malign by reducing the fertility of the farm, by depriving it of its full sustenance of organic manure? How far, in actual living, can its beneficence, in reducing the amount of human labour required, be turned to the true advantage of the individual members and the farm community as a whole? How much leisure can be achieved, say, by each of 18 members of a co-operative group farming 10 acres per member? Will such leisure in fact be creatively used: that is, used for the further fulfilment or enlargement of the individual and the common life?

These are questions of the first importance for determining a practical conception of the good life, in accord with the laws of Nature and of God ... If it can be proved that a group of men and women, co-operatively farming 10 acres for each person – 20 acres per family – using the power-machine in harmony, as far as possible, with the traditional art of agriculture, paying a reasonable rent for their land, and a reasonable return on the capital required, can live simple, decent, fulfilled and comely lives, then something of great significance for human living at the present time will have been proved. It will have been proved that it is possible to solve the real problem of mass-unemployment in a human, natural, and religious way, whereas all the other solutions – based as they are on full-employment of machine-factories – are inhuman, unnatural, irreligious, and lead straight to still greater enslavement, still greater frustration and still greater wars.[30]

This was the Charter of Lodge Farm, these the terms of reference within which the experiment was to be conducted. But the very nature of the experiment presupposed another problem: whether it was possible for a community, as it was for a prophetic man, to constitute an 'experiencing nature'?

Steele.

"Sir R^{t.} Steele hit the mark when he thus distinguished ... the Church of Rome & the Church of England: that the former pretended to be infallible, and the latter to be always in the right" Whitbread Life p.168

Swift's quarrel with S. which begins with S.'s letter to Addison, May 13, 1713 — the Bay on which the war rests for the 3 accounts were shewn to S. Therefore, the moment at which an attack on S. for infidelity might be expected to do the utmost harm, and at which S. was deeply agitated. S. was therefore fully justified in taking exception, and maintaining that Steele did have approached him first to find out whether, or to what, in any way, responsive. But S. went badly astray in refounding Steele with ingratitude, &

Steele offered again by not accepting S.'s disclaimer; but he, in turn, was justified in taking exception to S.'s claim to have kept him in office. "They laugh at you if they make you believe your interposition has kept me thus long in my office." The imputation that S. was a gull was calculated to irritate him in the extreme (though J. Swift ... was probably correct, and that Harley was only too anxious to retain a hold on Steele). In any case similar case S. could have guessed it was a piece of court-practice (a "refinement") to let him believe what Steele was retained "solely on my account. And it seems to me that S. deliberately misinterpretation of what Steele said, probably because he correct the correct interpretation thing S's vanity intolerably - It is a very illuminating episode. Swift's final letter is quicker, & more reasonable (May 31), when the Deanery is settled.

He married a Mrs Stretch, a Barbados widow, soon after Mar. 1705, when her first h. died. He said he estate (Roughcumbered by a debt of £2000) produced a rent of £850 yearly. It was left her by her mother. In Trinity Term 1705 (June 8 to 27) he sold part of his estate to Joseph Addison (apparently), & surprisingly not the Addison)

Mygod, his wife died at the end of 1706.

The unalloyed deprivation of S.: that Black Beau (think he in a post chariot, think yet, his eyes lost in his head, beetly eyebrows, inflamed face, & tallow complexion; agrees very well with the Thornhill portrait. He had got himself into serious embarrassment financing an alchemical theater's Gentleman—writes to P. George Aug. 1706. Gazetteer Ap-May 1707. Married lady Scurlock heiress to an estate of £800 a year in Caermarthen, Winchester 1707 — she was 23 & he 35. J Swift was vexed:

Ah, Dick Steele, that I were but more | May never rest me of my heart
Your love like mine so still endure; | which you have given of my heart
That brine or absence which destroys | Often diseased may bridge
The casts of lovers & their joys | whatever they think themselves

True died age 40 in Dec. 26, 1718

29. Facsimile of J. M. M.'s handwriting: Notes for *Jonathan Swift*

30. J. M. M. with Mary (left), Ruth Baker and Donald Soper, 1950

31. J. M. M. discussing Pacifism with Donald Soper, 1950

XXV

ANTICLIMAX

———◆⦁◆⦁◆———

IKE MURRY'S OTHER WAR-TIME books, *Adam and Eve* had
a bad press and a good public. The first impression went out of
print at once; a second, limited by paper restrictions to 2,000,
sold out before publication: 'so presumably it has struck a responsive
chord somewhere',[1] he remarked. On the other hand, coincident with
the news that he was living with Mary Gamble and filing a petition of
divorce (on grounds of 'mental cruelty'), it also created some scandal.
The prominent Quaker was not the only objector. The Anglican
Pacifist Fellowship asked Murry to resign, and two or three Nonconformist officers of the P.P.U. resigned themselves. They thought him
no fit representative of Christian Pacifism – and perhaps, though for
other reasons than theirs, they were right.

Had he not made his marriage the touchstone of his faith? It was
not by chance that, when hardening his heart against his wife, he had
advocated anti-Fascist war; when aiming at her conversion, he had
all but taken Orders; and when trying to reconcile her to Mary, he
had preached a negotiated peace. A shrewd observer, taking note of
the fact that he had finally written her off and thrown in his lot with
Mary, might even then have drawn certain deductions.

There was no such observer – not even 'Observer' himself. On the
contrary, 'I could no more cease to be a Pacifist than I could jump out
of my own skin,'[2] he wrote just after leaving Larling. In a civilization
which, he was more than ever convinced, was in its death-throes,
where else could a Church be looked for but in the interstices of a
decadent democracy? At the same time, the protests against his book
must have shaken his confidence in Pacifists. Could such doctrinaires
be fit pioneers of a new Christian society, with the motto, *Ama, et
fac quod vis?* The Thelnetham experiment was already giving him
to doubt.

The dozen young men and women composing the Farm Group were a quaint assortment, recruited from all parts of the country and all walks of life. George Lamb has described some of them, more charitably than Murry, in his autobiography, *Roman Road*. Their two or three years together at Langham had given them a certain solidarity and assurance; they were for the most part keen and hard workers; and they were prepared to make up by frugality for what they lacked in experience. Indeed, they had inured themselves to a standard of living which Murry, with his very individual ideas on the subject, found 'not merely spare but squalid',[3] and took immediate steps to raise. Yet their solidarity was that of a clique; their assurance ran easily to arrogance; they included only one married couple, which was childless, and none of them was over twenty-six. It was hardly to be expected that they should be much surer of their vocation, or much more socially responsible, than he himself had been at their age; nor can one suppress a smile on reading the address he delivered to them on February 12, 1944:

> I will take the risk of exaggerating the importance of our effort. Posterity will decide whether it is exaggeration. But I would at this moment unhesitatingly compare what we are trying to do here with what St Benedict tried to do in the 6th century at Monte Cassino, which our armies have just deliberately destroyed. The destruction of Monte Cassino struck home to me, because D. H. Lawrence taught me its full significance as the cradle and symbol of the Christian civilisation of Europe, which is now in its final death agony. The Lodge Farm is in my eyes nothing less than the Monte Cassino of a new Christian civilisation. With the same great motto as S. Benedict – *laborare est orare*: to work is to pray – we are trying to recolonise, to win to the service and the praise of God – the waste lands of the modern world.

Four years afterwards, re-reading this address and others like it, Murry himself could not suppress a rueful smile. 'I was a very sanguine chap in those days,' he confessed: 'What, strangely enough, I had forgotten was that the members of the group were all very young compared to me . . . It was very naive of me to have forgotten that.'[4] It was. So naive that one may reasonably wonder whether all the 'unawareness' was on their side.

As usual, his approach to the venture was strictly empirical. 'I profoundly distrust all preconceived ideas of community', he reaffirmed, four months later: 'because I am quite certain that community, if it is to have any practical validity for ordinary people and any real appeal to them, is a form of living which has yet to be discovered and manifested in the concrete':

> Community (as I imagine it and have faith in it) is the translation into terms of a group living and making its living of that attitude of mind which Keats described as 'making the mind a thoroughfare for all thoughts, not a select party'. And loyalty to community is primarily loyalty to that conception of it. It is the social embodiment – or an effort towards it – of what Keats again called Negative Capability. Community is, essentially, a new form of social organism that is capable of welcoming and digesting its own experience, without being disintegrated, and growing thereby.[5]

It was in accordance with this conception that Murry was in favour of everybody living under one roof, at any rate to start with. Just because of the difficulties (especially where women were concerned), he thought this a good way to promote a kind of survival of the fittest, to break down the bourgeois exclusiveness of individuals and families. There were, he stated, only two qualifications for membership of such a community: 'One is the determination to stay, whether you like it or not, whether or not you are unhappy, until you are asked to leave. The other is the determination to do more than earn your wages.'[5*] The latter was necessary in order that there should be a community at all; the former, in order that the members should be converted into 'experiencing natures' – 'discovering in themselves the willingness to have their personalities broken up and melted into a new form, "to die many deaths", and to be continually re-born'.[4] He conceived the community, in short, as a miniature Vale of Soul-making: and only when the Souls were being turned out to satisfaction was he prepared to devolve on the group a full measure of collective responsibility. That, he thought, might take seven years.

Unluckily (though no longer surprisingly), it was not until they had been installed at Thelnetham nearly eighteen months that he thought of explaining all this: 'Hitherto, I think, I had taken my own conception of "community" for granted.'[6] And what was

---

* I quote from the address as printed in *Community Farm* (p. 89). The manuscript reads rather differently: 'There is only one test which I have found valid in estimating a member of this place: that is, whether I find I have, first, a natural liking for them and, second, whether on future experience, this natural liking deepens and expands into a natural trust . . .'

'self-evidently true, a simple and luminous certainty',[7] to him was by no means so evident to others. Of one, he reports indeed, 'it seemed to him that I was trying to make him accept it because it was *mine*. Hence my astonishment.' [7]

In particular, it was by no means so evident why he, and he alone, should be the judge of who had 'the root of the matter' in him. Why, it occurred to some of them to ask, should the fittest to survive necessarily be the fittest to survive with Murry? It was all very well to talk of the members as committed to an experience of one another 'that might become almost unendurable':[7] only, whereas they were obliged to endure him, he was under no obligation to endure them. They were being required to commit themselves for life – on approval.

The feeling is understandable, especially as of 'the Big Three',[8] as he once called them – himself, Mary and Ruth – Ruth alone lived and worked with them continuously. It can scarcely have been reassuring to see Murry, after antagonizing Plowman and Watson by his infatuation with Walter, suddenly decide that they had been right after all, and from denouncing any who criticized Walter turn to trouncing some who did not. It must have been unsettling, to say the least, when, persuaded by his experience of the Centre that the worst possible basis for a community was an unsatisfactory marriage, he peremptorily dismissed the childless couple. At that juncture the 'seven years' began to revive memories of Laban, and the demand to make itself heard for an instalment of collective responsibility now, if only to the extent of consultation.

But on this score Murry was adamant – naturally. Consultation over crops was one thing, over personnel quite another. Frankly contemptuous of their claims to have learned as much from their two or three years' experience of communal living as he from his three or four months, he dismissed the suggestion roundly as one of those very preconceived ideas which community existed to dissolve. 'I am not accustomed to address myself to disembodied intelligences,' [9] he retorted; much less was he prepared to entrust his capital to 'a concentration of weakness, of unfitness, and unfittingness for life'.[9] The days were long past when he would venture his all in a cause as he had in *The Adelphi*.

Consequently, though it had struck him some years before that he, with his haggard cheeks and perfect tonsure, '*looked* like a Benedictine',[10] it did not take posterity to decide that Lodge Farm was no Monte Cassino. The details are of little interest. Enough that, by the end of four years, only one of the original group survived, and that mainly because he could not make up his mind to go; while Murry himself had been 'made sick of young pacifists' (perhaps he ought to have said, of the young) for the rest of his days: 'Instead of being a bit better than ordinary unpretentious folk in their social morality, they were a damned sight worse.' [11]

Meanwhile, a somewhat similar tale was being enacted in the P.P.U. at large: for, though he had decided – *ex cathedra*, so to speak – that this too was to constitute an 'experiencing nature', a community on a wider scale, there was nothing in the constitution to say so, nor did all its members concur. On the contrary, there were many who envisaged it less as a Church than a Party, and would have liked to see national policies adopted by majority vote and propagated through the columns of *Peace News* – at the risk of splitting the movement to fragments. As past-masters of minutes, motions and references-back, moreover, these were naturally well represented on all the elected bodies.

Murry was opposed to such a procedure on principle. The P.P.U., he insisted, could only be 'a catholic fraternity of constructive peacemakers',[12] active in whatever varied directions their talents and opportunities pointed, united simply as one body with many members; and the overriding duty of its leaders was to 'tender the whole'. In this he was at one with its Chairman, Alex. Wood, 'the finest figure in public life I have ever met'.[12] Of Wood he was to write in an obituary:

As I listened, during the memorial service at Cambridge on 21st April [1950], to the astonishing record of Alex. Wood's selfless activities in the cause of good, of which it seemed one-half at least were quite unknown to me, I felt wonder and gratitude that he had found the time to be my friend; and yet more wonder and more gratitude that he had never seemed to find it an effort. It is true I tried not to be an exacting one, for I was always conscious that the calls upon his devotion were unlimited; it is also true that my chief desire was to let him feel that, so far as it lay in me, he could always count on me, because I knew he was better, wiser, more patient and more forgiving than I, and my job was to follow. I am not, in general, fond of following, nor good at it. But with Alex. Wood I never had one moment of hesitation. I was proud to follow him. Even

when I was indignant and angry at others' treatment of him, I repressed
my indignation and my anger simply because I knew he preferred it that
way. Alex. always made me a better man than I am. I have never known
anyone else who did precisely that to me. In general, I do not want to be
a better man than I am; but Alex. simply made me want to be – [13]

Words which few who were acquainted with Wood would fail to
endorse.

If Murry was not good at following, however, neither was he really
good at leading. Unlike Shaw, for instance, whose capacity for comprehending a variety of viewpoints was as conspicuous in his political
as in his literary work, he was no committee-man. If he was far above
some of his associates in his detachment from the manœuvres and
intrigues that typify movements everywhere, he was far below Wood
in magnanimity, forbearance and understanding; and, while capable
of crediting his less articulate colleagues with insights so profound
that they were loth to disown them, he was incapable of suffering fools
gladly. His idea of Hell, he once said, was three committees a day.

His practice, moreover, was not always as sound as his principle.
For if *Peace News* was not to propound the short-term (and often
shorter-sighted) programme adopted by majority vote, there were
only two things it legitimately could do. One was to propagate
Pacifism, upon which all the members were agreed; the other to
provide a forum for the various policies on which they differed. And
Peace News did neither.

To propagate total unilateral disarmament and non-violent resistance to an invader was, Murry held, in war-time both futile and
immoral. It was merely to invite suppression – and he, for one, was
no more eager for public than domestic martyrdom. Sooner or later
the day might come when the Pacifist could commend this to the
nation again with some possibility of acceptance. In the meantime, his
only rational course was to 'try continually to make the wisest choice
among the inevitable limitations: the choice that will enable him to do
the work of most value to the cause of peace'.[14]

Ostensibly, therefore, *Peace News* was a forum. But Shaw's verdict
still held: Murry was too good a writer to be a good editor. He found
it so much easier to turn out a first-rate article himself than to get
second-rate ones from others that, as often as not, fully two of the
four pages were his. Again, while professing to exclude only such viewpoints as were 'explicitly intolerant' [15] of others, he was quite capable

of denouncing the 'official' policy of the Union in the leading article of its 'official' paper, promulgating his own instead. This was not the way to 'tender the whole'. It would not have been the way even if his own had been the more representative: and his own very seldom was.

It is certain, for example, that few Pacifists found his advocacy of defensive war compatible with a pledge to 'renounce war, and never support or sanction another'; and unlikely that many favoured collaboration with a 'new order' which their counterparts on the Continent were being hounded to death for resisting. Rose Macaulay was not the only one to question the will of God in this matter; nor was George Orwell alone in gaining the impression that Murry had no objection to violence, provided it was 'violent enough'.

To Orwell, he tried to explain that his attitude was much like Gandhi's: 'I do not, as a pacifist, say that no nation ought to defend itself. That is because I do not see any real good in a nation refusing to defend itself except out of pacifist conviction . . . In so far as people still believe in defending themselves as a nation, they had better do it than shirk the job.' [16] He had advanced a similar point of view in *Christocracy*:

> I acknowledge that I am in a paradoxical position: for my personal exercise of this Christian imagination compels me to be a pacifist. But at the same time I am a devoted citizen of my own country, and I am well aware that the vast majority of my fellow-countrymen are not pacifists, nor likely to be. I am therefore required to use what spark of Christian imagination is vouchsafed me on their behalf as well as to reach my personal conclusion. As a pure pacifist, I have no policy; but as the grateful citizen of a country where pacifism is permitted, I have. I am passionately concerned that the spirit of liberty and toleration which allows me to plead with my countrymen shall not perish from the earth.[17]

While he might legitimately invoke Gandhi on behalf of war as a second-best, however, he could not do so on behalf of collaboration. Far from preferring internal warfare to external, Gandhi himself thought even anarchy better than the *pax britannica* – and the majority of Pacifists agreed with him. In thinking even the *pax germanica* better than European anarchy, Murry was entirely unrepresentative.

Thus, in the P.P.U. as at Thelnetham, disillusionment was steady and mutual. It was well under way even before the end of the War; and that did nothing to stem it. On the contrary, though V.E. Day found Murry in hospital (undergoing his second sympathectomy), and therefore in no position to comment, enough had already transpired to set him thinking aloud in a way that was highly disconcerting, both to his readers and himself. ('The trouble with John', Wood said, 'is that he *will think aloud*.')

It was not that the event belied his prognostications. For the most part, these were too surely confirmed. If Dr Joad remembered the charge of 'inspissated gloom' he had brought against Murry in 1942, for suggesting that Russo-American friendship might not outlast the War, it must have brought a blush to his cheek. There was the super-Versailles being duly mapped out at Potsdam; there were the victors contending over the spoils; there, above all, were America and Britain sacrificing the very principles on which a world-peace organization must be built – the rights of small nations like Poland – to secure a nominal Soviet adherence: 'The net result is that the pre-war anarchy is fully restored, only it is now called world-security':

> Three and four years ago we used to weary our readers and ourselves in these pages by insisting that there could only be sense, instead of insanity, in this war if Britain became the champion of a better policy for Europe than Hitler's. The chance of giving sense to the war was missed. It is now revealed as pure insanity – not from Russia's point of view, for whom the destruction and downfall of Europe is so much gain; not from America's point of view, for America is remote and self-sufficient within her own hemisphere – but from our own.[18]

Even so, there was another side to the picture, which was not slow in coming home to Murry. His pessimism regarding the survival of democracy in Britain, for one thing, was shattered by the General Election – the repudiation of Churchill, the foundation of the Welfare State. For another, his optimism regarding Hitler's 'new order' sustained an overpowering shock from the exposure of the Nazi concentration-camps. He admitted this frankly in a review of Arthur Koestler's *The Yogi and the Commissar*, dated June 22, 1945:

> Though I am not ashamed that my faith in my countrymen was such that I believed them capable of both calling off the war with Hitler and offering a successful united and non-violent opposition to him, I think that I was a mistaken visionary. I misjudged two things. First, I misjudged the nature of the average decent man, for whom non-violent resistance is infinitely more difficult and less natural than violent. The second mistake

was even more serious. I gravely underestimated the terrible power of scientific terrorism as developed by the totalitarian police-States. I was deceived by the hush-hush and the propaganda applied to these, in the case of Nazis by the Right and the Centre, and in the case of the USSR by the Left and the Centre . . . As far as I am able to tell, the horrors in either case are substantially true. I am therefore constrained in honesty to admit that under neither the Nazi nor the Soviet system of systematic and applied brutality does non-violent resistance stand a dog's chance . . . You may try to believe, if you can, that the blood of the martyrs is the seed of the Church. I cannot. The martyrs in Germany and Russia run into millions, perhaps tens of millions. That is altogether too many for a Church to grow out of. The seed rots in the mass of mute, inglorious, intolerable suffering: under which men lose their human attributes, and nations their soul. In a word, it seems to me that the scientific terrorism of the totalitarian police-State – the wholesale reversion to medieval torture, with all the diabolic ingenuity of applied modern science – has changed the whole frame of reference within which modern pacifism was conceived.

For the first time, Murry had awoken to the political and ideological, as distinct from the economic, issue at stake in the War – to the force of the argument he had dismissed so lightly when it was advanced by Niebuhr (and Gandhi), that 'a virulent tyranny is worse than war because it comprehends both the present destruction of culture as an immediate consequence and war as an ultimate consequence'.[19] For the first time, he had come to doubt the betrayal of Christ by the democracies. As was to be expected, he leant over backwards. It would not be long now before he was pronouncing their morality quite adequate to averting war, and absolving them from all complicity.

This frank admission of error stands greatly to Murry's credit; as does his outspoken defence of some of the continental collaborators, who, he believed, might have been as misinformed as himself – Pierre Drieu la Rochelle, for instance, whom he had met in *Athenaeum* days, De Man, who had helped clarify his Socialism, even Laval, of whose corruption, he told Eliot, he could find no definite evidence in all the French charges he had read. At the same time, it was hardly to be supposed that so resounding a confirmation of their criticism would restore the Pacifists' faith in him, any more than their continued adherence to Gandhist principles would increase his respect for them – especially when combined, as it often was, with disdain for *ashrams* and sentimentalization of Russia. Quite the reverse. Within twelve months of the end of the War, 'I feel myself a fish out of water indeed',[12] he was confessing in his journal.

As the pilot who had weathered the storm, he continued to be elected to the top of the P.P.U. National Council, and he was unwilling to relinquish *Peace News* so long as there was any hope of its being 'a unifying influence in the movement'.[15] But this it certainly was not. As time went on, sales fell off, criticism grew more and more vociferous, his own revulsion more and more intense – until, at the Annual General Meeting of April 1946, a rude attack by Reginald Reynolds brought the issue to a head. Murry announced his resignation then and there, and retired the following October – sick not only of young Pacifists, but of old.

At bottom, it was the story of 'the Adelphi' yet again. Beyond doubt he would genuinely have liked to be the humble spokesman of a catholic fraternity: but it had to be a fraternity he agreed with, and the only way to ensure its agreement was to dominate it. Not that he saw it like that – in his own eyes, he was merely the vehicle of a supra-personal power – but others did. To them he appeared rather like Gladstone, who, a Frenchman once said, whereas he resembled every diplomat in keeping a card up his sleeve, differed in believing that God had put it there. Taking everything into account, his last year's editorship was a pity for all concerned, since it alienated the general public, which presumed that he must be talking Pacifism, without reconciling the Pacifists, who knew too well that he was not.

Was he, then, still a Pacifist himself? The question was asked in *Peace News*; and no doubt he was asking it too. 'Beneath everything are two deep-seated doubts,' he was confiding in his journal: 'One, whether pacifism has any answer to totalitarianism; two, whether one pacifist in ten has honestly faced the problem.' [12] Although he continued his Commentary even after ceasing to be editor, helped launch the Sheppard Press, the Pacifist publishing-house for which he had collected the funds (*Looking Before and After* was one of its first productions), and wrote a pamphlet, *Trust or Perish*, which ranks among his best, his mind was in a whirl. All that survived of the community were a couple of families, a single man and a woman, united by loyalty to himself; of the movement he had once been proud to belong to, some 15,000 nominal signatories, for the most part as tired as he, and as eager, if only subconsciously, to resume their pre-war avocations. The need to settle down quietly and re-think his position was growing urgent.

That autumn, 'the Big Three' moved out of the farmhouse, Ruth into a cottage of her own, where she continued to act as his secretary, he and Mary into a house further down the lane, The Poplars, which they bought for £1,600 and rechristened Lower Lodge. And there, at the end of November, he started composing the lecture which, as it came to engross him, expanded rapidly into a book, *The Free Society*:

> With this book, which is the first-fruits of my continuous thinking during the war, I discard my pacifism, and deliberately enter the political arena, in the hope that I may persuade my countrymen to make their political purposes completely unambiguous, and make it plain to all the world that they will contemplate war for one purpose and one purpose only, which they will declare with absolute clarity, and from which they will not deviate: the abolition of war, in the only way war can be abolished, by the establishment of a free society of nations.[20]

As usual, the *volte face* was more apparent than real. Personalities apart, *The Free Society* is neither more political nor less Pacifist than *Christocracy*, to the two parts of which its own two correspond. So far as foreign policy went, all that Murry had done was to dismiss unilateral disarmament (which, like most people, Pacifist or otherwise, he could never dissociate from conscientious objection) as chimerical, not merely for the present but for all time, and promote his second-best to the status of first.

That second-best had always been the same: the establishment of a supernational authority. Often in the past he had pleaded with Pacifists not to oppose such a thing, *if* it could be had. Now, he believed, it could. The atomic bomb had made it at once indispensable and feasible: indispensable, because 'ten more years of continued existence in a world of nations seeking merely to avoid war will witness such a degradation of human morality, such a continuous disintegration of purposeful living, that a war to abolish war will come as a moral and spiritual liberation';[21] feasible, because Mr Baruch, 'a member of the same sceptical and visionary race' [22] as Karl Marx, had proposed an Atomic Authority, which the Western Powers were actually sponsoring. Like Russell and Mosley, Murry contended that they should use their momentary monopoly of the bomb to enforce this Authority on the U.S.S.R.: and that if only the determination existed to enforce it, if need be by war, war might in fact prove unnecessary. As to the course to be followed in the more likely event of war being fought, actually or even ostensibly, for some other purpose, he gave no indication.

If his advocacy of a supernational authority was not new, neither, at first sight, was his theory of democracy, which occupied the bulk of the book. Indeed, he had expounded this so fully in *The Price of Leadership* and *The Defence of Democracy*, so succinctly in *The Pledge of Peace*, that it is with a start that one finds the birth of the 'free society' dated 1945. What he meant by this was, presumably, that full employment had made further evasion impossible: either men would voluntarily subordinate their sectional demands – for higher wages, higher profits – to the well-being of the commonwealth as a whole, realizing that new social morality which (he had been derided throughout the '30s for insisting) was the *sine qua non* of Socialism, or else the free society would perish. A problem remote before the War, and seemingly anachronistic during it, had suddenly become urgent and crucial.

In this situation, however, Murry had only to begin expounding the 'Idea' once more for it to come home to him, with the force of an illumination, that here, in the national society itself, was the very thing he had been seeking so long, in I.L.P., P.P.U., Church – an 'experiencing nature'. Here, before his eyes, was a community actually engaged in discovering 'the conditions of its own existence', and discovering them precisely as he had done, not by 'taking thought' beforehand, but by 'actual living'.[23]

That celebrated British empiricism, which approximates 'the correction of the action of the majority in the free society by the criticism, and eventually the advent to power, of the minority, to the correction of a scientific hypothesis, by further experiment'[24] – what was that but his own empiricism writ large? What was the belief underlying this practice, 'that formulations of the truth are provisional, save the one – that the free society is the sole means to truth – by which its own internal freedom and receptivity is guaranteed',[25] but the very belief which 'impresses upon men a continual self-annihilation: that is to say, a continual surrender of the finality of one's own truth'? And was not the mutual trust which alone made parliamentary democracy, as it made freedom of inquiry, possible, a diffused form of the love that lets the other one be?

[316]

Since the gradual emergence of this 'love' constituted, in Murry's eyes, the 'meaning of history', he could, and did, go on now to claim for the free society all that Marxists have claimed for the Communist:

> I have (I believe) the honour of being the first to make the claim explicitly on behalf of the fully free society . . . I claim that it sustains the meaning of history, whereas the Communist society annihilates that meaning. I claim that the conscience which unites the free society as a body of men dedicated to seeking truth is the only power which can give meaning to history. I claim that this conscience is essentially nothing other than the love of God and obedience to His will which were supremely manifest in Jesus Christ. I claim therefore that the free society is indeed the body of Christ in the sense in which the Christian Church – even though utterly divided against itself – has claimed to be that body.[26]

So, in the second part of *The Free Society* – which he himself deemed far the more important – Murry's quest for a society he can serve unreservedly culminates in a rediscovery of 'the free society of Britain'; his service, in 'exhibiting to it the moral beauty of its own hidden idea',[27] as Rousseau exhibited Geneva's. In this part, 'given' to him, he said, 'in a kind of illumination',[28] he thought he had composed our English *Social Contract*. It was not unfitting that his last and best exposition of the idea should have been delivered, two years later, before the *Rencontres Internationales de Genève*.

XXVI

ROUNDING OFF

———◆———

WITH *Adam and Eve* and *The Free Society*, Murry's 'thought-adventure' comes to an end. The lover had found his mistress, the cleric his Church. Both the great needs inspiring his urgent, all-absorbing, seemingly interminable quest for 'truth' were met; and with that, the quest subsided. Although he was to live another ten years and publish another half-dozen books, they would add nothing essential to his message. One might say of him what he had said of Wordsworth: 'Up to a point . . . we feel that we are being taken by him towards some splendid goal. After that point, we feel we are being led nowhere at all. In the deep sense, he has nothing more to say.' [1]

The reference to Wordsworth is pertinent. It was not for nothing that Murry had turned to him, on at least three occasions, for inspiration and guidance. 'I feel that if I am spared I shall do again what Wordsworth did,' he had exclaimed in 1918: and there was a real sense in which he did. For what he was then, he remained for the next thirty years – the poet *manqué*, the man with the vision but not the faculty divine. The growth of his mind was essentially the growth of a poet's mind – a major Romantic poet's. Hence, of course, that intimate understanding of the Romantics which is the unique distinction of his criticism.

To Plowman, who had criticized *The Necessity of Communism*, he once wrote:

> If it has something of the work of art about it, if as you say all my books have something of the work of art about them – and I've no doubt it's true – that is simply because Beauty is Truth, Truth Beauty. I am a man who comes at Beauty through Truth. It's a pity. Perhaps, if I hadn't been ill-used as a child, I should have been able to come at Truth through

Beauty as well: in fact, I should have been what I sometimes dream a Man might be. But I'm not. What I am not Keats might have become.[2]

To define the object of organic knowledge as 'truth' is obviously to beg a big question. An interpretation that satisfies the whole man is no more necessarily true than one that satisfies the intellectual man only. Poetic truths, as much as scientific, are working hypotheses at best, to be confirmed or refuted by experiment – in this case, the experiment of living. But what goes for *The Necessity of Communism* goes for each of Murry's nodal books. *Keats and Shakespeare, God, The Necessity of Pacifism, The Free Society* – each of these represents a fresh synthesis, at once of objective experience and of the experiencing subject. They are works of the whole man, addressed to the whole man. Hence their compulsive power, closely related to that of poetry. Of this series, *The Free Society* is the last.

When he finished it, Murry was, as usual on these occasions, confident that he had reached bedrock at last:

A just society is unimaginable unless it is based on the law of Love. This is the mighty and wonderful achievement of the Free Society: that it is, however crudely and clumsily, based on the law of Love. It is *the* Christian political Society. Here, it seems, is where I stop. I can get no further. This, it seems, is the conception towards which I have been struggling ever since I began *The Adelphi* – that is, for 25 years. I held it intuitively, and it shaped my original conception of *The Adelphi* itself – a magazine which *was* a society of people united by Justice and Love, moving forward, open-minded, learning by experience – a corporate mind which was 'a throughfare for all thoughts, not a select party'.[3]

The usual autobiography followed; the usual articles in *The Adelphi* re-defining and developing the theme (and, of course, demanding the suppression of those, Communists and Fascists, who undermine the society of justice and love). 'It seems that I have now got myself into a position where I shall have to go on saying the same thing over and over again, till people begin to listen,'[4] he told Ruth Baker. As usual, he expected them to listen.

And the result, also, was as usual. If anything, it was worse: for, unlike its predecessors, even the new 'visible Church' did not hail its latest recruit. *The Free Society* pleased nobody. It was more sympathetically received by Housman and Wood in *Peace News* than it was by Malcolm Muggeridge in *The Daily Telegraph* or Tomlinson in

John o' London's Weekly, both of whom made it a pretext for personal ridicule. Despite all Dakers' efforts, extending to posters on railway station platforms, it sold less than half the anticipated 10,000: whilst as for *The Adelphi* – which, with the help of a part-time assistant editor, Hogan, Murry had been trying to revive – it continued to lose £30 a quarter.

Yet this time there was no change of mind. Perhaps, if he had been ten years younger or twenty years stronger, there would have been. Perhaps some fresh initiative would have followed, culminating in some fresh *volte face*. As it was, there being nothing more he himself could do to put theory into practice, and finding it impossible after all to go on saying the same thing over and over again to the empty air, he threw in his hand. 'We cannot *live* under the shadow of impending annihilation,' he wrote soon afterwards, generalizing from his own limitations: 'We have to ignore it, and to behave as though it were not going to happen':[5] and with that, he stepped out of the arena of politics. In June 1948, just twenty-five years after the first number, he gave *The Adelphi* away.

All that he could do for the free society, Murry felt, reasonably enough, he was doing already at Thelnetham. For though, by the time he resigned from the P.P.U. in the autumn of 1947, the ideal of a multi-form community had long since receded, he still had hopes of a co-operative farm. In fact, it was only when he was rid of the irksome necessity of a weekly journey to London that he could devote himself fully to the work that lay nearest his heart. Not that there was much he could do in the practical line, beyond attend to the bees and summon all his strength for a periodical tour of inspection. But the accounts were his, and so were the selection and supervision of the workers. During the twelve months following his retirement, moreover, much of his best work went into the preparation of a cycle of sermons (*Not as the Scribes*), one for each Sunday of the year, which he would read to the community at Lower Lodge: some of them of particular application, some of more general purport.

These weekly services were not of his own initiation. He no longer believed that ritual and worship, any more than non-violence, were involved in the effort towards community. That belief he attributed now to the extreme disparity between the ideal and the real which had bedevilled his life in the '30s. 'The nature of my religion has subtly changed,' he confessed in one address: 'It always has been subtly

32. J. M. M. in argument, 1950

33. J. M. M. with Weg, Ruth Baker and his grandson John, Moselle, 1951

34. J. M. M. with Mary, Thelnetham, 1954

35. Lower Lodge, Thelnetham

changing.'[6] Not only ritual and worship, but God, had got left behind at Larling: he had reverted to his original view that 'the language of religion is, in so far as it is valid, one immense language of metaphor'.[7] Yet he would still have attended church, had he not been afraid of embarrassing the orthodox by the presence of an unmarried couple, and still liked to profess and call himself a Christian. To Eliot, who, reviewing *The Free Society* in the last *Adelphi*, raised the obvious question whether he had a right to do so, he replied:

> The issue about Christianity is an old one as between us. I remember your saying substantially the same thing more than 20 years ago. I think the trouble is that I, in some sense, am a sort of Christian mystic: in that the nearest I get to a conviction of transcendent truth is through the contemplation of the life and death of Our Lord. Therein I touch a new and totally different mode of experience; but I am somehow incapable of making ontological affirmations on the strength of it. I think I understand, – more than understand, find necessary and inevitable in an effort of intellectual apprehension and formulation of the transcendent truth revealed – the ontological affirmations of Christian Orthodoxy – but I feel them to be of *another order* than the revelation which they explicate. The immediacy is gone: and my mind (or soul) is in an essentially different condition – not exactly doubting, but no longer convinced of finality, wondering if it is not an ambiguity of utterance, imposed by the need of uttering the unutterable.[8]

Eliot's objection was warranted. Christianity has always been a system of ontological as well as experiential affirmations; and a conviction of their ontological validity alters the nature of the experience. Murry recognized this clearly enough when he insisted that belief in the bodily resurrection of Jesus would diminish, 'perhaps catastrophically',[9] the tragic appeal of the Cross and, in book after book, called on the Churches to discard this dogma. What he seems not to have realized is that it is equally true of all the dogmas that he who accepts them literally *feels* differently from him who sets his own construction upon them. Whatever he may have imagined when he knelt in church, he was not sharing the experience of the rest of the congregation, present or past.

If, as he admitted, to deny that 'the great first Cause of all being is the same as the God who reveals himself in us as love' is 'to part company with Christianity: for that is the very centre and essence of the Christian *faith*',[10] then he had parted company with it, and his retention of the terminology was misleading, to say the least. 'What do I gain by calling it [love] God?' he asked himself at the very end of his life: 'Except the palpable loss of having it mixed up with a very different – an *absolutely* different – Power, which I should be personally ashamed of obeying.' [11] It is a pity he did not ask himself sooner. Rather than indulge in such logomachies as mar *The Challenge of Schweitzer* (a pendant to the sermons), he might have done better to abide by the conclusion of *God*: 'The only verdict that can be accepted on what is, or what is not, God, is the verdict of the Catholic Church.' [12] By estranging the rationalists while failing to reassure the religious, this usage probably contributed more than anything else to bringing him into ridicule and neglect.

Even so, the temptation is understandable. Not only did it appeal to his passion for continuity in change, and his yearning for a language that would set no gulf between himself and the ordinary man, but, when he was addressing his friends, as he was in the sermons, it enabled him both to communicate what might otherwise have been incommunicable and to infuse fresh life and significance into the traditional dogmas. His treatment of the Pauline epistles provides a memorable instance.

The rump of the Thelnetham community were his friends. They understood his peculiar idiom and responded promisingly to his exhortations – with impressive unanimity pronouncing Russia antichrist, embracing the new militant gospel and changing overnight from a colony of Benedictines into 'a free society on a tiny scale'.[13] After years of acrimonious controversy, it must have been heartening to be treated as an oracle; and by March 1948, Murry's hopes were high. 'Our effort here', he was reminding them that month, 'is an effort to solve, in miniature, but in practice, the tremendous problem which confronts democracy':

> My own conviction is that we are going to make the grade, as the Americans say, – we are going to get to the top of the hill. I did not have that conviction a year ago; but to-day I have. Something has happened between us all – intangible and indefinable, but real. We have become members of one another; and I feel sure that the spiritual advance we have made will now have its outcome and expression in material success.[13]

It was the old story. The words were hardly out of his mouth before the last of the original Farm Group announced his departure: and with him appears to have departed the last hope of a co-operative farm. Crusaders were no better than monks. 'I have', Murry recorded, 'at the Adelphi Centre and here, proved the failure of Socialism on my pulses: the prodigious difficulty of creating a new co-operative ethos. Not that we have achieved *nothing* at Lodge Farm: but that we have learned, by hard experience, how little it is possible to achieve. Individualism must remain the chief social ethos.' [14] And with that, he stepped out of domestic as well as foreign politics, thenceforward voting Conservative.

Not even this disappointment, however, produced any major re-orientation. After all, there were substantial compensations. If he had failed to found a co-operative farm he had not failed as a gentleman farmer. 'To defend the soil against the exploiters, of *all* sorts, becomes a real mission,' he had told Eliot (who would consult him from time to time about Fabers' agricultural books), 'the more important because I am convinced that if a country has enough imagination to get its agriculture right, it will get everything else right – or not wholly wrong.' [15] As far as Lodge Farm was concerned, he could feel that this mission, at least, was discharged. From a huddle of dilapidated build-ings and neglected fields, it had become one of the most prosperous in the neighbourhood, graded up from C to A, an object of justifiable pride.

Again, the effort to restore it, although it had entailed the employ-ment of local and even prisoner-of-war labour, had welded the three families who remained – the Fergussons, the Hobsons and the Murrys – into something which, if not a 'community' in any strict sense, was assuredly the next best thing: a group of friends who could 'trust one another completely'. Thus, Murry could feel that he had realized the dream he had voiced to Plowman in 1937: and, drawing the lesson as usual, he found himself gravitating steadily towards Plowman's own belief, that only personal relationships counted. Notwithstanding the 'except', at any rate, it is a far cry from the 'nothing personal matters' [16] of 1931, to the journal entry of November 1954:

My views haven't changed – except in the sense that I have learned, by experience, that there is no way forward through voluntary community. But that's not a genuine impasse. It only means that I realise, more plainly than before, that the only thing to do is to work for the education of the individual into imagination and moral responsibility, – into a sense of real values.[17]

From the economic success of the farm and the 'normalisation' of its management, moreover, there followed one further consequence, which, though unforeseen, was dear to Murry's heart – a steady incorporation into the life of the village. From being an object of curiosity and amusement, good-natured or otherwise, 'Conchie Farm' had gradually acquired a reputation for fair dealing and neighbourliness – until the day came when a social initiative on the Murrys' part could evoke an immediate response.

It was Mary who first proposed that the group should put on a play for the village, and approached the schoolmistress for the use of her class-room. After that things moved quickly. Murry found himself Chairman of the parish council; the Christmas play became an annual institution; and so, since plays need halls, did the summer fête held at Lower Lodge, in aid of the Village Hall Fund. Before many summers had gone by, Historical Necessity itself was being invoked to bring about a rural renascence: 'The end of the effort which began with the Adelphi Centre is so different from anything I dreamed – yet it's the same thing – and so is begging my friends to buy tickets for a Great Christmas Draw for a Village Hall. And so is my great and novel reputation as the low comedian in the village theatricals.' [18]

The low comedian was in point of fact quite a good actor, as Dorothy Brett had noticed at Garsington; and it was typical of Murry that he devoted himself to these undertakings quite as earnestly as he had done to the world revolution. It was the same when, in 1952, he wrote the play himself. *The Gold-Diggers* was no masterpiece of dramatic art (and the local press, naturally, seized on it as a golden opportunity to ape its big brothers in Fleet Street), but it exactly fulfilled its purpose, which was to please, not journalists, but a village audience; and it would never have occurred to him to expend less pains upon it than upon the gravest Aspect of Literature. He never wrote down, never talked down, to his neighbours. Indeed, he would probably have been well content to think of that village hall – opened just after his death, with his photograph adorning the wall – as his most substantial memorial: *Si monumentum requiris circumspice.*

All this is sufficient to show why *Community Farm*, which he finished in 1949, far from being the most 'disillusioned' (in the contemporary sense of petulant), is quite the gayest of all his books. To be sure, its publication caused some resentment in the village, and even within the 'community' (from which he had kept it a deadly secret); and it may remind one a little of those satirical novels in which, amid a throng of cranks, humbugs and hobbledehoys, there is invariably one character of perfect good sense, in whom the discerning recognize The Author. Yet it is as rich in humour as in hindsight. Some passages, like the account of the farm valuation, have an almost Dickensian flavour, whilst the homely informality of the style, the unwonted sharpness of observation, match Richard Murry's illustrations.

Murry had once cited Ronald Duncan's *Journal of a Husbandman* as being 'almost too well-written, because it leaves behind the suspicion that Mr Duncan is still a good way from having sweated the intellectual out of himself. The journal of a husbandman would be a more humdrum affair: neither would it be so blithely innocent of a balance-sheet.' [19] 'Humdrum' is not the right word for *Community Farm* – the narrative is too lively, the reflections are too far-ranging, for that. 'Earthy' would be nearer the mark. But even overlooking the balance-sheet, one could hardly name a book more remote, in manner and matter alike, from *The Evolution of an Intellectual*. Emphatically, it is the work of a man who belongs, and is content to belong, to a particular patch of countryside – a stranger in a strange land no longer.

His contentment was indeed profound. If he rarely left Thelnetham now, that was not merely because he was a semi-invalid, unable to walk more than a couple of hundred yards without pain. He had not the least inclination to leave. Both farm and garden engrossed him. 'I don't find my limitations irksome,' he told Wordsworth:

> I accept them as natural as the casing air – probably because within my small radius of activity there is so much to do, and because the older I get the more engrossing do I find the simplest things. Life, in my experience, steadily becomes more 'sacramental'; the universal is more and more visibly present in the particular. I don't know how to explain this increasing coalescence of the ideal and the real, which seems almost anomalous at such a time of human and spiritual crisis – and no doubt it would not have happened were I not totally engaged in activities which my imagination tells me are the most significant in which *I* can engage. But as it is I am sustained by the deep feeling that I have found 'my line', as Matt. Arnold called it.[20]

His contentment was such that he could actually hold it against Schweitzer that to him the miseries of the world were misery, and would not let him rest.

But of course, as he also told Wordsworth, none of this would have been conceivable apart from his unbroken domestic happiness. 'Underneath everything, and enabling me to carry everything, is the blessedness of life with Mary. That is so extraordinary and so simple – so utterly unlike anything in my past experience – that I am never, in fact, overwhelmed, but always sustained by the sheer wonder of our love.' [21] That this was no exaggeration, a hundred passages in his letters and journals attest. Let one stand for many:

> I fear it will be very boring to anyone who reads this journal when I am dead; but I must, in simple honesty, put on record once more my exquisite happiness with Mary. It seems to me that it is the one thing of permanent value and significance I have achieved; the one thing worth listening to that I have to say: that man-woman love is the supreme felicity, and that it is attainable . . . Before I knew Keats,* I wrote about Katherine: 'Lo! I have made love all my religion, Nothing remains to me if it be gone.' Keats wrote the same: 'Love is my religion, and you are its only tenet.' And this sense of love as complete religious fulfilment is what fills my consciousness as I go to sleep with Mary at night and wake with her in the morning. I am in a new dimension of being, quite simple, quite real, quite familiar, yet every day absolutely new. And because of that I need no 'religion'; I *have* all that 'religion' promises, all that God could give. And yet I know that somewhere concealed, or lost, or perfectly realised in this enchanted simplicity of love, is a 'religion' in the more ordinary sense of the word. Were it not so, I should surely look with apprehension on the approach of death, as an end to this felicity. But it is not so. I feel I shall greet death when it comes with a song in my soul: *Nunc dimittis servum tuum.*' [22]

There were, of course, plenty of Murry's acquaintance to whom his 'mariolatry', as they called it, was boring; 'the idea that a man could not live, could not exist, could not breathe, apart from his beloved woman', [23] neither a tribute to his own philosophy nor a good testimonial to Keats's. And when, forgetting that 'religion in the more ordinary sense', he would proceed to preach Lady Chatterley's gospel 'that nothing matters except "love" between a man and a woman', [24] he certainly fell under the condemnation of *Son of Woman*: 'It is not physical tenderness to each other that men and women need to be taught as the one thing needful. What they need to learn is something to avail them when physical tenderness is torn away, and happy love

* A mistake: the poem was composed when he was already familiar with Keats, and may have contained an unconscious reminiscence.

is a faint and far-off dream; what they need to learn is how to endure suffering alone.' 25

Yet even those who scouted his conception of the happy marriage – or, in Thelnetham parlance, 'the true man-woman relation' – as a panacea for all the ills of the world, had to admit that, after what he himself had been through, it was more than pardonable. And it may be that in attaching such importance to his 'discovery' that the thing was attainable, Murry was not so deluded as he seemed:

> Why is it – I will not say so hard: for hard it has never been between Mary and myself – why is it such a long journey to bring the act and organs of physical love completely under the dominion of Imagination? So long a journey to so simple a conclusion? If I include, as indeed I must, my life with Katherine, Violet, B. in the journey, then it has been an exceedingly bitter one – so bitter that my mind is divided in its judgement. Part of me feels that the final discovery I have made must be very important, and that the Regeneration of Generation by the Imagination, the redemption of Sex by 'the Divine Humanity, the One Man, even Jesus', is the true gospel for this distracted and devil-invaded world; part of me feels that a journey so complicated, so utterly abnormal, can have precious little significance for the world, and that, even though the world might dimly recognise the quality of simplicity that I have attained – and that is not very likely – still it would be a baffling and exasperating simplicity, which would irritate rather than illuminate.26

The inference was true. There really was no means of ascertaining whether his belated fulfilment was a rarity or a commonplace of normal experience. Had there been – had others set their findings on record with the same unreserve as Lawrence – Murry's journey would not have been so bitter as it was. In the event, its very bitterness justified his determination to set on record his own.

'I wish you would write me a letter telling me what you really feel about love – a love autobiography, so to speak,' he wrote to Frieda: 'It seems to me so terribly important. And yet we go to our graves without really telling the *truth* about it. That is one thing I am determined not to do.' 27 And he did not. It was one of his ambitions in his journals to do what Lawrence had done, 'not quite successfully',26 in *Lady Chatterley's Lover*.

The Man who had Died had found his Priestess of Isis. Here in his domestic life, at any rate, there was no disillusionment – though of course there were difficulties in plenty. The 'family', after all, was no family in the accepted sense. For he had given up hope of a divorce, his attempts to discharge his responsibilities towards his two younger children were beset with difficulties, and there was little he could do for them now beyond ensuring Betty an adequate allowance. It was not until six years after leaving Larling that he was permitted to see them again – young Mary for a few minutes at her school in near-by Bury St Edmunds, David for a few weeks in the winter of 1947–8, when coaching him for his entrance to Christ's Hospital. This was a perpetual thorn in his side. Yet not even this could unsettle him for long at a time; and the sharp reminders of misery past which reached him week by week through the post served mainly as a foil to his present content. When, in the autumn of 1949, his wife left Larling for Winchester, and he revisited The Old Rectory for the auction, 'it did not cost me a single pang', he observed: 'Each room has its own particular memory of horror.' [28] Moreover, to offset his anxiety for Mary and David, came the satisfaction of seeing Weg at the Sorbonne and Col at Brasenose – and both, in the same year, engaged to be married.

Weg was married at Thelnetham church on July 5, 1949, the bridegroom a young Belgian producer and playwright, Jean de Coninck, whom Murry met for the first time then. The ceremony was a simple, homely affair, attended only by the families concerned, including Violet's father, and a few close friends and neighbours. Although he regretted, naturally enough, that Weg should be leaving England for good, Murry himself was profoundly happy. Next day, he was writing in his journal:

> There was a strange moment when everybody had left the house except Weg and me and we stood together on top of the stairs waiting the moment to drive to the Church. We stood arm in arm, just as we should be in walking up the aisle. Time stood still, while my mind moved back to my baby girl lying naked on my knees at the Old Coastguard, and I was held by the marvel of the thought of what would one day come out of that little womb in the unending continuity of life. My faith is realised. The love that held us together then, the love of which I was conscious and she was not, is now come to consciousness in her. She will pass it on. It lives and moves and has its being – a golden thread in the pattern. Love was in her making and her nurture: through love she suffered – those nights when I held her crying in my arms in the dark at Larling – through love she now has her happiness. All is well. Blessed be love. Its magic goes on, in spite of all – in spite of all.

The reminiscence of Katherine's farewell letter (which he misquoted consistently all his life) was not accidental. The following summer, Weg duly presented him with a grandson – fourth in the line of Johns – and it was after visiting them for the first time in Brussels, and while correcting the proofs of Katherine's *Letters*, that the thought came back to his mind:

I love to think (or dream) that Katherine – that Wig rather, for I never experienced her as Katherine – has watched all my life. And I am sure that this is not a pathetic fancy, because it is a way, and probably the only way, of expressing my experience of my darling. I feel that she has watched and is watching my life; that my communion with her through love is so simple and direct and intense at such a moment that all my life is subsumed under it. It is gathered up in such a moment and purified and vindicated. I am known even as I know. And there rises within me like a clear, silent spring the knowledge of the truth of her parting message: 'Truly I believe no two lovers ever walked the earth more joyfully – in spite of all, in spite of all.'

And this heritage of love I *saw*, renewed, incarnate, in Weg's little baby boy. I am convinced as I am of anything important in this life that Katherine's spiritual heritage has been passed on. I always felt, quite simply, that Violet's daughter was Katherine's daughter, and I named her accordingly. And I loved my little daughter as Katherine would have loved her – with *her* love as well as my own. And how vividly I remember one day in the upper room of the Old Coastguard Station at Abbotsbury, holding her flat on my knees (when she was not thriving) and brooding over her baby womb. Katherine's presence was there, while I was over-whelmed by the thought that in the fullness of time that little womb, so naked before me, would bear and bring forth a child of *love*. The marvel and the mystery of it. Everything was quiet except for the great sea thundering on the Chesil Beach. I was in the presence of God – the unnameable, unutterable, but infinitely tender God. And when in Brussels I saw that little boy the other day, I knew it had all come true. There *was* the continuity of Love. Love *is*.[29]

The wheel had turned full circle. It would have been unfitting if that expression, so long endeared to Murry's readers ('Has the wheel turned full circle this month?' they would ask, as they opened their *Adelphis*), did not apply to him. It did. Love, once again, was all his religion.

XXVII

DECLINING CURVE

❧❧❧

IN THE SUMMER OF 1950, *Picture Post* had the happy idea of featuring a discussion on Pacifism between Murry and the Rev. Donald Soper, who was driven down to Thelnetham for the purpose. It was a happy idea because, trailing the two round the garden and pig-sties, their photographer managed to capture the best of all likenesses of Murry. Here are all those quaint gestures and contortions that characterized him in earnest conversation, 'those sinuous movements, that mobility of feature', which, Eliot says, used to fascinate him, reminding him of 'an oriental, a Hindu'. Here he is, in his habit as he lived for the last few years of his life. For after his sixtieth year he altered little in outward appearance. Only his remaining hair began to whiten, his cheeks to redden, the elaborate tracery of furrows to be masked by the softness of age – so that, by his own account, he came closely to resemble his father.

Old John Murry had died in 1947, aged eighty-six. Murry's appearance of robustness, unfortunately, was deceptive. As he said of Gissing, 'no man can live through what he had lived through without a permanent loss of vitality'.[1] That the composition of *The Free Society* – a work of 100,000 words in a space of three months – should have been punctuated by headaches and left him with a feeling of lassitude, is not to be wondered at. Thenceforward any unusual exertion, mental or physical, was liable to prostrate him for days. He could carry on only by observing a strict routine, which, however trying to visitors, Mary understood to be necessary. 'The time comes', he told Henry Williamson, 'when it is one's duty to go more quietly – to acquiesce gracefully in the beginning of the declining curve.'[2]

Yet this did not trouble him much. On the contrary, 'It's very very nice to be old,'[3] he said, and he meant it. The inward transformation was astonishing. To those who had known the critic of thirty, or

[330]

the crusader of ten, years before, he scarcely seemed the same personality. He had come as near to being normal as a fundamentally healthy man can. The strain had gone out of his manner; every trace of fanaticism disappeared, and with it – most startling of all – even the compulsion to write:

> I find myself less and less inclined to do any serious writing . . . Deep down (I think) is the feeling that my bolt is shot. I haven't anything more to say. I was always, essentially, a man with a message; and, though nobody understands it, or thinks it worth understanding, it has been spoken. I've nothing really to add to *Adam and Eve* and *The Free Society*; what more I could add is a matter of living and doing. I feel that, if only I were sure of an income, I should 'mess about gaily' for the rest of my life, without any real qualms of conscience – superintending the farm, gardening, hatching out chickens and ducks, fattening pigs. I don't even want to read very much.[4]

For Murry this was indeed 'an unexpected and extraordinary condition'.[5]

He himself was inclined to attribute it less directly to age than to his happiness with Mary; and probably he was right. There is certainly some incompatibility between domestic and artistic fulfilment. This is a point he reverts to often in his journals, indicating the overwhelming preponderance of the unmarried or unhappily married among writers (he might have added artists, musicians and philosophers) of eminence; whilst in the 'Imaginary Conversation' between Keats and Coleridge, broadcast in 1946, he makes Coleridge say – no doubt with Wordsworth in mind: 'It is rare, I believe, that great poets attain domestic happiness, and when they do the faculty of poetry is apt to leave them.'[6]

As early as 1943, he had written to Mary, during one of their brief separations:

> Life is just utterly different without you. Not that it's bad – but the sheer *difference* is extraordinary. My old familiar sense of isolation comes back to me: the feeling that I'm a bit odd and queer – a sort of 'I, John Middleton Murry' feeling. When I'm with you I feel just an ordinary, but for some extraordinary reason, blessedly happy creature. If we were to be parted for a month (which God forbid) I might begin to feel myself a man with a mission again (which God forbid) –[7]

At which point, symbolically, his pen had run out. It recalls Mark Rutherford's, 'If I had been given you as a wife when I was thirty, I would never have let the public hear a syllable from me': and admirers of the man with a mission may be tempted to wish that Mary had stayed away longer and more often.

That, however, would be foolish and ungrateful – and not merely because, if Murry's explanation were complete, his bolt would have been shot with *Adam and Eve* and there would have been no *Free Society*. His whole significance is bound up with the fact that he never had been primarily an artist, or even an author:

> There is, indeed, no doubt at all that, in the last resort, art to me is nothing in comparison – with what shall I call it? My own 'personal happiness' gives the wrong slant. What could have made me endure the abject personal misery I endured from 1932–1939? My own personal reconciliation with life, much rather. And by life I mean the normal conditions of human existence: being married, having children, providing for them. A deliberately sterile marriage, because the added responsibility of children drains the energies that should be devoted to art, goes counter to my 'grain', *feels* somehow wrong. To find the true man-woman relation is, to me, more important than the achievement of artistic distinction. And these are with me not abstract 'principles', but the basic desires of the individual human being that is me: Conditions that must be satisfied in order to an immediate conviction of my own integrity. To this search for integrity – the reconciliation of Heart and Mind, Emotion and Intellect – I have sacrificed whatever talent for art I possessed. It was, probably, not much: but I think I had the makings of a good literary critic. But it was not really, or not wholly, a sacrifice: for criticism (as I wanted to practise it anyhow) depended on values – a determination of what is good for man: τὸ εὖ ζῆν. And I had to find out.[8]

That was true. What conflict there ever was in Murry's life between the claims of art and of love was decided almost before it was joined. Naturally he would have found his fulfilment in the normal conditions of human existence; it was only the deprivation caused, in the last resort, by his own insecurity and fear that launched him on such strange seas of thought – driving him on to create a religion and society which, by eliminating fear, should make those conditions possible. The quest had been long and arduous. If any man had earned the right to retirement, he had.

Actually, there were still some books he would have liked to write. He would have liked to finish his autobiography, for one: there were some things, he said, that he could communicate by no other means. But the attempt begun in November 1947 petered out – and six years later he had forgotten ever having made it. Coming on the last few pages in a notebook, 'I suppose', he has written at the end, 'this is the unfinished fragment of an autobiographical narrative of which the beginning is – somewhere.' Probably, like Gissing, he was 'afraid of the surging source of bitterness he might tap';[1] in any case, publication would have been difficult as long as Betty was alive. Again, he would have liked to expand the second part of *The Free Society* into a *magnum opus* incorporating all that he still endorsed of *Adam and Eve*. But this was not even begun. Lacking the excitement of discovery, he needed some outward incentive, and no incentive was forthcoming. By this time he had once more 'slid imperceptibly and completely "off the map" '.[9] Publishers refused to reprint his books; he was no longer asked for reviews; even his letters to the *Literary Supplement* were commonly ignored. 'I occasionally get what seems to me an over-whelming idea for a book', he told Hogan, 'and then I remember it would be incomprehensible.' [10]

For the best part of a year after winding up *The Adelphi*, therefore, he devoted himself to a task which had been on his conscience ever since his breakdown in 1939 – the preparation of a complete edition of his letters from Katherine. He wanted to transcribe them all, because no one else could so easily decipher her handwriting, much less assign dates; and he was resolved on publishing both them and the *Journal*, partly because he was more than ever convinced that 'Katherine's was an exquisite and unique personality, which she had exquisitely and uniquely revealed in her writings',[11] and partly in order to secure himself once and for all against the charges of falsification incurred by the earlier selections, in which he had aimed only at presenting 'the essential Katherine':[11] 'I do not like the idea that the few people who have loved me should discover that I had not been, to the utmost of my capacity, honest.' [11] With this end in view, he made it 'a point of honour' [12] to spare himself nothing, resisting even the 'momentary impulse to write a note or two, here and there, to say that there was another side'.[13]

It proved an exhausting occupation, physically and emotionally. 'Re-reading K.M.'s letters', he wrote in October 1950, while correcting the proofs, 'is to me at once *more* terrible and *less* terrible than reading Keats's':

> *More* terrible. I simply dread, shrink from, the approach of those passages which record the times I made her suffer. They are an agony

to me, and I have to brace myself to read them. I do read them, I read them indeed, very slowly, in order not to escape any of the pain. And it does not make much difference whether I know she was unjust to me (as at the time of the escape from Ospedaletti, in Jan. 1920, or the affair of the photograph, in Nov. 1920) or know she was justified (as in the case of my philandering with Elizabeth Bibesco, Nov. 1920). It is the fact that I caused her pain that is intolerable to remember – the experience an agony to renew. *Less* terrible. Because, at the same time, it is a renewal of intimacy, and of love – the anguish of love.[14]

He persisted, in spite of the strain, omitting from the *Letters* only those delivered to him after Katherine's death, and a couple mislaid among his papers; from the *Journal*, completed in 1953, some half-dozen passages which might have hurt others still alive, besides being more than even his own detachment could face. And it was in consequence of this undertaking that his next two productions came into being: the essay on Fanny Brawne, begun in February 1949, a month after finishing with the *Letters*; and *The Conquest of Death*, a year later. The one reflects the '*more* terrible', the other the '*less*', though a superficial reading would suggest the reverse.

At the time of *Keats and Shakespeare* he had indignantly rejected Amy Lowell's contention that Keats's charges against Fanny were unjust, symptoms of the emotional derangement wrought by phthisis: 'I wonder if Miss Lowell has ever *known* a writer of genius who suffered from consumption?'[15] In the new essay he rejects, almost equally indignantly, the contention that they were just. One would hardly need his own word to establish that it was Katherine's letters as much as Fanny's that had roused his suspicions. The evidence as to the changes wrought by phthisis had, indeed, been in his hands all along: 'But for some curious reason, I was blind to that evidence':

> Some strong unconscious motive was at work which forbade me to face the evidence of Katherine's emotional derangement – probably, since I was the one who suffered by it, a simple avoidance of pain. And mainly because of this I was impervious to the possibility of a similar emotional disturbance in Keats. I identified myself with him *too much*: as I identified myself with Katherine. It's an interesting example of how a bias may be produced.[16]

In *The Mystery of Keats* he made ample amends for the error, if error it was.

In Benjamin Constant's *Adolphe*, on the other hand, he found a story so closely resembling Katherine's that, newly sensitized as he was by the *Letters*, he could respond to it with peculiar intimacy – even to the extent of recapturing that sense of a 'presence', that assurance that 'all is well', which had overwhelmed him after her death, and was the root of his preoccupation, not only with tragedy, but with Christianity itself: 'For the Christian faith, in its origin and essence, appears to be nothing other than the declaration that love *is* self-validating, and veritably a new dimension of experience, in which alone the meaning of life is revealed.' [17]

Of course the actual events were not the same; and Murry was too good a critic to identify either Adolphe with himself or Ellenore with Katherine. He had never been so ignominious, nor she so altruistic, as the figures in Constant's *nouvelle*. Yet even here there were analogies enough to touch him to the quick. Could he read Adolphe's words, for instance, 'The unhappier you are, the more devoted I shall be', without recalling his own in 1920, 'When you're feeling things terribly hard just think that I'm loving you then, more intensely and warmly, more nearly, than at any other time?' [18] 'If you had read that in a book, what would you have thought?' [19] Katherine had cried. *The Conquest of Death* is Murry's answer:

> He is doomed to love, incapable of love, capable of knowing only that the angel troubled the waters of the pool while he was rooted immobile to the side, as in a horrible dream; capable of loving Ellenore only when love can be no more than an unappeasable regret, capable of loving Ellenore only when she is dying, and because she is dead. *Tendebatque manus ripae ulterioris amore.*[20]

In *Adolphe* he found a perfect text, or pretext, for his gospel of 'the liberation of the ego by simple love'.[21] Did he read more into it than was really there? Most of his critics presumed that he did. It is at least as likely that his experience enabled him to fathom it more deeply than they.

This translation and exegesis occupied him nearly three months: and 'I thought that I had had, and perhaps managed to convey, a momentary apprehension of something of importance',[22] he told Eliot, the only man, apart from his brother, to whom he sent a copy of the book. With that, the urge to write left him again. For a while he toyed with the idea of a further work on Shakespeare's tragedies, or on tragedy in general, re-reading all Aeschylus, Sophocles and Euripides in the Greek; but nothing came of this. Instead, he busied

himself with assembling the two selections of his essays published by
Peter Nevill; with a meticulous factual commentary on Keats's poems
and letters, resumed at intervals over the next six years; and with
long, largely retrospective entries in his journal, data for an unwritten
autobiography.

In June 1951, his mother died, aged eighty-two, in the old people's
home at Brighton, where she had passed the last years of her life
immersed in the world of Jane Austen. In 1955, Aunt Doll followed
her. As one after another of Murry's old friends found their way into
The Times obituary column – Walter de la Mare, Sir Edward Marsh,
Philip Tomlinson, Koteliansky – and he pasted their photographs into
the journal, it came to resemble an obituary itself. Sometimes he
would jot down his own recollections of them; and once the idea
occurred to him of compiling a volume of pen-portraits (how well he
could have done it, these jottings show) – only to vanish again when,
having imprudently started with Lawrence, he remembered that he
had written the *Reminiscences*.

He dwelt a good deal in the past now, especially the years of his
association with Lawrence and Katherine, which gradually became
enveloped in a rosy haze. Utterly dependent as he was upon Mary,
and happily dependent, he was unable to conceive how Lawrence
could have quarrelled with Frieda, though he had written a book to
account for it, and liked to fancy them all reunited and reconciled at
Lodge Farm. 'How true it is what you say', he wrote to Frieda in 1951,
'that our disagreements meant so much more and went so much deeper
than most people's so-called friendships':

> I feel that very strongly. In fact I sometimes feel that I have never had
> *any* friends except Lorenzo and you. Old Blake talks of 'the severe con-
> tentions of friendship'. Well, we have known them, and now they are a rich
> and joyful memory. The only thing I dislike about the past is that horrible
> grinding fear I used to have of not having any money.[23]

And again, four years later:

> You have been much in my mind for the last month: for I have been
> reading books about Lorenzo – Dr Leavis's book, in which he incident-
> ally wipes the floor with me (but I shall bob up again); Bunny Garnett's
> book of reminiscences: 'The Flowers of the Forest'; but chiefly Lorenzo's
> own books. And, of course, all the past has been flooding back on me
> again. Queer that the past should be more vivid than the present. Partly
> of course it's Lorenzo himself. Reading his books is like reliving so many

epochs of our lives. Queer, too, to read a book like Leavis's, making out Lawrence to be a classic, as it were the great successor to George Eliot, putting him on the very best shelf indeed, but on the shelf: quite right in one way, but yet how wrong in another. Lorenzo is an *experience*, not a classic.[24]

This correspondence with Frieda, resumed after the War, gave Murry particular pleasure. To her he could chat confidentially about 'the old times'; and for a season he and Mary quite seriously contemplated boarding a banana-boat for Mexico, so as to pay her a visit. When, in the summer of 1952, she herself flew over to England to see her children and grandchildren, one of her first requests of Laurence Pollinger was that he should ring Murry up and arrange a meeting in London. He and Mary drove to the Kingsley Hotel, where she was staying (for no better reason than that she had stayed there with Lawrence and could remember no other) – and 'it was there', Mary writes, 'that she told John how Lawrence had always looked on him as his greatest friend; how deeply he had loved him, and that he had held John's last letter to him in his hand when he was dying'.[25]

Frieda's was not the only old friendship to be renewed. Visitors to Thelnetham included Nehale and Vere Sullivan, Young (shortly before his death in 1950) and Rees. In 1949, moreover, being invited to address the Philosophical Society at Trinity College, Dublin, Murry took the occasion to stop with Gordon and Beatrice Campbell – now Lord and Lady Glenavy – whom he had not seen for forty years. 'Meeting him again was one of the happiest things that has happened to me for a long while.' [26] Thenceforward a trip to Dublin became a feature of the annual routine. It was the Glenavys who infected him with their own enthusiasm for croquet – the last of the long succession of ball-games.

Then there was Joyce Cary – though their reunion at Oxford in 1954, for all that it ended in Murry's being supported back to the Mitre, was not such an unalloyed pleasure:

> There was Joyce, for all the world just as I had left him in 1912, and there was I, not at all (I felt) as he had left me. He had had a long and happy married life; I a succession of disasters. He had achieved, deservedly, a huge success and was enjoying it vastly, loving all the lectures he was constantly invited to give – in Germany, Italy, Scandinavia, France; I a mediocrity and very glad of it, in the sense that to be dragged out of my isolation would be a horrible torment. But *really* glad of it?

Yes, I think, really: for I feel that anything else would have been false
to the inviolable, supra-personal me. But the sadness is: we now just don't
understand each other. He reads my books, I read his. I admire his; he
likes some at least of mine. But his don't *feed* me; and I'm pretty sure
mine don't feed him. It's strange, and disquieting.[27]

Disquieting, of course, because Murry could not help suspecting that
Cary had cultivated literature at the expense of 'the true man-woman
relation'. By this time, the liberation of the ego by love had all but
eclipsed its liberation by art. Shortly afterwards, he was adjuring
Henry Williamson: 'The moment her lip begins to tremble, throw
down all your weapons, don't care a tinker's curse what masterpiece
you may be spoiling, what plan upsetting' [28] – so far had the great
male purpose receded.

Williamson, though Galsworthy had drawn Murry's attention to
his writing as long ago as 1920, was a comparatively recent friend.
They had become well acquainted only since finding themselves farming within a few miles of each other. But Murry was attracted as he
had not been towards any man since Lawrence himself: and, indignant
at what he thought an unjust depreciation of his novels – for 'it is
much harder to feel a friend misprised than to have bricks thrown at
oneself' [29] – laid himself out to win them a wider public: composing
not only the long critical study which the publishers excluded from
Unprofessional Essays, but a shorter one which the Third Programme
rejected.* Privately, he encouraged Williamson to send him his manuscripts for criticism (a thing he very seldom did); while their correspondence shows how seriously he took his late-found belief in the
personal: 'I've told you before, I have always felt my function in
regard to H. W. is to be a sort of stand-by – a mooring that is after
all always there.' [30]

There were other new acquaintances also. One was his second cousin,
Mary Murry, whom he met for the first time in 1953, and whose plays
and novels he likewise appreciated and encouraged. Another was
Arthur Koestler, to whom Rees introduced him in 1955. Koestler's
writing he had long admired – it had helped to demolish his
Pacifism – and he would have liked to be of service to him too: for, he
wrote after their evening together, he seemed 'a man of genuine integrity . . . but very much at the end of his spiritual tether, badly in

* The first of these was subsequently published in *Katherine Mansfield and
other Literary Studies* (1959), the second in the *Aylesford Review* (Winter 1957-8).

need of a religion but not able to find one which does not do violence to his intellectual integrity'.[31] Unfortunately, Koestler's opening question, 'Have you got a new religion up your sleeve?' was not calculated to set Murry at his ease, nor does the 'true man-woman relation' appear to have supplied an adequate answer. It was not until a week or two later that he thought of recommending *God*.[32]

On the rare occasions when he did emerge from his isolation, however, it was usually to see his family, the high-lights of the year being the annual visit to Weg in Brussels, and her return visit to Thelnetham with little Johnnie – the apple of his eye. Recalling one of the last of these, she writes:

> Once, not so very long ago, when I went home for a few days in the winter, Dadda was standing up in the dining-room pouring out white wine (his famous 'Entre Deux Mers') for supper, to celebrate. I was there too, watching him, vaguely dreaming. Was it because he poured it out so carefully, so seriously, the way he used to do everything, that the tears came into my eyes and before I knew what I was doing I had rushed over to him almost jerking the bottle out of his hand and seized him in my arms? Whatever the reason may have been, he made nothing of the wine spilled on the table but hugged me and murmured 'You darling!'
>
> That was all. We spoke no more about it. It was just another moment that slipped easily and quietly into the continuous stream of his great love. My life with him was made up like that. Was it a wonder that I saw in him, so human, the face of God?

In the intervals between these visits, he would regale Weg every Sunday unfailingly with all the local gossip and family news – including the births, marriages and deaths of his beloved cats – very much as he had done Katherine.

Indeed, after his sixtieth year, Murry became, for the first time, quite a prolific correspondent. Col, who had married in 1950 (on the same day as he took his degree) and was now following in his mother's footsteps as a poet and story-writer, could count on him for unsparing criticism – also, like all the family, for financial advice and help. Old friends like Clare Farr and Mary Horsfall, Tomlinson and H. P. Collins, who had heard nothing for years, would be surprised by letters out of the blue (occasionally prompted by dreams) inquiring after them and theirs. Others were still more surprised, when the Adelphi School Co. was wound up, to have their twenty-year-old subscriptions refunded. It was as though, now that there was no longer any peremptory quest to overshadow them, all manner of minor interests could begin to burgeon freely at last, from rural crafts down to Test matches. ('How inconceivable it would have been to talk to Lawrence about cricket!')[33]

Nevertheless, he was not entirely content to give up writing. On the contrary, now that he had nothing to say, he felt, was the time to start saying it well; and, if only in order to avoid 'mental dissipation', to 'become, for the first time, and for a final brief period, what I have never been – simply a professional writer – in my case, a professional literary critic, who sets himself tasks of appreciation, purged of all *arrière pensée*, uncontaminated (and uninspired) by any effort to save my soul, by discovering what I do, or ought to, believe'.[34] It was in this spirit that, after considering and rejecting Gay and Pope in turn, he finally indentured himself to *Jonathan Swift*.

Why Swift? Because this was to be 'a sort of challenge to myself – to write a book on someone with whom I could not *possibly* identify myself',[35] on someone, therefore, who was 'the very antipodes of myself'.[36] And Swift was indisputably that. Here was a writer of genius who, at the age of thirty, had deliberately repudiated both 'the heart's affections' and the poetry they inspired; who had 'renounced marriage as an impediment when he determined to make his career' [37] and 'used his genius as the instrument of his ambition',[38] which was power; who, moreover, had ended his days in a state of insane revulsion against 'the act and organs of physical love'. Murry's elucidation of the brief 'romantic' phase of Swift's development was, he claimed, his one original contribution to the subject. For the rest, he was aiming at, and achieved, 'the *nec plus ultra* of objectivity'.[39]

It was no light undertaking to master, not merely a life, but a whole tract of history, with which he was quite unfamiliar: and this at a time when he was no longer capable of rapid composition. For, though his handwriting remained as firm and beautiful as when it had excited Galsworthy's admiration, five hundred words a day was now the limit of his output, working a four-day week. Begun in March 1951, the book took two and a half years; and in the end he was still dissatisfied, feeling that he had failed to realize imaginatively the life of the eighteenth century. He doubted whether it had been worth 'the really prodigious labour' [40] he had put into it: and we may doubt it too. It was rather as if Blake, after engraving *Jerusalem*, had spent the rest of his life painting *Hambledonian*.

Like *Hambledonian, Jonathan Swift* is a masterpiece in its kind. While one may regret that Murry lavished so much space on the women – all of them turning under his pen into incarnations of the Eternal Feminine – to the exclusion of such really interesting figures as Pope, Sheridan and Gay, one cannot deny that he fulfilled both his ambitions: to produce a 'standard book on Swift for a generation to come',[41] and to prove, to himself first and foremost, that he was 'at bottom a good sound literary critic'.[36] To those who are either unresponsive to Romantic poetry or unconcerned with the issues which had engrossed the better part of his life, it may well seem his finest book, as it is certainly his most artistically finished. Yet it is a book not only of a different, but of an inferior, kind to *Heaven and Earth* or *Keats and Shakespeare*. One need not endorse his own final verdict, 'anyone could have written my book on Swift, if he had taken an equal amount of trouble',[42] to admit that, alone of his works, it might have been produced by an exceptionally able don.

Hence the chorus of praise that greeted it. If Murry himself was as surprised and bewildered by this as he had been by the customary abuse, that only shows how out of touch he still was with the literary world. If he was gratified, that was the measure of his self-depreciation. 'Will the aged eagle stretch his wings sufficiently to uphold the splendid reputation of the past?' one reviewer was inspired to ask – to his intense amusement. The declining curve had brought the eagle so low that he was becoming visible even from Fleet Street.

XXVIII

LAST YEARS

———◆◆◆◆———

O N FEBRUARY 6, 1954, his daughter Mary, now a nurse in London, rang Murry up to tell him that her mother had died in hospital early that morning. Since the doctor had notified him a few days before that Betty was ill, and more ill than she knew, the news was not wholly unexpected; nor could he pretend to any emotion stronger than pity, and a profound relief that the family's long separation was drawing to an end. He and Mary senior drove down to Winchester that day, where the two Marys met for the first time – to his still greater relief, without any constraint on either side. They attended the funeral on the 8th.

Four weeks later, on March 10 – a day of brilliant sunshine, ushered in by the cooing of ring-doves in the chestnuts surrounding Lower Lodge ('which may be romantic, but is a fact')[1] – he and Mary were married at the registry office in Bury St Edmunds. Weg flew over from Brussels to be one of the witnesses; Ruth Baker was the other. Col was unable to be present, but only because his own wife, Ruth, had that morning given birth to a daughter – the final touch to 'an almost comic superabundance of happiness'.[1]

The same evening there was a party at Lower Lodge, attended by the two families from the farm, by Murry's erstwhile neighbours at Larling, the Hewetsons, and by Mr and Mrs Hewit ('Bodge'). On the 12th, he and Mary, with Weg, set off by car for Brighton – picking up Mary junior at Horsham and David at Christ's Hospital on the way – for the long-awaited family reunion. There the new grand-daughter, Jacqueline, was duly toasted with a bottle of champagne; and 'there', Murry recorded, 'were all my children, together for the first time for 14 years, and happy together'.[2] It was the fulfilment of his prophecy of February 1942.

Richard Murry was reminded of Job; and Murry himself was half-tempted to believe in a recompensing deity. At any rate, the event, in his own eyes, was the final vindication of his life-long faith in 'the holiness of the heart's affections'. Of his daughter he wrote immediately afterwards:

Nothing has been more wonderful to me than the discovery of little Mary's character. Her simpleness, her integrity, her poise, her affectionateness, her innocence – in a word, her loveliness – are to me like a wild but precious dream come true. I always did feel that the love I felt for her as a tiny girl – and the love she felt for me – could not *altogether* perish, and that some day it would emerge again. But even when I was most hopeful, I thought it would take patience and years for us to be again as we once were. To find that the seed has grown, aye and flourished, during this long separation – *ut flos in secretis nascitur hortis* – that she *is* what she would have been, if she had never been torn away from me – this is a miracle which I never could have imagined. Yet there it is. There *she* is: completely natural and entirely lovely. Let me not forget that it is a miracle.[2]

Thenceforward, Thelnetham became Mary's and David's home – David, a year or two later, entering the Merchant Navy.

Strange as it must still seem to those for whom literature is a matter of well-placed vowels, it was largely because of this that Murry was so deeply perturbed by the appearance, early in 1954, of Robert Gittings's book, *John Keats: The Living Year*, purporting to prove that Keats had 'written a perfect passionate love-poem to one woman (*Bright Star*) and polished it up to give to another'[3] – in other words, that 'Keats himself was utterly cynical about Love'.[4] The wide and uncritical welcome accorded this theory by reviewers self-evidently ignorant of Keats (one referred to a poem entitled 'The Eve of St Martin', another to the poet's acquaintance with Burton as a 'discovery') would have shocked Murry at any time – for 'loyalty to Keats is one of my few passions: *il y va de sa gloire, il y va de mon âme*'.[5] Coming just at the moment when his faith in Love was being put to the test, and vindicated, it upset him as nothing had done for years. He was 'consumed with indignation',[6] he told Clarence Thorpe, and could not rest till he had written a refutation.

He was aware, of course, that this would be 'put down to professional jealousy'[3] – for that reason he took pains to acknowledge Gittings's solid contributions to scholarship – 'but to refrain from protesting because of what people will, or may, say, seems to me ignoble'.[7] Equally he was aware of the temptation to dismiss out of hand a theory that ran counter to his prepossessions: but 'I feel convinced that if the evidence produced by Gittings were really cogent, – cogent enough to persuade me that his conclusion was probable – I would accept it. My loyalty to truth is even greater than my loyalty to Keats.' [3] In the event, his essay, 'Keats and Isabella Jones', was a deliberately restrained and objective examination of the evidence.

Yet the result was much as he had feared. The Oxford University Press refused to consider a new edition of *Studies in Keats* containing it; he could prevail on Cape to do so only by forgoing royalties on the first 1,500. It was received at best with embarrassment, by reviewers who had precipitately committed themselves to Gittings's theory; at worst with the charge of 'near-hysteria' which his name still provoked as a reflex-action. Apart from Thorpe and one or two other authorities, few attended to his argument. And the injustice rankled – as well it might, since Murry could truthfully claim to 'have studied Keats more closely and more lovingly than any of my living contemporaries outside the ranks of the exact professional scholars, such as Thorpe or Garrod or Rollins or De Selincourt'. [8]

Keats, as the new edition was simply called, was in fact a beautiful monument, not only to a lifetime's intimate study of the man and the poet, but also to a life uniquely moulded and inspired by that study. Other poets who had meant much to Murry at one time or another – Baudelaire, for example, or De la Mare – might come to stand in his mind as symbols for the emotions they had aroused: Keats never. Almost as often as he was called upon for an article or lecture on Keats, he would take the opportunity of re-reading the poems and letters from start to finish – for all that he must have had many of them by heart – and never without illuminating some fresh facet in the light of his own fresh experience. Conversely, his own experience would be illuminated by his reading:

> How much I owe to Keats is indeed past all computation. He has been the voice of Life itself, speaking to me – nay, even the voice of my own life, speaking to me. It is through him, and my slowly won understanding of him – an understanding continually deepened by love, and the love continually deepened by understanding – that I was carried on, irresistibly, to Jesus, to the same love and understanding of Him, and to that incessant grappling with the mystery of Christianity, which has become, in a sense, the main theme of my life. [9]

The essays comprised in *Keats*, composed as they were at three widely spaced moments in his life, and reflecting the preoccupations uppermost at those moments, testify to the truth of that statement.

This creative reciprocity between himself and his subject is what distinguishes Murry above all others as a critic. When, in a broadcast that November, Derek Savage happened to stress its desirability, Murry wrote to him citing Samuel Butler's aphorism: 'If you wish to preserve the spirit of a dead author, you must not skin him, stuff him, and set him up in a case. You must eat him, digest him, and let him live in you, with such life as you have, for better or worse.' Then he went on:

> The point is that this life-giving, life-changing contact between the reader and the good book is all-important. Yet criticism makes nothing of it. I mean modern criticism, for Coleridge and Hazlitt do take it into their reckoning. But contemporary criticism – of the influential sort, ranging from a Mortimer to a Leavis – completely disregards it, does not admit it as a possibility, or if it does, only to stigmatise it as a sentimental illusion to be contemptuously suppressed. The condition which it imposes as a necessary pre-condition of its own functioning is that there shall be *no* vital reciprocity between the critic and the work criticised. It has to be excluded, dismissed, as a sort of spurious magnetic 'disturbance' of the cold 'scientific' investigation. I am sure there is in this attitude a radical falsity, amounting to a real deathliness.[10]

It recalls Nietzsche's incisive comment on the philologists and the Greeks: 'They have nothing to say to each other, and that is what goes by the name of "objectivity".' It need hardly be added that it was this that made Murry – *Jonathan Swift* notwithstanding – *unzeitgemässe* still in the 1950s.

His 'line of life' might appear to have led him back from 'politics' through 'religion' to 'literature', but during his quarter of a century in the wilderness, the literary landscape had changed out of all recognition. 'I feel myself to be very old-fashioned: or rather like a sort of *revenant*,' [11] he told Eliot. The latest poetry (Dylan Thomas excepted) merely bewildered, the 'new criticism' (already senile) horrified him. He felt that 'a vast web of super-subtlety' [12] was being woven around something that was essentially as simple in its origin and direct in its appeal as love itself. He was, indeed, 'completely out of step with the age';[3] and there still came moments, naturally enough, when he regretted keenly his 'sense of estrangement from the modern way of thought, the modern idiom; of incommunicability'.[13]

However, now that he was no longer dependent upon literature for a livelihood, there were also compensations. 'I am not distracted by any desire to please. I can go my own way, unperturbed, "the world forgetting, by the world forgot" – trying to set down the truth as it appears to me, and getting real – though laborious – enjoyment out of the effort.' [13] He was reading widely, mainly fiction, ancient and modern, and – the old reviewer's habit persisting – recording his judgements day by day in his journal. It was between May 1954 and April 1955, moreover, that – encouraged, perhaps, by Cape's decision to reissue *Son of Woman* and *Shakespeare* – he slowly completed the four studies contained in *Unprofessional Essays*: of Whitman as poet-prophet of the free society, Clare as elegiast of the moribund village community, Fielding as protagonist and Eliot as antagonist of the 'true man-woman relation'.

His criterion of value was now very simple. Far distant the days when a novelist or playwright, in order to appeal to him, had to reflect a 'thought-adventure', a quest for personal or collective salvation. Not that he was tempted to rank Dostoevsky below Scott Fitzgerald or Salinger, much as he admired these two, Hardy below L. P. Hartley or that 'great virtuoso of prose', [14] Evelyn Waugh. But what counted above all, in his eyes, was the writer's attitude, implicit or explicit, to love. In a broadcast, his last, on *Generosity in Literature*, he was to point out how rightly congenial the 'love-interest' must be to any true artist, being a manifestation of the same self-forgetful imagination as art itself. He had advanced a similar thesis in *Rhythm*.

It was for this reason that Fielding was dear to his heart; for this reason, equally, that Eliot was remote. For Eliot he always regarded as a poet who had sought refuge from 'the heart's affections' in a citadel of intellectual mysticism, purchasing literary eminence at the expense of self-abeyance – as a very minor Swift, in fact, and therefore his own 'antipodes', now as in the 1920s. It was while he was at work on 'The Plays of T. S. Eliot' that he observed in a letter to Hogan: 'I put myself as representing something in between T. S. Eliot and D. H. Lawrence. They are antipodal to one another; my something – a veritable *nescio quid* – is friendly antipodal to each of them; much in the way of a saturated solution that either of them can precipitate into the certainty "Thou art not that!" ' [15] As Rees has written, it is a poor tribute to the intellectual vitality of our time that nobody has yet found the forty-years' debate between these two writers worth an extended study.

At the same time, the word 'friendly' should be stressed. No more now than in the 1920s did their intellectual or spiritual opposition interrupt the personal *rapport*. If anything, that was closer than it had been for a long while. Following a copious correspondence concerning Eliot's play, *The Cocktail Party*, Murry was writing in May 1954:

> I *should* like to see you one day, and have a long talk with you. I have an obscure, but persistent and definite feeling, that we have something to say to each other, though I have no idea what it is. I have a hunch – nothing more – that this feeling of mine is connected with my conviction that my strange and weary pilgrimage (or whatever it should be called) is over.[16]

Actually, it was more than a year before that wish was granted; but when they did meet again, it was to find his apprehension that they too might 'shake hands as 'twere across a vast' quite groundless. Although Eliot struck Murry as 'very frail', and he left on Eliot the impression of a man somewhat older than himself, talking of Gide and Valéry, Lawrence and Simone Weil, they lost count of time: 'It was as it used to be between us 35 years ago.' [17] And when, a few weeks afterwards, Murry learned of Eliot's forthcoming marriage, his gratification was boundless.

This meeting – their last – took place in November 1956. In the meanwhile, he had rallied all his strength for what, he must have foreknown, would be his final treatment of the main theme of his life – the book, *Love, Freedom and Society*.

The initial impetus to this was a request – itself unexpected and heartening – to review F. R. Leavis's *D. H. Lawrence* for *The Literary Supplement*. Murry promptly seized the occasion, as he would have done had the subject been Keats, to re-read Lawrence's works from beginning to end: with the natural result that a bare 2,000 words could not accommodate all he wished to say of his other antipodes – and the much longer essay came into being which was the germ and gem of the book. His sentiments at the time of writing it (October 1955) deserve to be recorded:

> I go on reading Lawrence. In spite of myself, it gets me down. I am torn between a heart-rending sense of the pity of it, and a kind of exaltation at the splendour of it. Sometimes I am uplifted into a realm where I understand that it all had to be, and the pity and the beauty and the terror become one; then I come down to earth and think only that it might have

been humanly so different if I had only been able to understand, and to 'go along with him' as he pleaded. And then again I am struck dumb with the strangeness of those who treat his writings as those of 'a literary man' – a 'genius' of course – who has to be placed and judged, as someone who 'wrote well' or didn't 'write well', or sometimes one and sometimes the other. That attitude is just impossible for me. His stature, his nature, his achievement, are altogether different – different in kind. He is a symbolic and prophetic man. And then it seems a strange mystery that I knew him – knew him and didn't know him. In my bones I am sure I am right: he is the Jesus of our times – and God knows they are apocalyptic enough. 'And I, if I be lifted up, shall draw all men unto me.' He was lifted up, he lifted himself up. And one day, perhaps, he will draw all men unto him; and a new consciousness will be born of that act of the imagination which he compels from us.

And then, after thinking such thoughts, moving in that realm, I say to myself: Here I am, 66, writing laboriously at my desk in the October sunshine, looking forward to a game of croquet in the afternoon, modestly glad to be alive, conscious of a quiet happiness, accepting a little incredulously the fact that I am four times a grandfather, smoking a lot of cigarettes, completely unable to remember as a living fact the hydrogen bomb – What have I to do with Lawrence? What has Lawrence to do with me?

And yet it is true, I should not be what I am, or where I am, without him. Just as Katherine is, he is part of me. My life would have been utterly different without those two. I owe it to them – and to Keats – that I have this life with Mary. Perhaps he would disown me; perhaps, from his 'different Hades' he is contemptuous of me and my ordinariness now. If so, it can't be helped. But I don't really believe it. I think he is glad that a fragment of him lives on in me.

The simple mystery of life – the infinite mystery of it. Lawrence enlarged our awareness of it: brought together our bodies and our souls. We shall never be the same as we were before him. We struggle with him and, though he does not prevail, his virtue passes into us. We have been quickened.[18]

Possibly there are still people who think of Murry as Lawrence's traducer. If so, let them read the essay. Although he was actually so carried away by his sympathy that it took a 'meaningful dream' to prevent him from leaning over backwards ('I must not go too far in endorsing L's rejection of democracy: I must make clear that his bias towards authoritarianism, violence, human sacrifice even, was "compensation" for frailty'),[19] it turned out to be not merely the best he had written on the subject, as he knew, but the best that anybody has written. Here all the defects of *Son of Woman* – the over-emphasis on one side of Lawrence's message, the under-estimate of his later works, the stark oppositions – are made good. *Son of Woman* is not denied, but transcended, as he said it should be – and it was a grievous disappointment to him that Frieda was never able to read this. How much her appreciation would have meant to him is revealed, not only by their correspondence, but also by the tribute he wrote for *The Times* on her death, in August 1956.

It was not until a month after finishing 'D. H. Lawrence' that he thought of re-casting *The Challenge of Schweitzer* as a companion-piece: and that was not such a happy conception, since, as he once remarked, one of his idiosyncrasies as a critic was that he loved to admire, welcoming nothing so much as the chance to add another to his pantheon of heroes – and Schweitzer was antipathetic as well as antipodal. Indeed, it is questionable whether Murry understood either him or his problem – the problem of justifying love to the intellect in a world that bears no witness to the reality of a loving God. His own philosophy, as M. C. D'Arcy once said, ends where metaphysics begins.

He was certainly mistaken (as George Seaver had pointed out in his reply to *The Challenge of Schweitzer*, *Albert Schweitzer: A Vindication*) in supposing that Schweitzer denied a 'meaning of history', as he himself understood that. The 'meaning' that Schweitzer denies is a meaning guaranteed by God, in the Christian or Hegelian sense. Far from disputing that men may draw inspiration from history, or confer a meaning on it by their own exertions, he himself does both – with the result that Murry wasted pages convicting him of self-contradiction. This was one of the unfortunate results of his use of 'God' as a synonym for 'meaning'.

He was probably mistaken again in thinking the supreme value of love so self-evident as to stand in no need of intellectual justification. Were that really the case, it would not be 'now threatened as never before':[20] for the challenge comes, not from men who do not, or cannot, love, but from men who believe they ought not to – or rather, from those biological pragmatists who affirm the supreme value, not of love, but of integration, and invoke both human and pre-human history in its support.

There had been a time when Murry could have answered them, and Schweitzer too. He could have said that 'love is an acquired metabiological faculty making for integration in the individual and further development in the race' [21] – and then he likewise could have invoked both human and pre-human history. As it was, though these words occur in his journal at this time, he failed to draw the moral. He failed to reaffirm his earlier conclusion, 'It is better to be whole than to be good',[22] and was forced in consequence to posit an impassable gulf between man and the rest of creation. This was one of the unfortunate results of his use of 'love' as a synonym for 'integration'.

At first sight, these misunderstandings are odd, since, as Seaver maintained and Murry admitted, the standpoint of *Civilization and Ethics* is not unlike that of *God*; nor is Schweitzer's effort to escape from esotericism, to express his religion in words and ways intelligible to the ordinary man, at all remote from Murry's. Their loyalty is one and the same. But Murry's final conception of history as the progressive embodiment of Christ's vision of human brotherhood, culminating in the free society, satisfied his imagination so completely that he was impatient, not only of Schweitzer's elusive rationalization, but equally of the Catholic contention that 'respect for the dignity of the person is unintelligible, or irrational, unless it is based on a belief in the Christian God'.[23] It seemed to him far more irrational for the intellect to call in question the precondition of its own free expression: and here, notwithstanding his impatience, he may well have stood on firm ground.

Originally, *Love, Freedom and Society* concluded with 'A Political Meditation'. Only when it was in the publisher's hands did he decide that 'after all politics, in the practical sense, is not really my pidgin, and anything detailed is bound to date horribly' [24] – and substitute the present epilogue. It was a wise decision. Over the ensuing months, his views on the world situation did, in fact, oscillate violently – from hope that Krushchev's denunciation of Stalin might spell the liberalization of Russia to despondency over the repression of Hungary and the British failure to recapture Suez (the 'one just war') – settling finally into weary disgust: ' "Tired with all these for restful death I cry." ' [25]

Into 'Beyond the Prophets', on the other hand, he put 'all he had' [26] – the fruits of a lifetime's meditation on tragedy, and the Crucifixion as the archetype of tragedy. This was a theme on which he could, and did, speak with authority: the experiences he was treating of here being, as he said, more real to him than any others, 'in that they have a continuous effect upon my life: all that is most intimate, most personal, in my personality is bound up with and nourished by them; and this is supremely so in the case of the experience of Jesus into which they all coalesce'.[27] It is worth noting that just beforehand he had consulted Karl Jaspers's *Tragedy is not Enough* – Jaspers being, of all the speakers he had met at Geneva, the most congenial to his own way of thinking. This was as might have been expected. As he observed in connexion with Lawrence, we do not need to look to the Continent for our existentialists – or did not as long as Murry was alive.

He had reverted to the standpoint of Dostoevsky, simultaneously rejecting the last of his ontological affirmations – 'The conditions of this world really forbid giving ontological status to the world of spirit'[28] – and reaffirming the reality from which they had been derived, that 'impassioned contemplation of the Cross which has been the mystical centre of the Christian religion and the source from which love has been renewed'.[29] This being the reality by which both empirical Christianity and Christian civilization had been inspired, it was to this, he submitted, that men must turn for the renewal of their inspiration, in face of that civilization's cataclysmic collapse:

> I believe that those who are overwhelmed by their sense of the pathos of the Christian civilisation: its failure, its disruption, its self-betrayal, of which they share the guilt, may find relief, and purification, and peace by learning to regard the history of Jesus as the archetypal tragedy and by entering into the spiritual experience that comes from it. This re-awakening of the tragic consciousness would involve no escape from reality, no violation of integrity. On the contrary, it would proceed from a more resolute acceptance of the truth concerning the human condition. It would not weaken our determination to know what we fight for and love what we know. On the contrary, it would greatly strengthen it. It would give a focus to our shattered imagination, and an object to our emotional and ethical loyalty.[30]

This being the contemplation to which Murry himself had returned unfailingly, and which alone had enabled him to receive, digest and assimilate an experience of the twentieth century as extreme, and yet as representative, as any Englishman's of his generation, he had the best possible warrant for his belief. Whether his religion was what he called it, a Christianity purged by the historical consciousness and therefore appropriate to a new historical epoch, or, as some would contend, a Christianity purged of Christianity itself, is immaterial beside the fact that it was a religion grounded and tested in such experience. Into this lucid, profound and beautiful essay he distilled the quintessence of all his thinking – religious, literary and political. It was a fitting last word.

Love, Freedom and Society was published at the beginning of March 1957. During the foregoing months, Murry had been cheered by the reception of *Unprofessional Essays* and by an invitation to contribute to *The London Magazine*. It had begun to look as if his 'faint star' [31] might be rising again. But it was too late for him to take much advantage of it. He could work only very slowly; his strength was manifestly ebbing. Although, in November, a specialist had pronounced his heart still sound, his inability to walk far enough for exercise made the winter months irksome; and with the arrival of the first mild days he lost no time in getting out into the garden, digging, planting and sawing. It was these exertions that brought on his first heart-attack, on the night of February 23.

He did not take it very seriously. Despite a recurrence three nights later, forcing him to take to his bed again, he received the diagnosis, angina pectoris, cheerfully, continuing to read and dictate letters as usual. By March 5 he was declared out of danger and allowed to get up. The same night, however, a more violent and prolonged attack caused Mary (overriding his protests against disturbing anyone at such an hour) to summon the doctor. Morphia had to be administered, and he was conveyed by ambulance to the hospital in Bury St Edmunds.

Mary and Ruth took rooms in a hotel near by, at the same time notifying the family, except for David, who was at sea. Young Mary came down from London; Col drove through the night from Brighton; Weg flew over from Brussels. Though the situation was critical, they were told, every day that he lived made recovery more likely: and after two days he was already so far recovered that Col was able to go back to work. By the 12th he was almost out of pain.

Yet, when Mary went to see him that afternoon, it was clear to her at once that he had 'something very important to say':

> He was in complete command of the situation, perfectly clear in mind and voice. From what he said I realised at once that he was sure the time had come for him to die – that indeed he was ready to go. He seemed to be taking complete responsibility for his own death. At first I felt I could not bear it, and tried to persuade him to go on living. Then he said: 'I should not have asked Katherine to go on, I should not have asked Lawrence to go on,' and added; 'I should be so happy to die to-night.' Then, as I knelt beside the bed, he looked at me and said: 'You have

never let me down.' And, suddenly, I knew that if I tried to keep him, even in my heart, I *should* be letting him down. For a moment I struggled within myself and, as soon as I could 'let him go', a strange peace came to both of us.[32]

He was still in this state of mind when, a few minutes later, his two daughters joined him. 'I can't go back there,' he said. Weg thought he was referring to another room in the hospital, which he had occupied before and disliked. 'Dadda', she assured him, 'there's no *question* of your going back.' 'No', he murmured, 'I don't suppose there is, really' – and it was only then that she knew what he meant. He died soon after midnight.

The funeral, attended by his family and some two dozen friends and neighbours, took place on March 16. He was buried in Thelnetham churchyard, where a stone, designed by his brother, bears the inscription:

In Loving Memory of
JOHN MIDDLETON MURRY
AUTHOR AND FARMER
1889–1957
'Ripeness is All'

The Works of John Middleton Murry

━━━━━━◅◦◌◦▻━━━━━━

Still Life. Constable, 1916. [SL.]

Dostoevsky: A Critical Study. Secker, 1916. [FD.]

Poems: 1917–1918. Heron Press, 1918.

The Critic in Judgement. Hogarth Press, 1919.

The Evolution of an Intellectual. Cobden-Sanderson, 1920: 2nd ed. Cape, 1927. [EI.]

Cinnamon and Angelica. Cobden-Sanderson, 1920: 2nd ed. Dakers, 1941.

Aspects of Literature. Collins, 1920: 2nd ed. Cape, 1934. [AL.]

Poems: 1916–1920. Cobden-Sanderson, 1921.

The Problem of Style. Oxford University Press, 1922. [PS.]

The Things We are. Constable, 1922. [TWA.]

Countries of the Mind (1st Series). Oxford University Press, 1922: 2nd ed. 1931. [CM1.]

Pencillings. Collins, 1922.

The Voyage. Constable, 1924.

Discoveries. Collins, 1924: 2nd ed. Cape, 1930. [D.]

To the Unknown God. Cape, 1925. [TG.]

Keats and Shakespeare. Oxford University Press, 1925. [KS.]

The Life of Jesus. Cape, 1926. [LJ.]

Things to Come. Cape, 1928: 2nd ed. 1938. [TC.]

God. Cape, 1929. [G.]

D. H. Lawrence: two essays. Gordon-Fraser, 1930 (Minority Pamphlets, No. 4).

Studies in Keats. Oxford University Press, 1931: 2nd ed. *Studies in Keats, New and Old*, 1939: 3rd ed. *The Mystery of Keats*, Nevill, 1949: 4th ed. *Keats*, Cape, 1955.

Countries of the Mind (2nd Series). Oxford University Press, 1931. Issued in one volume with 1st Series, 1937. [CM2.]

Son of Woman. Cape, 1931: 2nd ed. 1954. [SW.]

The Necessity of Communism. Cape, 1932. [NC.]

The Fallacy of Economics (Pamphlet). Fabers, 1932 (Criterion Miscellany, No. 37).

Reminiscences of D. H. Lawrence. Cape, 1933. [RDHL.]

The Wanderer. Issued by private subscription, 1933–4. [W.]

William Blake. Cape, 1933. [B.]

Between Two Worlds. Cape, 1935. [BTW.]

Shakespeare. Cape, 1936: 2nd ed. 1955. [S.]

The Necessity of Pacifism. Cape, 1937. [NP.]

God or the Nation? (Pamphlet). Peace Pledge Union, 1937.

Heaven – and Earth. Cape, 1938. [HE.]

The Pledge of Peace. H. Joseph, 1938. [PP.]

Peace at Christmas (Pamphlet). City of Birmingham School of Printing, 1938.

The Price of Leadership. S.C.M. Press, 1939. [PL.]

The Defence of Democracy. Cape, 1939. [DD.]

Europe in Travail. Sheldon Press, 1940. [ET.]

Democracy and War (Pamphlet). Nisbet, 1940.

The Brotherhood of Peace (Pamphlet). Peace Pledge Union, 1940 (Bond of Peace, No. 4).

The Betrayal of Christ by the Churches. Dakers, 1940. [BC.]

Christocracy. Dakers, 1942. [C.]

The Dilemma of Christianity (Pamphlet). J. Clarke, 1942 (New Foundations, No. 3).

The Economics of Peace (Pamphlet). Peace News, 1943.

Adam and Eve. Dakers, 1944. [AE.]

The Third Challenge. National Peace Council, 1946 (Peace Aims Pamphlets, No. 33).

Trust or Perish (Pamphlet). Peace Pledge Union, 1946.

The Free Society. Dakers, 1948. [FS.]

Looking Before and After. Sheppard Press, 1948. [LBA.]

The Challenge of Schweitzer. Jason Press, 1948.

Katherine Mansfield and Other Literary Portraits. Nevill, 1949. [KMP.]

John Clare and Other Studies. Nevill, 1950.

The Conquest of Death. Nevill, 1951. [CD.]

Community Farm. Nevill, 1952. [CF.]

Jonathan Swift. Cape, 1954.

Swift (Pamphlet). Longmans, Green, 1955 (Writers and their Work, No. 61).

Unprofessional Essays. Cape, 1956.

Love, Freedom and Society. Cape, 1957. [LFS.]

Katherine Mansfield and Other Literary Studies. Constable, 1959. [KMS.]

Not as the Scribes. S.C.M. Press, 1959.

Books on John Middleton Murry

John Middleton Murry: A Study in Excellent Normality, by Rayner Heppenstall. Cape, 1934. (An intelligent examination and appreciation of Murry's thought up to this date.)

Albert Schweitzer: A Vindication – Being a reply to 'The Challenge of Schweitzer' by John Middleton Murry, by George Seaver. James Clarke, 1950.

John Middleton Murry, by Philip Mairet. Longmans, Green, 1958 (Writers and their Work, No. 102). (A fine appreciation of Murry's work as a literary critic.)

To Keep Faith, by Mary Middleton Murry. Constable, 1959. (A memoir, covering the last twenty years of Murry's life.)

References

The initial letters are printed in brackets after the titles to which they refer in the foregoing list of Murry's works. J. stands for Murry's journal. Except where otherwise stated, the page numbers given are those of the latest English editions.

CHAPTER

1. W. 21.
2. *Coming to London.* Ed. J. Lehmann. Phoenix House. 1957.
3. Conversation with G. Sainsbury.
4. BTW. 11.
5. J. 28.4.46.
6. BTW. 34.
7. To Mrs Parkhouse: 1916.
8. BTW. 32.
9. J. 6.8.50.
10. MS.: 'A London Suburb in the '90s.' 1950.
11. J. 22.2.55.
12. *Adelphi*, Nov. 1930.
13. To M. Plowman: 26.5.31.
14. BTW. 44.
15. To H. Williamson: 1.2.52.
16. To Mother: 10.2.01.
17. BTW. 35.
18. BTW. 81.
19. BTW. 47.
20. BTW. 62.
21. BTW. 65.

CHAPTER II

1. *Coming to London.*
2. To Mrs Parkhouse: 24.10.08.
3. BTW. 87.
4. BTW. 92.
5. BTW. 106.
6. To P. Landon: Jan. 1911.
7. To P. Landon: 31.12.10.
8. To P. Landon: 14.12.10.
9. BTW. 154.
10. SL. 4.
11. F. Carco: *Bohème d'Artiste.* Albin Michel. 1940. 246.
12. J. 28.9.52.
13. To P. Landon: 30.3.11.
14. To L. Duke: April 1911.
15. To Mrs Parkhouse: 29.1.11.
16. To P. Landon: 5.4.11.
17. To P. Landon: April 1911.
18. BTW. 170.
19. J. 19.4.53.
20. SL. 9.
21. To R. Murry: 1911.
22. SL. 3.

CHAPTER III

1. E. H. W. Meyerstein: *Of My Early Life*. Spearman. 1957. 70.
2. *Blue Review*, May 1913.
3. To L. Duke: Summer 1911.
4. *Coming to London*.
5. BTW. 174.
6. *Rhythm*, Winter 1911.
7. BTW. 184.
8. J. 17.9.53.
9. SL. 9.
10. J. 19.4.53.
11. J. 1.11.53.
12. BTW. 78.
13. J. 26.4.53.
14. BTW. 209.
15. BTW. 219.
16. E. Marsh: *A Number of People*. Heinemann. 1939. 226.
17. J. 4.9.33.
18. BTW. 224.
19. F. Carco: *Bohème d'Artiste*. 250–1.
20. BTW. 278.
21. BTW. 264.
22. Notes, Nov. 1913.
23. BTW. 307.
24. *Blue Review*, July 1913.

CHAPTER IV

1. D. H. Lawrence to J. M. M.: Nov. 1913.
2. BTW. 319.
3. BTW. 267.
4. KMP.
5. RDHL. 56.
6. *The Journal of Katherine Mansfield*. Constable. 1954: 16.11.14.
7. *Katherine Mansfield's Journal*: 1.1.15.
8. J. 10.11.14.
9. Katherine Mansfield to S. Koteliansky: 20.1.15 (British Museum MS.).
10. *Katherine Mansfield's Journal*: 23.1.15.
11. D. H. Lawrence to O. Morrell: Feb. 1915. *London Magazine*, Feb. 1956.
12. BTW. 337.
13. *Katherine Mansfield's Letters to John Middleton Murry*. Constable. 1951: 12.
14. J. 26.4.53.
15. J. 25.1.55.
16. D. Brett: *Lawrence and Brett*. Secker. 1933: 17–18.
17. Katherine Mansfield to J. M. M.: 10.2.20.
18. *Katherine Mansfield's Journal*: 29.10.15.
19. BTW. 320.
20. Katherine Mansfield to J. M. M.: 15.12.15.
21. To Katherine Mansfield: 22.12.15.
22. BTW. 390.
23. BTW. 393.
24. BTW. 368–9.
25. FD. 44.
26. FD. 219.
27. FD. 241.
28. FD. 79.
29. FD. 69–70.
30. FD. 253–4.

CHAPTER V

1. J. 11.7.34.
2. D. H. Lawrence to J. M. M.: ? Feb. 1916.
3. D. H. Lawrence to J. M. M.: 18.3.16.
4. RDHL. 77.
5. D. H. Lawrence to S. Koteliansky: 9.4.16 (British Museum MS.).
6. Katherine Mansfield to S. Koteliansky: 11.5.16 (British Museum MS.).
7. RDHL. 79.
8. D. H. Lawrence to J. M. M.: 20.5.29.
9. D. H. Lawrence to O. Morell: 24.5.16.
10. BTW. 421.
11. J. 20.11.55.
12. BTW. 428.
13. BTW. 430.
14. R. Merlin: *Le Drame Secret de Katherine Mansfield*. Editions du Seuil. 1950. 147.
15. G. 17.
16. TC. xvi.
17. G. 21.
18. BTW. 437–8 (quoted).
19. BTW. 443.
20. BTW. 446.
21. BTW. 447–8.
22. BTW. 450.
23. BTW. 460.
24. G. 19.
25. *Katherine Mansfield's Letters to J. M. M.:* 246.
26. *Poems: 1916–20.* 26.
27. EI. 74.
28. G. 23.
29. To Katherine Mansfield: 21.2.18.
30. BTW. 492.
31. To Katherine Mansfield: 1.3.18.
32. To Katherine Mansfield: 30.3.18.
33. EI. 15.
34. BTW. 491.
35. EI. 180–1.
36. *Adelphi*, Oct. 1937.

CHAPTER VI

1. *Katherine Mansfield's Letters to J. M. M.:* 309.
2. F. Swinnerton: *The Georgian Literary Scene*. Hutchinson. 1935. 204.
3. D. H. Lawrence to S. Koteliansky: 7.11.16 (British Museum MS.).
4. To Katherine Mansfield: 17.10.19.
5. RDHL. 219.
6. J. 28.5.37.
7. G. B. Shaw to J. M. M.: 25.8.19. (By courtesy of the Society of Authors.)
8. *Adelphi*, Jan. 1937.
9. To Katherine Mansfield: 12.2.20.
10. *Nation*, March 10, 1920.
11. To Katherine Mansfield: 14.11.19.
12. To Katherine Mansfield: 25.11.19.
13. AL. 154–5.
14. To Katherine Mansfield: 7.5.15.
15. To Katherine Mansfield: 29.10.19.
16. *Athenaeum*, Dec. 12, 1919.
17. AL. 79.
18. *Nation*, Feb. 26, 1921.
19. AL. 185.

20. *Athenaeum*, Nov. 19, 1920.
21. W. 26.
22. T. Hardy to J. M. M.: 28.10.19.
23. T. Hardy to J. M. M.: 8.11.19.
24. AL. 141.
25. CM1. 90.
26. AL. 61.
27. J. 17.2.34.
28. To Katherine Mansfield: 9.11.19.
29. J. 29.5.54.
30. To Katherine Mansfield: 30.3.20.
31. KMP. 11.
32. *Katherine Mansfield's Journal:* 15.12.19.
33. MS. 1947.
34. AE. 37.
35. To Katherine Mansfield: 8.12.19.
36. To Katherine Mansfield: 26.1.20.
37. *Katherine Mansfield's Journal:* 29.1.20.
38. To Katherine Mansfield: 7.2.20.
39. *Katherine Mansfield's Letters to J. M. M.:* 467.
40. To Katherine Mansfield: 2.2.20.
41. Katherine Mansfield to J. M. M.: 5.2.20.
42. To Katherine Mansfield: 5.2.20.
43. J. 24.5.54.
44. J. 4.1.51.
45. J. 23.5.54.
46. Katherine Mansfield to J. M. M.: June 1920.
47. To Katherine Mansfield: 10.2.20.

CHAPTER VII

1. H. G. Wells to J. M. M.: 11.2.21.
2. W. de la Mare to J. M. M.: 31.1.21.
3. D. H. Lawrence to S. Koteliansky: 2.3.21 (British Museum MS.).
4. J. 11.7.32.
5. *Katherine Mansfield's Letters to J. M. M.:* 625.
6. To Katherine Mansfield: 20.5.21.
7. To Katherine Mansfield: 19.5.21.
8. To Katherine Mansfield: 26.3.18.
9. To Katherine Mansfield: 17.5.21.
10. To Katherine Mansfield: 26.5.21.
11. *Katherine Mansfield's Letters to J. M. M.:* 643.
12. To Katherine Mansfield: 6.4.20.
13. PS. 26.
14. PS. 27.
15. PS. 95.
16. D. 1st edn. 140.
17. To Katherine Mansfield: 23.11.19.
18. To Katherine Mansfield: 3.11.19.
19. CM1. 14.
20. CM1. 150.
21. *Katherine Mansfield's Letters to J. M. M.:* 641.
22. *Katherine Mansfield's Letters to J. M. M.:* 644.
23. To Katherine Mansfield: 8.2.22.
24. J. 10.8.48.
25. J. 2.9.37.
26. MS. 1936.
27. MS. 1947.
28. F. Carco: *Bohème d'Artiste.* 254.
29. Katherine Mansfield to S. Koteliansky: 23.8.22 (British Museum MS.).
30. TWA. 268.
31. *Adelphi*, June 1933.
32. D. 137.
33. TC. 71.

34. *Aryan Path*, Jan. 1938.
35. J. 8.5.35.
36. G. 26.
37. Katherine Mansfield to J. M. M.: 26.12.22.
38. Katherine Mansfield to J. M. M.: 9.12.22.
39. To Katherine Mansfield: ?11.12.22.
40. To Katherine Mansfield: 31.12.22.

41. Katherine Mansfield to J. M. M.: 1.12.22.
42. To W. Wordsworth: 1.10.35.
43. *Katherine Mansfield's Letters to J. M. M.:* 700.
44. To V. Bartrick-Baker: 26.2.23.
45. *Adelphi*, Oct.–Dec. 1946.
46. G. 31.
47. *Katherine Mansfield's Letters to J. M. M.:* 701.

CHAPTER VIII

1. MS. 1947.
2. J. 11.8.53.
3. TG. 42–4.
4. TC. iii.
5. AE. 153.
6. G. 40.
7. G. 39.
8. RDHL. 104.
9. D. H. Lawrence to J. M. M.: 2.2.23.
10. To V. Bartrick-Baker: 10.3.23.
11. AE. 152.
12. RDHL. 105–6.
13. *Nation & Athenaeum*, March 31, 1923.
14. To H. P. Collins: 29.3.22.

15. BTW. 444.
16. MS. 1936.
17. J. 25.1.55.
18. TG. 22.
19. *Adelphi*, June 1933.
20. G. B. Shaw to J. M. M.: 27.4.23. (By courtesy of the Society of Authors.)
21. J. Galsworthy to J. M. M.: 6.5.23.
22. To H. P. Collins: 1.5.23.
23. TG. 39–40.
24. TG. 156–7.
25. W. 84.
26. TG. 35.

CHAPTER IX

1. J. 3.8.56.
2. To J. P. Hogan: 31.1.29.
3. J. H. Watson, *London Magazine*, May 1959.
4. G. 43.
5. D. H. Lawrence to S. Kotelian-sky: 22.6.23 (British Museum MS.).
6. A. Bennett to J. M. M.: 1923.
7. H. G. Wells to J. M. M.: 1923.
8. J. 30.1.55.

9. *Nation*, June 4, 1921.
10. W. 84.
11. J. 6.8.32.
12. MS. 1947.
13. *Katherine Mansfield's Journal:* 13.1.22.
14. MS. 1936.
15. To V. Bartrick-Baker: 11.3.23.
16. To V. Bartrick-Baker: 23.3.23.
17. To V. Bartrick-Baker: 4.4.23.
18. J. 12.4.53.

19. J. 13.3.55.
20. To T. S. Eliot: 1923.
21. J. 5.9.53.
22. J. 18.12.55.
23. RDHL. 110.
24. RDHL. 111.
25. To Katherine Mansfield:
    19.12.15.
26. J. 21.7.32.

27. J. 12.7.53.
28. J. 4.8.32.
29. RDHL. 175.
30. G. Deghy & K. Waterhouse:
    Café Royal. Hutchinson. 1955.
    163.
31. RDHL. 177.
32. TG. 222.

CHAPTER X

1. MS. 1947.
2. MS. 1936.
3. T. Hardy to J. M. M.: 9.4.24.
4. H. Moore: *Life and Works of
   D. H. Lawrence.* Allen &
   Unwin. 1951. 186.
5. S. 278.
6. *Adelphi,* Jan. 1925.
7. *Adelphi,* Nov. 1924.
8. TC. 254.
9. *Aryan Path,* May 1930.

10. G. 60.
11. TC. 171.
12. To C. du Bos: 12.7.25.
13. AL. 79.
14. *Criterion,* May 1927.
15. To T. S. Eliot: 18.3.27.
16. *Adelphi,* Oct. 1924.
17. TC. 119.
18. TC. 5.
19. To T. S. Eliot: 18.3.27 (quoted).

CHAPTER XI

1. *Now and Then* (Cape), Christmas, 1924.
2. S. Koteliansky to J. M. M.:
   7.10.24.
3. S. Koteliansky to J. M. M.:
   21.10.24.
4. J. S. Collis: *Farewell to Argument.*
   Cassell. 1935. 200.
5. To Katherine Mansfield: 26.3.20.
6. S. Koteliansky to J. M. M.:
   7.10.24. (quoted).
7. J. 25.7.32.

8. J. 6.6.35.
9. J. 21.5.46.
10. J. 2.6.35.
11. To J. W. N. Sullivan: 2.8.32.
12. *Katherine Mansfield's Journal:*
    1.4.14.
13. MS. 1947.
14. RDHL. 199.
15. To F. Lawrence: 24.9.53.
16. D. H. Lawrence to S. Kotelian-
    sky: 28.6.26 (British Museum
    MS.).

CHAPTER XII

1. MS. 1936.
2. MS. 1947.
3. LJ. 63.

4. To T. S. Eliot: 28.4.28.
5. W. 42.
6. To T. S. Eliot: 28.1.27.

7. *Adelphi*, April 1927.
8. W. 124.
9. *Adelphi*, May 1931.
10. G. 66.
11. To C. du Bos: 31.7.29.
12. To T. S. Eliot: 22.9.27.
13. J. 15.8.50.
14. G. 74.
15. G. 313.
16. G. 315.

17. *Adelphi*, Feb. 1931.
18. G. 214.
19. G. 246.
20. G. 247.
21. G. 253.
22. G. 312.
23. *Adelphi*, Jan. 1925.
24. *Criterion*, Dec. 1927.
25. *Criterion*, July 1930.
26. W. 92.

CHAPTER XIII

1. HE. 185.
2. To G. B. Shaw: 23.9.29.
3. G. B. Shaw to J. M. M.: 26.9.29. (By courtesy of the Society of Authors.)
4. J. 31.5.32.
5. G. K. Chesterton to J. M. M.: 30.6.30.
6. J. 3.1.30 (quoted).
7. To R. Rees: ? May 1929.
8. To F. A. Lea: 25.9.35.
9. RDHL. 122.
10. D. H. Lawrence to J. M. M.: 20.5.29.
11. To Clare Farr (Mrs C. Walter): 25.12.30.
12. To M. Plowman: 27.1.31.
13. BTW. 124.
14. J. 15.8.50.
15. To T. S. Eliot: 6.1.45.
16. MS. 1936.
17. J. 21.10.56.

18. KS. 98.
19. G. 138.
20. SW. 185.
21. G. 260.
22. To M. Plowman: 6.3.30.
23. J. 12.7.53.
24. G. 264.
25. W. 19.
26. HE. 327.
27. SW. 88.
28. H. Moore: *Life and Works of D. H. Lawrence*. 186.
29. W. 45.
30. *Nation & Athenaeum*, Sept. 30, 1922.
31. SW. 171.
32. SW. 183–4.
33. SW. 340–1.
34. SW. 389.
35. To V. M. Sheppard (Mrs C. Johnson): 20.8.31.

CHAPTER XIV

1. To M. Plowman: 6.3.30.
2. J. 22.6.31.
3. MS. 1936.
4. To M. Plowman: Nov. 1930.
5. To M. Plowman: Sept. 1930.

6. M. Plowman to J. M. M.: 25.10.29. (*Bridge into the Future*, Dakers, 1944.)
7. M. Plowman to J. M. M.: 9.11.29.

8. SW. 352.
9. J. 2.12.30.
10. J. 21.12.30.
11. J. 6.1.31.
12. M. Plowman to M. Marr: 5.6.31.
13. J. 7.1.31.
14. J. 4.2.31.
15. J. 3.2.31.
16. J. 13.2.31.

17. M. Plowman to O. MacKenzie: 5.3.31.
18. J. 6.3.31.
19. J. 24.2.31.
20. M. Plowman to P.A.: 31.12.29.
21. SW. 205.
22. J. 19.1.31.
23. J. 26.1.31.
24. J. 1.4.31.

CHAPTER XV

1. W. 87.
2. J. 2.4.36.
3. M. Plowman to G. West: 7.2.38.
4. J. 25.4.31.
5. To M. Plowman: 19.5.31.
6. To H. Williamson: 30.12.55.
7. To M. Plowman: 30.5.31.
8. M. Plowman to H. I'A. Fausset: 2.6.31.
9. To M. Plowman: 14.5.31.
10. To R. Rees: 4.6.31.
11. To R. Rees: 1931.
12. J. 21.6.34.
13. J. 8.8.31.
14. J. 3.9.31.
15. MS. 1947.

16. J. 16.9.31.
17. J. 12.8.31.
18. J. 13.9.31.
19. J. 7.6.31.
20. W. 95.
21. To M. Plowman: 27.1.31.
22. *Adelphi*, Aug. 1931.
23. *Adelphi*, June–Aug. 1929.
24. TC. xxvii.
25. W. 94.
26. NC. 54.
27. NC. 41.
28. NC. 93.
29. NC. 117.
30. J. 9.11.31.

CHAPTER XVI

1. W. 77.
2. To R. Rees: Nov. 1931.
3. W. 70.
4. W. 95.
5. J. 10.11.31.
6. To M. Plowman: 19.11.31.
7. To R. Rees: 29.1.32.
8. To R. Rees: 13.11.31.
9. W. 76.
10. To M. Plowman: 27.11.31.
11. To C. Farr (Mrs C. Walter): 3.5.32.

12. To R. Rees: 29.2.32.
13. *Adelphi*, Nov. 1932.
14. To A. W. Votier: 7.1.32.
15. To R. Rees: Jan. 1932.
16. *Adelphi*, Nov. 1932.
17. J. 26.7.32.
18. J. 16.8.32.
19. J. 5.8.32.
20. *Adelphi*, Oct. 1932.
21. J. 30.1.33.
22. *Adelphi*, Feb. 1933.
23. J. 18.1.33.

24. To M. Plowman: 10.11.32.
25. J. 6.2.33.
26. To R. Rees: Summer 1933.
27. J. 16.7.33.
28. W. 56–7.
29. NP. 70.
30. *Adelphi*, Jan. 1934.
31. *Adelphi*, Feb. 1934.

32. *Adelphi*, May 1934.
33. *Adelphi*, Nov. 1934.
34. To R. Rees: ? Summer 1934.
35. J. 26.7.34.
36. *Adelphi*, Sept. 1934.
37. NP. 72.
38. To M. Plowman: 20.9.34.

CHAPTER XVII

1. PL. 93.
2. J. H. Watson, *London Magazine*, May 1959.
3. W. 186.
4. To C. Farr (Mrs C. Walter): 21.7.33.
5. W. 3.
6. G. 268.
7. TC. ix.
8. MS. 1936.
9. J. 19.9.56.
10. MS. 1947.
11. B. 261.
12. B. 363.
13. B. 275.
14. B. 276.

15. B. 294.
16. M. Plowman to O. MacKenzie: 5.12.32.
17. M. Plowman to M. Marr: 3.3.33.
18. J. 7.7.32.
19. J. 6.5.52.
20. *Adelphi*, April 1932.
21. J. 11.1.32.
22. J. 10.7.55.
23. S. ix.
24. S. 200.
25. S. 297.
26. S. 116.
27. *Adelphi*, July 1935.

CHAPTER XVIII

1. J. 2.3.35.
2. To M. Plowman: 3.2.35.
3. J. 8.6.33.
4. To R. Rees: ? 23.1.35.
5. To R. Rees: 14.2.35.
6. To R. Rees: 16.1.35.
7. To R. Rees: 30.1.35.
8. W. 111.
9. To R. Rees: July 1935.
10. J. 14.3.35.
11. To R. Rees: 29.8.35.
12. *Adelphi*, Oct. 1935.
13. To N. Gill: 28.8.35.

14. *Adelphi*, Jan. 1936.
15. To M. Plowman: 17.9.35.
16. J. 8.9.35.
17. J. 11.8.35.
18. W. 19.
19. J. 29.10.35.
20. To J. P. Hogan: 2.12.35.
21. J. 18.2.36.
22. Address, 12.2.44.
23. To T. S. Eliot: 25.3.56.
24. To V. Cooley: 1.3.36.
25. J. 10.3.36.
26. J. 1.4.36.

27. J. 18.2.36.
28. J. 9.12.33.
29. J. 13.4.36.

30. J. 21.4.36.
31. MS. 1936.

CHAPTER XIX

1. *Adelphi*, Oct. 1936.
2. MS. 1936.
3. J. 20.1.32.
4. *Adelphi*, Sept. 1936.
5. M. Plowman to G. West: 21.10.36.
6. M. Plowman to J. Common: 10.9.36.
7. J. 25.9.36.
8. J. 6.9.36.
9. J. 4.4.36.
10. RDHL. 175.
11. J. 19.9.56.
12. J. 12.11.36.
13. To W. Wordsworth: 21.10.36.
14. To M. Plowman: 27.5.37.
15. J. 16.11.36.
16. NP. 13.
17. NP. 101.
18. NP. 97.
19. NP. 104–5.
20. NP. 90.

CHAPTER XX

1. To M. Plowman: 27.5.37.
2. W. 69.
3. Conversation with F. A. Lea: 25.4.38.
4. LBA. 56–7.
5. LBA. 58.
6. PP. 134.
7. To M. Gamble: 18.1.38.
8. J. 15.9.36.
9. PP. 133.
10. PP. 131.
11. PP. 146.
12. PP. 145.
13. To T. S. Eliot: 20.1.38.
14. PP. 185.
15. PP. 183–5.
16. Conversation with F. A. Lea: 15.4.38.
17. HE. 347.
18. HE. 333.
19. AL. 40.
20. HE. 198–9.
21. DD. 216.
22. DD. 278.
23. HE. 195.

CHAPTER XXI

1. MS. 1947.
2. J. 28.2.38.
3. To S. Miles: 14.1.38.
4. To J. Young: 9.5.38.
5. *Katherine Mansfield's Journal:* June 1919.
6. To M. Plowman: 28.12.37.

CHAPTER XXII

1. MS. 1947.
2. Mary Murry: *To Keep Faith*. Constable. 1959. 14.
3. HE. 286.
4. To M. Gamble: 24.7.39.
5. Mary Murry: *To Keep Faith*. 20.
6. To M. Gamble: 1.8.39.
7. J. 12.5.46.
8. Conversation with F. A. Lea: 3.9.39.
9. PP. 11.
10. To M. Plowman: 6.7.47.
11. To N. Gill: 9.9.39.
12. To G. Marshall: 22.3.55.
13. ET. 66–7.
14. ET. 46.
15. *Adelphi*, Oct. 1939.
16. Verbatim report of conference, published by National Peace Council, 1940.
17. H. Mister: *Peace News*, March 23, 1957.
18. *The Brotherhood of Peace*.
19. BC. 142.
20. *Procs. Archbishop of York's Malvern Conference*. Longmans, Green. 1941. 197.
21. BC. 45–7.
22. *Peace News*, Jan. 19, 1940.
23. J. 16.4.41.
24. *Adelphi*, Feb. 1941.
25. *The Times*, May 29, 1940.

CHAPTER XXIII

1. LBA. 248.
2. *Adelphi*, July 1940.
3. To M. Gamble: 10.6.40.
4. J. 21.1.40.
5. To M. Plowman: 30.12.39.
6. Mary Murry: *To Keep Faith*. 70.
7. Mary Murry: *To Keep Faith*. 69.
8. *Peace News*, May 17, 1940.
9. *Peace News*, Jan. 31, 1941.
10. Report of 4th A.G.M. of P.P.U., 1941.
11. *Peace News*, Aug. 16, 1940.
12. *Peace News*, Sept. 6, 1940.
13. *Peace News*, Nov. 8, 1940.
14. *Peace News*, March 7, 1941.
15. *Peace News*, July 25, 1941.
16. C. 69.
17. C. 58.
18. C. 78.
19. HE. 124.
20. *Peace News*, Dec. 6, 1940.
21. *Peace News*, Feb. 21, 1941.
22. *Peace News*, Aug. 23, 1940.
23. *Peace News*, April 19, 1940.
24. *Peace News*, Jan. 21, 1941.
25. *Peace News*, Dec. 10, 1943.
26. *Peace News*, March 26, 1943.
27. C. 71.
28. C. 148.
29. C. 141–2.
30. *Adelphi*, April–June 1943.
31. C. 127.
32. C. 128.
33. C. 118.
34. C. 109.
35. C. 119–20.
36. C. 124.
37. C. 110.
38. *Peace News*, Feb. 20, 1942.
39. *Adelphi*, April–June 1945.

CHAPTER XXIV

1. To W. Wordsworth: 10.7.41.
2. To M. Gamble: 9.6.41.
3. To M. Plowman: 2.4.40.
4. To M. Plowman: Dec. 1939.
5. To F. A. Lea: 2.8.41.
6. To F. A. Lea: 4.9.41.
7. J. 4.9.41.
8. J. 19.9.41.
9. J. 2.1.40.
10. Mary Murry: *To Keep Faith*. 82.
11. J. 15.10.41.
12. J. 12.12.41.
13. J. 19.2.42.
14. AE. 194.
15. CF. 22.
16. *Adelphi*, Dec. 1940.
17. CF. 33.
18. To Brasenose College: 9.6.42.
19. J. 14.10.42.
20. To R. Murry: 6.10.42.
21. J. 23.10.42.
22. AE. 58.
23. AE. 35.
24. AE. 87.
25. AE. 63.
26. AE. 115.
27. Letter, 12.10.43.
28. AE. 43–4.
29. AE. 44.
30. AE. 55–6.

CHAPTER XXV

1. To W. Wordsworth: 1.3.45.
2. J. 22.10.41.
3. CF. 51.
4. Address: 11.1.48.
5. CF. 88.
6. CF. 87.
7. CF. 91.
8. J. 29.7.56.
9. Address: Feb. 1944.
10. J. 25.8.32.
11. CF. 84.
12. J. 14.4.46.
13. *The Objector*, May 1950.
14. *Peace News*, March 28, 1941.
15. Report of 9th A.G.M. of P.P.U., 1946.
16. To G. Orwell: 9.8.44.
17. C. 151.
18. *Peace News*, April 20, 1945.
19. LBA. 93.
20. FS. 163–4.
21. FS. 68.
22. FS. 55.
23. TC. viii.
24. FS. 216–17.
25. FS. 126.
26. FS. 238.
27. HE. 213.
28. To F. A. Lea: 28.2.48.

CHAPTER XXVI

1. HE. 296.
2. To M. Plowman: 30.11.31.
3. J. 31.5.48.
4. To R. Baker, ? 1947.
5. CF. 154.
6. Address: 15.6.44.
7. To J. Young: 6.6.47.
8. To T. S. Eliot: 8.4.48.
9. LFS. 246.
10. LFS. 194.

11. J. 27.10.56.
12. G. 246.
13. Address: 7.3.48.
14. J. 5.3.56.
15. To T. S. Eliot: 14.5.46.
16. To M. Plowman: 5.11.31.
17. J. 20.11.54.
18. To W. Wordsworth: 29.11.49.
19. *Adelphi*, April–June 1944.
20. To W. Wordsworth: 23.12.47.

21. To W. Wordsworth: 23.12.48.
22. J. 27.2.54.
23. *Keats*, 58.
24. SW. 369.
25. SW. 379.
26. J. 24.12.47.
27. To F. Lawrence: 4.9.46.
28. J. 8.11.49.
29. J. 9.10.50.

CHAPTER XXVII

1. KMS. 48.
2. To H. Williamson: 5.10.52.
3. To F. Lawrence: 9.12.51.
4. J. 11.5.49.
5. J. 20.11.50.
6. KMP. 40.
7. To M. Gamble: 21.8.43.
8. J. 14.2.53.
9. J. 13.3.50.
10. To J. P. Hogan: 7.6.49.
11. J. 30.1.55.
12. J. 29.11.53.
13. J. 24.5.54.
14. J. 11.10.50.
15. *Adelphi*, April 1925.
16. J. 11.1.49.
17. CD. 159.
18. To Katherine Mansfield: 31.1.20.
19. Katherine Mansfield to J. M. M.:
    31.1.20.
20. CD. 174–5.
21. J. 27.7.53.

22. To T. S. Eliot: 5.8.53.
23. To F. Lawrence: 9.12.51.
24. To F. Lawrence: 26.10.55.
25. Mary Murry: *To Keep Faith.*
    153.
26. To H. Williamson: 7.9.52.
27. J. 10.6.54.
28. To H. Williamson: 12.3.55.
29. To H. Williamson: 30.12.54.
30. To H. Williamson: 5.10.52.
31. To Mme de Coninck: 4.12.55.
32. J. 28.5.55.
33. J. 22.12.54.
34. J. 12.8.53.
35. To F. A. Lea: 12.4.53.
36. To R. Murry: 21.4.54.
37. *Swift.* 8.
38. *Swift.* 7.
39. To H. Williamson: 7.9.53.
40. To F. A. Lea: 20.4.53.
41. J. 18.4.54.
42. J. 26.12.54.

CHAPTER XXVIII

1. J. 10.3.54.
2. J. 14.3.54.
3. J. 31.1.54.
4. J. 9.5.54.
5. J. 17.10.54.

6. To C. Thorpe: 14.5.54.
7. J. 9.4.54.
8. J. 17.1.54.
9. MS. 1947.
10. To D. S. Savage: 20.11.54.

11. To T. S. Eliot: 4.4.54.
12. J. 6.12.53.
13. J. 10.4.55.
14. To J. M. Murry Jr.: 27.12.53.
15. To J. P. Hogan: 8.3.55.
16. To T. S. Eliot: 26.5.54.
17. J. 16.11.56.
18. J. 16.10.55.
19. J. 15.10.55.
20. LFS. 231.
21. J. 29.4.56.
22. Address: 10.8.47.

23. *Adelphi*, Oct.–Dec. 1944.
24. J. 27.5.56.
25. J. 13.11.56.
26. J. 2.7.56.
27. LFS. 232.
28. J. 29.4.56.
29. LFS. 227.
30. LFS. 251.
31. J. 12.5.54.
32. Mary Murry: *To Keep Faith.* 189–90.

INDEX